SH█████ ████ ████ █████ ██ARY
D0226011

WOMEN WRITERS IN
RUSSIAN
LITERATURE

Recent Titles in
Contributions to the Study of World Literature

SHENANDOAH UNIVERSITY LIBRARY
WINCHESTER, VA 22601

WOMEN WRITERS IN RUSSIAN LITERATURE

EDITED BY

Toby W. Clyman & Diana Greene

CONTRIBUTIONS TO THE STUDY OF WORLD LITERATURE,
NUMBER 53

Greenwood Press

WESTPORT, CONNECTICUT • LONDON

54.95

Library of Congress Cataloging-in-Publication Data

Women writers in Russian literature / edited by Toby W. Clyman and
   Diana Greene.
     p. cm.—(Contributions to the study of world literature,
  ISSN 0738–9345 ; no. 53)
   Includes bibliographical references and index.
   ISBN 0-313-27521-1 (alk. paper)
   1. Russian literature—Women authors—History and criticism.
  I. Clyman, Toby W. II. Greene, Diana. III. Series.
  PG2997.W66   1994
  891.709′9287—dc20   93–21143

British Library Cataloguing in Publication Data is available.

Copyright © 1994 by Toby W. Clyman and Diana Greene

All rights reserved. No portion of this book may be
reproduced, by any process or technique, without the
express written consent of the publisher.

A paperback edition of *Women Writers in Russian Literature* is
available from the Praeger Publishers imprint of Greenwood Publishing
Group, Inc. (ISBN: 0–275–94941–9).

Library of Congress Catalog Card Number: 93–21143
ISBN: 0–313–27521–1
ISSN: 0738–9345

First published in 1994

Greenwood Press, 88 Post Road West, Westport, CT 06881
An imprint of Greenwood Publishing Group, Inc.

Printed in the United States of America

(∞)™

The paper used in this book complies with the
Permanent Paper Standard issued by the National
Information Standards Organization (Z39.48–1984).

10 9 8 7 6 5 4 3 2 1

PG   Women writers in Russian
2997   literature
.W66
1994

891.709 W842

For Joel
and Katherine
D.G.

To Bob, Larry, and Johnathan
T.W.C.

Contents

Acknowledgments

We wish to thank Mary Zirin and her annual discussion group on Women in Slavic Literature and Culture at the University of Illinois, Urbana-Champaign. Our thanks also to Ellen Hurwitz and Carol Olechowski. We are grateful to the Summer Research Laboratory of the Russian and East European Center at the University of Illinois, Urbana-Champaign, for providing access to its fine Slavic Collection and to the librarians for their gracious and unstinting help. Our special thanks to our spouses for their understanding and support.

Introduction

This book examines the often-ignored or forgotten contributions that women writers have made to Russian literature. While scholars of other literatures have been recovering women's contributions since the women's movement of the 1970s,[1] in Russian literature we have only recently begun the process.[2] Women writers (except for a few token poets such as Zinaida Gippius, Anna Akhmatova, and Marina Tsvetaeva) still have not become part of the literary canon—that collection of authors and works considered central to the understanding of Russian literature as reflected in teaching and scholarship.[3] We hope this book will add to the recovery effort now under way.

Over the last twenty-five years, feminist scholars working in other literatures have developed an impressive body of feminist scholarship and theory. We in Russian literature, as relative newcomers to the recovery of women writers, can learn a great deal from this work.

For example, the rediscovery of Russian women writers raises many of the same basic questions already addressed by feminist scholars in relation to their own literatures: Why have we never heard of these women writers before? Are they good writers? Can we speak of a separate women's literary tradition?

The scholar Nina Baym, in discussing American women writers suggests three possible reasons for their obscurity, reasons that apply equally well to Russian writers:[4] Women writers made real contributions which biased critics did not recognize;[5] social conditions hindered them;[6] or literary theories created by later critics retroactively eliminated them.[7] (The last certainly applies to socialist realism.)

In asking why we have never heard of these writers, feminist scholars have also had to consider the more traditional answer to the question: These writers' work was not worth preserving as part of the literary canon. Recently, however, some scholars have begun to challenge the idea that canons embody universal, ahistoric values, passed down intact from generation to generation. Rather, they suggest, canons constantly evolve and reflect cultural biases and ongoing literary political struggles; indeed, canons may be the means by which people in aesthetic power—literary gatekeepers such as critics, book reviewers, editors, book and journal publishers—keep out other interests, values, and world views.[8]

The second question raised by the rediscovery of women writers—Are they good writers?—in turn raises other questions: What do we mean by good? Is "good" a gender-neutral concept? Or, like the personal, is the aesthetic political? Some critics have suggested that "good" literature reflects the attitudes and experiences that men typically share, as expressed in such "stylistic, thematic and aesthetic norms," as "economy, irony, well-articulated structure, complexity, detachment, emotional restraint."[9] If "good literature" describes the attitudes and experiences typical of men, and if, as one scholar suggests, we have all unconsciously learned to look at literature in a way that supports and perpetuates the male canon, perhaps we need to develop new ways of reading, new "interpretative strategies" that will help us appreciate the achievements of women's writing.[10] Ultimately, such thinking leads us beyond the idea of expanding literary canons to questioning their meaning altogether.

As feminist scholars have pointed out repeatedly, such scholarship demands that we rethink the history of literature, literary periods, literary standards, the hierarchy of genres, the very definition of literature itself. It is tempting to reject such demands. After all, the old assumptions and definitions have served for a long time and at least give the illusion of certainty. Accepting this challenge, however, will yield a broader, richer, more exciting concept of literature.[11]

Our last question—Can we speak of a separate women's literary tradition?—arises from the recent deliberate focus on women writers to the exclusion of men.[12] The common sense answer would seem to be yes, and no. Yes, women writers in comparison to men writers read other women writers more avidly and tend to be more deeply influenced by them. Yes, it enriches our appreciation of women's writing to trace those mutual influences among women writers. Yes, it may make sense temporarily to look at women's writing exclusively in its own terms; to ask how our understanding of the world and literature would be changed if we accepted women's experiences and viewpoints as the norm instead of as deviations from the norm. On the other hand, we cannot speak of a separate Russian women's literary tradition because clearly, all Russian women writers were deeply influenced by the writings of Russian men. Indeed, we cannot fully understand women's achievements without also considering what men were writing at the time. Eventually, as Barbara Heldt has stated, men's and women's literatures have to be put back together.[13]

Why has it taken so long to start recovering Russian women writers? Certainly during the Soviet period, Russian literary scholars would have found it difficult to concern themselves with questions of gender, as their government permitted them only one approach to literature, socialist realism.[14] Despite the Soviet claim that the Revolution had "resolved the woman question,"[15] socialist realism did not promote sexual equality, but rather a male heroic world view.[16] In Soviet novels, women and their values often represented temptation or decadence, while in literary scholarship, women writers were labeled "unprogressive" when they wrote about the domestic sphere in which they lived rather than focusing on revolutionary politics.[17] Even dissident Soviet writers and critics who resisted socialist realism (Boris Pasternak, Aleksandr Solzhenitsyn, the Strugatsky brothers, Joseph Brodsky, Andrei Siniavsky, Iurii Daniel) challenged the Soviet heroic ideal without generally questioning the sex roles that cast women as temptresses or handmaidens, but never as subjects of their own stories. Despite the Cold War, American Slavists may have been affected by the hypnotic, monolithic force of socialist realist literary criticism, or by a long Russian tradition, predating the Revolution, that united literature with male political resistance.[18] Nonetheless, the significance of Russian women's contributions to folklore and all aspects of literature has attracted increasing interest and can no longer be ignored.

We intend this book for several different audiences and purposes. First, we hope these chapters about the role of women writers in Russian literature will intrigue both specialists and nonspecialists interested in literature, in women's studies, and in Russian culture. In addition, we expect that the scholarly apparatus will be helpful to those scholars, critics, and translators engaged in recovering Russian women writers and their works. Finally, it is important to us that this book be accessible to students of women's studies, history of Russian literature, and women in Russian literature classes, and useful to their teachers. To this end, we have organized the book by period and genre and committed ourselves to clarity of language and presentation.

For convenience we have divided the essays on nineteenth- and twentieth-century writers into prose, poetry, drama, and memoir. We have no wish to enter the very lively debate around the validity and definition of genres.[19] Our divisions simply reflect broad literary traditions that both writers and readers recognize, although, of course, most writers and many works cannot be pigeonholed in one of these traditions.

Ziolkowski examines women's roles in literate medieval culture and traces the changing images of women in Old Russian literature from the tenth to the seventeenth centuries. She shows that the dualistic concept of the good and evil woman Christianity introduced to Russia in the tenth century influenced and gradually replaced earlier depictions of women derived from folk tradition.

Kononenko questions why the lament is performed exclusively by women, whereas the epic is man's province, and she locates the answer in the wedding. The wedding, she postulates, was a late addition, introduced by men to subjugate an existent women's culture and to ensure paternity; she shows that the women's wedding ritual is analogous to her funeral, that it enacts her death. The funeral lament, Kononenko further demonstrates, had been a common ancestor of both the lament and the epic. With the introduction of the wedding, however, this changed. Because the woman became associated with death, the lament, the genre of death, became women's exclusive domain and the epic was restricted to men.

Nikolai Karamzin made the language and tastes of society "ladies" the standard of literary excellence, Vowles points out. Leading eighteenth-century writers went about creating a literary language and national literature based on premises about women and language. Vowles examines the assumptions some of these male writers made about women; she then looks at the contributions eighteenth-century women authors made to literature and language and shows how they themselves perceived their own relation to culture.

The history of the woman question (debates concerning women's work, education, and their place in the family), Costlow indicates, was largely framed by men; women, the critics said, failed to play a role in the public and literary articulation of the woman question. Examining the fiction women wrote in the second half of the nineteenth century, Costlow shows the literary ways women framed the issues concerning women's emancipation. Costlow demonstrates that women authors, by retaining traditional love plots and notions of female characters, explicitly and implicitly advocated changes in women's education and women's choices, and challenged accepted ideas about love, family, and dependence on men.

Zirin notes that women authors wrote mostly about private experiences because they were excluded from the public sphere. They depicted the world of women in an age that expected them to describe the broader social sphere. Zirin points to the rich but largely ignored literature these women left, examines features characteristic of their fiction, and notes the private and public handicaps under which these prosaists worked.

Greene shows how male critics viewed the poetry of several recognized and less well known nineteenth-century female poets and demonstrates that their literary reputations were shaped by cultural categories available for speaking about women. Greene re-examines these women's writings to show the irrelevance of cultural categories to the self-definition of these women poets.

Women physicians' memoirs constitute a large body of nineteenth-century Russian women's autobiographical literature. Their autobiographical texts—valuable as historical documents and literary works—are part of the recovery of Russian women's literature now under way. Clyman examines several of these physicians' memoirs, noting their literary features, the memoirist's self-image as it unfolds in her writing, and the extent to which the memoirist's awareness of her gender shapes the form and content of her recollections.

Holmgren identifies and analyzes "cause serving texts," twentieth-century Russian women's autobiographies, written to protest political and moral injustice. These include recollections of revolutionaries Vera Figner and Olga Liubatovich; memoirs of political prisoners Irina Ratushinskaia and Evgeniia Ginzburg; and reminiscences of cultural conservators Nadezhda Mandelstam and Lidiia Chukovskaia, among others. Holmgren argues that some of these autobiographies, called forth in protest, impose their own conformist stance. They articulate the position and standards of privileged women.

By the end of the nineteenth century, women's fiction had become a staple on the literary scene and could no longer be ignored. Rosenthal provides a broad, critical survey of the fascinating but largely overlooked women's prose fiction at the turn of the century. She notes and analyzes the salient features of women's writings, points to their literary models, identifies characteristic themes in their fiction and the types of female characters they depict. She also examines more closely the works of several women authors, each of whom has made a distinct contribution to women's prose of the Silver Age, 1885–1925.

Taubman examines a number of prominent as well as less well known women poets of the Silver Age, focusing especially on their use of the female persona. In the early years of the Symbolist movement, women poets, Taubman demonstrates, avoided female themes and sought a neutral voice. Akhmatova was the first to intentionally mark her female gender.

Twentieth-century women playwrights have received scant attention in Slavic scholarship, Smith notes; few anthologies of twentieth-century drama have included women playwrights. Since *glasnost*, women playwrights have been making sizable contributions to the theater. Smith examines the texts of nine twentieth-century women playwrights, focusing primarily on the development of their female characters.

Goscilo shows that contemporary women's fiction is gynocentric, emphasizing women's experiences and psychology. Unlike male writers, women authors neither universalize political issues nor treat them directly. In a discussion of four generations of contemporary female writers, Goscilo demonstrates that the later generation of prosaists has moved away from the gender paradigm imposed by official orthodoxy. Current female authors reject the gender stereotypes and offer alternatives to sanctioned models or write as though there were none.

Since *glasnost*, Ueland points out, new works by women poets are being issued, and previously unpublished verse by established and lesser-known women poets are being printed in increasingly larger numbers. She notes that no other period or genre of Russian literature is as ripe for recovery and re-evaluation. Ueland traces the poetry of Ol'ga Berggol'ts, Anna Barkova, and Mariia Petrovykh and shows the complexity and diversity of their poetry. She then surveys the poetry of contemporary women poets, whose literary careers began in the fifties, and notes the impact of Tsvetaeva's and Akhmatova's art on this younger generation of Russian women poets.

Ledkovsky notes that prominent women writers such as Gippius, Tsvetaeva, Berberova, Odoevtseva, and Teffi, who began writing in prerevolutionary Russia, have been amply represented in anthologies and in scholarship. Most women authors who began their careers in emigration, however, are sadly ignored. Ledkovsky surveys a number of those "lesser known" female writers of the first, second, and, most recently, third wave of emigration.

Diana Greene
Toby W. Clyman

NOTES

1. For example, Sandra Gilbert and Susan Gubar, *The Madwoman in the Attic* (New Haven: Yale University Press, 1979); Dale Spender, *Women of Ideas and What Men*

Have Done to Them (Boston: Routledge & Kegan Paul, 1982); Ruth Ellen Joeres and Mary Jo Maynes, eds., *German Women in the 18th and 19th Centuries: A Social and Literary History* (Bloomington: Indiana University Press, 1986); Jane Snyder, *The Woman and the Lyre: Women Writers in Classical Greece and Rome* (Carbondale: Southern Illinois University Press, 1989); Joan DeJean and Nancy Miller, eds., *Displacements: Women, Tradition, Literatures in French* (Baltimore: Johns Hopkins University Press, 1991).

2. See Barbara Heldt's pioneering *Terrible Perfection* (Bloomington: Indiana University Press, 1987); Marina Ledkovsky, Charlotte Rosenthal, and Mary Zirin, eds., *Dictionary of Russian Women Writers* (Westport, CT: Greenwood Press, forthcoming); P. A. Nikolaev, *Russkie pisateli 1800–1917: biograficheskii slovar'* (Moscow, 1990, 1992), which contains many previously forgotten Russian women writers as well.

3. For a discussion of literary canons, see Wendell Harris, "Canonicity," *PMLA* 106.1 (January 1991): 110–21.

4. Nina Baym, "Melodramas of Beset Manhood: How Theories of American Fiction Exclude Women Authors," *American Quarterly* 33 (1981): 123–39.

5. This is a view Dale Spender has also developed in suggesting that women have been made to "disappear" from intellectual and literary history. Spender, *Women of Ideas*, and Spender, *Mothers of the Novel: One Hundred Good Women Novelists Before Jane Austen* (New York: Pandora, 1986).

6. Virginia Woolf, *A Room of One's Own* (London: Hogarth, 1929), a view also developed by Tillie Olsen, *Silences* (New York: Delacorte Press, 1978) and Alice Walker, *In Search of Our Mother's Gardens* (San Diego: Harcourt Brace Jovanovich, 1983).

7. A view also developed by Berenice Carol, "The Politics of 'Originality': Women and the Class System of the Intellect," *Journal of Women's History* 2:2 (Fall 1980): 136–63; Gay Tuchman, *Edging Women Out: Victorian Novels, Publishers and Social Change* (New Haven: Yale University Press, 1989); Catherine Belsey and Jane Moore, eds., *The Feminist Reader: Essays in Gender and the Politics of Literary Criticism* (Houndsmills, Basingstoke, Hampshire: Macmillan Education, 1989).

8. See Peter Berger and Thomas Luckmann, *The Social Construction of Reality* (New York: Doubleday, 1967); Jane Thompkins, *Sensational Designs: The Cultural Work of American Fiction 1790–1880* (New York: Oxford University Press, 1985); Paul Lauter, *Canons and Contexts* (New York: Oxford University Press, 1991); Olsen, *Silences*; and Walker, *In Search of.*

9. Lauter, 104.

10. Patricinio Schweickart, "Reading Ourselves: Toward a Feminist Theory of Reading," *Gender and Reading*, ed. Elizabeth Flynn and Patricinio Schweickart (Baltimore: Johns Hopkins University Press, 1986). Also, Lillian Robinson, "Treason Our Text: Feminist Challenges to the Literary Canon," *The New Feminist Criticism*, ed. Elaine Showalter (New York: Pantheon, 1985), 105–22; Thompkins, *Sensational Designs.*

11. On literary periodization as it applies to women's writing, see Elaine Showalter, "Feminist Criticism in the Wilderness," *Writing and Sexual Difference*, ed. Elizabeth Abel (Chicago: University of Chicago Press, 1982), 33; on hierarchies of genres, see Anne Cranny-Francis, *Feminist Fiction: Feminist Uses of Generic Fiction* (New York: St. Martin's Press, 1990) and Naomi Schor, "Idealism in the Novel: Recanonizing Sand," *Displacements: Women, Tradition, Literatures in French*, ed. Joan DeJean and Nancy Miller (Baltimore: Johns Hopkins University Press, 1991).

12. Elaine Showalter, *A Literature of Their Own* (Princeton: Princeton University

Press, 1977); Elaine Showalter, "Toward a Feminist Poetics," *The New Feminist Criticism*, ed. Elaine Showalter (New York: Pantheon, 1985), 125–67; Flynn and Schweickart, eds., *Gender and Reading*.

13. Heldt, *Terrible Perfection*, 9.

14. "Soviet" is used throughout this book to refer to Russia during the existence of the Soviet Union (1917–1991).

15. For descriptions of the paradoxes of women's position under communism, see Norma Noonan, "Marxism and Feminism in the USSR: Irreconcilable Differences?" *Women and Politics* 8. 1 (1988): 31–49; Mary Buckley, *Women and Ideology in the Soviet Union* (Ann Arbor: University of Michigan Press, 1989). Also see Lynne Attwood, *The New Soviet Man and Woman* (Bloomington: Indiana University Press, 1990).

At the end of the Soviet period, some previously forgotten Russian women writers began to be republished. Even these editions, however—which probably represented a response to Western feminist criticism—tended to keep women writers ghettoized as secondary "poetesses" or "authoresses" who derived their significance from more famous male contemporaries. For example, M. Sh. Fainshtein, *Pisatel'nitsy pushkinskoi pory* (Leningrad, 1972); N. V. Bannikov, *Russkie poetessy XIX veka* (Moscow, 1979).

16. Socialist realism was officially defined as "a truthful, historically concrete representation of reality in its revolutionary development . . . combined with . . . ideological transformation and education of the working man in the spirit of socialism." Marc Slonim, *Soviet Russian Literature* (Oxford: Oxford University Press, 1964), 165.

17. Katerina Clark, *The Soviet Novel: History as Ritual* (Chicago: University of Chicago Press, 1981), discusses woman as temptress in socialist realist novels.

18. See Rufus Mathewson, *The Positive Hero in Russian Literature* (Stanford, CA: Stanford University Press, 1975).

19. See, for example, Alastair Fowler, *Kinds of Literature: An Introduction to the Theory of Genre and Modes* (Cambridge: Harvard University Press, 1982); Joseph P. Strelka, *Theories of Literary Genre* (University Park: Penn State University Press, 1978); Anne Cranny-Francis, *Feminist Fiction*.

WOMEN WRITERS IN RUSSIAN LITERATURE

1

Women in Old Russian Literature

Margaret Ziolkowski

Medieval Russian literature, traditionally called Old Russian literature, lasted from the eleventh until the end of the seventeenth century. This chapter explores the role played by women in the literate culture of medieval Russia and the images of women in Old Russian writings. Examination of a variety of texts suggests that certain types of female characters achieved enduring popularity, even though they did not strictly conform to the code of feminine virtue prescribed by the Russian Orthodox Church.

In 1051 Anna Iaroslavna, one of the daughters of the renowned Kievan ruler Iaroslav the Wise (1036–1054), married Henry I of France. As queen and later regent, Anna was the signatory of several documents; on one the name "Anna Regina" appears in Cyrillic characters.[1] Anna could not only write, she possessed a personal library as well.[2] While this might seem unusual for its time, she was by no means unique among elite Kievan women. Iaroslav's sister Predslava is known to have corresponded with her brother. The daughter of Vsevolod I (1078–1093), Ianka, founded a convent school for girls later in the eleventh century.[3] These details suggest that female literacy was far from uncommon among the princely families of early Russia. The evidence of hagiography bears out this surmise. The Life of the twelfth-century abbess and convent founder, Evfrosiniia, daughter of a prince of Polotsk, mentions that she copied manuscripts.[4] Other princesses, nuns, and women of the boyar class are also known to have engaged in this literary activity.[5] On a more mundane but equally significant level, the birchbark documents and inscribed distaffs (staffs to which flax, wool, or tow are tied in spinning) found in the environs of Novgorod and some other ancient Russian cities include numerous missives and inscriptions composed by and for women. They indicate that as early as the eleventh and twelfth centuries privileged women, including those from the merchant class, were frequently literate.[6] In later centuries this situation changed, however. By the sixteenth and seventeenth centuries there had been a marked decline in female literacy that reflected a general decrease in literacy.[7]

The ability of some early Russian women to read and write is a matter of justifiable national pride, particularly if one remembers that Russians had had access to a written language only since the late tenth century, when Prince Vladimir of Kiev first adopted Christianity. Yet there is also a sad irony inherent in examples like that of Anna Iaroslavna or Evfrosiniia of Polotsk cited earlier, for in spite of this auspicious beginning, Russian women ultimately made no contribution to the extant written literature of medieval Russia.

One may speculate that some literate woman must at some time have written a chronicle entry or composed a saint's Life, but in fact, in the course of seven centuries, there were no known women authors.[8] The participation of women in the production of oral literature seems to have been more significant, but the composition of written medieval Russian literature was very much the province of men.[9] The apparent absence of women from the Russian medieval literary scene resulted from a confluence of religious, social, and political factors. Most importantly, this absence of women is linked to a pervasive deterioration in their position in Russian society from the period before the invasion of the Tatars in the thirteenth century to the heyday of Muscovy in the sixteenth and seventeenth centuries. Although most recent scholarship suggests that women had more rights in the later period than has previously been recognized,[10] nonetheless, there was an objective decline in the status of women that reached its nadir in the seventeenth century. Women were increasingly excluded from public life. They were also the objects of intense and growing suspicion by the Orthodox Church, which encouraged patriarchal regimentation of their domestic existence. Ecclesiastical hostility was such that even women who entered convents did not enjoy the same respect as did their Western sisters.[11]

The comparatively lesser status of Russian nuns was undoubtedly one of the factors involved in a related cultural development; namely, the remarkable paucity of female Russian saints. Although there were hundreds of male holy men, there were only a few venerated women; a list of locally venerated women compiled by the nineteenth-century scholar Fedor Buslaev includes only about two dozen names. Moreover, as Buslaev observes, virtually all of the women mentioned are from princely families, and many of them are wives or relatives of venerated men.[12] In other words, religious achievement alone did not guarantee sanctification for women; in addition, indications of status derived from family background were frequently necessary. This was not true of male saints, many of whom were of relatively humble social origin.

The marginalization of women by medieval Russian literary culture extended not only to authorship, but also to subject matter. The official state culture was vehemently religious in its orientation. This extreme religiosity meant that there were no romances or love lyrics available even in translation. Russian scribes who scorned the classical heritage of Byzantium because it had been produced by pagans limited themselves mostly to the dissemination of biblical and patristic works and edifying parables. In these religious works as well as in similar native compositions, women figured most often in theoretical discussions of good and evil female types often inspired by the Proverbs of Solomon, particularly Chapter 31.[13] An early formulation of this popular theme of the good and evil woman is found in one of the earliest Old Russian works, the chronicle compilation *Povest' vremennykh let*, often referred to as the *Primary Chronicle* or the *Tale of Bygone Years*, produced by the monk Nestor in the early twelfth century on the basis of now-inextant earlier chronicles:

> The charm of woman is an evil thing. As Solomon in his repentance said of woman: "Listen not to an evil woman. Honey flows from the lips of a licentious woman, and for a time it delights thy palate. But in the end it will become bitterer than wormwood. They who cleave to her shall die in hell; for she walks not in the path of life, but unstable and foolish are her ways" (Proverbs 5:3–6). Thus spoke Solomon of adulteresses, but of a good woman he said, "More precious is she than jewels. Her husband rejoices in her, for she brings him blessedness all the days of her life. She seeks wool and flax, she makes useful things with her hands. . . . She rises also while it is yet night, she gives food to the household and tasks to the servants. . . . She has proved how good it is to labor, and her candle goes not out by night. . . . She stretches out her hand to the poor, and has given her wealth to the beggar. Her husband is not concerned with the household. . . . She has opened her lips with wisdom, she speaks fittingly with her tongue. . . . and her husband has commended her. For a wise woman is blessed; let her praise the fear of God" (Proverbs 31:10–31).[14]

The various motifs that occur in this compilation of biblical passages—the wantonness, deceptive charm, foolishness, and unreliability of the evil woman and the piety, industriousness, charity, and wisdom of the good woman—reflect the duality that often characterized both ancient and medieval perceptions of the female sex. Such motifs are reiterated countless times in medieval Russian chronicles, homiletic works, and didactic compositions of various kinds.[15] The most notorious example of a didactic work is the sixteenth-century prescriptive manual, the *Domostroi (Household Management)*, a joyless guide to domestic existence that outlines the recommended behavior for women and insists on the complete subordination of wife to husband.

The dichotomous ecclesiastical theory of the female personality provides a valuable source for examining the impact of Christianity on medieval Russian attitudes toward the family.[16] It can also prove helpful in the analysis of the few portraits of women found in major works of medieval Russian literature. The extent to which these female characters diverge from or adhere to the standards of behavior delineated by discussions of stereotyped good and evil women suggests a great deal about the relative conformity of particular works. Divergences from stereotypes may also point to the potential importance of other influences on the development of the image of women in Old Russian literature.

The earliest extended description of a woman in an Old Russian work is that of Ol'ga, in the *Primary Chronicle*. Like her grandson Prince Vladimir, Ol'ga was an early convert to Christianity. The *Primary Chronicle* (the oldest extant Old Russian annalistic compilation) gives considerable attention to Ol'ga's activities both before and after her conversion. She first attains prominence in the discussion of the events following the death of her husband, Prince Igor' of Kiev (912–945). He was slain by members of the East Slavic Derevlian tribe when he attempted to extort tribute from them for the second time in one season. According to tribal custom, Ol'ga was bound to avenge Igor's death, but the Derevlians hoped to convince her to marry their prince. The story of how Ol'ga foiled this scheme and avenged her husband's murder is one of the most gripping passages in the *Primary Chronicle*.

When the Derevlians arrive in Kiev, Ol'ga pretends to give serious consideration to their proposal. She tells the delegates to return the next day and to insist that the Kievans carry them in their boat as a sign of honor. Meanwhile, the princess commands that a deep trench be dug, and when the delegates appear the next morning, she has them dropped into the trench and buried alive. Using similar ploys, Ol'ga tricks the Derevlians twice more, until her revenge is complete.

While the historical Ol'ga apparently wreaked destruction on the hapless Derevlians, the precise details of the account given by the *Primary Chronicle* have a readily apparent folkloric basis. The triplicity of the princess's revenge is reminiscent of the triple repetitions that occur so frequently in fairy tales. The use of dramatic dialogue and riddling language is also typical of folklore.[17] In this instance, Ol'ga's fatuous interlocutors are not even aware that her speech contains an ominous subtext, that, for example, in pagan ritual transportation in boats is associated with death. As a whole, the episode illustrates an important point about Old Russian literature in general and accounts of women in particular: Motifs and techniques borrowed from the pagan oral tradition could be and often were effectively adapted by written works produced in the service of a far different ideology.

The use of folkloric devices does not cease when Ol'ga converts to Christianity. Indeed, the events surrounding her baptism are couched in evocative dialogue that also exploits the device of the unrecognized riddle. According to the *Primary Chronicle*, Ol'ga's conversion took place in Constantinople.[18] The Byzantine emperor Constantine is so impressed by Ol'ga's beauty and intelligence that he contemplates marrying her. Ol'ga cleverly declares that she will accept baptism only if he performs it, and when Constantine later proposes marriage, she refuses on the grounds that this would represent a violation of the paternal role assumed by him during her baptismal ceremony. " 'Ol'ga, you have outwitted me,' " declares the confounded emperor.[19]

The hallmark of Ol'ga's behavior both before and after her conversion is intelligence combined with intransigence. No one whom the princess encounters is cleverer than she, and the chronicler repeatedly speaks admiringly of her intellect. Ol'ga always operates according to a cunningly devised plan, constantly faithful to a stringent code of virtue. Yet as Horace Dewey and Ann Kleimola observe in their study of admired medieval Russian women, her actions remain "within the limits of prescribed female behavior."[20] Although her willfulness means that Ol'ga does not embody the stereotype of the good woman, neither is she in any sense evil.[21] The chronicler assumes that the princess possesses post-conversion Christian values but focuses on the manifestations of a consistent wit and integrity. Perhaps equally important for purposes of comparison with subsequent portrayals of women in Old Russian literature is the fact that the Ol'ga so enthusiastically described in the *Primary Chronicle* is a widow, un-constrained by the demands of a spouse. As we shall see, such is the status of most of those few women treated in prominent medieval Russian works.

By contrast, there is little that appears folkloric about either the personality or the actions of another very early medieval Russian woman, the mother of St. Feodosii, who is described in the *Life of Feodosii of the Cave Monastery* (*Zhitie Feodosiia Pecherskogo*). This work was composed late in the eleventh century by the same monk, Nestor, who was responsible for the compilation of the *Primary Chronicle*.[22] Feodosii, one of the most beloved of the early Russian saints, according to Nestor's Life, wished to pursue a religious career from an early age, but his mother hindered him in the fulfillment of his desires. As in the case of Princess Ol'ga, discussion of Feodosii's mother assumes prominence in the Life after the death of Feodosii's father when the boy is thirteen.

St. Feodosii was one of the foremost practitioners of kenoticism—that is, the imitation of Christ's extraordinary humility—a practice that led to conflict with his mother. In the Life, Feodosii's willingness to abase himself reveals itself in his youth when he works in the fields along with peasant laborers. Feodosii's mother, though herself a Christian, disapproves of this behavior, considering it unsuitable for someone of his social station. When the youth persists, she frequently becomes angry and beats him. The description of her physique and speech is intimidating: "she was robust and strong in body like a man. If someone who didn't see her heard her speaking, he would think that she was a man" (310).[23]

Physical violence rapidly becomes the leitmotif of relations between Feodosii and his mother. Their strained relations continue until Feodosii successfully escapes to Kiev and becomes a monk. When his mother finally discovers him after four years, she weeps at the sight of his emaciated body and begs him to return home, citing her great love: "I cannot endure living without seeing you" (320). However, Feodosii also possesses great strength of will, and he convinces his mother to enter a convent in Kiev and from there to visit him.

The parent reluctant to permit a child to adopt a religious calling is a frequent topos in the Lives of holy men and women, both Russian and non-Russian (Abraham of Edessa, Athanasia of Aegina, Amelbert of Bavaria, Clare of Assisi, Paisii Velichkovskii). Yet Nestor's descriptions of Feodosii's mother eloquently testify to the probable historically reliable basis for this topos. The account of her actions and motivation is buttressed by such realistic details that one is tempted to assume a high degree of veracity. A loving mother whose frustration leads her to persecute the very son whom she adores, Feodosii's mother is, in the words of Antonia Glasse, a "formidable woman," a type that becomes especially prominent in nineteenth-century Russian literature.[24] She is neither good nor evil, but misguided.

The hysterical anger of Feodosii's mother is far different from the coldblooded machinations of Princess Ol'ga, but it is noteworthy that neither rage nor craftiness is traditionally associated with the stereotype of the good woman. The characters of Feodosii's mother and the princess share more than negative similarities, however. Both are strong-willed to the point of ruthlessness and attach great importance to family considerations. Both also are or become Christians, but neither makes the practice of religious precepts central to her existence. For this subordination of existence to religion, one must look to other representations of women in Old Russian literature.

Among the handful of female Russian saints, there is only one whose religious career is comparable to that of Feodosii Pecherskii. Like her counterpart, Evfrosiniia of Polotsk (d. 1173) is described in her Life as religiously inclined from an early age, but inhibited in the realization of her desires by her father, who wishes her to marry soon after her twelfth birthday. Evfrosiniia escapes this unsought fate by going secretly to a convent and convincing the abbess to permit her to become a nun. She causes her father further grief by asking him to allow her sister to visit, ostensibly only to learn to read and write, but she then encourages her to become a nun. When she becomes an abbess, Evfrosiniia is, like St. Feodosii, associated with the expansion of monastic life and the construction of various ecclesiastical buildings. Toward the end of her life, she decides to visit the holy sites of Jerusalem and to die there. Her wish is fulfilled.

Evfrosiniia, unlike Feodosii, is not distinguished by remarkable demonstrations of humility. Dewey and Kleimola aptly describe her as "a genuinely 'formidable woman.' "[25] While Feodosii is initially sometimes frustrated in his quest for spiritual perfection by his mother's actions, Evfrosiniia never yields to anyone. She is as strong-willed as either Ol'ga or Feodosii's mother and has the advantage over the latter of always being in the right religiously. But while she is unfailingly virtuous, the stereotype of the good woman does not apply directly to Evfrosiniia in part because she is always unyielding, in part because she never marries. She shows her virtue in her single-minded dedication to Christ rather than in unstinting efforts for the benefit of a husband.

Old Russian literature does include some portraits of devoted wives whose husbands are still living. Many of these portraits describe women's responses to their husbands' involvement in military actions. The most famous example is Princess Iaroslavna in the *Tale of Igor's Campaign* (*Slovo o polku Igoreve*).[26] Iaroslavna's outpourings on behalf of her captured husband represent one of the most poignant poetic achievements of medieval Russian literature. Traditionally called a lament, these lines have been said to resemble the incantation of a pagan goddess.[27]

In these lines the princess speaks of her desire to bathe Igor's wounds and addresses the wind, the sun, and the Dnieper River, both reproachfully and beseechingly. As elsewhere in the *Tale of Igor'* , the influence of oral literature is very pronounced, both in the use of the lament form and in the apostrophizing of the elements.[28] Iaroslavna can be included in the category of biblically and patristically defined good women only with some difficulty. Though she is clearly devoted to her absent husband, she exhibits none of the traditional signs of Orthodox piety. Instead, she embraces a kind of pantheism, very different, as we shall see, from Evdokiia's more religious lament in the later *Story of the Mamai Battle* (*Skazanie o Mamaevom poboishche*).

Preceding Iaroslavna's lament in the *Tale of Igor'* is a brief lament by all the Russian women, who bemoan their husbands' defeats and probable deaths. Both laments subsequently influenced the *Zadonshchina*, a late fourteenth-century composition by Sofonii of Riazan' and one of several works that describes the Battle of Kulikovo in 1380.[29] The widows of princes and others slain in the battle bewail their husbands' deaths and address the Don and Moscow rivers in terms particularly reminiscent of the *Tale of Igor'*. As in the latter case, the women's laments in the *Zadonshchina* do not evoke a noticeably Christian ideology. Although the wicked women of Old Russian literature do not typically have recourse to laments, the laments spoken by good women do not serve primarily as expressions of virtue. Indeed, they seem to reflect a folk ethos of sorrow for the deceased unleavened by the consolations offered by faith.

A very different tone is apparent in another work devoted to the battle, the *Story of the Mamai Battle*. Though influenced by the *Zadonshchina*, this early fifteenth-century composition is more overtly religious in its orientation. When Prince Dmitrii and his comrades set out against the Tatars, Dmitrii's wife Evdokiia and the other Russian wives weep as they say farewell to their husbands, but Evdokiia's sorrow inspires her to address God, not the rivers or the elements:

My Lord God, Most High creator, observe my humility, permit me, Lord, to see again my sovereign, Grand Prince Dmitrii Ivanovich, glorious among men. Give him, Lord, help with Your strong hand to defeat the pagan Polovtsians opposed to him. . . . Do not allow the Christendom that remains to perish, and may Your holy name be glorified in the Russian land.[30]

The folkloric lament has been subordinated here to a religious vision, and Evdokiia approaches the ideal of the good woman more closely than any of the married women discussed thus far. Her piety and her devotion to her husband are inextricably linked.

Evdokiia also appears in another fifteenth-century work, dedicated not specifically to the Battle of Kulikovo, but to the biography of Prince Dmitrii. Couched in language frequently reminiscent of a saint's Life, the *Discourse on the Life of Grand Prince Dmitrii Ivanovich* (*Slovo o zhitii velikogo kniazia Dmitriia Ivanovicha*) portrays its subject as a paragon of Christian virtue and repeatedly describes the marriage of Dmitrii and Evdokiia in idealized terms:

"after their marriage they lived chastely, like a gold-breasted dove and a sweet-voiced swallow, they contemplated their salvation tenderly, with a pure conscience, ruling the earthly kingdom with strength of mind and taking an oath to the heavenly one, and they did not partake of pleasures of the flesh'' (210).[31] The high-minded image suggested here owes much to a monasticized conception of an ideally celibate marriage that was increasingly upheld as an Orthodox model in the later Russian medieval period.

The *Discourse* is not consistent in its evocation of an intensely Christian world view, however. This is particularly apparent in the lengthy lament of Evdokiia at Dmitrii's death, which reverts to the use of folkloric metaphors to characterize the prince ("my sun," "my bright moon" [218]) and describes a despair largely unrelieved by any optimism engendered by Orthodoxy. Only toward the end of the lament does Evdokiia appear to remember the possible relief her religion may afford her, when she asks Dmitrii to pray for her and entreats: "My great God, tsar of tsars, be an intercessor for me! Most pure Lady Mother of God, do not abandon me, do not forget me in the time of my sorrow!" (220). Considered in its entirety, the image of Evdokiia presented by the *Discourse* constitutes an uneasy synthesis of the folkloric and the religious. While the princess is a good woman, her behavior cannot be characterized solely in terms of this stereotype, for in the course of the work, the model Christian wife becomes a traditional, breast-beating widow.

A more elaborate fusion of folkloric and religious motifs and themes occurs in an extremely popular sixteenth-century work, the *Tale of Petr and Fevronii of Murom (Povest' o Petre i Fevronii Muromskikh)*.[32] In her study of feminine images in Old Russian literature and art, Joan Grossman calls the *Tale of Petr and Fevroniia* "practically the only love story in Old Russian literature.''[33] Unlike the works in which the above laments appear, the *Tale of Petr and Fevroniia* features a female character whose actions are central to many of the events recounted. In contrast to Princess Ol'ga or Evfrosiniia of Polotsk, Fevroniia achieves such narrative prominence even though she is juxtaposed throughout the *Tale* to a male figure. In fact, it may be argued that Fevroniia gradually comes to dominate the narrative just as she dominates her husband.

The *Tale of Petr and Fevroniia* is ostensibly the story of two early thirteenth-century rulers of the city of Murom who were canonized in the sixteenth century. However, there is little historical basis for their story. Instead, it constitutes an amalgam of various hagiographical and folkloric motifs. Fevroniia first appears in the capacity of a healer. Blood from the body of a serpent slain by Petr has spattered the prince, leaving him covered with ulcerous sores. Fevroniia, the daughter of a wild-honey farmer, asserts that she can heal Petr, but only if he will marry her. She foils the prince's clumsy attempts to test her and to evade marriage. After their marriage, boyars who wish to rid themselves of a princess of such lowly birth annoy the couple, but eventually they are able to rule in peace. Toward the end of their lives, Peter and Fevroniia take monastic oaths.

After their simultaneous deaths, their bodies are miraculously found together in a tomb, as they had requested they be buried.

The *Tale of Petr and Fevroniia* has much in common with other European narratives that drew heavily upon the oral tradition, most notably the story of Tristan and Isolde.[34] Entire episodes, such as the slaying of the serpent, have an obvious broadly European folkloric basis. With her penchant for riddling language and with her clear intellectual superiority to those around her, Fevroniia calls to mind the beautiful and wise maiden of numerous tales, as well as Princess Ol'ga.[35] Much of the action of the story is structured according to folkloric compositional principles. When, for example, Petr is near death, he must send three messages to Fevroniia before she will finish her embroidery and die with him.

The *Tale of Petr and Fevroniia* also has a pronounced hagiographical slant that becomes increasingly apparent in the course of the story. After their marriage, the prince and princess are said to live "in great piety, observing God's commandments" (112). Although the boyars resent her, Fevroniia's goodness makes her popular with other inhabitants of Murom. Miracles are associated with her and, to a lesser extent, with Petr, both before and after their deaths. When the two are finally able to govern Murom without hindrance, they emerge as ideal Christian rulers: "They were true shepherds for their city, and not like mercenaries. They ruled their city with truth and meekness, and not with rage. They received pilgrims, fed the hungry, clothed the naked, and saved the poor from misfortune" (113).

The figure of Fevroniia represents a successful blend of the folkloric and the hagiographical; the two tendencies complement rather than conflict with one another. At the same time, the princess's image does not conform to the stereotype of the good woman. Fevroniia is clearly too superior to her partner, in both intelligence and virtue, to play the role of a subordinate helpmate. Significantly, Petr, not Fevroniia, must wait for his spouse's permission to die. Although she is less strident, Fevroniia has something in common with earlier examples of unyielding righteousness, like Princess Ol'ga and Evfrosiniia of Polotsk. Yet her continuing demonstration of virtue after her marriage is ironically facilitated by her apparent domination of her husband. The popularity of the *Tale of Petr and Fevroniia* attests to the fact that such a contravention of ecclesiastical models for submissive feminine behavior was not only possible in a literary context, but it was well tolerated by medieval readers.

A more conventional vision of marriage is offered by the seventeenth-century *Tale of Marfa and Mariia (Povest' o Marfe i Marii)*. It describes the involvement of two sisters in the divinely directed creation of a miraculous cross endowed with curative powers. The story is relatively unusual among Old Russian works in that it features a pair of virtuous female protagonists. Marfa and Mariia are married to men who refuse to allow their wives to meet with each other. When their husbands die, the sisters, each ignorant of the death of the other's spouse, decide to visit each other's home. The two women meet en route and share a vision in which they receive gold and silver intended for a cross and its shrine. As instructed by an angel, they give the precious metal to three passing monks. Their skeptical relatives berate Marfa and Mariia for such carelessness and initiate a search for the strangers. After further adventures, the monks, who are actually angels in disguise, reappear with the finished cross.

A Soviet scholar described Marfa and Mariia as "typical submissive wives of the Middle Ages."[36] They submit first to their husbands and later to their relatives. In both cases they endure behavior that is clearly unjust. In fact, the two sisters become agents of God's will only when they stop adhering to a conventional code of feminine ethics that attaches primary importance to compliance with masculine authority. This paradox suggests the difficulties that may have been inherent in creating a female character who consistently embodied the stereotype of the good woman and yet retained the interest of a medieval audience.

In many respects, the *Tale of Iulianiia Osor' ina* (*Povest' ob Ulianii Osor'inoi*), composed by Iulianiia's son, Druzhina Osor'in, in the early seventeenth century describes such a happy coincidence of stereotype and individual. Dewey and Kleimola observe that, in her piety, Iulianiia more closely approaches the medieval ideal than either Ol'ga or Fevroniia and that "many aspects of her conduct as housewife and estate manager would have met with the approval of the *Domostroi*'s compiler."[37] T. A. Greenan has demonstrated in detail how Iulianiia's behavior is deliberately shown to reflect the precepts of a popular book of devotional readings, the *Izmaragd* (*Emerald*).[38]

Although the *Tale of Iulianiia* is pathbreaking because it describes a female saint who was not a princess and never became a nun, it is unabashedly traditional in its hagiographical orientation. After a precociously pious childhood, Iulianiia marries the wealthy Georgii Osor'in. Her behavior as a young married woman is a model of Christian femininity construed according to medieval Russian Orthodox prescriptions; her devotion to the management of her household is matched only by her humility and fondness for prayer and charity. After the deaths of two of her sons, Iulianiia begs Georgii to allow her to enter a convent. He refuses, but agrees to practice sexual abstinence, an extreme expression of piety for a medieval Russian couple. Even after her husband dies, Iulianiia does not become a nun. She continues to live in the world, indulging her ascetic and charitable inclinations even more than when Georgii was alive. Miracles are associated with her both before and after her death. When the time finally comes for Iulianiia to die, she instructs her children and serfs in her conception of virtue and laments her failure to become a nun: "From my youth I had a desire for the angelic, monastic way, but I did not have the honor because of my sins and wretchedness. Since I was unworthy, being a sinner and wretched, God willed it thus, glory be to His righteous judgement."[39]

The observance of Christian precepts to the fullest is the focal point of Iulianiia's existence. In this respect she differs greatly from those female characters discussed earlier for whom religion represented a secondary, or even peripheral, concern. The only impediment to Iulianiia's practice of her religion is her husband. Ironically, what most distinguishes Iulianiia as an idealized realization of the type of the good woman is submission to her husband's will and the monasticization of her existence within marriage rather than her entrance into a convent. From this point of view, the fact that Iulianiia does not become a nun even after Georgii's death is consistent with the specifically female-oriented teachings of the medieval Russian Orthodox Church, which argue for the practice of goodness in the world. It is also significant, however, that Iulianiia performs her greatest feats as a widow.

Other powerful images of women that date from the seventeenth century are found in works by and about the schismatic Old Believers. The martyr Archpriest Avvakum Petrovich (1620?–1682), a major opponent of the ecclesiastical reforms initiated by Patriarch Nikon of Moscow, described his own sufferings and those of his co-religionists and family in his autobiography.[40] The archpriest's long-suffering wife is portrayed in this work as both devout and devoted to her husband. A popular episode that illustrates her readiness for martyrdom and uxorial devotion occurs when she expresses frustration during their Siberian exile: "the poor [woman] reproached me, saying, 'Will these sufferings go on a long time, Archpriest?' And I said, 'Markovna, right up to our very death.' And sighing, she answered, 'Good enough, Petrovich, then let's be getting on.' "[41] His wife's respect for Avvakum does not lead to a craven submissiveness, however. When the archpriest falters briefly in his struggle against the reformers, his wife exhorts him in strong terms, and he bows in acknowledgment of her righteousness. Avvakum's wife is a good woman, but one with more spirit than the compiler of the *Domostroi* might have wished.

Another seventeenth-century female schismatic is herself the subject of a Life. The boiarynia Feodosiia Morozova (1639?–1675) was a wealthy conservative Muscovite who was very close to Avvakum and who herself eventually died a martyr's death. The *Tale of Boiarynia Morozova (Povest' o boiaryne Morozovoi)* was written by someone in her immediate circle soon after her death.[42] The nineteenth-century artist Vasilii Surikov later exploited the *Tale* as a source for his famous painting of Morozova.[43]

The *Tale of Boiarynia Morozova* is above all an account of her persecution and martyrdom. The first two paragraphs of the work discuss Morozova's entire childhood and married life; no details are given about her relationship with her husband, who died when she was still a comparatively young woman. The narrator then touches upon Avvakum's influence on the boiarynia and describes her pious widowed existence. Her spiritual aspirations culminate in her decision to become a nun, which she does while remaining in her own home. Increasing conflict with Tsar Aleksei because of her fidelity to pre-reform rituals culminates in the arrest of Morozova and her closest associates. Three years of imprisonment, torture, and physical abuse end only when Morozova starves to death in a dungeon. These experiences are treated in great detail through dialogue.

A stubborn refusal to compromise her faith is the hallmark of Morozova's behavior throughout her years of persecution. One of her tormentors, Archimandrite Ioachim of the Chudov Monastery, criticizes her intransigence: "You did not know how to live in subjugation, but were confirmed in contradiction" (135).[44] Like Iulianiia, Morozova has made her faith the center of her existence, more important even than her family. In response to advice to take her son into greater account, she declares: "I live for Christ, and not for my son" (136). In confrontation after confrontation, the boiarynia manifests both intellect and courage. Morozova is far too independent to fit the stereotype of the good woman.

The *Tale of Boiarynia Morozova* is one of the last major works of Old Russian literature. The late seventeenth and early eighteenth centuries constituted a transitional period in Russian literature, as the conventions of medieval Orthodox culture yielded to Western influence. In a work like the *Tale of Savva Grudtsyn* (*Povest' o Savve Grudtsyne*), one still finds an example of the evil adulteress inspired by the devil and the poor young man who is her victim. But in another late seventeenth-century work, the *Tale of Frol Skobeev* (*Povest' o Frole Skobeeve*), the questionable morality of the hero and his lover, Annushka, wins them nothing but success. Frol dresses in women's clothing to gain access to Annushka's bedroom, and Annushka later elopes with him. Eventually, Annushka's parents relent and make Frol the heir to all their wealth. The mores of the fictional world in which these young characters act are quite different from those of Old Russian literature.

The *Tale of Boiarynia Morozova* is a fitting work with which to conclude a survey of Old Russian women because, in a sense, the depiction of Morozova represents a logical culmination of various trends associated with the image of women in medieval Russian literature over the centuries. The *Tale of Boiarynia Morozova* focuses on Morozova's experiences as a widow. This is also true in many of the works discussed here. Where a major female character is not a widow, she is either single (Evfrosiniia of Polotsk), left alone while her husband is in battle (Iaroslavna), or clearly the dominant spouse in the marriage (Fevroniia). This pattern suggests that women without men were more likely to command narrative attention in Old Russian literature, perhaps because in such circumstances women's freedom of action was greater. Many of the female characters considered in the preceding pages are also distinguished by their stubbornness, a quality considered unfeminine by medieval Russian standards. This would appear to support the notion that it was not the submissive wife who was likely to become an important figure in an Old Russian work.

It is also apparent that over the centuries, the portrayal of women in Old Russian literature became increasingly Christianized and, simultaneously, less reflective of the oral tradition. The Christian faith of the post-conversion Ol'ga and sorrowful Iaroslavna seems incidental, while the folkloric underpinnings of their behavior and speech are very pronounced. Fevroniia, a figure from later in the medieval period, represents a harmonious mixture of both tendencies, a cross between a saint and a fairy-tale heroine. In the cases of Iulianiia and

Morozova, the practice of religious precepts completely dominates their existence, while the impact of the oral tradition on their representation is scarcely visible. Paralleling developments in medieval Russian life, the influence of religious thought became increasingly significant in the portrayal of women in Old Russian literature. This did not necessarily entail attention to the constructs of the good and evil woman. Considered in the context of evolving tendencies in the literary treatment of women, Boiarynia Morozova, a widowed martyr to her fate, is an ideal embodiment of the Old Russian woman. The representation of her uncompromising spiritual commitment is achieved without the use of folkloric motifs, while widowhood facilitates her narrative centrality. In a sense, the depiction of Morozova thus constitutes the logical culmination of Old Russian literary trends in the representation of women from the tenth through the seventeenth century.

NOTES

1. George Vernadsky, *Kievan Russia* (1948; reprint, New Haven: Yale University Press, 1973), 342.
2. N. L. Pushkareva, *Zhenshchiny Drevnei Rusi* (Moscow, 1989), 68.
3. Vernadsky, *Kievan Russia*, 154.
4. "Povest' o Efrosinii Polotskoi," in *Pamiatniki starinnoi literatury*, ed. N. Kostomarov (St. Petersburg, 1860; The Hague: Mouton, 1970), vypusk 4, 174.
5. Pushkareva, *Zhenshchiny Drevnei Rusi*, 68.
6. A. A. Medyntseva, "Gramotnost' zhenshchin na Rusi XI–XIII vv. po dannym epigrafiki," in *"Slovo o polku Igoreve" i ego vremia*, ed. B. A. Rybakov (Moscow, 1985), 237–88; Dorothy Atkinson, "Society and the Sexes in the Russian Past," in *Women in Russia*, ed. Dorothy Atkinson, Alexander Dallin, and Gail Warshofsky Lapidus (Stanford, CA: Stanford University Press, 1973), 22.
7. Susanne Janosik McNally, "From Public Person to Private Prisoner: The Changing Place of Women in Medieval Russia" (Ph.D. diss., SUNY Binghamton, 1976), 150; E. Likhacheva, *Materialy dlia istorii zhenskovo obrazonvaniia v Rossii (1086–1796)* (St. Petersburg, 1890), 23.
8. Marie A. Thomas, "Moscovite Convents in the Seventeenth Century," *Russian History* 10 (1983): 240.
9. The role played by women in the production of oral literature will not be treated here, in part because of the difficulties involved in this dating.
10. On this point, see especially Ann M. Kleimola, "Moscovite Dowries and Women's Property Rights," *The Russian Review* 51 (1992): 204.
11. Christine D. Worobec, "Accommodation and Resistance," in *Russia's Women: Accommodation, Resistance, Transformation*, ed. Barbara Evans Clements, Barbara Alpern Engel, and Christine D. Worobec (Berkeley, CA: University of California Press, 1991), 26.
12. F. Buslaev, "Ideal'nye zhenskie kharaktery drevnei Rusi," in his *Istoricheskie ocheri russkoi narodnoi slovestnosti i iskusstva*, 2 vol. (St. Petersburg, 1861), vol. 2, *Drevne-russkaia narodnaia literatura i iskusstvo*, 244–45.

13. Cf. Joan Delaney Grossman, "Feminine Images of Old Russian Literature and Art," *California Slavic Studies* 11 (1980): 51.

14. *The Russian Primary Chronicle: Laurentian Text*, trans. and ed. Samuel Hazzard Cross and Olgerd P. Sherbowitz-Wetzor (Cambridge, MA: The Medieval Academy of America, 1953?), 94–95. For the Russian text, see *Pamiatnik literatury Drevnei Rusi. Nachalo russkoi literatury. XI-nachalo XII veka*, ed. D. S. Likhachev and L. A. Dmitriev (Moscow, 1978), 94–106.

15. On the popularity of this theme, see especially M. D. Kagan-Tarkovskaia, "Slovo o zhenakh o dobrykh i o zlykh' v sbornike Evfrosina" in *Kul'turnoe nasledie Drevnei Rusi. Istoki. Stanovlenie. Traditsii*, ed. M. B. Khrapchenko et al. (Moscow, 1976), 382.

16. Pushkareva, *Zhenshchiny Drevnei Rusi*, 6.

17. For a detailed analysis of the use of dialogue and riddling language in the story of Ol'ga's revenge, see D. S. Likhachev, *Russkie letopisi i ikh kul'turnoistoricheskoe znachenie* (Moscow-Leningrad, 1947; The Hague: Europe Printing, 1966), 132–40.

18. There is some uncertainty as to whether the historical Ol'ga was actually baptized in Constantinople or in Kiev. See Vernadsky, *Kievan Russia*, 40.

19. *The Russian Primary Chronicle*, 82; *Pamiatniki literatury Drevnei Rusi. XI-nachalo XII veka*, 76.

20. H. W. Dewey and A. M. Kleimola, "Muted Eulogy: Women Who Inspired Men in Medieval Rus'," *Russian History* 10 (1983): 193.

21. Cf. P. V. Snesarevskii, "Otnoshenie k zhenshchine v pamiatnikakh pis'menosti i istoricheskie problemy russkoi srednevekov'ia (XI–XV vv.)," in *Istoriographicheskie i istoricheskie problemy russkoi kul'tury*, ed. L. N. Pushkarev et al., (Moscow, 1983), 33–34.

22. On the composition of the *Zhitie Feodosiia Pecherskogo*, see *Pamiatnik literatury Drevnei Rusi. XI-nachalo XII veka*, 456.

23. For the text of the *Zhitie Feodosii Pecherskogo*, see *Pamiatniki literatury Drevnei Rusi. XI-nachalo XII veka*, 304–91.

24. Antonia Glasse, "The Formidable Woman: Portrait and Original," *Russian Literature Triquarterly* 9 (1974): 447–48.

25. Dewey and Kleimola, "Muted Eulogy: Women Who Inspired Men in Medieval Rus'," 191.

26. The dating and authorship of this work have at times been hotly debated, but it is assumed by most scholars to date from the end of the twelfth century, soon after Prince Igor's unsuccessful campaign against the nomadic Polovtsians in 1185.

27. Joanna Hubbs, *Mother Russia: The Feminine Myth in Russian Culture* (Bloomington: Indiana University Press, 1988), 171.

28. On laments, see, in this volume, Natasha Kononenko, "Women as the Performers of Oral Literature: A Re-examination of Epic and Lament."

29. At this battle the Russian forces under the leadership of Prince Dmitrii of Moscow defeated the Tatars for the first time since the Tatars invaded in the thirteenth century.

30. *Skazanie o Mamaevom poboishche*, in *Pamiatniki literatury Drenei Rusi. XIV-seredina XV veka*, ed. L. A. Dmitriev and D. S. Likhachev (Moscow, 1981), 152.

31. The text of the *Slovo o zhitii velikogo kniazia Dmitriia Ivanovicha* is found in *Literatura Drevnei Rusi. XIV-seredina XV veka*, 208–29.

32. On the popularity of the *Povest' o Petre i Fevronii Muromskikh*, see for example, Vladimir Kuskov, *A History of Old Russian Literature*, trans. Ronald Vroon (Moscow,

1980), 211. The text of the *Povest' o Petre i Fevronii Muromskikh* is found in *Russkie povesti XV–XVI vekov*, 108–15.

33. Grossman, "Feminine Images in Old Russian Literature and Art," 47.

34. D. S. Likhachev, *Chleovek v literature drevnei Rusi* (Moscow, 1970), 94.

35. On the folkloric motifs employed in the *Povest' o Petre i Fevronii Muronskikh*, see, for example, *Russkie povesti XV-XVI vekov*, ed. M. O. Skripil' (Moscow-Leningrad, 1958), 447, 450–51. For an unconventional discussion of the work's possible mythic components, see Jack V. Haney, "On the 'Tale of Peter and Fevroniia, Wonderworkers of Muron,' " *Canadian-American Slavic Studies* 13 (1979), 139–62.

36. *Russkaia povest' XVII veka*, ed. I. P. Eremin, comp. M. O. Skripil' (Leningrad, 1954), 362.

37. Dewey and Kleimola, "Muted Eulogy: Women Who Inspired Men in Medieval Rus'," 195.

38. T. A. Greenan, "Iulianiya Lazarevskaya," *Oxford Slavonic Papers* 15 (1982): 28–45.

39. The text of the *Povest' ob Ulianii Osor'inoi* is found in the *Russkaia povest' XVII veka*, 39–47.

40. The reforms initiated by Nikon included, among others, extensive emendation of religious texts and certain changes in ritual, such as the use of the three rather than the two fingers to make the sign of the cross.

41. *Zhitie protopopa Avvakuma, im samim napisannoe, i drugie ego sochineniia*, ed. N. K. Gudzii (Moscow, 1960), 78. In my translation, I relied extensively on Kenneth N. Brostrum's translation, *Archpriest Avvakum: The Life Written by Himself* (Ann Arbor, MI: University of Michigan Press, 1979).

42. On dating and authorship of *Povest' o boiaryne Morozovoi* see A. I. Mazunin, ed., *Povest' o Morozovoi boiaryne* (Leningrad, 1979), 50, 66, 71, 74–77.

43. A. M. Panchenko, "Boiarynia Morozova—Simvol i lichnost'," in *Povest' o boiaryne Morozovoi*, 4.

44. The text of the oldest extant redaction of the work is found in *Povest' o boiaryne Morozovoi*, 127–55.

2

Women as Performers of Oral Literature: A Re-examination of Epic and Lament[1]

Natalie Kononenko

A knowledge of folklore is essential to understanding the image of women presented in Russian literature and the prejudices encountered by women writers. Folklore is much closer to the Russian consciousness than to the consciousness of the average American, and it would not be an exaggeration to say that virtually all Russian writers used elements of folklore in their works. Nikolai Gogol took characters from folk puppet theater. Nikolai Karamzin and Mikhail Lermontov incorporated beliefs about the *rusalka*, or Russian mermaid. Fedor Dostoevsky used folk motifs and folktale structural elements. Marina Tsvetaeva drew on folk-song form, imagery, and literary devices. Writers from the village prose school, such as Vasilii Shukshin, saw peasants as a paragon of the Russian ethos and tried to capture their lifestyle, world outlook, and language.

Numerous studies examine the use of folklore by Russian authors. Many folklore textbooks end with a section on folklore in literature.[2] Handbooks for the community centers that Communists established in virtually every town and city neighborhood detail ways of adapting folklore to community functions.[3] Since folk belief affected all strata of Russian society, folklore helps us understand not only peasant women and their songs and tales, but also beliefs encountered by upper-class women who chose to write.

Folklore is a huge field. It includes the study of folk housing, clothing, food, and decorative arts, the study of wedding rituals, funerals, and calendary rites such as Easter, and the study of folktales, folk songs, proverbs, riddles, and other verbal forms. Discussing all of these areas in their relationship to written literature is impossible in one chapter. Therefore, I shall examine oral literature, the analog of written literature, and look at women as performers of oral literature, the position analogous to that of women writers. Because the various aspects of traditional culture are so tightly interwoven, my examination of oral literature will, necessarily, bring in the other areas of folklore.

The genres of oral literature that women, as opposed to men, performed show an association between women and poetry parallel to the one Barbara Heldt found in her examination of nineteenth- and twentieth-century Russian written literature.[4] More important, my investigation of why both men and women were allowed to perform most genres while a certain few were gender-restricted reveals something fundamental about Russian culture and women's position in it. Oral literature, I believe, offers a clear indication that marriage was a late addition to Slavic society and that it was introduced to subjugate powerful, independent women. A further implication is that marriage was imposed by patriarchal peoples and that the Slavs were originally matriarchal.

The domain of oral literature is enormous. There are stories to entertain the old and stories to educate the young. Some narratives are believed to be true and some are frankly fantastic, their action set three times nine kingdoms away. Some songs are said to affect the future and help crops grow; others are sung simply to express feelings. There are miniature forms such as proverbs and riddles and narratives that take hours to tell. Interestingly, access to this vast realm of oral literature was remarkably egalitarian.

We are accustomed to division by gender—in folklore as well as in other fields. In the house and farmstead, for example, there are separate areas for men's work and for women's work, both indoors and outside. In oral literature, however, it seems that almost every genre could be performed by either women or men. Thus, there are limericks that voice women's anger at a two-timing man, as well as songs that express a man's point of view.[5] There are lyric songs in which a man longs for his beloved and songs in which a woman voices the same emotion. Where collectors of oral literature provide information about their sources, we see that both women and men tell folktales, both women and men recount personal experiences, and so forth, for almost all genres of oral literature.[6] When Russian scholars classify genres of oral literature, they do not use performer gender as a distinguishing criterion. Propp, for example, discusses other performance features such as choral versus solo singing, but not gender.[7] If there is a gender distinction, it is that only women sing weaving songs, because only women weave, and only men sing songs to accompany chopping wood, because that is man's work. Such a distinction is outside the realm of oral literature, because what is gender-specific is the type of work, not the song.

One gender distinction existed, however, until the turn of this century: Women and only women sang laments (*plachi, prichitaniia, prichity*) while only men sang epic (*byliny*). As Roman Jakobson points out, in all of the Slavic areas where epic and lament exist—Russia, Ukraine, and the Balkans—"the former genre has a string accompaniment and is monopolized by men, while the latter is performed by women only."[8] Poetic forms that developed out of epic, such as historical and religious songs, were also primarily men's genres. In short, oral literature was equally accessible to women and men, but epic and lament and only these two genres and their direct relatives were gender-restricted.

In addition to gender-restriction, epic and lament share other features. Most of the discussion has focused on their formal similarities. Both epic and lament are narrative poetry and both are sung in a chanting style called recitative (*re-chitativ*). As Jakobson has shown, the two genres have similar verse and line structure. The prosodic features are nearly identical. There are long lines and short lines in both, and in both, the long line is used for a more elevated tone. In fact, Jakobson notes that "in all three Slavic areas where these genres exist, the epics and the laments prove to be closely interconnected structurally (and, in particular, in their metric form)."[9]

The content of epic and lament have much in common as well: Both combine narrative and tragic elements. Laments frequently tell about events in the life of the deceased, sometimes describing the way he or she died.[10] Thus, laments, in addition to expressing bereavement, have a narrative component. Epics, on the other hand, which we normally associate with narration of armed conflict, deal with death as well. Whether under the influence of Western scholarship, which is based on Western epic, or in an attempt to disassociate epic from lament, a genre strongly connected to women, Russian and Soviet epic scholars concentrate on battle themes rather than on death themes.[11] Although the tragic content of Russian epic poetry has not been emphasized, it is very much a part of the tradition. Sviatogor,[12] a hero so mighty that the earth can barely support his weight, finds a coffin that is just his size. He decides to try it out and lies down in it. He then tries to rise, but the more he struggles to get out, the more tightly he is entrapped. Before he dies, Sviatogor manages to breathe some of his strength into the hero Il'ia Muromets, but Sviatogor dies nonetheless. Sukhman, a mighty hero who battles an entire Tatar army single-handedly, is insulted when Vladimir does not believe that he could accomplish such a feat. Once Sukhman's conquest of the Tatars has been confirmed by witnesses, he repays Vladimir by committing suicide, removing his own bandages and bleeding to death. Dunai murders his wife because she outperforms him in archery and other contests of military prowess. When he learns that she was indeed pregnant with the beautiful child she said she was carrying, he plants a spear into the ground and kills himself by falling on it. Il'ia slays his own son. Before the boy is born, Il'ia abandons the woman who will bear him a child. Therefore, when he meets his son as an adult, he does not recognize him and engages him in battle with tragic results. Vasilii Buslaev kicks a skull lying on the side of a mountain and is cursed to die on the same mountain. Churilo is murdered in bed. Skopin is poisoned.[13]

Tragic elements abound in epic. The death of a hero's wife is almost as frequent a topic as the death of the hero himself. Dunai is not the only one who murders the woman he loves. Mikhailo Potyk kills Mar'ia the White Swan, the most beautiful of women. Dobrynia kills Marinka and Ivan Godinovich kills Nastasiia; both do it in a very cruel way, first by chopping off the woman's lips, then her arms, then her legs.[14]

Death is not characteristic of all Russian *byliny*, but it is prominent in the tradition. Furthermore, if no one dies, there is other misfortune. Friends fight. Friends and lovers betray each other, often unwittingly. There is tragic misunderstanding. Heroes are unjustly punished. Russian *byliny* may not be as sad as Ukrainian epics, which have a tragic element in virtually every song.[15] Nonetheless, this is poetry with elegiac content as well as lament form.

The connection between epic and lament extends still further. Russian tradition has laments for three occasions. In addition to funeral laments, the most familiar category and the one that we have discussed up to this point, there are also Russian laments for the departure of recruits and for weddings.[16] Epic is connected to all three lament types.

The link between laments for recruits and epic is not difficult to establish. Epics are songs about war, and the Russian songs tell about battles between the Slavs and the Turkic peoples and about struggles against the Polish-Lithuanian Commonwealth. Putilov, the leading scholar of epic alive today, considers the conflict with the Turkic peoples the core of Russian heroic narrative.[17] Thus, epics have military subject matter and the tragic tone discussed above. Laments for recruits share this tragic tone and military setting, because they are songs sung by mothers, wives, and sweethearts lamenting over men departing for battle and possible death.

The connection between epic, lament, and the wedding is more unexpected. Nonetheless, matrimony is another of the central topics of epic poetry. There are numerous *byliny* about getting married. Dobrynia sees Nastasiia Filipovna riding across a field and attacks her with his mace. She is so large and so strong that she barely notices the blows. When she finally realizes that she is being attacked, she decides to marry Dobrynia, picks him up, and puts him in her pocket. After they marry, she becomes the best of wives, but, in another *bylina*, Dobrynia almost loses her to Aliosha Popovich when Dobrynia stays away from home too long. Solovei Budimirovich wins Vladimir's niece as his bride by building a palace beneath her window. Sadko charms the king of the sea by playing his *gusli*, and he is rewarded with the offer of marriage to one of the king's daughters. Volkh Vseslavevich attacks India and commands his troops to slaughter old and young alike, leaving only enough beautiful women for each warrior to have a bride. The song ends with a mass wedding. When the prospective bride's mother refuses the marriage offer made by the mother of Khoten Bludovich, Khoten ruins her house and kills six of her nine sons. To save her remaining children, the woman agrees to the marriage proposal, and Khoten shows his good will by procuring the water of life and reviving his six new brothers-in-law.[18] We would not consider the actions of Dobrynia, Volkh, and Khoten appropriate courtship behavior, but these are, nonetheless, songs of courtship and marriage.

Marriage is the subject of all of the epics about unhappy spousal relationships that were listed above. Most of the songs that end with the death of the wife begin with courtship and happy marriage, making the end more tragic by contrast. There are also songs of happy unions, such as the one between Dobrynia and Nastasiia. In one such story, Staver Godinovich boasts too much of his possessions and of his young wife. This behavior makes Vladimir jealous and the king has Staver thrown into prison. Staver's wife arrives in court dressed as a warrior and eventually succeeds in outwitting Vladimir and freeing her husband. Perhaps in keeping with the sorrowful tone of the *byliny*, however, marital problems appear more frequently than does wedded happiness. This seems especially true of the secondary characters, and even Vladimir's wife Apraksiia is ready to offer herself to the gluttonous villain Tugarin when she thinks he is stronger than the Russian warriors.[19] Happy or unhappy, marriages are an important theme in *byliny*. There is even a pattern of sorts. Weddings occur early in a narrative if the marriage will eventually fail and at the end if the song will end happily. Sometimes, as in the *bylina* of Mikhailo Potyk, there is a wedding at the beginning and one at the end.

The reason epics and laments resemble each other to such an extent, is that epic and the three types of lament all had one ancestor: the funeral lament. This is the likely progenitor because it is more basic than epic or the other two lament types. Funeral laments are widespread and exist among a variety of peoples, while epics are rare and occur only under special social and historical circumstances. Wedding laments and laments for recruits are rarer still and are found primarily among the Slavic peoples. We also know that there were once men's and women's funeral laments, just as there are now men's and women's work songs, lyric songs, limericks, and tales. Medieval documents attest that both men and women lamented and that the laments they sang were for the deceased. Russian and Soviet scholars, working from these manuscripts and other sources, agree that funeral laments were once performed by both sexes.[20] Even if they make no connection between epic and lament, these scholars nonetheless concede that, in the distant past, men as well as women sang funeral laments. Thus, unlike epics and the other two types of lament, funeral laments once followed the pattern we now see in the rest of Russian oral literature. If funeral laments were once like the other genres, then they are likely the precursor for the other two types of lament and for epic.

It is not difficult to see laments for recruits as an outgrowth of the funeral lament. Even if one disregards the nature of Russian military service, which took men away from their families for twenty-five years, and if one ignores the Russian belief in the parallel between travel and death, sending a man off to battle and the possibility of being killed has a certain funereal nature, and lamenting on such an occasion seems logical.[21] It is also not difficult to suppose that epics developed out of men's laments for their comrades fallen in battle, even though some scholars, like Kolessa and Jakobson, do not see such a generic relationship.[22] Lamenting on the occasion of a wedding, however, does not seem to develop logically out of songs of death.

The wedding is the key to the puzzle. At some point in the past, there were no epics, wedding laments, or laments for recruits. Only the funeral lament existed and both women and men performed it. The introduction of the wedding, at least in the form that we know it, brought gender restrictions into Russian oral literature. The wedding accrued the lament to itself and was so drastic and peculiar a rite that it caused lament to fragment. Instead of there being a single genre—lament—with men's and women's forms, there now arose two separate genres: epic for men and lament for women. To support this theory, I shall show that the Russian wedding was no ordinary mid-life rite of passage, but a ritual much like a bride's funeral, where lamenting would be most appropriate.

The Russian wedding rite is performed primarily for the woman. Whatever description one examines, from whichever region, one finds that very little is done for the groom. What is done for the woman—symbolically, at least—seems like an attempt to take a powerful being who does not want to get married and force her into matrimony. It appears that the woman must be convinced that she no longer has a will and is now like an object, exchanged between men for goods, since she is "sold" by her father to the groom's family for a bride price. The woman must be turned into someone who is no longer a being in her own right, but a submissive and subservient daughter-in-law, the protector of her husband's fortune, a mother of children. Ideally, a married woman should be as good as dead. She should cease to exist for herself and live for and through others.

The wedding process typically begins when the groom's family approaches a woman's family with a marriage proposal. If the woman's family is favorably inclined, the prospective bride's father and either her mother or elder brother go to see the groom's home to examine his possessions and his cattle.[23] If the bride's family remains interested in the union, the ritual of the "covering" of the bride (*zaporuki, zakryvanie, zaveshivanie*) is performed. The groom's family returns to the bride's home for the negotiation of the bride price, which signals that the first two steps have gone smoothly and that the two families are about to conclude the marriage agreement. The bride is supposed to react by running away and trying to hide, usually in one of the outbuildings of the farmstead such as the barn or the bathhouse. The bride is found and forcibly brought back to her house, either by family members or by her girlfriends. She is then covered with a large scarf or shawl.[24] From this point on, the bride laments, asking her parents why they want to sell her to a stranger and begging them not to do so. She asks her parents how she has displeased them that they should want to be rid of her. She begs her parents for mercy and expresses fear of her future husband and the new household.[25] The bride usually remains dressed in the shawl, even sleeping in it, until the ritual bath preceding the wedding.

The next step is a period of preparation for the wedding, called the *nedelia*. The father of the bride brews beer for the wedding. The bride and other women cut and make the wedding dress and work on various cloth items that are to be part of the wedding. These items include the gifts that the bride will distribute to the groom and his family and the dowry that she will bring with her, mostly linens for herself, her husband, and their future children. Except for the dress, most of the gifts and dowry are prepared well in advance; girls are supposed to start working on their dowries at the age of eight.[26] During the period of preparation, the bride, usually very lightly dressed in spite of the cold weather, goes out to the street in the evening in the company of her girlfriends. She laments

again, beats herself, and flings herself into the snow. This is called *vykhodit'
na ugor*. In some regions this behavior happens every night and, in others, three
or four times during the preparation week. As the last event of the *ugory*, the
bride walks around the entire village and says good-bye to it, to all of its
inhabitants, rivers, fields, and forests.[27]

The actual wedding begins with a ritual bath for the bride, which is usually
followed by the *devichnik*, the bride's farewell to her maidenhood. The *devichnik*
is a party, with food and drink served to the bride's girlfriends and sometimes
to members of the groom's wedding party. During the *devichnik*, the bride
laments the loss of her beauty (*krasa, krasota*) or freedom (*volia*). She then
either hands an object such as a wreath, which represents the beauty or free will,
to another person, or she assigns the abstract concept of her beauty and will to
the church, a birch tree, or a river.[28]

The other elements of the wedding day include the arrival of the groom's
party. When they arrive, they have to gain entrance into the bride's house either
by offering money or answering riddles. The groom's lack of participation in
the wedding rite is evidenced by the fact that whichever multiform is used, these
actions are performed by the best man (*druzhko*). The groom's party "buys" a
place for the groom at the table, symbolically repeating the purchase of the bride.
The groom's party then demands to see the bride. After some delay, she is led
in, dressed in her wedding clothes. The members of the groom's party greet her
and compliment her on her beauty as her father seats the bride next to the groom.[29]
There is apparently some variation in the sequence of wedding day events.
Sometimes the *devichnik* precedes the formal interaction with the groom's party.
Sometimes, especially if the church wedding is held the following day, the
devichnik occurs in the evening, following the arrival of the groom and his men.
If the *devichnik* occurs with the men present, the house is partitioned into men's
and women's sections.[30]

The church wedding begins with the couple seated at the table in the bride's
home. The bride gives gifts of the various items she has embroidered and woven
to the members of the groom's party. After the ceremonial meal, the groom's
party leads the bride from her home, often in an unusual way such as out the
back door and through the yard. In the yard, the bride receives her parents'
blessing. Once she has joined the groom's party, the bride is supposed to stop
lamenting.[31]

After the church wedding, the bride is brought into her new home. Since she
has given gifts to the male members of the groom's party at her own house, she
now distributes presents to the groom's female relatives here. There is some
ritual humiliation of the bride: assigning her impossible tasks such as carrying
buckets of water from the river that members of the groom's family knock over
and spill. A festive meal takes place at the groom's home, followed by the ritual
of preparing the bridal bed, paying for the bed, and again ritually debasing the
bride by having her remove her husband's boots.[32]

The following morning, the couple is awakened by the wedding party. They then travel to the bride's former home where the bride's mother treats the groom to *bliny* (wheatcakes) or scrambled eggs and the groom pays for the food. In the past, the payment was optional and was made only if the bride was a virgin. It was the groom's way of thanking his mother-in-law for keeping the bride pure. The couple returns to the groom's household, which will be their home, where the wedding ritual concludes with a final festive meal.[33]

The traditional Russian wedding is complex. The previous descriptions are only a brief summary of what is usually documented in book-length works. This outline, although brief, reveals many links between the wedding and the funeral in addition to the laments that accompany both rites. The shawl covering the bride has some resemblance to the shroud. The ritual washing of the bride is comparable to the bathing of the corpse, and both are followed by public display: the presentation of the bride to the groom's party and the laying out of the corpse for viewing. Removing the bride through the back door is analogous to removing the coffin through an unusual aperture, again, the back door or a window, and both precede a trip to church.[34] There are many more details that could be included, and the entire wedding process and its symbolism could be discussed at much greater length. For our purposes, it is sufficient to say that there are a number of parallels between the treatment of a bride during her wedding and the treatment of a corpse during a funeral.

All of the parallels between the wedding and the funeral, if taken individually, could be rationalized in one way or another. After all, the wedding is multifaceted and its components function on many psychological and social levels. Taken as a whole, however, the death imagery of the wedding cannot be ignored. It is striking and overwhelming. Van Gennep, Turner, and other anthropologists have pointed out that all rites of passage have elements of death and rebirth. They also believe that the person for whom a rite is performed is seen to die, from the viewpoint of his or her former social position, to be reborn in the new one.[35]

In the Russian wedding, however, death symbolism goes far beyond that commonly seen in a rite of passage. This is not just a normal mid-life transition from one position in society to another. The Russian woman dies, in terms of her previous existence as a single girl in her household of birth, but there is little imagery that suggests she is reborn as a married woman in her husband's household. She is supposed to die symbolically and stay that way. Her rebirth is not to a new position in society, as would be typical of a rite of passage, it is through others.

In an article that applies Van Gennep's theories to the Russian wedding, Baiburin and Levinton call the bride's ceasing to lament when she leaves her house for the trip to church a rebirth element.[36] This is "stretching" the evidence because the bride ends an activity; she does not perform a new act. I believe that there is no symbolic rebirth in a Russian wedding and that its position in the ritual process is filled by the physical birth of the woman's first child. At this point, the woman's position begins to improve, and although she never fully achieves the status elevation that Turner says concludes a rite of passage, the birth of a child is the beginning of the long climb to prominence in the household of marriage.[37] Balashov, Marchenko, and Kalmykova, by using a picture of a woman holding a baby as their final illustration, reflect the sense that the real culmination of the wedding is the birth of a child.[38] I should emphasize that these authors label the second festive meal at the groom's home the last step of the wedding, while their choice of illustration contradicts their words and shows that they, too, feel the process is not complete until a baby is born.

The belief that a woman's wedding was like her funeral is seen in her treatment during other rites. Because the wedding was a woman's symbolic death, when her biological death came, there was little need to lament her passing. Thus, descriptions of funerals tell what is done to the male deceased, and the majority of published funeral laments are laments for men. In the Biblioteka poeta edition, for instance, there are forty-three funeral laments, of which thirty-two are for men and eleven are for women.[39] The pattern seems to be that the wedding for a woman was what the funeral, or being called up as a recruit, was for a man. The distribution in texts was not that some were performed by women and others by men; rather, it was that certain types, namely wedding laments, were about women and others were about men.

Perhaps the clearest indication that the wedding is a woman's fundamental rite of passage is that, if a woman died unwed, her funeral was celebrated as a wedding. All of the steps of the wedding were not performed, but the deceased was dressed in wedding clothes and given a ring. The laments sung were modifications of wedding laments, and some of the decorations were also modifications of objects used in a wedding. Unmarried young men were also "married to death," but performing the funeral as a wedding was much more important if the deceased was female. All accounts of such "weddings of the dead" among the East Slavs describe rites performed for women.[40]

Considering marriage to be a woman's death explains the presence of laments in the wedding ritual: The wedding, being so much like a funeral, accrued various elements from this rite, laments included. Why the wedding had to be a woman's symbolic death is another question. The best answer is that it was part of an attempt by men, perhaps an invading patriarchal group, to control women, possibly those of a native matriarchal culture, and to guarantee paternity.[41]

Interestingly, images of force, subjugation, and control appear not only in the wedding rite but also in epic. According to Russian epic, a woman is very strong and rather frightening. She is the huge Amazon (*polianitsa*) whom Dobrynia marries. She is a powerful warrior who must be conquered by Dunai. She can get the better of even the king himself, as does the wife of Staver Godinovich.[42] In epics, a woman is not monogamous by choice. Most of the women killed in *byliny* die because they betray the hero by having sexual relations with another man. This is what Mar'ia the White Swan does to Mikhailo Potyk and Marinka does to Dobrynia. It is the reason Ivan Godinovich kills his beloved. Female fickleness extends to the highest social positions. It is not clear whether Vladimir's wife Apraksiia ever actually betrays him, but there is no doubt that she is ready to do so. Women can deceive even the mightiest of men. In one of the Sviatogor *byliny*, Il'ia first encounters the hero asleep. While her husband sleeps, Sviatogor's wife makes love to Il'ia. Sviatogor eventually kills her, but he is a cuckold nonetheless.[43]

Most important, Russian epics also express the hope that marriage will subdue a woman. Nastasiia the *polianitsa*, once she marries Dobrynia, not only becomes a model wife, but she is reduced in size and power from mountainous to normal proportions. According to Stephen Dunn, epic expresses the male point of view.[44] What happens to Nastasiia as the result of marriage seems like fulfillment of male wishes. Perhaps the Russian wedding was instituted with hopes for a transformation like Nastasiia's in mind. Propp connects the origin of epic to the introduction of marriage. He theorizes that epic came into being when society shifted from clan to feudal organization; he argues that epics often deal with the establishment of the monogamous family.[45] Propp's ideas are based on a Marxist interpretation of history and are out of vogue at the moment. But they deserve more attention, especially in light of the discussion here.

If the Russian wedding was indeed a relatively late development, it would explain the gender assignation we find in oral literature. It would signify that the system of oral literature, with its lack of gender restrictions, was in existence when the wedding was introduced. The introduction of the wedding and its emphasis on death would have affected the genre connected with death, namely the lament. As the wedding was a rite done unto the woman and the woman only, so the lament became a genre restricted to women.

Excluding men from lamenting and calling lament specifically a women's activity may have provided the stimulus for the evolution of lament performed by men into a separate, male genre—epic. If men could no longer lament, then what had been men's lament might have retained its elegiac tone and its formal features but moved to a distinct setting. War, as a strictly male activity, was the logical choice for such a setting, and epics may well have evolved from laments for fallen comrades.

The wedding acts as the key to another set of beliefs that are important to both Russian folklore and written literature. Because women are seen as dying during the wedding ritual, they are associated with the other world. Like the biological dead, the women become spiritual beings. Again, this is a complex phenomenon in which pagan religion and beliefs about the closeness of the dead to the living play a role. What is important for us here is that women are supposed to be spiritual in two senses. They are to be uninterested in themselves and in physical things. They are expected to sacrifice themselves, especially for their children and the men they love. If they live up to the ideal of the feminine, they are considered morally superior. These themes are expressed throughout oral literature. As Heldt points out, these themes are common in Russian written literature. The other sense in which women are spiritual beings is that they are assigned a great deal of spiritual power. They are expected to interact with the spirit world, at least in its non-Christian manifestations.

The concept of female spiritual power appears in the belief that women take care of the boundary between the human and the spirit worlds. All aspects of the entry of the human soul into this world and its departure from it, which were not part of Christian rite, were supervised by women. Thus, married women delivered babies and washed and prepared the dead, while baptisms and church services for the deceased were activities done by males. Women, married and of marriageable age, could interact with the spirits and tell fortunes. But women of the same two groups could be accused of bad spirit contact, namely witchcraft.[46]

The pattern is that non-Christian spirituality belongs to women, which suggests that the pre-Christian Slavs were not only matriarchal, but they also practiced goddess worship. Traces of goddess beliefs among the Slavic peoples are numerous: from archeological evidence to attestations of female supernaturals in nineteenth- and twentieth-century folk belief.[47] One of the most important of these, the *rusalka*, should be mentioned here, because she is very much linked to the Russian wedding.

The *rusalka* is believed to be the unquiet spirit of a girl who committed suicide by drowning because she was pregnant out of wedlock. She lives in the body of water in which she died, along with the child who is born after her death. She has legs rather than a fishtail and is believed to sit in trees at night, luring men with her singing. When men approach and gaze at the beauty of her image reflected in the water, the *rusalka* is supposed to jump on them and drown them, forcing them to join her in her watery home.[48] Even this cursory description of the *rusalka* shows that the way she comes into being is almost the inverse of the wedding. The *rusalka* bears a child first, outside of wedlock; while for the bride, the child is the culmination of the wedding process. The *rusalka* actively seeks a mate, though not a husband, and the man is forced to join her in her domain while the human bride must move into her husband's household, something the bride resists. It is tempting to see the *rusalka* as a remnant of a pre-Christian deity, forced underground or, more literally, underwater by a new religion. It is also tempting to see the *rusalka's* life as a reflection of an early social order where there was no marriage and women accepted men into their domain to father children. Speculation aside, folk belief articulates clearly that a woman who resists marriage, especially one who becomes pregnant outside marriage, is bad. A woman who does not submit to the symbolic death of the wedding must accept the literal death of the *rusalka*. A woman who does not become spiritual as a married woman should, must become a spirit and a bad one at that, because the *rusalka* is associated with the "unclean force" (*nechistaia sila*). It is not surprising that the *rusalka*, like Nastasiia the *polianitsa*, can be transformed by marriage. If a man succeeds in putting a cross around her neck and marrying her, a *rusalka* becomes a most desirable wife.

Examining folklore and oral literature shows us that, for a woman, marriage is like death, and, like death, its desired effect is to turn her into a spiritual being. Spirituality, moral power, and self-sacrifice are all qualities that Heldt includes in her idea of "terrible perfection." It would be useful to examine this idea and the lives of the women writers Heldt discusses in terms of folk belief.

Examining folklore also shows us that the wedding may well be a late addition to Russian ritual, which affected access to certain genres of oral literature. Because a woman's wedding was believed to be so much like a funeral, death became an exclusively female domain and the genre of death, the lament, was restricted to women. As suggested here, the restriction of lament probably caused the genesis of epic. The strength of the link between women and lament can be seen in what happened to oral literature in this century. As epic began to die out, women were allowed to sing it and, because so many women knew all of the requisite poetic devices from lament, they did just that. In fact, some women *skaziteli* were recognized as top performers.[49] Thus, epic assumed the pattern of gender access seen in the rest of oral literature. Lament, to this day, is sung only by women.

The effect of folk patterns of gender access on written literature is a fruitful area for further investigation. In written literature, according to Heldt, men dominated prose fiction, and women chose the more personal and immediate forms of poetry and autobiography. Certainly folk laments are poetry. Like autobiography, they are personal narratives that recount events and express the emotions of the lyric "I." Conversely, the male oral genre, epic, attempts to name women and assign them the qualities of terrible perfection, much as Heldt says occurs in literature written by men. Thus, the phenomena observed in nineteenth- and twentieth-century writing may have a basis in folk belief.

Oral literature offers a hopeful precedent as well. Most genres of oral literature were performed by women as well as by men and epic eventually entered this system. Since women became among the best singers of epic, they may achieve full status as writers of all forms of literature.

NOTES

1. I would like to thank Jeannette Lacoss and Rebecca Bowman for their assistance with background research.

2. Mahdu Malik, "*Vertep* and the Sacred/Profane Dichotomy in Gogol's Dikanka Stories," *Slavic and East European Journal* 34.3 (Fall 1990): 322–47. Natalie K. Moyle, "Mermaids (*Rusalki*) and Russian Beliefs about Women," in *New Studies in Russian Language and Literature*, ed. Anna Lisa Crone and Catherine V. Chvany (Columbus, OH: Slavica Publishers, 1986), 221–38. V. E. Vetlovskaia, "F. M. Dostoevskii," in *Russkaia literatura i fol'klor (Vtoraia polovina XIX v)* (Leningrad, 1982), 12–75. V. Iu. Aleksandrov, "Fol'klorno-pesennye motivy v lirike M. Tsvetaevoi," in *Russkaia literatura i fol'klornaia traditsiia* (Volgograd, 1983), 103–12. Examples of studies of folklore in written literature are E. V. Pomerantseva, *Pisateli i Skazochniki* (Moscow, 1988); Bazanov et al., *Mif/Fol'klor/Literatura* (Leningrad, 1978); F. Ia. Priima et al., *Russkaia Literatura i Fol'klor (Pervaia polovina XIX v)* (Leningrad, 1976); and the two collected works cited above. A recent example of a folklore collection with a section on folklore

and written literature is Iurii Georgievich Kruglov, *Russkoe Narodnoe Poeticheskoe Tvorchestvo. Khrestomatiia po fol'kloristike* (Moscow, 1986), 536.

3. See, for example, N. V. Novikov, *Fol'klor i Khudozhestvennaia Samodeiatel'nost'* (Leningrad, 1968).

4. Barbara Heldt, *Terrible Perfection: Women and Russian Literature* (Bloomington: Indiana University Press), 7.

5.

Off of a steep bank	So krutogo berezhka
The girls pushed a guy:	Stolknuli devushki druzhka:
Sink to the bottom, dear one,	Idi ty, korovochka, ko dnu,
If you love more than one.	Koli liubish' ne odnu.

Kruglov, *Russkoe narodnoe poeticheskoe tvorchestvo*, 409.

6. Collectors provided practically no information about performers until the second half of the nineteenth century because they assumed that the oral literature originated among the upper classes and that the folk from whom they collected merely remembered the texts created elsewhere and remembered them badly at that. Among the first collections to give performer information were *Pesni, sobrannye P. N. Rybnikovym*, vol. 1–41 (1861–1867); reprinted *Pesni sobrannye P. N. Rybnikovym*, ed. A. E. Gruzinskii, *s portretom, biografiei i ukazatelem* (The Hague: Europe Printing, 1968) and Aleksandr Fedorovich Gil'ferding, *Onezhskie byliny, zapisannye A. E. Gil'ferdingom letom 1871 goda. S dvumia portretami onezhskikh rapsodov i napevami bylin* (St. Petersburg, 1873).

7. V. Ia. Propp, "Printsipy klassifikatsii fol'klornykh zhanrov," *Sovetskaia Etnografiia* 4 (1964): 147–54.

8. Roman Jakobson, "Slavic Epic Verse: Studies in Comparative Metrics," vol. 4 of *Selected Writings* (The Hague and Paris: Mouton, 1966), 444. Elsa Mahler, *Die Russische Totenklage; Ihre Rituelle und Dichterische Deutung (Mit Besonderer Berucksichtingung des Grossrussischen Nordens)* (Nendeln/Liechtenstein: Kraus Reprint, 1968) of original Leipzig (1935), 52–55, using some very reliable sources, contradicts Jakobson and finds male lament among the Ukrainians. She even includes examples of men lamenting over their wives. (Ukrainian material cannot be discussed here for lack of space.) The existence of men's laments, specifically among the Ukrainians, does not contradict the argument presented here. Ukrainian marital patterns differ from Russian patterns in such a way that male access to lament would be fully expected.

9. Jakobson, 414–63, 445.

10. See, for example, Iurii Sokolov's discussion of laments as social protest. To make his point, Sokolov cites a lament that tells the circumstances under which a village elder died. Y. M. Sokolov, *Russian Folklore*, trans. Catherine Ruth Smith (Detroit: Folklore Associates, 1971), 230–32.

11. Two short histories of epic scholarship by leading scholars are V. I. Chicherov, "Itogi rabot i zadachi izucheniia russkikh bylin i istoricheskikh pesen," in *Osnovnye problemy eposa vostochnykh slavian*, ed. V. I. Chicherov (Moscow, 1958), 15–47 and B. N. Putilov's introduction to the Biblioteka poeta collection of *byliny*, "Russkii bylinnyi epos," in *Byliny*, 2d ed., ed. B. N. Putilov (Leningrad, 1957), 5–44.

12. As oral literature, *byliny* do not have titles. The custom, both among oral performers and among folklorists, is to refer to a *bylina* by the name of its hero. When published in collections, *byliny* are usually assigned a title, such as *"Bylina about Sviatogor."*

13. Because the Biblioteka poeta edition prepared by Putilov is carefully done and

readily available, all further citations of *bylina* texts will be from this collection unless otherwise noted. In terms of recording accuracy, the classic collections are *Pesni sobrannye P. N. Rybnikovym*, most readily available in the 2d ed.; *Onezhskie byliny, zapisannye A. F. Gil'ferdingom letom 1871 goda*, most readily available in 4th ed.; and *Byliny Severa*. "Podgotovka tekstov, vstupitel'naia stat'ia i kommentarii," A. M. Astakhovoi, vol. 1–2 (Moscow, 1938, 1951). Sviatogor, Sukhman, Dunai, Il'ia and his Son, Vasilii Buslaev, and Churilo are Putilov, 48–52; 170–75; 276–84; 112–17; 374–81; and 424–27, respectively. Skopin is Astakhova, vol. 1, 432–34.

14. Putilov, 240–63, 264–70, 292–98.

15. Filaret M. Kolessa, "Rechytatyvni formy v ukraiisns'kii narodnii poezii," in *Pervisne Hromadians'tvo* (1927), 60–113, discusses the form and content of Ukrainian epic, *dumy*, in relationship to laments.

16. The classic collection is Elpidifor Vasilevich Barsov, *Prichitaniia severnogo kraia sobrannye E. V. Barsovym* (Moscow, 1872–1882), in 2 vols. It is divided into funeral laments, wedding laments, and laments for recruits.

17. Putilov, "Russkii Bylinnyi Epos," 33–34.

18. Dobrynia and Nastasia Filipovna are in M. Speranskii, ed., *Russkaia ustnaia slovesnost': Byliny*, vol. 1 (Moscow, 1916), 67–71; Dobrynia and Aliosha: Speranskii, 55–66; Putilov, 400–406; Solovei Budimirovich: Putilov, 382–88; Sadko: 224–39; Volkh Vseslavevich: 53–58. This is a rather extreme form of courtship and one not likely to instill great love for the groom in the bride. Scenes of attack and bride capture, especially in *byliny* based on the earliest historical periods, do support the Marxist and feminist sequences of historical epochs. Khoten Bludovich: Putilov, 428–32.

19. Staver: Putilov 344–53; Tugarin: 97–101. Please note that Staver Godinovich is not the same character as Ivan Godinovich, a hero mentioned on page 31. Staver Godinovich and Ivan Godinovich may be based on the same historical person or on different historical figures. What is certain is that, in the *bylina* texts that we have, the two Godinoviches appear in separate and rather different songs and are not linked in any way. In the Ivan *bylina*, the hero discovers his wife's infidelity and deals with it cruelly. In the Staver *bylina*, the couple survives a threat from a jealous monarch and is actually pictured as together and happy at the end of the narrative.

20. B. E. Chistova and K. V. Chistov, eds., *Prichitaniia* (Sovetskii pisatel', 1960), 14–15; Mahler, 19–35. Please note that Ukrainian men sing funeral laments; Mahler, 52–55; K. V. Chistov, "Russkaia Prichet' " in *Prichitaniia*, 14–15.

21. For discussion of beliefs about travel and death, see Natalie K. Moyle, "Spacey Soviets and the Russian Attitude Toward Territorial Passage," in *Folklore Groups and Folklore Genres*, ed. Eliot Oring (Logan, UT: Utah State University Press, 1989), 87–97.

22. Putilov, *Russkii Istoriko-pesennyi fol'klor XII–XVI vekov* (Moscow/Leningrad, 1960), 43–48.

23. There is a great deal of variation in the wedding, especially in a country as huge as Russia. I chose to use one region for consistency and will follow D. M. Balashov, Iu. I. Marchenko, and N. I. Kalmykova, *Russkaia svad'ba: Svadebnyi obriad na Verkhnei i Srednei Kokshen'ge i na Uftiuge (Tarnogskii raion Vologodskoi oblasti)* (Moscow, 1985), 390. There are a number of wedding descriptions, but this one is thorough and done following current fieldwork standards. The descriptions of the beginning of matchmaking and the viewing of the groom's property are on pp. 26–32. The overall structure

of the wedding is given in synopsis on p. 25 and in charts on pp. 356–67, which also show regional variation.

24. Balashov, Marchenko, and Kalmykova, 33–42.

25. Lament texts are available from a number of sources: Barsov, the Biblioteka poeta collection of laments, Balashov, Marchenko, and Kalmykova's *Russkaia svad'ba*, which gives the laments appropriate to each ritual act. In the laments given in *Russkaia svad'ba*, the bride complains that military service and indentured service are rewarded with pay and are only for a limited time, whereas she will be in servitude forever and be paid nothing. In the second text given, she promises her father that she will work for him in any capacity if only he will not give her away. In the fourth text, she accuses her parents of having betrayed her. She says that they promised not to give her away and here they are doing just that. She then says that she has heard that the man to whom she will be married is a drunkard and will beat her. These are only three samples. The total number of texts given in the *zaporuki* section is nineteen.

26. Balashov, Marchenko, and Kalmykova, 43–99. This section describes the ritual and lament texts with melodies. For a discussion of all of the cloth items used ritually in the wedding and also for a somewhat different description of the wedding rite, see Galia Semenovna Maslova, *Narodnaia odezhda v vostochnoslavianskikh obychaiakh i obraidakh XIX-nachala XX v* (Moscow, 1984), 8–84. This book also contains photos of the chest in which the dowry was collected, the dowry itself on display at the home of the groom, and others.

27. Balashov, Marchenko, and Kalmykova, 48–50. The meaning of *ugor* is not known. It is possibly related to *gora* (hill) and thus *vykhodit' na ugor* would be "going out to the hill," but this translation is not certain. See same source, footnote 5, under *zaporuki* (372), for an account of how the bride "beats herself" (*khleshchetsia*). What she is supposed to do is collapse from a standing position onto her hands and knees. The note adds that people say a bride would sometimes end up with bloody elbows and knees by the time the wedding rite was complete.

28. Balashov, Marchenko, and Kalmykova, 103–217. This section again gives a description of the ritual, lament and other texts, and melodies. In lament 243 (215–16), the bride asks what to do with her beauty and will (*krasnaia krasota, vol' naia voliushka*). She contemplates placing it on the door step; then decides against this because her beauty and freedom will be trod upon and soiled there. She then contemplates placing it in the window. This, too, she decides is no good because her sister will open the window in springtime and the beauty and freedom will fly into the forest and the swamps. The bride then offers her beauty and free will to her father, her mother, her sister, and her brother, in turn. All refuse to take it because they are afraid. The bride then tries to plait the ribbons representing her beauty and free will back into her own hair and decides that this is not the place for them either because her time has passed. Finally, the bride gets her sister to accept the beauty and free-will ribbons and to dole them out to the bride's girlfriends. As this is done, she reassures all of the women receiving the ribbons that they need not be afraid because her ribbons will not dishonor them.

29. Ibid., 207–52.

30. Ibid., 359–64.

31. Ibid., 253–92.

32. Ibid., 293–97. The ritual humiliation appears in Nikolai Vladimirovich Zorin, *Russkaia svad'ba v Srednem Povolzh'e* (Kazan', 1981), 112 (the mother-in-law greets

the bride in a bearskin coat turned inside out and tries to frighten her), 115–16 (bride removes groom's boots), 122–23 (fetching water).

33. Balashov, Marchenko, and Kalmykova, 293–300. The description of the post-wedding rituals in Zorin, 118–33, is more detailed.

34. Descriptions of funeral rites are much harder to find than descriptions of wedding rites; perhaps because this was a rite performed exclusively by women. Collectors would record laments, usually outside the context of the funeral, but not document the rite itself. Barsov's classic collection, for example, devotes only twelve pages to the description of the funeral rite. In addition to Barsov, see Maslova, 85–92 and Mahler, 643–65.

35. Arnold van Gennep, *The Rites of Passage*, trans. Monika B. Vizedom and Gabrielle L. Caffee (Chicago: The University of Chicago Press, 1960); Victor Turner, *The Ritual Process: Structure and Anti-Structure* (Ithaca, NY: Cornell University Press, 1969).

36. A. K. Baiburin, G. A. Levinton, "K opisaniiu organizatsii prostranstva v vos-tochnoslavianskoi svad'be," *Russkii narodnyi svadebnyi obriad: issledovania i materialy*, ed. K. V. Chistova and T. A. Bernshtam (Leningrad, 1978), 89–105; see especially 98.

37. The clearest statement of the link between bearing a child and achieving status appears in Andrei Simic, "Machismo and Cryptomatriarchy: Power, Affect, and Authority in the Contemporary Yugoslav Family," *Ethos* 11, No. 1/2 (1983): 66–86. For Russian material, see Christine D. Worobec, *Peasant Russia: Family and Community in the Post-Emancipation Period* (Princeton: Princeton University Press, 1991). Although Worobec does not specifically link childbirth with status, this can be deduced from her discussion of Russian family dynamics.

38. Ibid., 298.

39. Barsov describes the funeral of a man. Mahler works primarily from a funeral for a man. The description of a funeral given in Mary Matossian, "The Peasant Way of Life," in *The Peasant in Nineteenth-Century Russia*, ed. Wayne S. Vucinich (Stanford, CA: Stanford University Press, 1968), 1–40, is that of a man. The lament texts used are B. E. Chistov and K. V. Chistova, eds., *Prichitaniia*. The account given excludes laments for recruits, which are a type of lament for a man. Laments about one's fate and about accidents are also excluded. It should also be noted that, of the eleven laments for women, two and possibly five are laments for women who died unwed. These are closer to wedding laments than to funeral laments.

40. The most extensive treatment of this phenomenon is Gail Kligman, *The Wedding of the Dead: Ritual, Poetics, and Popular Culture in Transylvania* (Berkeley: University of California Press, 1988). This book, however, treats not the Slavs, but their neighbors, the Romanians. The funeral of the unmarried as wedding among the Russians is discussed by Mahler, 391–408, and Maslova, 92–93. Of the laments for women in the Biblioteka poeta collection (total eleven), two are for daughters who died unmarried; three are for sisters and whether or not they were married is unclear—the lament stresses the woman's untimely death; six are for mothers.

41. Interestingly, elements that indicate concern with paternity are present in the most contemporary fieldwork. There is certainly a great deal of emphasis on the virginity of the bride. In addition to making sure that the bride was a virgin so that any children produced from the marriage would be certain to come from the husband, there were also attempts to consider the relatedness of the couple and its influence on the genetic makeup of the children; Zorin, 44–48.

42. Speranskii, 67–71; Putilov, 276–84, 344–53.

43. Putilov, 240–63; 292–98; 264–70; 97–101; Rybnikov, 2d ed., vol. 1, 318–23; vol. 2, 290–92.

44. Stephen P. Dunn, "The Family as Reflected in Russian Folklore," *The Family in Imperial Russia: New Lines of Historical Research*, ed. David L. Ransel (Urbana: University of Illinois Press, 1978), 163.

45. Vladimir Propp, *Russkii Geroicheskii Epos* (Leningrad, 1955), 30–55.

46. The available descriptions of funerals have already been cited. Descriptions of birth customs are even harder to find than accounts of the funeral. See Maslova, 101– 109. Presumably, both rites were poorly documented because they were women's rituals and thus not collected by male ethnographers. For fortune-telling and witchcraft beliefs, see Linda J. Ivanits, *Russian Folk Belief* (Armonk, NY, and London: M. E. Sharpe, 1989), 59–60 and 83–124. See also, S. V. Maksimov, *Nechistaia Sila. Nevedomaia Sila*, vol. 18 of *Sobranie sochinenii* (St. Petersburg, 1908–1913), 55–60.

47. For a discussion of archeological evidence for goddess worship in the Slavic area, see Maria Gimbutas, *The Goddesses and Gods of Old Europe, 6500–3500 BC; Myths and Cult Images*, 2d ed. (Berkeley: University of California Press, 1982). An interesting but poorly documented discussion of other manifestations of goddess worship is Joanna Hubbs, *Mother Russia; The Feminine Myth in Russian Culture* (Bloomington: Indiana University Press, 1988).

48. Moyle, "Mermaids," 229–32.

49. Texts collected from women appear in all of the major collections starting with Rybnikov and Gil'ferding. Kriukova was such an adept performer of epic and composer of new songs honoring Lenin and the Revolution that she was asked to appear at various Soviet festivals of folklore and oral literature, such as the 1939 All-Republic Conference of Folk Artists held in Kiev, Ukraine, where she was the one to represent Russian *byliny*.

3

The "Feminization" of Russian Literature: Women, Language, and Literature in Eighteenth-Century Russia

Judith Vowles

At the close of the eighteenth century, in the course of debates about the character of the Russian literary language, the writer Nikolai M. Karamzin (1766–1826) and his followers crystallized ideas and assumptions about women's influence on literature and language that first appeared at the beginning of the century.[1] The Karamzinists made women's taste and women's language the standard of literary and linguistic excellence. They accorded women such authority over Russian language and literature that later scholars have spoken of a "feminization" of Russian culture.[2] The detailed history of that "feminization" remains to be written. In its most general outline, it accompanied the rapid Westernization and secularization of Russian society that took place in the eighteenth century. Writers now found themselves writing for a society transformed by the presence of aristocratic women, who had formerly been sequestered in the terem.[3] There was no clearly articulated argument or debate about women's role, but it is possible to trace the underlying assumptions about women's relation to language that leading writers incorporated into their texts as they set about creating a literary language and a national literature equal to those of Western Europe. Before turning to the ways in which some women writing in the eighteenth century perceived their own role, I shall sketch the background against which they worked.

Among the first to articulate assumptions about women and the Russian language was the poet and scholar Vasilii K. Trediakovskii (1703–1769).[4] Like other writers, he confronted the ever-widening gap between the spoken language and Church Slavonic. Church Slavonic, which had long functioned as the written language of high culture dominated by the church, could no longer adequately serve as the language of a society whose literary interests were increasingly secular and oriented toward the West. Some writers sought to reform Church Slavonic. Others, Trediakovskii among them, attempted to create a new literary language based on the Russian vernacular in conjunction with the introduction of literary genres and themes long established in European culture, but unknown in Russian society.[5]

Trediakovskii marked his departure from the Church Slavonic tradition with *Voyage to the Isle of Love* (1730), a translation of Abbé Paul Tallemant's *précieux* novel *Voyage de l'isle d'Amour, ou la Clef des coeurs* (1663). Trediakovskii's choice of text marked his intention to model the creation of a Russian literary language on the example of seventeenth-century France and the literary culture associated with the *précieuses*, the women in whose salons the French language was refined and cultivated.[6] By translating the *Voyage to the Isle of Love*, Trediakovskii attempted to imitate French writers who based the literary language on the spoken language of polite society where the pleasures of love and conversation had created a refined and supple language untainted by scholarly pedantry offensive to women's softer nature and their naturally delicate taste. Just as French women spoke a pure French untainted by the scholarly languages of Latin and Greek, Russian women were a source of pure Russian untainted by the learned language of Church Slavonic.[7] In his introduction to the novel, Trediakovskii justified his use of the spoken language of society rather than the learned language of Church Slavonic on the grounds that the latter was obscure to all but a scholarly elite, and that the soft Russian tongue was more appropriate than harsh Church Slavonic for a secular genre on "the delights of love," a subject considered profane by churchmen.

In later years Trediakovskii disavowed his earlier work. He rejected *préciosité* as a model and returned to Church Slavonic and the language of books as the standard for the literary language. Where he had once translated a *précieux* novel celebrating the delights of love, he now translated into the "manly Slavonic tongue" Fénelon's anti-*précieux* novel *Les Aventures de Télémaque*, in which the hero must, among other trials, learn to flee the pleasures of love and the company of women. Nevertheless, he retained the gendered distinction between Church Slavonic and Russian. His contrast between the "manliness of the Slavonic language" and "the tenderness of Russian" and "tender ladies' speech," and the association of women with the lighter genres, the theme of love, and Western influences persisted throughout the century.[8]

Similar distinctions were made both by writers of the neoclassical school and the sentimentalists in the second half of the eighteenth century. In his programmatic "Conversation with Anacreon" (1756–1761), one of the leading exponents of neoclassicism, the poet and scholar Mikhail V. Lomonosov (1711–1765), defined the proper character and direction of a national literature by contrasting his own patriotic cultivation of the solemn ode with its lofty themes and high style to the lighter genres practiced by Anacreon, whose poems of wine, women, and song were ill-suited to represent the literature of a great nation.[9] Where Anacreon sings of love's pleasures, Lomonosov sings the praises of great Russian heroes and warriors. Where Anacreon details his beloved's charms, Lomonosov celebrates the abstract glories of Mother Russia. Lomonosov's preference for the solemn ode rather than songs of love reflects his neoclassical allegiance and the aesthetic values of the neoclassical hierarchy of genres he had elaborated more systematically and influentially in his "Foreword on the Utility of Ecclesiastical Books in the Russian Language" (1757). The poem reveals women's association with the lesser, lighter genres (lyric poetry, the song, and so on), which required a middle style blending the spoken language with Church Slavonic elements rather than the "high" genres (the epic, tragedy, and solemn ode) demanding the loftier language of Church Slavonic.

Lomonosov's "Conversation with Anacreon" was polemicizing with writers whose attention to anacreontic verse was gradually to erode neoclassical ideals.[10] The decline of neoclassicism and the rise of sentimentalism with its emphasis on the lighter, more personal, genres, reliance on individual poetic inspiration rather than rules and norms, the development of a single style suitable for all genres and themes, and the transformation of the literary milieu from the public life of the court to journals and more intimate literary circles were foreshadowed by the poet and writer Mikhail Kheraskov (1733–1807) in his Anacreontic *New Odes* (1762). Kheraskov's opening poem, "To My Lyre," defined the poet's literary credo in terms of his ideal reader, the "intelligent Russian woman." The poet rejects the rhetoric and high style ("thunderous strings and bombastic words") associated with Lomonosov's solemn odes and the court ("the worldly splendor of a magnificent life") in favor of a more intimate and private world. He defines himself not as a poet who strives to be "a famous creator" and aspires to the heights of Parnassus, but as one whose verses are "the work of idle hours, of hours not many, my un-serious endeavor," written not for glory but so that his beloved will "read these songs . . . and say that you are content with them."[11]

Kheraskov's appeal to the "intelligent Russian woman" reflects a certain ambivalence toward women and love found among many other writers. "To My Lyre" presents the poet's beloved as a sympathetic friend and love as spiritual friendship rather than the celebration of love's pleasures more characteristic of Anacreontic verse. The moral and didactic poems the poet reads to his beloved are similarly out of keeping with the more lighthearted Anacreontic tradition. They reflect Kheraskov's more serious side, which emerged in his later work, fortified by the teachings of freemasonry. His attempt to revise the Anacreontic tradition by purging love of its carnal and sensual elements also reveals the fear that love was a corrupting as well as a civilizing force. His misgivings were shared by many other writers, who were often sharply critical of women's presence in society.

The most eloquent discussions about women, language, and literature came from the satirists who inveighed against the deleterious effects of Western influence and women's presence in society in satirical journals and plays from the late 1760s onward. The writer and journalist Nikolai Novikov (1744–1818) produced some of the most vivid portraits of Russian society corrupted by exposure to Western, especially French, culture in his journals *The Drone* (*Truten'*) and *The Painter* (*Zhivopisets*). He had only harsh words for the Russian ladies and their gallant companions, the men and women dandies (*shchegol'* and *shche-*

golikha) whose vice and corruption were most fully embodied in their disdain
of the Russian language and what Novikov called their "dandified jargon" or
"women's language" (*zhenskii slog*).[12] This "women's language" was the coin
of a Westernized society corrupted by frivolity and fashion, love affairs, and
contemptuous of Russian manners and morals. It was characterized by its idiosyncratic and affected pronunciation, its excessive use of Gallicisms and other
foreign words, and its horror of "coarse" and "vulgar" words and Church
Slavonicisms. Novikov deplored the dandies' disdain for serious literature and
religious writings and their preference for frivolous comedies, novels, love
poems, and songs. He even authored a number of letters purporting to be written
by female dandies written in the highly stylized "women's language" he
abhorred. His satires were designed to reform and shape Russian society and to
define and create the virtuous man and his helpmate, the ideal Russian wife and
mother. Novikov and other satirists frequently contrasted the ignorant female
dandy to the educated virtuous woman, but women's education was to be placed
in the service of women's proper role as wife and mother. There was a thin line
between education and "dandification." Thus, despite the seriousness and piety
of Elizaveta Kheraskova, Kheraskov's wife, the original "intelligent Russian
woman" and a minor poet in her own right, the writer Vasilii Maikov, a member
of Kheraskov's circle and a friend of Novikov, attacked her as "a dandified
young lady. If she writes her husband won't have good cabbage soup: he writes,
she writes, so who's going to cook the soup?"[13]

The same virtuous feminine ideal promoted in satirical writings was encouraged by the teachings of freemasonry, the quasi-religious movement to which
many leading literary figures, including Kheraskov and Novikov, subscribed in
the second half of the century. The freemasons' extensive educational and philanthropic projects were devoted to social reformation and the creation of the
virtuous man. They were generally hostile to the manners and morals of polite
society and the court.[14] The virtuous feminine ideal promoted by the masons
was embraced by some women. A. E. Labzina, wife of a leading mason, grate-
fully recalled her education in the Kheraskov household, "I was fifteen then . . .
And I was told that what was required of me was complete and unlimited
obedience, humility, meekness and patience, and that I was to offer no opinions,
but only to listen, be silent and obey."[15] Other women, like the young poet
Anna Volkova, were more critical. Volkova rebuked the masonic fraternity as
"the proud masons,/ Who call us immodest,/ And consider our conversations
an impediment in their mysterious work,/ Who consider the female sex weak,/
Not only in body but in mind."[16]

Karamzin had received much of his early literary training from the freemasons,
but when he began to formulate his views on women and language, and made
polite society and the salon the locus of literary life, he broke with his former
friends. They in turn labelled him a dandy. In his classic essay "Why Are There
So Few Authorial Talents in Russia?" (1802) Karamzin invoked Trediakovskii's
early proposal to use *préciosité* as a model for Russian.[17] Karamzin and his

followers, most notably the writer and journalist P. Makarov, established the usage of polite society as the standard for the Russian literary language. Woman in her various incarnations as the "worldly lady," "amiable woman," "dear woman," and "beautiful woman" became the writer's ideal reader. Karamzin's careful cultivation of what he termed a "tender style" in prose was directed at this ideal reader, the woman whose naturally refined feminine taste he sought to please and whose language he sought to emulate. Society, the salon, and what P. Makarov termed the "luxurious boudoirs of Aspazias" were the laboratories where the Russian literary language was to become as cultivated and elegant as the French language had become in the seventeenth-century salons.[18] By "moving the throne of Philosophy into their boudoirs," Makarov hoped that women would raise Russian culture to the heights to which French women had brought French civilization.[19] In the poet Konstantin Batiushkov's famous formulation, the writer should be he "who writes as one speaks,/ whom ladies read."[20]

Whether women themselves should write was a matter on which the Karamzinists disagreed. As Batiushkov's phrasing suggests, women were imagined as readers rather than writers. This was not merely because, as the Karamzinists frequently lamented, women preferred French to Russian. The Karamzinist Vladimir Izmailov translated an essay attacking women writers in his journal *The Patriot* in 1804: "I do not know how one can wish [to hear] the conversation of a woman who has said the best of everything she has to say in a book printed in two thousand copies; whose most tender feelings and most delicate thoughts are sold at a reasonable price in all the book shops."[21] Such objections reflect polite society's general disdain for professionalism and commercialism, but this view of the woman writer marks her not only as vulgar but immoral: "a woman in print is the same as a woman in ill-repute, whose adventures are common knowledge."[22] In a footnote Izmailov applauds the author's sentiments, congratulates Russia on being spared the plague of women writers found in France, but fears the contagion may spread. P. Makarov, on the other hand, encouraged women to write. "To get rid of pedantry," he wrote, "and, moreover, to bring the language of books into harmony with the language of good society, we could wish that women would take up literature; with their fine taste, their ardent imaginations, and their tender souls, we could expect good Authors."[23] Moreover, he gallantly, if inaccurately, assured women they would be well received: "What pedant, what Barbarian would dare not to praise that which a tender, white, lovely hand has written? . . . We can assure the amiable woman writer that our critics will always have the most sacred respect for all the works issuing from her pen."

Despite the protestations of Admiral Aleksandr Shishkov (1754–1841) and his followers, who attacked the Karamzinists and urged a return to Church Slavonic and the language of books as the basis for the literary language, the "feminization" of Russian culture accorded women unprecedented prestige and authority.[24] However, the history of that "feminization" of Russian language and literature has been written almost entirely on the basis of what men wrote about women. Although women themselves wrote in increasingly large numbers, Novikov's satirical letters from women dandies are probably the most famous specimens of "women's writing" in eighteenth-century Russian literature. How women perceived their own relation to language and literature and the various ways in which they responded to the "feminization" of Russian culture has received scant attention.[25] Catherine II and the Princess Ekaterina Romanova Dashkova were the two best-known women writing in the eighteenth century. The range and depth of their work goes far beyond the light "feminine" genres, and neither accepted the feminine ideal imagined by various writers, although their attitudes to the worldly lady differed sharply. Other women, like the poet Ekaterina Sergeevna Urusova, happily embraced that ideal as a fruitful way of imagining their own poetic vocation. Similarly disparate views can be seen at the end of the century when the "feminization" of Russian culture encouraged many women to take up the pen, but provoked others to reject an ideal that seemingly offered authority and prestige.

The most prolific and powerful woman writing in eighteenth-century Russia was an obscure German princess, born Sophia Augusta Frederika, princess of Anhalt-Zerbst, who became Empress of Russia, Catherine II (1729–1796). Catherine II desired glory. She was, as one of her contemporaries declared, "insatiably desirous of renown and ambitious of wearing every wreath which fame can bestow. She courts celebrity with unremitting eagerness, and her every word, her every action, are directed with a view to immortality."[26] Catherine II wanted more than a well-turned compliment and elegant madrigal. Aside from moments of cheerful and self-mocking bragging, Catherine herself realized that of the two paths to glory and immortality open to her—to write or to be written about— her own writings were unlikely to bring her fame. She therefore relied on others to tell the history of her words and deeds. To that end she assiduously cultivated her reputation among the philosophes, with many of whom, including Diderot, Voltaire, Grimm, and Madame de Geoffrin, she corresponded.[27] Of all her writings, the text she most valued was her *Great Instruction* (1768), a lengthy and scholarly political treatise on the principles of good government and an orderly society incorporating the thinking of leading Enlightenment figures.[28] The *Instruction* was to serve as a blueprint for a reign she hoped would bring her the glory she desired, in the role she reserved for herself, that of the ruler-philosopher. The treatise did indeed bring her the reputation for which she hoped. The *Instruction* was applauded by the philosophes, and Catherine was much gratified by the praise of her rival as ruler-philosopher, Frederick the Great, who described the *Instruction* as "a masculine, nervous Performance, and worthy of a great man," and wrote, "We have never heard of any Female being a Lawgiver. This Glory was reserved for the Empress of Russia."[29]

Catherine's patronage of Russian culture was designed to achieve renown for herself and her reign. In her essay "Nachertanie o Rossiiskikh sochineniiakh i Rossiiskom iazyke" ("A Sketch of Russian Compositions and the Russian Language"), published anonymously in 1783, Catherine outlined her views on Russian language and literature as a reflection of and testament to the glory of her own reign. She solemnly congratulated herself on the accomplishments she predicted under her rule thanks to "the great intelligence of the Great Female Monarch leading Russia on the road to glory." She reversed the more customary relation of woman and poet in which the poet confers immortality on the name of the beloved; instead, her glory confers immortality on the poet.

How enviable the fate of Russian writers will be! Because of the sacred name of *Catherine* their name will be engraved in the temple of immortality, and their never-to-be-extinguished glory will be spoken by their descendants for all time; when, in contrast, the ringing voices of thousands of earthly rulers will be mingled with the dust of decay and disappear into the eternal darkness of merited oblivion.[30]

Although the end of Catherine's long reign was marred by repression of writers and literary enterprises she had once encouraged, under her patronage learning and the arts flourished.[31] Her encouragement of all aspects of literary and artistic life is reflected in the breadth (if not the quality) of her own extensive writings.[32] Her work includes some twenty-five comedies and historical plays, written mainly in Russian, although some are in French.[33] She founded the first Russian satirical journal, *All Sorts* (*Vsiakaia vsiachina*), successfully encouraging the genre of satirical moral weeklies that had done so much to create a reading public in Britain and Germany.[34] She wrote numerous essays and feuilletons for various journals, including Novikov's. She contributed many items to the *Conversational Journal of Lovers of the Russian Word* (*Sobesednik liubitelei rossiiskago slova*), the official journal of the Russian Academy, notably her imitation of Sterne, *Facts and Fictions* (*Byli i nebylitsy*, 1783), as well as a long historical study *Notes Concerning Russian History* (*Zapiski kasatel'no rossiiskoi istorii*, 1783–1784). She wrote a number of pedagogical works as well as children's stories, the most well known of which was *Tale of Prince Khlor* (*Skazka o tsareviche Khlore*, 1782). Her more scholarly works include *Antidote* (1770), a description of Russian society rebutting Abbé Chappe D'Anteroche's criticisms of her empire in *Voyage en Siberie*. The only genres and arts Catherine did not cultivate were poetry and music, those arts thought most pleasing to women's taste and character. Her memoirs, to which she turned at various periods in her life and which are perhaps her liveliest and most interesting work, reflect not only her love of what she considered serious "masculine" pursuits, but also her love of pleasure and society and "feminine" interests.

Catherine did not disdain the ideal of the lady and polite society or the prestige and pleasure of the more worldly life, and she aspired to make her court as brilliant as that of Louis XIV. Cultivated women were essential to polite society and Catherine encouraged aristocratic women to follow her lead.[35] So successfully did she promote the pleasures of worldly society that the artist and connoisseur of polite society, Elisabeth Vigée Lebrun, who visited Russia in the 1790s, recalled, "There were innumerable balls, concerts and theatrical perfor-

mances, and I thoroughly enjoyed these gatherings, where I found all the ur-
banity, all the grace of French company. It seemed as though good taste had
made a jump with both feet from Paris to St. Petersburg.''[36] In particular, she
observed ''it would be impossible to exceed the Russian ladies in the urbanities
of good society.''[37] Many foreign visitors observed the numbers of well-educated
Russian women with European tastes to be found in the capitals, providing grist
for the satirists' mills, and creating the salons and drawing rooms where Karamzin
and his followers were to shape the literary language. Although Catherine occasionally satirized the foibles of worldly women and society, in practice she
reconciled the demands of both worlds. In doing so she was very different from
the ''other'' Catherine, Princess Ekaterina Romanova Dashkova (née Voront-
sova, 1743–1810), who shared the satirists' contempt for society and the worldly
lady.

As director of the Academy of Sciences and founding president of the Russian
Academy, appointments she held simultaneously from 1783 to 1796, Dashkova
exerted considerable influence over the direction of Russian language and literature.[38] It is ironical that a woman occupied these positions at a time when
satirists inveighed against women's corruption of the Russian language. Moreover, the very year that Dashkova received her double appointment to the academies, Karamzin embarked on his literary career and began to define the salon
and polite society as the locus of literary life, and the worldly lady as the
legislatress of the Russian language. As director of the Academy of Sciences
and president of the Russian Academy with its charter ''to purify and enrich the
Russian language and make rules for the use of words in speech and poetry,''
Dashkova displayed the most conservative views of language, far removed from
the Karamzinian ideal or the much-satirized ''women's language.''

Dashkova's views on the Russian language can be seen in two of the many
projects she initiated and oversaw during her tenure at the two academies: the
publication of the journal *Conversational Journal of Lovers of the Russian Word*
(*Sobesednik liubitelei rossiiskago slova*, 1783–1784), the Russian Academy's
official journal; and the production of the first dictionary of the Russian language.[39] The preface to *Conversational Journal of Lovers of the Russian Word*
declared Dashkova's determination to encourage the cultivation of Russian literature and learning by publishing only original Russian works, excluding the
translations hitherto a staple of Russian periodicals, and by accepting only contributions conducive to good morals. Dashkova's own pieces, a short verse
dedication to Catherine II and her ''Epistle to the Word 'So' '' (''Poslanie k
slovu 'Tak' '') which followed Derzhavin's famous introductory ''Ode to Fel-
itsa,'' set the tone for the journal. ''Epistle to the Word 'So' '' attacked various
specimens of poor morals found in Russian society, reserving particular scorn
for the morals and manners of the fashionable lady, especially her dandified
jargon.[40] Dashkova's promotion of the Russian language and criticism of those,
especially women, who were ignorant of Russian became a constant feature of
the journal.[41]

Dashkova's work on the first Russian dictionary also incorporated long-held and cherished views of the Russian language. She approached the dictionary as a learned work for scholars rather than as a dictionary of usage, based on the spoken language, designed for the ordinary reader. She organized it on etymological principles in order to show the roots of words, instead of organizing the dictionary alphabetically, and drew heavily on Church Slavonic writings. The dictionary caused Dashkova considerable unpleasantness at court and roused Catherine's anger because it was too learned to be useful and convenient for her courtiers to use. Nevertheless, it was Dashkova's most enduring contribution to the Russian language, and a testament to her preference for the academy rather than the salon, the library rather than the boudoir.

Dashkova wrote numerous Russian works in the course of her life, including verse, plays, and essays on a variety of social and political subjects.[42] Her most enduring contribution to Russian literature was a memoir that she wrote in French for her young friend Martha Wilmot, who did not speak Russian, in 1804–1805.[43] Her description of the British artist and scholar Anne Seymour Damer, whom she met during her travels in Italy, defines a view of women that runs throughout the memoir: "The mornings we spent in sight-seeing and excursions which usually ended at Mrs. Damer's studio. For it was not in her boudoir that her friends found her—rather did they find her wrestling with a block of marble, trying to impart to it the shape she wanted."[44] Dashkova's satisfaction at finding the artist at work in her studio marks a lifelong rejection of the boudoir as woman's realm, and rebuts those writers like P. Makarov who would locate women's authority and prestige in the salon and boudoir.

Unlike Catherine II, Dashkova never reconciled the claims of worldly society and the intellectual life. Indeed, she blames the collapse of the original friendship between herself and Catherine, the only two women in Russia "who did any serious reading," on Catherine's love of the pleasures of the boudoir.[45] Catherine, on her part, frequently ridiculed what she saw as Dashkova's pedantry and moralistic views. Throughout her memoirs, Dashkova criticizes the ladies of polite society, beginning with the attempts made to educate her as a lady. "According to the ideas of the time we received the very best education," she wrote, "for we had a perfect knowledge of four languages, particularly French; we danced well and drew a little; . . . we were attractive to look at and our manners were lady-like. Everyone had to agree that our education left nothing to be desired." Nothing, she observes tartly, but the "improvement of our hearts and minds."[46] Her lifelong contempt for superficial "feminine" accomplishments and dress is epitomized in the self-satisfaction with which she recalls first acquiring the *Encyclopedia* and Morelli's dictionary. "Never," she writes, "would the finest piece of jewellery have given me such pleasure."[47] Throughout her memoirs, she recalls with pride her disregard for dress on various occasions and her manners, often blunt to the point of rudeness.

Her memoirs inscribe the life of a woman of considerable intellect and erudition. She recalls her travels, readings, conversations with leading thinkers of her time, visits to galleries and museums, factories and mills, ruins and studios, libraries and academies. The life that she made for herself and the figure that she cut as a learned woman was by no means unusual in eighteenth-century Europe. Her memoirs include numerous references to the educated women of her day. The names of Anne Damer, the sculptress Marie Anne Collot (1748– 1821), the Irish blue-stocking and philanthropist Lady Arabella Denny (1708– 1792), the salonnières Suzanne Necker (1739–1794) and Marie Thérèse Geoffrin (1699–1777), and others appear alongside the names of Diderot, Voltaire, and other famous men. In her day Dashkova's intellectual curiosity, her "serious" reading and enthusiasm for the *Encyclopedia* and Morelli's dictionary would have seemed natural.[48] But even as she kept company with learned women, Enlightenment attitudes toward women were eroding.[49] The writer Jean-Jacques Rousseau was an eloquent and influential critic of women's role in intellectual life. "By themselves," he declared, "the men, exempted from having to lower their ideas to the range of women and to clothe reason in gallantry, can devote themselves to grave and serious discourse without fear of ridicule."[50] His views came to be shared by many of his contemporaries and found a ready audience in Russia. Even though she belonged within a tradition of women whose seriousness belied such criticisms, Dashkova shared such views, including the insistence on women's proper role as wife and mother. Her presentation of herself as a serious, intellectual woman is punctuated by claims of self-abnegation and assertions that many of the activities, like her extended stay in Europe, were undertaken primarily for the sake of her children and their education. She makes protestations of incapacity and modesty, even as she details her capabilities and accomplishments. The contradictions of her narrative reveal much of the tension experienced by educated women in those years as changing attitudes made women's intellectual aspirations incompatible with women's newly defined domestic role.[51]

Catherine II and Dashkova were the most prominent and influential women writing in eighteenth-century Russia. Their lives and work, and the Enlightenment tradition to which they belonged, counter the image of the lady as she emerged by the end of the century, although Catherine by no means shared Dashkova's contempt for the lady. Other women, however, embraced the ideas offered by Trediakovskii, Kheraskov, and others. The poet, princess Ekaterina Sergeevna Urusova (1747–after 1817), was perhaps the most well known of these women.[52] She found the association of women with love rather than learning a useful way of imagining women's place in Russian culture.

Like most of the women writers in the second half of the century, Urusova belonged to the literary circles that gathered around Kheraskov and the poet Gavriil Derzhavin.[53] Urusova was one of the few women to produce a large body of original poetry rather than the translations, which account for most of the work published by women in this period. Her poetry began appearing in print in the early 1770s and included lyric verse published in journals as well as a number of longer works published separately. "Pis'mo Petru Dmitrievichu

Eropkinu'' ("Epistle to Petr Dmitrievich Eropkin") an account of Eropkin's heroic endeavors in Moscow during the plague first appeared in 1772. It was republished in 1774 together with *Polion, ili Prosvetivshiisia Neliudim, Poema* (*Polion, or the Misanthrope Enlightened, a Poem*), an allegory in five cantos describing a young man's corruption by false learning and his redemption by a feminine spirit. This was followed in 1777 by *Iroidy, muzam prosviashchennyia* (*Heroides, Dedicated to the Muses*), a collection of nine heroides. Although Urusova abandoned poetry in the 1780s, she began to publish again in the 1790s. A small but steady stream of lyric verse and occasional odes to members of the royal family appeared in various literary journals over the next twenty years. In 1811 she became an honorary member of Shishkov's conservative literary society "Society of Lovers of the Russian Word" ("Beseda liubitelei russkogo slova"). A collected edition of her poems appeared in 1817, shortly before her death, the precise date of which is unknown.

In her early work, Urusova presents an eloquent defense of the civilizing power of women and love in Russian culture. In *Polion* (in Russian, "the sex and he"), an allegory about the secularization and "feminization" of Russian society, Urusova rejects the view of Novikov and others that feminine society and conversation corrupts, and she asserts that without love and without women there can be no civilization and no enlightenment. While the satirists provide the general context for Urusova's argument, Trediakovskii's translation of Fénelon's *Les Aventures de Télémaque* provides a more specific subtext for her poem. In particular, she polemicizes with the chapters relating Telemachus's visit to the island of the nymph Calypso, where the hero must preserve his virtue from the corrupting influence of feminine company. Where Trediakovskii had once written of the "delights of love" in *Voyage to the Isle of Love*, he now wrote of love as a "shameful tyrant," who seduces Telemachus into "a life soft and without honor amidst women," a life "without liberty, without virtue, without glory."[54] The deleterious effects of this seductive life are embodied in the disintegration of Telemachus's command of language. The chapters reflect not only Trediakovskii's rejection of his earlier celebration of the "delights of love" and *préciosité* but also his preference for "the manliness of the Slavonic language" over the "tenderness of the Russian language."[55] Urusova's opening lines evoke and reject Trediakovskii's arguments:

> I sing of severe manners, the vanity of learning,
> The Triumph of Love, and the enchantment of beauty.
> Reveal to me, Muse, into what error,
> False learning deludes the judgment;
> Promising brilliance and light to the mind,
> They lead it into the darkness by arduous paths;
> However, often love enlightens us,
> And softens and tames our rough manners.
> Love, although stern, your law is pleasant,
> Through you Polion became learned and happy.[56]

Polion tells of how only love and the company of women make Polion a fully civilized, virtuous man. His enlightenment is embodied in his repudiation of Church Slavonic and ecclesiastical culture and his embrace of Russian speech and society.

Urusova tells of Polion's corruption by false wisdom when he abandons society to dedicate himself to "coarse Learning."[57] Polion acquires "a coarse and unwise education" in a so-called temple of learning situated in a gloomy forest, the wild wood of barbarism and ignorance, representing Russian culture in the days untouched by the civilizing presence of women and love. Neither Nature nor Truth finds a home in this barren land ruled by a grey-haired tsar seated on a crumbling throne, where "Pomona [the goddess of love and marriage] had no sway."[58] His education complete, Polion returns to society a misanthrope, a term often used in Urusova's day as a synonym for "misogynist." Polion's hatred of society and his disgust for all social ties is epitomized by his contempt for women whom he considers only as slaves, and whom he has learned to fear as sirens or pagan devotees of Cythera (Venus). He takes refuge in the country where he seeks to re-create the "temple of learning." He erects a high wall around his home, lays waste the arcadian countryside, and spreads misery and unhappiness throughout his domain. Only when Eros, "that God to whom the race of mortals is subject," sees Polion in the forest reading Seneca's writings against the passions and pierces him with a dart of love to punish him for his hubris, does Polion's redemption and his return to civilization and humanity begin.[59]

In a series of scenes containing a complex set of allusions and reworkings of Telemachus's flight from Aphrodite's beautiful and seductive worshippers at Cythera, and his escape from Calypso's isle and the chaster pleasures of feminine society, Urusova relates how Polion is redeemed through love of a beautiful maiden in whose face shines "the spirit of intelligence."[60] Through conversation with the naiad of the woods and countryside, Polion casts off his old education and becomes a civilized man once more. In Fénelon's/Trediakovskii's narrative, the hero must flee Calypso's isle, shunning the feminine company and love that make men soft and weak. Urusova teaches a very different lesson. She ends her poem with Eros's words: " 'There is nothing more useful than the heart's passion!/ It warms cold blood;/ And where light shines, there reigns love.' "[61] The naiad's conversation enlightens, Calypso's conversation destroys. Thus Telemachus's companion, Mentor, warns his charge, "Beware of listening to the gentle and flattering words of Calypso which will glide like a serpent beneath the flowers; fear the hidden poison; mistrust yourself, and always wait for my advice."[62] Urusova rejects such a view of women's conversation. To Polion's declaration of love the naiad replies, "learn to know yourself if you want to know the Naiad."[63] Her words answer Fénelon's/Trediakovskii's objections that the influence of women destroys the self, and passions hinder self-knowledge and control. Feminine society and love make Polion more fully, not less, himself.

In both texts, the hero's integrity is associated with control of language.

Fénelon had written his novel against *préciosité* and women's influence over language and literature. Trediakovskii had found the novel an ideal vehicle for rejecting his former allegiance to *préciosité* and asserting the claims of Church Slavonic as the foundation of the literary language. Urusova, in turn, rejects Trediakovskii's preference for the language of learning and books instead of the spoken language of society. Polion's "coarse learning" ("uchen'e gruboe") in the "temple of learning" is readily identifiable with Church Slavonic and ecclesiastical culture. His ignorance of the spoken language is evident in the phrase, "Learning gave no freedom to his lips and tongue."[64] He only regains that freedom of speech after his conversations with the naiad. In contrast, Telemachus, famous for his eloquence, loses all his mastery of language on Calypso's isle. Speaking of Calypso's nymphs, "he blushed without knowing why. He could not prevent himself from speaking; but hardly had he begun to speak than he could not continue: his words were cut short, they were obscure, and sometimes they had no meaning."[65] He only regains his capacity for language once he leaves the isle. Urusova underlines the debate about the language of books and the spoken language in a final account of the naiad's temple, which is contrasted to the temple of false learning. Polion is startled by the absence of books in the naiad's temple. " 'But where are the books,'/ he cried beside himself,/ 'which made you wise?'/ 'The books I read,' said she,/ 'Are the things visible among which I dwell;/ They are inscribed in the hand of the Divine,/ They do not consist of letters, but of Nature's words;/ Although they are despised by scholars,/ They are open for all mortals to read.' "[66] Urusova's vision of the world and nature as a book open to all stands in sharp contrast to the "temple of learning" and its restricted and misanthropic library. The book of nature is open to all, perhaps especially women, who are not among the learned and who preside over this library.

Urusova's vision of the naiad and her realm draws on the ideas of Kheraskov and his circle, but she makes the naiad a far more powerful presence and a far deeper reader than Kheraskov's ideal woman reader, the "intelligent Russian woman," to whom the poet speaks, but who has few words of her own. Polion listens to his beloved's superior wisdom, not she to Polion. Urusova's allegory provides not only an account of a man's education, but also a way for women to imagine their own relation to culture that she carries into her next long work. In her introduction to the *Heroides*, Urusova claims love, the civilizing passion, as the woman writer's particular contribution to Russian culture: "And to encircle the throne of the sacred Muses,/ The female sex began to sing among us:/ They hasten to tenderness in their songs/ And prepare crowns for virtue,/ They sing pleasantly of merriment/ And allow one to feel the workings of the passions;/ In Russia we see Saphos, de la Suzes,/ I strive to follow in their footsteps. . . . "[67]

By the end of the century, it seemed that the naiad's realm was well established, as the "feminization" of Russian language and literature accorded women a central civilizing role. Women began to write in large numbers, a phenomenon that has been attributed in large measure to Karamzin's creation of a "tender style" agreeable to women. Most of the names from this period appear only fleetingly, attached to one or two poems, short prose pieces, and translations published primarily in the leading sentimental journals of the time, *Readings for Taste, Intelligence, and Sensibility* (*Chteniia dliia vkusa, razuma i chuvstvovanii*, 1791), *A Pleasant and Useful Way to Spend Time* (*Priiatnoe i poleznoe preprovozhdenie vremeni*, 1794–1798), and *Hippocrene* (*Ippokrena*, 1799–1801), edited by the Karamzinists P. A. Sokhatskii and V. S. Podshivalov.[68] The sentimental, "feminine" appeal of these journals was defined by *A Pleasant and Useful Way to Spend Time*'s open rhapsody to the "sensitive heart" and *Hippocrene*'s elegant frontispiece depicting a beribboned lady's basket full of flowers upon which rest a scroll and a laurel branch. The editors printed some charming and accomplished pieces by women, including the lovely verses by the sisters Ekaterina and Anastas'ia Svin'ina, and Natal'ia and Aleksandra Mikhailovna Magnitskaia. On the whole, the majority of women's writings were no better, although often no worse, than most of the items that appeared in the journals and almanacs of the period, which were increasingly ridiculed for their lacrimose sentimentality.[69] Occasionally women published slender volumes of their own. *Aoniia*, a collection of sentimental verse by the sisters Mariia and Elizaveta Osipovna Moskvina, appeared in 1802. Aleksandra Petrovna Khvostova (née Kheraskova, 1767–1853) published her sentimental and Ossianic reveries *Fragments. The Hearth and the Stream* (*Otryvki. Kamin i Rucheek*) in 1796 to some acclaim, thanks mainly to her position in society. Mar'ia Alekseevna Pospelova (1784–1805) published two volumes of prose and poetry on various sentimental themes, *The Best Hours of My Life* (*Luchshie chasy zhizni moei*, 1797) and *Some Characteristics of Nature and Truth, or Shades of My Thoughts and Feelings* (*Nekotoryia cherty prirody i istiny, ili ottenki myslei i chuvstv moikh*, 1801), both of which were admired in literary circles.

Although they were encouraged to write occasional verse, few of these women aspired to become writers. Most of their work falls into the category of "ladies' dilletantish sentimental verse" and can be defined by the credo: "I am a woman, I have a heart; consequently I feel the need to impart my feelings. Tell me, is it necessary to read philosophers to have the right to reveal one's thoughts?"[70] Those who did wish to write more than light verse had serious reservations about the "feminization" of Russian society and the feminine ideal that accompanied it. The aging poet, Urusova, the obscure writer, Aleksandra Petrovna Murzina, and Russia's first well-known woman poet, Anna Petrovna Bunina, offer three different perspectives on the woman writer's place in literary life.

In her late poems, Urusova re-examines the ideas expressed in her early work. In "Stream" ("Ruchei"), one of her finest late poems, Urusova encounters the naiad's realm once again, but where the naiad had formerly urged Polion to embrace love and the passions, the naiad now teaches the poet to struggle against them.[71] As the poet sits beside a clear stream watching her image in the waters, she desires to see not only her outer form, but her innermost soul: "But, oh, stream, why, oh why,/ Do you not lay bare my soul/ In your ripples?/ Reveal my heart, my thoughts;/ Be a mirror of my soul;/ Number its sins;/ Paint them vividly.'' In answer, churning waves break the smooth surface of the enchanted stream, the waters darken, and the poet hears, not the naiad's sweet conversation, but the ''terrible voice of the naiad'' speak of the destructive passions that lie hidden in her soul beneath the smooth surface of her outward appearance.

Urusova's desire to look beyond the lovely surface of the naiad's arcadian realm was born of old age. The underlying theme of Urusova's contemplative late poems is the confrontation not only with her own death, but with being an old woman in a society that valued youth and beauty in women. P. Makarov argued in favor of women's education primarily because women must grow old and lose their beauty:

The Empire of beauty knows no bounds; but beauty soon withers, youth flies away,— and when the icy hand of Time disfigures the Angelic, heavenly features, what is to become of a woman accustomed to the sweetness of seeing everyone at her feet if she has not made agreeable each wrinkle of her face in good time, if she has not prepared consolation for herself in her old age?[72]

He wrote more bluntly and less gallantly in review of a novel by Mme. de Genlis, ''After all a book is not a *woman*: it does not lose its value with *time*.''[73] He had urged women to write, gallantly asking, ''What pedant, what Barbarian would dare not to praise that which a tender, white, lovely hand has written?''[74] But what if the hand that pens the poem is now wrinkled and withered?

Urusova records the loss of her youth and beauty in the poem ''Spring'' (''Vesna''). She sees the coming of spring and the rebirth of nature, ''The face of Nature has been renewed,/ The face of spring beauty . . . / What was dead in winter/ Has been reborn in its finest face.''[75] Her description of spring—''The quick waters have begun to murmur,/ Meadows and flowers have bloomed;/ Gentle butterflies fly,/ Herds lie in the fields,/ Little birds sing in the groves,''— deliberately employs the most conventional sentimental terms for a common sentimental subject, one that conventionally provided the basis for a comparison between spring and the young girl. But the poet can no longer read nature and those lines in the way she used to. She no longer sees her own face reflected in the face of Nature: ''I delight in Nature;/ She captures my gaze; But I turn to myself: Where are you, my spring, where?/ Where are you, former joys/ That drew me to you?/ Where are amusements, games and laughter?/ You have vanished, flowed away!/ Mournful Autumn has come;/ Behind her winter will flow . . . / I have withered away irretrievably;/ Death awaits me at the grave.'' By reading the book of nature more deeply, however, she is able to overcome her sorrow. She can no longer compare herself to spring, but she can read spring as a figure for the rebirth of her soul. ''But when death comes my soul will be renewed;/ Then spring will be reborn,/ Then will come the spring of my immortal days.'' ''Spring'' breaks off with a remonstrance to herself not to become too solemn—a tone unsuitable for a sentimental journal. She wrote a number of lighthearted poems in the 1790s, including several charming poems to young women that bear witness to her continued love of life and the naiad's arcadian realm.[76] Gradually, however, the naiad's "terrible voice" comes to dominate her poems.

As Urusova grew older and faced death, her poems became more severe, detached from the world, and preoccupied with her inner world and spiritual life.[77] In "My Seventieth Year" ("Moi semidesiatiy god"), she writes of the rapidity with which death approaches, returning to the image of the stream once again: "Like stormy whirlpools the floods of water churn,/ Just so were days gone by harrowed up by passions,/ And my feelings weighed to the earthly realm./ My seventieth year found me still amidst vanities."[78] In poem after poem she reiterates her struggle with herself, worldly vanity, and the passions, as she contemplates her approaching death. In "To My Genius" ("K moemu geniiu"), she begs her guardian spirit to "Teach me to struggle/ Against worldly vanity;/ Teach me reason/ To oppose the passions."[79]

The peculiar poignancy of Urusova's late poems lies in their being spoken by an aging woman. But her concerns were echoed by many younger women who wrote at this time and feared that their male readers valued outward beauty alone. The lines of an anonymous woman written in reply to a compliment on her love of literature expressed a view shared by a number of other women: "When you weave flattering praises of me/ You call me lovely in vain./ Spiritual beauty alone captivates me;/ I want to shine in such beauty for ever;/ Its light will never fade."[80] Just as male writers imagined their ideal reader, so women reflected on their readers.

Aleksandra Petrovna Murzina offered an original solution to the problem of the male reader. She dispensed with the male reader altogether and imagined a community of women readers. In her collection *The Blooming Rose, or Various Essays in Prose and Verse* (*Raspuskaiushchaisia roza, ili raznyia sochineniia v proze i stikhakh*, 1799), Murzina imagines a world in which the woman writer will find a home and an audience in a female community of friends and readers. The volume is divided into two parts, a series of prose essays followed by a collection of poetry. In the long poem "To Readers" ("K chitateliam"), the first poem and the central work of the volume as a whole, Murzina considers how women's writing is read.[81] The poet describes how she began to write poetry for her own pleasure and to occupy herself, only to be surprised by her readers' reactions to her poems:

I was astonished to hear,/ That Satire was wholly/ Against my sex,/ As if the female sex/ Spent their lives in darkness;/ While man, despising the low earth,/ Flew among the stars with his mind.// As though the Creator/ Had not endowed us with minds,/ But let tenderness of heart/ Rule over us;/ That vanity alone/ Surrounds us,/ And only beauty/ Draws others to us.// Behold how they think,/ Loving their own talents,/ Despising us, they/ Number only themselves among the intelligent.

Where men blame women for corrupting society, she concludes to the contrary, that men have no right to speak ill of women:

Inspired by pride/ They sin against us and despise us,/ And wholly deadened/ They shamelessly reproach us./ Did wise God/ Have it in His plan?/ That man alone could judge the world?// O proud being!/ How impudent and offensive/ Is your dream!—/ Everyone can see from experience/ That women have minds.

Although she acknowledges that there are some enlightened men who do not scorn women and who can see "That the Creator made all mortals/ Equal in their gifts," rather than seeking those men out, she imagines a sympathetic female reader and a female community.

How the poet finds that reader is the subject of the six prose essays that make up the first part of the book and sketch the writer's life, her character and beliefs, and her discovery of a female community. Rejecting worldly society and the dandy preening and primping before the mirror, as well as the domestic life of a wife and mother, she resides quietly in the country until chance leads her to the gates of a monastery. Within the wall of the monastery she discovers a female community, headed by the Abbess Amaliia, in whom she finds a beloved friend for whom she gladly forsakes the world. She and her friend spend their days together in conversation, drawing, gardening, reading, and prayer, bound by mutual love in a meeting of hearts and minds. The final essay "The Image of True Love" ("Obraz istinnoi liubvi"), a rhapsody to love as sympathy and virtue, characteristic of the sentimental cult of friendship, prepares the way for the poetry in the second part of the volume. The poet has now found a world and a reader who can read her poems and understand her. The reader she finds bears no relation to the harsh readers of "To Readers." Although she says that there are some enlightened men who "know how to be captivated by spiritual beauty," she finds her true reader in Amaliia. She has found her beloved "intelligent Russian woman" capable of understanding that "the pleasantness of learning captivated my soul."[82]

The poetry that follows can be read as the creative work that flows from the woman poet's participation in the community. The poems are made possible by her muse and reader, her beloved Amaliia, who acts as friend and teacher. In "A True Testament of the Heart Ecstatic with Friendship" ("Istinnoe veshchanie serdtsa, druzhboiu upoennago"), the poet addresses her muse, who is "in conversations cheerful, charming,/ Dear, feeling, not flattering—" with the words: "I do not speak with invention of the mind;/ I will leave the style of pomposity:/ And I will lay bare my feelings/ Before she whom I have long been accustomed/ To think of as my soul,/ She who shines in her virtue/ Like a ray of sun that has driven away the waves of dark storm clouds."[83] The poems return to many of the themes and subjects raised in the first part of the book. Many are deeply religious poems in which she beseeches God to help her overcome the passions. Other poems speak of the vanity of the world and in praise of country life, love, and friendship. The volume also includes a number of more lighthearted pieces and word games, and ends with a series of forty love songs set to popular romances. The poems belong to the female community and to Amaliia, whose wisdom and conversation the poet treasures, and with whom she can speak her mind and heart. Murzina's ideal female reader and community offers an original way around the difficulty posed by ideas of feminine nature that sundered beauty and intellect, heart and mind, and that could so easily transform beauty and tenderness of heart into marks of frivolity and lack of intellect.

For a final commentary on the Karamzinists' ''feminization'' of Russian culture, I shall turn briefly to the poet Anna Petrovna Bunina (1774–1829) and her poem ''A Conversation Between Me and Women'' (''Razgovor mezhdu mnoiu i zhenshchinami'') published in her first collection of poetry *The Inexperienced Muse* (*Neopytnaia muza*, 1809–1812). Bunina more properly belongs to the nineteenth century, but her ''Conversation Between Me and Women'' stages a witty commentary on the legacy of ideas about women and language bequeathed by the eighteenth century.[84]

By the time Bunina wrote the ''Conversation'' she was already well established as a poet and translator. Her work first appeared in the sentimental journals of the 1790s. Over the next decade she published verse, both original and in translation, in the leading literary journals of the day, as well as *The Rules of Poetry* (*Pravila poezii*), a translation and adaptation for women of Abbé Charles Batteux's classic text in 1808, and a translation of Boileau's neoclassical manifesto, *L'Art Poétique* the following year. The first volume of *The Inexperienced Muse* appeared in 1809; a collection of tales, *Village Evenings* (*Sel'skie vechera*), followed in 1811, and the second volume of *The Inexperienced Muse* in 1812. She became an honorary member of Shishkov's ''Society of Lovers of the Russian Word'' in 1811. Her collected works, the *Collected Poetry of Anna Bunina* (*Sobranie stikhotvorenii Anny Buninoi*, were published by the Academy of Sciences in three volumes from 1819 to 1821.[85]

A ''Conversation Between Me and Women'' dramatizes an exchange between a woman poet (akin to Bunina herself) and several Karamzinian ladies who speak in chorus about the woman writer, what she writes, and what she might, as a woman, be expected to write. The ladies first hail the woman poet rapturously, expecting to find in her a writer who will write for and of them: ''Sister darling, how delighted we are!/ You are a poetess! You have ready various inks/ For odes, fables and fairy tales,/ And you undoubtedly have a special feeling for panegyrics.'' They expect to find her a woman's writer, a poet who will write for women. They complain of men's language which is ''like a sharp knife.'' And they say they hear ''Only curses—and how the ladies suffer!/ We wait for madrigals—and we read epigrams./ From brothers, husbands, fathers and sons/ Don't expect to hear words of praise./ We have long wanted our own singer!'' Unfortunately, they have to ask her to tell them what she has written because they cannot read Russian, it is ''strange and difficult'' and, besides, not at all the fashion. But when the poet describes her writings to them, they are cruelly disappointed. Instead of madrigals and poems of their own world, the pleasures of the capitals and their elegant boudoirs and salons, she tells them of her poems of peaceful pastoral pleasures and the sublimity of nature's harsher designs. Instead of panegyrics to the ladies, the woman poet writes in praise of famous men, warriors, and poets, physicists, chemists, and astronomers. Finally, the ladies repudiate the woman poet as one of themselves: "And not a word there about us!/ That's truly doing us a service!/ What's there for us in you? What do you do for us?/ Why have you learned to write verse?/ You should have taken [poems] from your own sphere;/ And you started praising men!/ As though their sex alone deserves praise!/ Traitress!''

The breach between the woman poet and the ladies marks Bunina's repudiation of Karamzinism and the "feminization" of Russian culture. Her repudiation takes place on two levels. The first and most obvious is her refusal to write for the inhabitants of the "luxurious boudoirs of Aspazias" and be a writer "whom ladies read." Accordingly, she presents the ladies in their most vilified form, as they appeared to satirists like Novikov and Shishkov, whose arguments she echoes. On a second level, she rejects the Karamzinists' ideal of the woman writer by means of her portrayal of the woman poet. Her poet stands in sharp contrast to a young woman who perhaps most fully embodied the Karamzinian sentimental ideal, Mar'ia Pospelova who poured out her feelings in her two books *The Best Hours of My Life* (*Luchshie chasy zhizni moei*, 1797) and *Some Characteristics of Nature and Truth, Or Shades of My Thoughts and Feelings* (*Nekotoryia cherty prirody i istiny, ili ottenki myslei i chuvstv moikh*, 1801).[86]

Young, innocent, and modest, Pospelova embodied many of the most cherished images of sentimentalism and the sentimental woman. Although her writings are accomplished and show considerable craft and mastery of meter and rhyme, she presents herself as a child of nature and her work as the outpourings of her childlike heart rather than a work of learning. In the introduction to her second volume, she emphasizes her lack of education. She had no teachers, but a few books from which she taught herself, although she often erred, not realizing, she says, how nearly wise men resemble children. "Nature gifted me with sensibility, and made my mind capable of reflection," she writes.[87] Nature became her true teacher and "taught me from my infancy to reflect and set down on paper the shades of my thoughts and feelings. I sing, imitating the little singers of spring; I sing by nature's inspiration alone." Pospelova's readers particularly admired the young girl's modest and retiring nature. "Neither glory, nor the sound of praises animate me, but only the delight I feel," she writes. And she appeals to her readers' indulgence, "Your smile and a tear is for me a crown more precious than laurels! I hope that true simplicity and the voice of feeling will touch your tender hearts and that you will not judge severely the failings of an unlearned and inexperienced child of nature."

In contrast to Pospelova, Bunina presents her woman poet as a craftsman, not as a creature of spontaneously overflowing emotion or a poet of the heart merely echoing the voice of nature. She does not dissolve the difference between the child and the sage, for she values learning. Bunina's poet emphasizes that her poetry is a work of craft in which she exercises power over her words and their form. The world of nature she describes is her work: She makes the shepherds dance and prevents their feet from crushing a single blade of grass; she sets the hornèd moon in the water; she orders the winds to blow. Unlike Pospelova, she does not stand and admire nature, of which she herself is a part, and the work of the Creator; she herself creates her world. Where Pospelova becomes modest and humble in the face of God's creation, Bunina's poet is emboldened by the beauty she herself has created, "Strengthening my timid voice/ By the beauty of nature,/ Suddenly I become braver!" Bunina's poet wants more than the smile or tear that satisfies Pospelova. The poet wants glory and the laurel crown, hence her reply to the ladies' accusations that she is a traitress for writing in praise of men instead of her own sex: "You are right my dears! You are no lower than they,/ Ah! But men, and not you sit in judgement over authors' crowns,/ And authorial glory lies in their hands,/ And each man is drawn involuntarily to his own!" Her words deny a central tenet of the Karamzinists' view of language and literature. Women are not the judges of literature and language. However gallantly men say otherwise, men, not women, bestow the literary laurels. Gallantry and politeness only conceal the fact that women do not share in the literary conversation on the same terms as men. To Bunina's mind, madrigals and compliments were not much better than the "sharp knife of language." In reply to a compliment in her album, she wrote, "Madrigals please frivolous women. A woman accustomed to reflection, wants only to be treated with respect." Moreover, she added, "a poet showers a woman-writer with praise more willingly than a fellow poet; for he is accustomed to thinking that he knows more than she."[88] Bunina does not refuse to make common cause with the ladies because she rejects her sex; rather, she rejects their solution—the "feminization" of women and the woman writer. In doing so she rejects the ideas about women, language, and literature that the eighteenth century bequeathed to the nineteenth.

NOTES

1. See V. D. Levin, *Ocherk stilistiki russkogo literaturnogo iazyka kontsa XVIII–nachala XIX v.* (Moscow, 1964); Iu. M. Lotman, B. A. Uspenskii, "Spory o iazyke v nachale XIX veka kak fakt russkoi kul'tury," in *Uchenye zapiski Tartuskogo universiteta*, vyp. 358 (1975), 168–323; Boris A. Uspenskij, "The Language Program of N. M. Karamzin and Its Historical Antecedents," in *Aspects of the Slavic Language Question, vol. 2, East Slavic*, ed. Riccardo Picchio and Harvey Goldblatt (New Haven, CT: Yale Russian and East European Publications, No. 4-b, 1984), 235–96; Boris A. Uspenskii, *Iz istorii russkogo literaturnogo iazyka XVIII–nachala XIX veka* (Moscow, 1985); V. V. Vinogradov, "Russko-frantsuzskii iazyk dvorianskogo salona i bor'ba Pushkina s literaturnymi normami 'iazyka svetskoi damy'," in *Iazyk Pushkina* (Moscow-Leningrad, 1932), 195–236.

2. Vinogradov appears to be the first to use the term "feminization" in *Iazyk Push-*

kina, 216. It has been used most recently by Uspenskii, *Iz istorii russkogo literaturnogo iazyka*, 58.

3. See Dorothy Atkinson, "Society and the Sexes in the Russian Past," in *Women in Russia*, ed. Dorothy Atkinson, Alexander Dallin, and Gail Warshofsky Lapidus (Stanford, CA: Stanford University Press, 1977), 3–38; Lindsey Hughes, *Sophia, Regent of Russia 1657–1704* (New Haven and London: Yale University Press, 1990), 16–22; Richard Stites, *The Women's Liberation Movement in Russia. Feminism, Nihilism, and Bolshevism, 1860–1930* (Princeton, NJ: Princeton University Press, 1978), 3–25. Valuable older studies include V. Mikhnevich, *Russkie zhenshchiny XVIII stoletiia* (Kiev, 1895); Elena Likhacheva, *Materialy dliia zhenskago obrazovaniia v Rossii* 4 vols. (Spb., 1890–1893).

4. On Trediakovskii, see William Edward Brown, *A History of 18th Century Russian Literature* (Ann Arbor, MI: Ardis, 1980), 54–73; Irina Reyfman, *Vasilii Trediakovsky: The Fool of the 'New' Russian Literature* (Stanford, CA: Stanford University Press, 1990).

5. See Iu. M. Lotman, " 'Ezda v ostrov liubvi' Trediakovskogo: funktsiia perevodnoi literatury v russkoi kul'ture pervoi poloviny XVIII v.," in *Problemy izucheniia kul'turnogo naslediia* (Moscow, 1985), 222–30.

6. On Trediakovskii's linguistic views, see A. A. Alekseev, "Evoliutsia iazykovoi teorii i iazykovaia praktika Trediakovskogo," *Literaturnyi iazyk XVIII veka. Problemy stilistiki*, ed Iu. S. Sorokin (Leningrad, 1982), 86–128; Uspenskii, *Iz istorii russkogo literaturnogo iazyka*, 70–199. On the *précieuse*, see L.-F. Flutre, "Du rôle des femmes dans l'élaboration des *Remarques* de Vaugelas" *Neophilologus*, XXXVIII, No. 4 (1954): 241–48. For a feminist reading of the scholarship on *préciosité*, see Domna C. Stanton, "The Fiction of Préciosité and the Fear of Women," *Feminist Readings: French Texts/ American Contexts*, *Yale French Studies*, No. 62 (1981): 107–34.

7. In the later "Conversation on Orthography" (1748), Trediakovskii proposed that "tender ladies' speech" ("nezhnyi damskii vygovor") might usefully serve as the model for the linguist, like himself, trying to standardize Russian orthography. The quotation is from "Razgovor ob ortografii," in Trediakovskii, *Sochineniia*, vol. 3 (Spb., 1849), 285.

8. See Lotman and Uspenskii, "Spory o iazyke" 230, and Alekseev, "Evoliutsiia iazykovoi teorii i iazykovaia praktika Trediakovskogo," 121.

9. M. V. Lomonosov, *Izbrannye proizvedeniia*, 3d ed. (Leningrad, 1986), 269–74.

10. See P. N. Berkov, *Lomonosov i literaturnaia polemika ego vremeni 1750–1765*. (Moscow and Leningrad, 1936), 6–53; James von Geldern, "The Ode as Performative Genre," *Slavic Review* 50, No. 4 (Winter 1991): 927–43; Pierre Hart, "Continuity and Change in the Russian Ode," *Russian Literature in the Age of Catherine the Great, A Collection of Essays*, ed. Antony Glenn Cross (Oxford: Meeuws, 1976), 17–43.

11. M. M. Kheraskov, *Izbrannye proizvedeniia* (Leningrad, 1961), 74–75, trans. Brown, in *A History of 18th Century Russian Literature*, 252. On Kheraskov and his circle, see Brown, ibid., 246–67; Grigorii A. Gukovskii, *Russkaia poeziia XVIII veka* (Leningrad, 1927), 9–182; Doris Schenk, *Studien zur anakreontischen Ode in der russischen Literatur des Klassizismus und der Empfindsamkeit*, *Frankfurter Abhandlungen zur Slavistik*, 13 (1972): 28–74.

12. See, for example, the letter from a dandy, "It is absolutely necessary that I speak the current dandyfied women's jargon ("nyneshnee shchegol'skoe zhenskoe narechie"), for in our time it is considered not the least of the skills essential to the art of love-making." (*Zhivopisets*, I, list 4, 1772, in *Satiricheskie zhurnaly N. I. Novikova*, ed.

P. N. Berkov (Moscow-Leningrad, 1951), 293. On the dandies and women's language, see V. I. Pokrovskii *Shchegoli v satiricheskoi literature XVIII veka* (Moscow, 1903), and *Shchegolikhi v satiricheskoi literature XVIII veka* (Moscow, 1903); Uspenskij, "The Language Program of N. M. Karamzin," 242–47; Uspenskii, *Iz istorii russkogo literaturnogo iazyka*, 46–65.

13. Quoted in P. V. Vladimirov, *Pervyia russkiia pisatel'nitsy XVIII veka* (Kiev, 1892), 26. Ivan Krylov's play *The Mischief Makers* (1788) also satirizes the female dandy and poetess, the mistress of a disorderly household (the satire was directed at the poet Ekaterina Aleksandrovna Khniazhnina, née Sumarokova). For a brief analysis of Denis Fonvizin's play *The Minor* (1782) from this perspective, see Joe Andrew, *Women in Russian Literature, 1780–1863* (London: Macmillan Press, 1988), 12–18. Andrew's reading emphasizes the connection between the restoration of a patriarchal social order and the silencing of women and views the play as a more general attack on Catherine II's rule.

14. On freemasonry, see Stephen Lessing Baehr, *The Paradise Myth in Eighteenth-Century Russia* (Stanford, CA: Stanford University Press, 1991); G. Gareth Jones, *Nikolay Novikov: Enlightener of Russia* (Cambridge: Cambridge University Press, 1984).

15. A. E. Labzina, *Vospominaniia, 1763–1819* ([Spb., 1914]; republished, Cambridge, Mass.: Oriental Research Partners, 1974), 49.

16. "Stikhi k 'Besede liubitelei russkogo slova,' " *Chteniia v Besede liubitelei russkogo slova*, 1 (1811): 82.

17. "Otchego v Rossii malo avtorskikh talantov?" in N. M. Karamzin, *Sochineniia v dvukh tomakh*, vol. 2 (Leningrad, 1984), 123–26. On Karamzinism, see Levin, *Ocherk*, 115–293; Uspenskii, *Iz istorii russkogo literaturnogo iazyka*, 16–69.

18. Review essay of Aleksandr Shishkov's *Razsuzhdenie o starom i novom iazyka* in *Moskovskoi Merkurii*, ch. 4 (1803), 155–98, quoted 175. On Makarov, see G. Gennadi, "P. I. Makarov i ego zhurnal 'Moskovskii Merkurii'," *Sovremennik*, vol. 47, 2 (1854): 65–94; Lotman and Uspenskii, "Spory o iazyka," 168–254. Aspazia was a Greek courtesan known for her beauty and cultivation.

19. Makarov, "Nekotorye mysli Izdatelei 'Merkuriia,' " *Moskovskoi Merkurii*, ch. 1 (1803), 4–18.

20. "Pevets, ili Pevtsy v Besede slaveno-rossov" in K. N. Batiushkov, *Sochineniia v dvukh tomakh*, vol. 1 (Moscow, 1989), 393.

21. "O vospitanii devits i ob uchenykh zhenshchinakh. Pis'mo materi k docheri" ("On the Education of Girls, and On Learned Women. A Mother's Letter to Her Daughter") *Patriot*, vol. 3 (1804): 291–304.

22. On the clash between the polite society and professionalism, see William Mills Todd III, "Institutions of Literature in Early-Nineteenth-Century Russia: Boundaries and Transgressions," in *Literature and History*, ed. Gary Saul Morson (Stanford, CA: Stanford University Press, 1986), 57–89.

23. P. Makarov, "Nekotoryia mysli Izdatelei 'Merkuriia,' " 10–11.

24. On Shishkov and the Shishkovites, see Mark Al'tshuller, *Predtechi slavianofil'stva v russkoi literature. (Obshchestvo "Beseda liubitelei russkogo slova")* (Ann Arbor, MI: Ardis, 1984); Lotman and Uspenskii, "Spory o iazyke"; Uspenskii, *Iz istorii russkogo literaturnogo iazyka*, 158–99.

25. One exception is A. A. Alekseev's essay, "Iazyk svetskikh dam i razvitie iazykovoi normy v XVIII veke," in *Funktsional'nye i sotsial'nye raznovidnosti russkogo literaturnogo iazyka XVIII veka*, ed. V. V. Zamkov (Leningrad, 1984), 82–95. However,

Alekseev essentially treats women's language as a biological phenomenon. A more historical view of the folk-linguistics of women and language can be found in Jennifer Coates, *Women, Men and Language* (London: Longmans, 1986); and Dennis Baron, *Grammar and Gender* (New Haven and London: Yale University Press, 1986).

26. Quoted in David Griffiths, "To Live Forever: Catherine II, Voltaire and the Pursuit of Immortality," in *Russia and the World of the Eighteenth Century*, ed. R. P. Bartlett, A. G. Cross, Karen Rasmussen (Columbus, OH: Slavica Publishers, 1988), 444–68, 452.

27. On her relation to the philosophes, see Léonce Pingaud, *Les Francais en Russie* (Paris, 1886), ch. 2, "Catherine II et l'esprit philosophique," 27–60; *Voltaire and Catherine the Great: Selected Correspondence*, ed. A. Lentin (Cambridge: Cambridge University Press, 1974).

28. See Isabel de Madariaga, "The Great Instruction," in *Russia in the Age of Catherine the Great* (New Haven and London: Yale University Press, 1981), 151–63; *Documents of Catherine the Great. The Correspondence with Voltaire and the Instruction of 1767 in the English Text of 1768*, ed. W. F. Reddaway (Cambridge: Cambridge University Press, 1931).

29. Quoted in John T. Alexander, *Catherine the Great. Life and Legend* (New York and Oxford: Oxford University Press, 1989), 101.

30. *Sobesednik liubitelei rossiiskago slova*, 7 (1783): 142–61.

31. Recent general histories of literature in Catherine II's reign include Brown, *A History of 18th Century Russian Literature*; *Russian Literature in the Age of Catherine the Great. A Collection of Essays*, ed. Antony Glenn Cross; de Madariaga, "Court and Culture," in *Russia in the Age of Catherine the Great*, 327–42; Gary Marker, *Publishing, Printing, and the Origins of Intellectual Life in Russia, 1700–1800* (Princeton, NJ: Princeton University Press, 1985).

32. Many of her writings are collected in *Sochineniia Ekateriny II* 12 vols., ed. A. N. Pypin (St. Petersburg, 1901–1907). See N. N. Golitsyn, *Bibliograficheskii slovar' russkikh pisatel'nits* (St. Petersburg, 1889), 91–109; Grigorii A. Gukovskii, "The Empress as Writer," in *Catherine the Great. A Profile*, ed. Marc Raeff (New York: Hill and Wang, 1972), 64–89; V. P. Stepanov, "Ekaterina II," *Slovar' russkikh pisatelei XVIII veka* vyp.1 A-I (Leningrad, 1988), 291–302.

33. On Catherine and the theater, see P. N. Berkov, *Istoriia russkoi komedii XVIII v.* (Leningrad, 1977), 144–53, 290–91; Simon Karlinsky, *Russian Drama From Its Beginnings to the Age of Pushkin* (Berkeley, CA: University of California Press, 1985), 83–92; Charles Hyart, "Le Théâtre de l'Hermitage et Catherine II," *Revue de Littérature Comparée* vol. 61 (January-March 1987): 81–103.

34. On the satirical journals, see P. N. Berkov, *Istoriia russkoi zhurnalistiki XVIII veka* (Moscow-Leningrad, 1952), 225–29; Jones, *Nikolay Novikov*; Kevin J. McKenna, "Empress Behind the Mask: The *Persona* of Md. Vsiakaia Vsiachina in Catherine the Great's Periodical Essays on Morals and Manners," *Neophilologus* 74 (1990): 1–11.

35. On her educational policies for women, see J. L. Black, "Educating Women in Eighteenth-Century Russia," in *Citizens for the Fatherland, Education, Educators and Pedagogical Ideals in Eighteenth-Century Russia* (New York: Columbia University Press, 1979), 152–71; Likhacheva, *Materialy*, vols. 1–3; Carol S. Nash, "Educating New Mothers: Women and the Enlightenment in Russia," *History of Education Quarterly* 21 (1981): 301–16.

36. *Memoirs of Madame Vigée Lebrun*, trans. Lionel Strachey (London, 1904), 108.

37. Ibid., 100.

38. On Dashkova, see L. Ia. Lozinskaia, *Vo glave dvukh akademii* (Moscow, 1978); Tatyana Mamonova, "The Two Catherines," *Russian Women's Studies* (New York: Pergamon Press, the Athene Series, 1989), 9–19; M. I. Sukhomlinov, *Istoriia Rossiiskoi Akademii*, 8 vols. (Spb., 1874–1887), vol. 1, 1–57; V. A. Teplova, "Dashkova," *Slovar' russkikh pisatelei XVIII veka*, vyp. A-I, 243–47.

39. For her work at the Academy, see Berkov, *Istoriia russkoi zhurnalistiki XVIII veka*, 330–48; V. P. Semennikov, *Materialy dlia istorii russkoi literatury i dlia slovaria pisatelei epokhi Ekateriny II* (Spb., 1914), 29–39, 151–55; Sukhomlinov, *Istoriia Rossiiskoi Akademii*, 1–57.

40. *Sobesednik*, ch. 1 (1873): 15–23.

41. See, for example, a note from the editors, *Sobesednik*, ch. 1 (1783): 86–87; "Otvet ot slova Tak," ibid., ch. 3 (1783): 141–47; and Catherine II's "Nachertanie o Rossiiskikh sochineniiakh i Rossiiskom iazyke."

42. See Golitsyn *Bibliograficheskii slovar' russkikh pisatel'nits*, 77–82.

43. *The Memoirs of Princess Dashkov*, trans. and ed. Kyril Fitzlyon (London, 1958). On the memoirs, see S. S. Dmitriev and G. A. Veselaia, "Zapiski kniagini Dashkovoi i pis'ma sester Vil'mot iz Rossii," introduction to E. R. Dashkova, *Zapiski. Pis'ma sester M. i K. Vil'mot iz Rossii* (Moscow, 1987), 5–32; Barbara Heldt, *Terrible Perfection. Women and Russian Literature* (Bloomington: Indiana University Press, 1987), 64–76.

44. *Memoirs*, 177.

45. Ibid., 28.

46. Ibid., 24.

47. Ibid., 27.

48. On this tradition, see Sylvana Tomaselli, "The Enlightenment Debate on Women," *History Workshop* 20 (Autumn 1985): 101–24; *French Women in the Age of Enlightenment*, ed. Samia I. Spencer (Bloomington: Indiana University Press, 1984).

49. See Dena Goodman, "Seriousness of Purpose: Salonnières, Philosophes, and the Shaping of the Eighteenth-Century Salon," *Proceedings of the Annual Meeting of the Western Society for French History*, vol. 15 (1988): 111–21; Dena Goodman, "Enlightenment Salons: The Convergence of Female and Philosophic Ambitions," *Eighteenth-Century Studies*, vol. 22, No. 3 (Spring 1989): 329–50; Joan B. Landes, *Women and the Public Sphere in the Age of the French Revolution* (Ithaca, NY, and London: Cornell University Press, 1988).

50. Jean-Jacques Rousseau, *Politics and the Arts: Letter to M. d'Alembert on the Theater*, trans. Allan Bloom (Ithaca, NY: Cornell University Press, 1960), 101–105.

51. See Margaret Darrow, "French Noblewomen and the New Domesticity, 1750–1850," *Feminist Studies*, 5, No. 1 (Spring 1979): 41–65; Dorinda Outram, "Words and Flesh: Madame Roland, the Female Body and the Search for Power," in *The Body and the French Revolution: Sex, Class and Political Culture* (New Haven and London: Yale University Press, 1989), 124–52.

52. On Urusova, see Golitsyn, *Bibliograficheskii slovar' russkikh pisatel'nits*, 254–55; M. N. Longinov, "Kniazhna Ekaterina Sergeevna Urusova," *Russkaia starina*, vol. 13 (1873), 336–37.

53. See P. V. Vladimirov, *Pervye russkie pisatel'nitsy XVIII veka* (Kiev, 1892).

54. *Tilimakhida ili stranstvovanie Tilimakha syna Odyseeva*, in Trediakovskii, *Sochineniia*, vol. 2 (Spb., 1849), 189–90.

55. See Alekseev, "Evoliutsia iazykovoi teorii i iazykovaia praktika Trediakovskogo";

A. S. Orlov, *"Tilemakhida* V. K. Trediakovskogo" *XVIII vek.*, sb. 1 (Moscow-Leningrad, 1935), 5–55; Uspenskii, *Iz istorii russkogo literaturnogo iazyka*, 70–219.

56. *Polion ili Prosvetivshiisia Neliudim, Poema* (Spb., 1774), 5.

57. Ibid., 5.

58. Ibid., 8.

59. Ibid., 31.

60. Ibid., 35.

61. Ibid., 55.

62. *Tilimakhida*, 11.

63. *Polion*, 39.

64. Ibid., 15.

65. *Tilimakhida*, 187.

66. *Polion*, 53.

67. See N. V. Guberti, *Materialy dliia russkoi bibliografii. Khronologicheskoe obozrenie redkikh i zamechatel'nykh knig XVIII stoletiia napechatannykh v Rossii grazhdanskim shriftom 1725–1800, Chteniia v imperatorskom obshchestve istorii i drevnosti rossiiskikh pri moskovskom universitete*, 1 (1879), 1–112, quoted 13.

68. On sentimentalism, see M. A. Arzumanova, "Russkii sentimentalizm v kritike 90-kh godov XVIIIv.," *XVIII vek*, 6 (Moscow-Leningrad, 1964), 197–223; A. G. Cross, "The Russian Literary Scene in the Reign of Paul I" *Canadian-American Slavic Studies* 7, 1 (1973): 39–51; Rudolf Neuhäuser, *Towards the Romantic Age: Essays on Sentimental and Romantic Literature in Russia* (The Hague: Nijhoff, 1974); P. A. Orlov, *Russkii sentimentalizm* (Moscow, 1977).

69. See Vladimirov *Pervyia russkiia pisatel'nitsy XVIII veka*, 32–35.

70. "Florisa," in *Ippokrena*, trans. G. Kamen'ev, ch. 6 (1800), 225.

71. *Aonidy*, 1 (1796), 131–34.

72. *Moskovskoi Merkurii*, 1 (1803), 11–12.

73. Ibid., 72, Makarov's italics.

74. P. Makarov, "Nekotoryia mysli Izdatelei 'Merkuriia,' " 13.

75. *Aonidy*, 1 (1796), 67–69.

76. See, for example, "Stepnaia pesn" ("Steppe Song"), *Aonidy*, 3 (1798–1799), 27–30; "K Val'mine" ("To Val'mina"), *Patriot*, 1 (1804), 222–23.

77. See, for example, "Ot sochinitel'nitsy 'Ruch'ia.' Otvet na otvet" ("From the Writer of the Stream. A Reply to a Reply"), *Ippokrena*, 3 (1799), 303–304; "K tvortsu Kadma" ("To the Creator of Cadmus"), *Chtenie v Besede liubitelei russkago slova*, 1 (1811), 78–81.

78. *Syn otechestva*, 31 (1816), 160–61.

79. *Chtenie v Besede liubitelei russkago slova*, 8 (1813), 65–66.

80. *Moskovskii zhurnal*, ch. 3 (1791), 131.

81. *Raspuskaiushchaisia roza, ili raznyia sochineniia v proze i stikhakh* (Moscow, 1799), 46–49.

82. Ibid., 4.

83. Ibid., 99–101.

84. The poem was first published in *Neopytnaia muza*, vol. 2 (Spb., 1812), 57–61. It is included in the anthology *Tsaritsa muz. Russkie poetessy XIX-nachala XX vv.* (Moscow, 1989), 21–24. A discussion of the poem appears in Heldt, *Terrible Perfection*, 108–10.

85. See A. K. Baboreko, "Bunina," *Russkie pisateli 1800–1917. Biograficheskii slo-*

var', vol. 1, A-G (Moscow, 1989), 362–63; A. K. Baboreko, ''Bunina,'' *Russkie pisateli. Biograficheskii slovar'*, 2 vols., vol. 1, ed. Nikolaev (Moscow, 1990), 128–31.

86. On Pospelova, see B. Fedorov, ''O zhizhni i sochineniiakh devitsy Pospelovoi,'' *Otechestvennye zapiski* ch. 17, No. 46 (1824), 185–201; No. 47, 457–70; ch. 18, No. 48, 75–86; Mordovtsev, *Russkiia zhenshchiny novago vremeni*, vol. 3, 39–46; M. D. Khmyrov, ''Russkie pisatel'nitsy proshlogo vremeni. Anna Bunina, Mariia Pospelova i Elisaveta Kul'man,'' *Rassvet*, vol. 7, No. 11 (1861): 257–63.

87. *Nekotoryia cherty prirody i istiny, ili ottenki myslei i chuvstv moikh* (Moscow, 1801), 5–9.

88. K. Grot, ''Al'bom Anny Buninoi,'' *Russkii arkhiv*, 1 (1902): 500–506.

4

Love, Work, and the Woman Question in Mid Nineteenth-Century Women's Writing

Jane Costlow

"We are not 'the woman question' asked by somebody else; we are the women who ask the questions."

Adrienne Rich[1]

"Where am I to go? Run away? Where is there to run?"

Nadezhda Suslova[2]

In an essay published in 1884 for a volume entitled *The Woman Question in Europe*, Mariia Tsebrikova (1835–1917) set out to describe for foreign readers the status of Russian women.[3] "How is it," Tsebrikova had repeatedly been asked, "that Russia, which by no means occupies the foremost rank in European civilization, is first in this matter of women's emancipation? For no country in the Old World can vie with Russia in this respect."[4] The paradox of apparent emancipation in a country more renowned for repression was—as we will note—paramount to Tsebrikova and her contemporaries and formed the substratum of much of their writing. For nineteenth-century Russians, the woman question was the term that served to designate the whole complex of issues regarding women's education, work, and position in the family. First raised explicitly in the period following the Crimean War and the death of Nicholas I in 1855, the "woman question" came to refer to public discussion of social and economic changes in women's lives (participation in the political life of Russia remained beyond debate for women as for men).[5] For Tsebrikova, there was generous evidence of Russian women's achievements in science, education, and literature, as well as in the legal and economic order. She frames her brief history of the "woman question" with reference to women's efforts in science and literature: She begins with Nadezhda Suslova, the first Russian woman to practice as a doctor, and ends with a discussion of women writers. Implicit in both references is women's entry into public life and professional work, as well as the social and economic aspect of transformation of women's lives.

Tsebrikova's essay notwithstanding, the history of the "woman question" in Russia has in large part been framed by male intellectual figures; questions of women's education and of their abilities to work entered public discourse in the late 1850s, most prominently in a series of essays written by M. L. Mikhailov, *Women: Their Education and Position in the Family and Society.*[6] Similarly, the publicists Dmitrii Pisarev and Nikolai Chernyshevsky both contributed in fundamental ways to articulation of what the woman question meant to educated Russia, the first in his essays on literature and education, the second in his novel of 1863, *What Is to Be Done?*[7] Women enter this history of their own emancipation as philanthropic agents and revolutionary terrorists, but their role as articulators of public and literary discourse remains largely unstudied.[8] Nikolai Shelgunov, a literary critic and social commentator, himself a prominent figure in the radical politics and lifestyle experiments of the 1860s, could in fact claim that women had played no role in the written articulation of the "woman question." In an essay written in 1870, Shelgunov raised what was for him a rhetorical question: "Who among our women writers—and we have many of them—has studied the woman question and written about it? Not a one."[9] Could Shelgunov possibly have been right? Were women silent in the matter of their own freedom? Were they not, as Adrienne Rich puts it, "the women who ask the questions," content instead to be talked about rather than enunciating their own words and fates?

As this chapter will show, Shelgunov was wrong. But our initial concern will be to understand how struggles for the power of naming did in fact enter criticism of woman writers and discussions of the woman question: What was the woman question and who got to define it, if not women? One of the central assumptions of feminist scholarship is that the power of naming is central to the power to constitute history.[10] The texts that form the central focus of this chapter are literary rather than programmatic or journalistic; the best of them demonstrate the complexity and subtlety of fictive statement and make it difficult, if not impossible, to reduce them to simple propositions regarding women's lives. It is in their complex interaction with legacies of culture—with inherited plots and notions of feminine character—that these women writers "name" the woman question. Their writing needs to be read with attention to the literary ways in which they framed women's aspirations, and with a historical sense of how their activity as writers was shaped by contemporary polemics and socioeconomic change.[11]

Nikolai Shelgunov tendered his claims about women's literary silence in an essay entitled "Women's Heartlessness" ["Zhenskoe bezdushie"], an essay devoted to one of the finest women writers of the nineteenth century, Nadezhda Khvoshchinskaia (1824–1889).[12] Shelgunov claimed that Khvoshchinskaia was concerned with "unnecessary details" ("all the folds of a woman's dress and all the trivia of a woman's boudoir");[13] Mariia Tsebrikova, a far more sympathetic memoirist, remembered having been told that Khvoshchinskaia "didn't sympathize with women's emancipation," a rumor that Tsebrikova considered "rubbish."[14] What is apparent in these claims and rumors and counterclaims about a woman's writing is a specific understanding of what, exactly, the "woman question" was: Shelgunov and other critics and readers could only perceive a woman writer as addressing the woman question if she wrote in a certain way, about certain things. Shelgunov wanted to discover in women's writing the same kind of "positive heroine" that Chernyshevsky had created in Vera Pavlovna, the liberated heroine of *What Is to Be Done?*. He refused to read Khvoshchinskaia's nuanced psychological tales as narratives critical of the constraints on women's lives.[15] What becomes impeccably clear to the modern reader, however, is the extent to which women of the 1860s and 1870s did in fact take the constraints and conditions of women's lives as their central topic, advocating both implicitly and explicitly fundamental changes in women's education, women's choices, women's work, and in the impulses of love that shaped women's inner lives. That they did not produce "positive" heroines as conceived by Shelgunov speaks not of their failure to address the woman question, but of their disinclination to imagine utopian solutions to what were, for them, intimate and intractable problems. The variety of their narratives as well as the diversity of their talents and strengths is apparent in their own efforts to name the "woman question."

An 1864 essay by Dmitrii Pisarev provides a cogent instance of the ways in which discussions of women's writing and of the woman question became disputed terrain, with various writers claiming the "right" to define the woman question and be accepted as its legitimate exponent.[16] Pisarev's essay is a review of a novel by Avdotiia Panaeva (1819–1893), a novelist and publicist of the 1850s and 1860s who is best known for her memoirs of the period.[17] Panaeva's novel, *A Woman's Lot* [Zhenskaia dolia], is true to its title in addressing the "fate" of a young woman within the upper reaches of Russian society. The plot follows Sonia, who falls in love with a man her father induces to court her as a jest; unheeding of her mother's warnings about the perfidy of men, Sonia is "caught" by her father's friend and is subject for the rest of the novel to the various erotic machinations of her husband and father's circle of debauched aristocrats.

In its concern with the fate of an innocent in the erotic world of high society, *A Woman's Lot* shares much with society tales of the 1830s and 1840s. Many of those earlier tales became, in women's hands, protests against gentry women's lot; their protest, however, remained largely covert and implicit. Panaeva, on the other hand, is quite explicit in the way she approaches the "woman question" in her novel. *A Woman's Lot* is an adamant and indignant protest against women's victimization in upper-class marriage, but Panaeva's narrator repeatedly invokes the dangers of women's emancipation when emancipation is primarily erotic. Her narrator proclaims early in the novel, "And for now don't expect anything of women's emancipation! . . . Don't you see that a woman who's carried away with emancipation and gives herself to a man without all civil rights [*grazhdanskie usloviia*][18] will also perish in humiliating slavery—and in addition will be covered with shame!'"[19] *A Woman's Lot* poses the problem of women's dependence on men, but views emancipation as inevitably working against the woman, since it is identified (by the novel's male "liberals," interested primarily in romantic adventure) largely with George Sand and the "freedom of the heart" imagined by her novels.[20] Like another of Panaeva's novels, *An Affair in the Petersburg Demi-monde* [*Roman v Peterburgskom demi-monde*], *A Woman's Lot* describes a world of romance that seems inescapable and doomed; her narratives rail melodramatically at women's "fate" but cannot imagine a world in which there might be resolutions other than death or entrapment.[21]

Pisarev's attack on Panaeva is twofold: In a brief introduction, Pisarev charges Panaeva with "distorting with phrase-mongering the bright and broad ideas" advanced in *The Contemporary (Sovremennik)*—the leading journal of Russian radicalism in the early 1860s; the thrust of Pisarev's venom in this section of his essay is that "second rate" authors—of whom he finds Panaeva exemplary—debase otherwise lofty ideas by their efforts to articulate them "in their own words."[22] Most of Pisarev's essay is a detailed examination of *A Woman's Lot*, but in this introduction, Pisarev's attack is broader and suspiciously gendered: The metaphors he uses to describe the "debasement" of lofty ideas are all associated either with the domestic realm or with (purported) feminine aesthetics: "[second-rate authors'] novels are usually sewn with living threads according to the latest fashionable patterns"; people and events are reflected in a "cheap mirror"; Dobroliubov's ideas are distorted with "innocent gossip."[23] Regardless of the justice of Pisarev's subsequent analysis of the novel (and a contemporary reader can find much to agree with in his reading of a weak narrative), the hostility of Pisarev's metaphors reveal an inclination to delegitimate all women's writing about the "great ideas" of women's emancipation as propounded in *The Contemporary*. Pisarev assumes that the power to control those ideas belonged to figures like Dobroliubov and himself, not to the phrase-mongering gossipers who wrote "heart-rending novels" ("razdiratel'nye romany").

The remainder of Pisarev's essay, which explicates Panaeva's novel, raises issues of more substance for writing about "the woman question," issues that would in fact be taken up by women writers. Most pertinent in this regard is Pisarev's analysis of the nature of jealousy, something that Panaeva attributes to women alone. Pisarev wants to take Panaeva's insights further than she herself does by questioning the origins of jealousy. For Pisarev, they lie in the absence of "inner content" in the lives of those whose entire being is invested in love; jealousy erupts as a reaction to powerlessness, when one's possibilities for happiness lie entirely in another's hands. In Pisarev's view, this represents a "tormenting and shameful dependency" that can be overcome only by positioning the center of one's life somewhere else, not in love, but in work. Pisarev doesn't suggest a wholesale rejection of love, but he insists that women's traditional immersion in love as the fabric of their lives is in fact the central wellspring of other kinds of dependence.[24] Panaeva's narrator's attacks on women's emancipation imply the danger of romance for women; Pisarev wants to define emancipation itself as liberation from romanticized love and the acceptance of the necessity of work.

What Pisarev's essay works to do is deconstruct the genre of romance and delegitimate it as a vehicle for writing about "a woman's lot." Panaeva's novel is in fact a good example of the plot and assumptions that women writers of the 1860s worked against. Public discussion of the woman question focused on the importance of serious education and work for women, as ways of liberating them from the oppressiveness of the patriarchal family; culturally, the 1860s were marked by an effort to deromanticize love, even to discredit feeling per se.[25] Women's writing on the woman question is obviously framed by these assumptions. Women writers, however, tend to preserve the centrality of the love plot even while moving towards other resolutions and meanings; such conservatism on their part may express the extent to which they saw love and intimacy as central to the processes of women's transformation. In varied ways, women writers will attack romance and insist on the social conditioning and material dependence that condition love; implicit even in the narratives most critical of love, however, is a kind of grudging acknowledgment of its power.

My intention is to focus on a series of writings by women that re-imagine women's lives; these writings challenge traditional assumptions about romance, marriage, and the shape of women's stories, although they do so in ways that differ significantly from each other. I begin with a story by Nadezhda Khvoshchinskaia, "The Boarding School Girl" ["Pansionerka"] (1861), that ends the traditional narrative of a young girl's awakening to love with a very different form of closure. I follow with a brief discussion of elaborations of love, work, and economics in the 1860s and then look closely at *A Living Soul* [*Zhivaia dusha*] (1868), a novel by Marko Vovchok (1833–1907) that narrates the heroine's choice of autonomy but is more reluctant than "The Boarding School Girl" to give up romance. I close with another story by Khvoshchinskaia, "The Meeting" ["Svidanie"] (1879), which focuses on love and class in the period of emancipation. This final story suggests a wholly new configuration of women's lives and loves, in which resolutions might be structured around affections between women rather than between a man and a woman. The transition from *A Woman's Lot* to novels that imagine "ways out" for women is not merely a matter of chronology and economic necessity; Panaeva's novel was, in fact, written after "The Boarding School Girl." More than chronology, the transition marks an aesthetic and ideational shift. These narratives begin to help us understand what love, work, and the "woman question" meant to women of the mid nineteenth century.

Richard Stites, in his history of the women's movement in Russia, points to Nadezhda Khvoshchinskaia's "The Boarding School Girl" as articulating, "for the first time in Russian literature, the philosophy of the New Woman: 'I swear that I will give no one authority over me and that I will not serve the barbaric old law in word or in deed. . . . On the contrary, I say to all: do as I am doing. Liberate yourselves, all of you who have two hands and a strong will! Live alone. Work, knowledge, and freedom—this is what life is all about.' ''[26] ''The Boarding School Girl'' is an account of Lelen'ka, a young girl in the provinces who is awakened to the constraints of her life and the possibilities of a world beyond by an idealistic gentleman who spends the summer in a house adjoining her family's.[27] In the lush surroundings of their gardens, the gentleman—Veretitsyn—expostulates to Lelen'ka on the emptiness of her boarding school education, and suggests that she should reject her family and their values.[28] While Veretitsyn is waxing eloquent (with no suggestion of how to break free) Lelen'ka is set to work sewing what is, unknown to her, her dowry: As it turns out, Veretitsyn is a man of words alone, like Turgenev's Rudin, unable to be a true mentor to Lelen'ka. Caught in the narrowing space between empty idealism and arranged marriage, Lelen'ka does something that no Turgenev heroine ever did: She escapes to St. Petersburg to live, as she says in the passage quoted above, ''alone,'' supporting herself through translations and the copying of paintings at the Hermitage.

Khvoshchinskaia's story works through love and awakening to autonomy and work: Lelen'ka later concedes that she had loved Veretitsyn; but it was her emotion rather than the man himself that becomes the vehicle of her awakening and freedom. In the story's ending, Lelen'ka and Veretitsyn meet again, by chance, in St. Petersburg eight years later. Their meeting serves both to illustrate the spirit and richness of this ''new woman's'' life and becomes the occasion for a dialogue between the two that makes explicit many of the story's oppositions. Their dialogue is a debate on love and work, entities that for Lelen'ka (and presumably for Khvoshchinskaia) must remain opposed: Love could only appear to Lelen'ka as a ''yoke'' that enforces the effacement of self: ''I understood . . . that [love] forces one to look through the other's eyes, and disappear before another's will.''[29] What Lelen'ka rejects is that erasure of will and the rhetoric of self-sacrifice that upholds it. Veretitsyn holds up Sof'ia, the woman he had loved long ago, as an ideal of love and womanhood: She married without love but as a gesture of obedience to her parents; her life is structured as a sacrifice for her children. For Veretitsyn, the idealist Sof'ia—like the nurses of the Crimean War—represents an image of perfection because she embodies sacrificial love; for Lelen'ka, such self-sacrifice only perpetuates the misery it sets out to ameliorate.[30]

Khvoshchinskaia's story does offer instances of affection that are not self-effacing: Lelen'ka has been helped in getting to St. Petersburg by a widowed aunt, and the two share an apartment where they welcome a circle of friends. Clearly, Lelen'ka is less ''alone'' than the rhetoric of her words suggests, but in the lexicon of the day, such attachments did not constitute ''love.'' Love, self-sacrifice, and the idealistic poetizing that enforces them are for a woman like Lelen'ka a ''yoke'' that only work can throw off. Work, moreover, is conceived of as achieving something beyond Lelen'ka's autonomy; when Veretitsyn asks, ''but is this labor for everyone?''[31] he voices the assumption of progressives that one's work should be useful to the Russian people. Lelen'ka's response is that even her humble work is "one part of those labors; I'm still making my contribution, I'm serving thought . . . " Lelen'ka has gained autonomy, but it is important nonetheless for her to conceive of her private labors as connected to a larger "global" cause, however hazily defined, a cause in which one works, not for oneself, but "for everyone."

In its provincial setting and in the significant encounter of an ingenue and an older idealist, Khvoshchinskaia clearly writes *contra* Ivan Turgenev, whose heroines embody the strength of pure love and sacrificial impulse. In the emphasis she places on economic independence, and in her use of work as an element of plot resolution, Khvoshchinskaia joins company with numerous other voices articulating the woman question. Aleksandra Kollontai (1872–1952), the feminist author and figure in the first Soviet government, held that the woman question was in its essence "the question of a crust of bread."[32] That is, the issue of women's economic autonomy—their ability and willingness to work—was at the center of the woman question. Efforts to improve women's education and their position in the family—the other two issues that someone like Mikhailov points to as comprising the woman question—finally collapse if educated women have nowhere to work, hence, no way to gain some economic autonomy.

The triumph of independence and labor that Khvoschinskaia imagines at the end of "The Boarding School Girl" resolves the dilemma set by her contemporary, Sof'ia Soboleva (1840–1884),[33] in the story "A Hopeless Situation" ["Bezvykhodnoe polozhenie"].[34] Soboleva, not unlike Khvoshchinskaia, sets out to deromanticize love, by illustrating the extent to which romance depends on economics.[35] Soboleva's lovers, a provincial teacher (Ilarii) and a musician who gives lessons (Alexandra Pavlovna), are caught in a "hopeless situation" because Ilarii's sisters depend on him economically and refuse to work. Work of any sort is beneath their dignity (and something for which they have no training); they expect him to finance their interest in balls and modish dresses from his limited salary. When Alexandra Pavlovna assures Ilarii's sisters that they, too, could be "obligated to no one," they interpret her words as evidence of her marital maneuvering.[36] Since Ilarii can barely support his mother and sisters, he and Alexandra cannot marry; if the sisters could work (or find husbands to support them), the pair would be free to make their own happiness.

Love and happiness in "A Hopeless Situation" are inextricably dependent on money. Most of the story is concerned with the unfortunate marriages that the structure of women's dependence leads to. Soboleva effects a sudden (and fairly contrived) happy ending when Ilarii and Alexandra defy societal opinion at the end of the story and go off to St. Petersburg, despite the fact that Ilarii is married (to a woman who had feigned affection and then deceived him). The somewhat melodramatic *peripeteaia* of Soboleva's story do not work to condemn marriage per se, but to illustrate that bad, loveless marriages emerge in part from the fact that women do not work but remain wholly dependent on men's support.[37]

Soboleva views women's degrading position in society as, at least partly, of their own making. When Ilarii's provincial sisters refuse to work, they illustrate a point that was central to the argument of Mariia Vernadskaia (1831–1860), an economist who published a series of essays on economic aspects of women's lives in the early 1860s.[38] In "Women's Work" ["Zhenskii trud"], an essay that received considerable attention, both favorable and condemnatory,[39] Vernadskaia emphasized the importance of changing women's attitudes toward work. For Vernadskaia, the crucial problem was not the unavailability of positions (she considers all paths open to women except the military and the bureaucracy). The problem lay rather in an attitude of disdain, even shame, toward labor. Women surrender their autonomy, Vernadskaia suggests, in exchange for lives of leisure supported by men; men then demand women's domestic labor, a demand that Vernadskaia saw as being largely justified, given what seemed to her women's voluntary participation in the "division of labor."[40] What is crucial is that women begin to take pride in work rather than disdain it; "There is no degrading work!" proclaims Vernadskaia. "A person can, perhaps, degrade some undertaking, but no honest labor can degrade a person."[41] Vernadskaia's arguments, in effect, are grounded in an attack on class privilege; she writes about and for gentry women, women whose lives of leisure were grounded in the economics of serfdom. The fields of activity she suggests that are open to women, and worthy of respect, include kinds of labor associated with the peasantry; one could work as a nanny or as a midwife, she insists. Vernadskaia, like other of her contemporaries, assumed that women of the peasantry had relatively greater freedom within the family, a freedom that derived in part from the fact that they worked.[42] As with other discussions of women's work and economic position in the 1860s, the shadow of economic dislocation and profound changes in Russia's class structure is ever present. The economic background of the "woman question" was a world in which the lives of leisure led by women would be increasingly impoverished, as incomes generated by serf labor disappeared. As contemporary observers were well aware, the economic consequences of 1861—the year in which the serfs were liberated—were profoundly felt by women.[43] The promises of romance, in which the sole occupation of a woman's life was to wait for a husband who would support her economically, were becoming increasingly illusory, even as a generation of women questioned romance for more abstract reasons.

Marko Vovchok, who wrote in both Ukrainian and Russian, participated in elaborations of the "woman question" in a particular way, since her work deals both with women of the peasantry and with gentry women.[44] While the structure of romance is central to Vovchok's writing from the outset, she is never unaware of the ways in which class structure and economics impinge on the possibilities of love. In her early peasant stories, there are numerous examples of love blighted by serfdom. In "Sasha" (1859), a nobleman falls in love with a house serf, but lacks the courage of his emotion when he must defy his parents to marry her; in "After Finishing School" (1860), the narrator Ustenka is separated from her husband by a mistress who punishes his courage by sending him off to serve in the army. The question of women in serfdom, that is, runs throughout Vovchok's shorter narratives of Ukrainian and Russian peasant life. Her novel *A Living Soul*, on the other hand, takes as its heroine a young woman of the gentry, Masha, and makes a more explicit attempt to describe the experience and choices of a "new woman."[45] In elaborating Masha's choice to refuse the offers of wealthy suitors and seek a life of work and autonomy, Vovchok plays out some of the same concerns as do Khvoshchinskaia or Soboleva, although she reveals a surprising unwillingness to give up the resolutions of romance, attempting rather to envision a life of labor and love intertwined.

Vovchok's novel includes an explicit attempt to demystify the extent to which women's expectations for romance and marriage are a "fairy tale" that results in boredom and empty lives. At the beginning of the novel, her heroine overhears a nanny telling bedtime stories to Katya, Masha's young cousin. The bedtime stories exemplify the plots young women are led to believe can be theirs: The prince will arrive on a white horse, clothe them in elegant garments, and carry them off to marriage and affluent ease. Vovchok's heroine is presented with one suitor who embodies the role of the prince and has the requisite "palace," an elegant country estate that he tries in vain to make more modest in order to please the unconventional Masha.

Masha spurns both the affluent "prince" and the liberal intellectual of more humble means, choosing, instead, to run away from her suitors and her aunt's home to find work as a seamstress and tutor in the poorer section of her provincial town. The plot turns here on a choice of work, autonomy, and modest dwellings. Vovchok represents her heroine's life alone as difficult but not penurious. Two things are striking in Vovchok's resolution of Masha's story: Masha's departure from her aunt's home means she must sever her relationship with Katya, and Masha's decision to live out her aspirations for autonomy are inspired in large part by a shadowy radical, Zagainy, who shows up in the provincial town and then abruptly leaves. Implicit in Vovchok's plot is a trade-off between relationships with women and the inspiration of a beloved heroic man: While most of the women in *A Living Soul* are thoroughly compromised by the comforts of their dependent, affluent lives, Katya is a spirited, rebellious child for whom Masha serves as friend, confidante, mother, and image of autonomy. By the novel's end, Katya is wasting away in Masha's absence; Masha, on the other hand, is reunited with Zagainy. They are described as sharing a small house, in which Masha sits awaiting her husband's return.[46]

Vovchok's novel, unlike "The Boarding School Girl," wants to imagine the possibility of a woman having autonomy, work, *and* love. The closing chapter, in which Zagainy suddenly returns to the plot and we learn that he and Masha are married, is brief and unelaborated. Vovchok's description nonetheless reinscribes the traditional gendered oppositions of the fairy tales she had earlier critiqued: Masha is at home, associated with domesticity and stasis, while Zagainy emerges from the distance, associated with the larger world and various kinds of danger. Vovchok's novel may well stand as an articulation of what even "new" women did not want to give up—the intimacy and love implicit in conventional romance. Her ending, however, bespeaks just how difficult it was to imagine love beyond traditional roles. And the ''abandonment'' of Katya to the world Masha spurned reminds us of another narrative turn Vovchok could not take: There is no imagination in this novel of a world in which the relationships of women might be able to constitute the strength and promise implicit in narrative closure.

For evidence of how relationships between women might emerge more positively, we must turn to another story by Nadezhda Khvoshchinskaia, written nine years after *A Living Soul*. ''The Meeting'' is an excellent example of the ways in which gender, sexuality, and class could emerge as profoundly intertwined from a woman's pen.[47] The story was published in 1879, a moment already well beyond the first flush of discussions of the woman question in Russia. It is nonetheless a story that makes a significant contribution to women's imaginings of what it meant to ''question'' woman—or raise women as questions—precisely because it insists on the continuity and enduring relevance of what had been a movement of the 1860s. Khvoshchinskaia's story addresses the ways in which women's issues are inextricably qualified by the class structure of Russian society. But it moves beyond the other stories we have examined as narrative examples of the woman question, by posing a visionary form of closure that is no longer bound to heterosexual romance. This chapter closes with ''The Meeting,'' both because it comes last in chronological terms and because it seems to adumbrate a wholly new way to imagine the resolutions and significances of women's lives.

''The Meeting'' opens on the balcony of Alexandra Sergeevna's country home where she is receiving Altasov, a writer and old flame of her youth. Their conversation dwells largely on the disappointments of their lives; Alexandra did not marry, her brother squandered their fortune on the enthusiasms of youth (providing schools and hospitals for the peasantry in the years immediately preceding and following the emancipation of 1861), and she has been forced to open an institute for young girls in a provincial town. Altasov, on the other hand, is largely a failure and has designs on Alexandra's remaining money as a way to shore up his own finances. This dialogue of *ennuie* and failure is interrupted by the entrance of Anna Vasil'evna, Alexandra's brother's widow: Both Alexandra and Altasov are embarrassed by Anna's energy, good cheer, and enthusiastic tales of her students (she teaches at Alexandra's school and manages Alexandra's household).[48] The story pivots on the appearance of Anna: Altasov repeats gossip from St. Petersburg about a ''kept woman'' who is, it turns out, Anna's daughter; the remainder of the story is told from Anna's point of view, focusing on Anna's memories of love and her resolve somehow to rescue her daughter.

''The Meeting'' is at one level a story of the daughter of a marriage of the 1860s: A young member of the gentry returns from the Crimean War filled with lofty ideas, sets up a school for the peasants on his estate, falls in love with one of his serf women, lives with her, has a daughter by her, and ultimately marries

her.[49] The legacy of that marriage is the "fallen" daughter of Altasov's gossipy
tale: Educated in an institute but impatient with provincial life, Anna's daughter
Sasha leaves for St. Petersburg, where the life of a glamorous prostitute is all
that awaits her. Read allegorically, the story is a narrative of the collapse of
hopes following the period of emancipation, a period that stands in Anna's
memory as an idyllic moment of love and the collapse of class boundaries. The
story ends with Anna's departure for St. Petersburg to seek out her daughter,
an ending that seems to articulate the longing of Khvoshchinskaia's own generation to retrieve and resurrect its ideals, embodied in a child of love who has
been lost and squandered.

But the allegorical possibilities of Khvoshchinskaia's story should not blind
us to its strength as a narrative of women's affection and bonds. There are three
meetings in this story: one between a jaded *literateur* and a woman he can still
take advantage of; one between a noble idealist and a serf woman; and finally,
one only implied, between mother and daughter. This story, like several others
by the Khvoshchinskaia sisters, begins to illustrate what Virginia Woolf suggested would change the history of literature: the bonds of friendship and affection
between women that come to displace marriage and heterosexual romance as
forms of literary closure.[50] Vovchok, even in her most obviously "woman-
centered" works, seems committed still to romance in ways that blind her to
the failure of women's support for each other; Nadezhda Khvoshchinskaia and
her sister Sof'ia (1828–1865) repeatedly explored in their fiction the possibilities
inherent in women's support and love for each other:[51] Lelen'ka in "The Boarding
School Girl" is helped to autonomy by the widowed aunt with whom she shares
an apartment; two elderly aunts in Nadezhda Khvoshchinskaia's "First Battle"
["Pervaia bor'ba"][52] serve as the existential and moral centers of the novel; the
heroine of Sof'ia Khvoshchinskaia's "City Folks and Town Folks" ["Gorodskie
i derevenskie"][53] frustrates the machinations of society grande dames, not to get
married, but in order to return to peaceful life with her mother.

This last narrative involves a plot that echoes those of the society tales,
including Karolina Pavlova's *A Double Life*. Unlike earlier versions, however,
the heroine of "City Folks and Town Folks" is not trapped in a loveless marriage,
nor is she alienated from a cruel and conniving mother. What it might mean to
be a "new woman" is given an unexpected twist in this story that combines
bucolic frivolity and unabashed affection for provincial life.[54] Like her sister
Nadezhda, Sof'ia Khvoshchinskaia longs to imagine a world sheltered from
moneyed aristocracy, a world marked by the love of women. In "The Meeting,"
the idyllic mother/daughter bond is broken by money and debauched eroticism;
in "City Folks and Country Folks," the rapacious urbanites and feather-headed
intellectuals do not succeed in separating the two. These are perhaps utopian
narratives, but the nature of their guiding vision is significant, speaking as they
do for transfigured feeling in any vision of the "new woman" and the new world
she might inhabit.

In her review of women's writing in Russia, Mariia Tsebrikova called on women to address the fundamental issues confronting Russian society in the post-Emancipation era; she asked that women's writing might frame women's concerns for autonomy and education without ignoring the larger context of social inequity. She is critical of women writers of the 1830s and 1840s for the narrowness and solipsism of their vision: "Women's field of observation of life was very narrow, and in women's stories of that period we see no allusion to the social relationships of that period, even to the extent that one could address them at that time . . . "[55] Clearly, what Tsebrikova has in mind here is serfdom; the heroines of her account are the Khvoshchinskaia sisters and Marko Vovchok, writers in whom she found attention to women's position as it is structured by class. Women, insisted Tsebrikova, will find "no exit from their narrow corner" except in the context of larger transformations of the economic and social injustice of Russian society.[56] The "woman question," in other words, is really a question of what divides women as much as of what might unite them; her call was for women writers who might be able to address the disabilities of women's lot without retreating to an intimate world that ignored the extent to which even their unhappiness was grounded in privilege.

Histories of the women's movement in nineteenth-century Russia focus primarily on three issues: on women's emancipation from familial despotism, on women's aspirations to education, and on their desire for work and economic autonomy. Clearly, all three issues are intertwined, and all three surface continually in women's writings of the period. It may be, however, that shifting our vision will enable us to see the literary and existential issues of the woman question in new ways. Inherited plots of love acted as cultural texts, ascribing to women particular capacities for feeling; women's writing struggles with that ascription and those plots, cognizant of the ways in which issues of class structure the possibilities of love. Women's writing struggles with the burdens that history, gender, and economics have laid on affection, as yet only imperfectly able to imagine ways in which love might be reborn.

NOTES

1. Adrienne Rich, "Notes toward a Politics of Location," in *Blood, Bread and Poetry: Selected Prose, 1979–1985* (New York: Norton, 1986), 216.

2. Nadezhda Suslova, "The Dreamer" ["Fantazerka"], *Sovremennik* 9 (September 1864): 218.

3. Mariia Konstantinovna Tsebrikova was a writer, critic, and publicist active in women's causes, best known for her 1889 letter to Tsar Alexander III, in which she implored him to end repression and address Russia's deep social and economic ills. As a result of this letter, which was printed abroad and circulated in Russia illegally, Tsebrikova was sent into internal exile.

4. Marie Zebrikoff [Mariia Tsebrikova], "Russia," in *The Woman Question in Europe*, ed. Theodore Stanton (New York: G. P. Putnam's Sons, 1884), 391.

5. For general discussions of the woman question and the women's movement in Russia, see Richard Stites, *The Women's Liberation Movement in Russia: Feminism,*

Nihilism and Bolshevism, 1860–1930 (Princeton: Princeton University Press, 1978); Barbara Alpern Engel, *Mothers and Daughters: Women of the Intelligentsia in Nineteenth-Century Russia* (Cambridge: Cambridge University Press, 1983); and G. A. Tishkin, *Zhenskii vopros v Rossii: 50–60-e gody XIX v.* (Leningrad, 1984).

6. Mikhail Mikhailov, *Zhenshchiny: Ikh vospitanie i znachenie v sem'e i obshchestve* (St. Petersburg, 1903); first published in 1860 as articles in *Sovremennik*. On these essays and their significance for public life in Russia, see Richard Stites, "M. L. Mikhailov and the Emergence of the Woman Question in Russia," *Canadian Slavic Studies* 3.2 (1969): 178–99.

7. On Pisarev's role in the dissemination of emancipatory ideas to young women, see Barbara Heldt Monter, "*Rassvet* and the Woman Question," *Slavic Review* 36.1 (1977): 76–85.

8. On women's philanthropic activities, see Stites, *The Women's Liberation Movement*, 191–232; on women's role in revolutionary terrorism, see Barbara Alpern Engel and Clifford N. Rosenthal, eds., *Five Sisters: Women Against the Tsar* (Boston: Allen & Unwin, 1987); and Margaret Maxwell, *Narodniki Women: Russian Women Who Sacrificed Themselves for the Dream of Freedom* (Elmsford, NY: Pergamon Press, 1990).

9. Nikolai Shelgunov, "Zhenskoe bezdushie," *Delo* 9 (1870): 11.

10. Sandra Gilbert and Susan Gubar, *The Madwoman in the Attic* is a ground-breaking example of feminist efforts to reconstruct literary history by reading women authors' texts in such a way as to "name" their subversive potentials. Implicit in Gilbert and Gubar's study is the notion that women could not be wholly forthright about their subversions because of assumptions about women's use of language and women's proper place in society. *The Madwoman in the Attic: The Woman Writer and the Nineteenth-Century Literary Imagination* (New Haven: Yale University Press, 1979).

11. For a good overview of feminist discussions of the importance of "naming" to women's cultural activity, see Deborah Cameron, ed., *The Feminist Critique of Language* (London: Routledge, 1990), in particular, part 2, "Naming and Representation."

12. Nadezhda Dmitrievna Khvoshchinskaia (who published under the pseudonym V. V. Krestovskii) began her writing career in 1847 as a poet but devoted herself thereafter almost exclusively to prose. While Nadezhda Dmitrievna had some supporters in literary circles, her life was marked by limited means, provincial isolation, and the burdens of supporting her family.

13. Shelgunov, "Zhenskoe bezdushie," 11.

14. Mariia Tsebrikova, "Ocherk zhizni N. D. Khvoshchinskoi-Zaionchkovkoi," *Mir Bozhii* 12 (1897): 21.

15. A similar impatience with a woman writer whose heroine is not "positive" enough is apparent in Tkachev's review of Marko Vovchok's *A Living Soul*: P. Tkachev, "Podrostaiushchiia sily," *Delo* 9–10 (1868). On the "positive hero" and his elaboration in literary criticism of the 1860s, see Rufus Matthewson, *The Positive Hero in Russian Literature* (Stanford, CA: Stanford University Press, 1975). Richard Stites briefly discusses the "positive heroine," *The Women's Liberation Movement*, 94.

16. Dmitrii Pisarev, "Kukol'naia tragediia s buketom grazhdanskoi skorbi," in *Sochineniia D. I. Pisareva. Polnoe sobranie v shesti tomakh*, vol. 4 (St. Petersburg, 1901), 148–96. (Originally published in *Russkoe Slovo*, 1864).

17. On Panaeva, see Marina Ledkovsky [Astman], "Avdotya Panaeva: Her Salon and Her Life," *Russian Literature Triquarterly* 9 (1974): 423–32.

18. The "civil rights" referred to here are the legal rights conferred by marriage.

19. Avdoti'ia Panaeva, *Zhenskaia dol'ia, Sovremennik* 3 (1862): 50.

20. On the influence of George Sand in Russia, see Martin Malia, *Alexander Herzen and the Birth of Russian Socialism, 1812–1855* (Cambridge, MA: Harvard University Press, 1961) and Leslie Hermann, "*Jacques* in Russia: A Program of Domestic Reform for Husbands," *Studies in the Literary Imagination* 12.2 (1979): 61–81.

21. *An Affair in the Petersburg Demi-monde, Sovremennik* 3–4 (1860); the novella ends with the attempt of ill-fated adulterous lovers to escape Russia and an evil husband; they are caught at the last posting-house before the border and brought back to Petersburg, husband, marriage, and unrequited love. Nadezhda Suslova's "The Dreamer," from which this chapter's epigraph is taken, is another narrative of the period that deals with the inescapability of a woman's "fate"; the heroine can't escape the "pleasures" of an affluent world and ultimately commits suicide.

22. Pisarev, 148.

23. Ibid., 148. There is a long history to the notion that women's association with "domestic" speech disqualifies them from participation in serious moral or political discourse. See Jean Bethke Elshtain, "Feminist Discourse and Its Discontents: Language, Power, and Meaning," *Signs* 7:31 (1982): 606–607.

24. Pisarev, 179–80.

25. See, for example, Elizaveta Vodovozova's memoirs of the period: "Feeling was at a disadvantage, it was given minimal significance, and manifestations of it were even laughed at: 'Now you've gone saccharine!'—one heard that phrase not infrequently then." *Na zare zhizni*, vol. 1 (Moscow, 1964), 188.

26. Stites, *The Women's Emancipation Movement*, 48.

27. Nadezhda Khvoshchinskaia, "Pansionerka," in *Povesti i rasskazy* (Moscow, 1984), 62–158. (The story was first published in *Otechestvennye zapiski*.)

28. As Stites points out, Verititsyn's name suggests inconstancy, as it is etymologically linked to the verb "to turn around." Stites, 48.

29. Khvoshchinskaia, "Pansionerka," 156.

30. On the role of women nurses during the Crimean War, see Stites, *The Women's Emancipation Movement*, 30–33.

31. Khvoshchinskaia, "Pansionerka," 155.

32. Quoted in Tishkin, 133.

33. Sof'ia Pavlovna Soboleva (who published under the pseudonym V. Samoilovich) published short prose works throughout the 1860s; after 1867, she concentrated on works for children and journalistic writing.

34. "Bezvykhodnoe polozhenie," *Russkoe Slovo* 2–3 (1864): 117–58, 29–79.

35. Mariia Tsebrikova, in an 1870 review of Ivan Goncharov's *The Precipice* [*Obryv*], insists that "A difference of opinions and understanding, even of social position creates a deep chasm that no passion can overcome." "A Pseudo-New Heroine," ["Psevdo-novaia geroinia"] *Otechestvennye zapiski* 5 (1870): 45.

36. Samoilovich, 133.

37. Soboleva's concern for women's economic position in marriage is apparent in several other of her stories: "Both *pro* and *contra*" ["I pro i contra"] is the fictionalized memoir of an "emancipated woman" who refuses to cede control of her money to her husband, and gains considerable autonomy within marriage. "I *pro i contra*," *Otechestvennye zapiski* 6 (1863): 295–337. "The Good Old Days" ["Dobroe staroe vremia"] depicts the failure of love in a household where the father (a bureaucrat who has risen in the service) refuses to bless his daughter's marriage to a doctor (*lekar'*), whose work

is too plebian. Once more, Soboleva makes the case for the interdependence of class concerns and romantic possibilities. "Dobroe staroe vremia," *Russkoe slovo* 7.4–5 (1865): 1–40, 38–72.

38. M. Vernadskaia, *Sobranie sochinenii* (St. Petersburg, 1862). Mariia Nikolaevana Vernadskaia was Russia's first woman economist; together with her husband, I. V. Vernadskii, she published *The Economic Indicator*.

39. On the journalistic response elicited by Vernadskaia's work, see Tishkin, 111–14.

40. Vernadskaia, 99.

41. Vernadskaia, 110.

42. N. I. Kostomarov, in his history of domestic life in the sixteenth and seventeenth centuries (*Ocherki domashnei zhizni i nravov velikorusskogo naroda v XVI i XVII stoletiiakh* (St. Petersburg, 1860), made a similar argument. Tishkin, 117.

43. Stites, *The Women's Liberation Movement*, 56–60. Elizaveta Vodovozova notes the impact of economic factors on women's attitudes toward work; Vodovozova, 195–96.

44. Marko Vovchok (pseudonym of Mariia Viliinskaia/Markovich) was a writer and translator whose stories of peasant life, published in the late 1850s, were enthusiastically greeted by contemporary critics.

45. Marko Vovchok, *Zhivaia dusha*, in *Tvori v tr'okh tomakh*, vol. 3 (Kiev, 1975). The novel was originally published in *Otechestvennye zapiski*.

46. Vovchok, 354–55.

47. Nadezhda Khvoshchinskaia, "Svidanie," in *Svidanie: Proza russkikh pisatel'nits 60–80-kh godov XIX veka*, ed. V. Uchenova (Moscow, 1987), 363–416. The story was originally published in *Otechestvennye zapiski*.

48. One measure of the contrast between the two women is their differing investments in this provincial school: Alexandra's involvement is nominal and cursory; Anna's, real and intense. Despite criticisms of institute education as superficial, it is represented in this story as the only possibility for provincial girls to get some education.

49. Eizaveta Vodovozova recounts an instance of the "real life" occurrence of such a marriage; in her story, however, the young man was unable to sustain his idealism and the marriage failed. Vodovozova, 226–29.

50. Virginia Woolf's argument is that the narrative exploration of women's friendships will mark a fundamental change in the history of writing. Virginia Woolf, *A Room of One's Own* (New York: Harcourt, Brace and World, 1957), 86–90.

51. It is worth noting that the love for her sister Sof'ia seems to have been the most significant relationship of Nadezhda's life; herself a gifted writer (she published under the pseudonym Vesen'ev), Sof'ia died at the age of 37 in 1865. Nadezhda's subsequent marriage was, by all accounts, a response to loneliness rather than a matter of intense affection.

52. Nadezhda Khvoshchinskaia, "Pervaia bor'ba," *Povesti i rasskazy*, 159–335.

53. Sof'ia Khvoschinskaia, "Gorodskie i derevenskie," *Svidanie*, 95–234.

54. Nikolai Shelgunov, in "Zhenskoe bezdushie," makes Nadezhda Khvoshchinskaia's "provincialism" the object of violent attack: for Shelgunov, it was unthinkable that a serious writer would live in the provinces.

55. Mariia Tsebrikova, "Russkie zhenshchiny pisatel'nitsy," *Nedelia* (1876), 13–14, 21–22, 436.

56. Tsebrikova, "Russkiia zhenshchiny pisatel'nitsy," 435.

5

Women's Prose Fiction in the Age of Realism

Mary F. Zirin

Encouraged by the example of the first active generation of prose writers of their sex in the late 1830s (Nadezhda Durova, Elena Gan, Mariia Zhukhova), scores of women began writing and continued refining their craft throughout the decades when Realist fiction was the major genre of Russian literature.[1] By the late 1840s, women writers were shaking off the spell of Romanticism and beginning to depict the constraints of women's situation and the domestic milieu in sober and muted terms. From the late 1850s, they showed their heroines taking part in the work of social reconstruction then under way. Russian intellectuals greeted women's literary efforts with reactions ranging from generous enthusiasm to snarling dismissal—and, all too frequently, with an admixture of condescension toward the efforts of the frail sex.

The lives of these writers reflect the handicaps that women had to overcome in order to establish independent careers. Almost all of them came from the miniscule (3 percent) gentry class.[2] Under Russian autocracy, nobody enjoyed full autonomy, but women suffered under a double burden: To the restrictions on civil freedom imposed to a greater or lesser degree on everyone was added a concomitant tutelage by men. Although women enjoyed a legal right to inherit and dispose of a small percentage of the family property (where there was any), in practice their portion was often treated as dowry.[3] Custom decreed that their overriding mission, married or spinster, was to remain the angel in somebody's house. Well into the latter half of the century, women's autobiographies and fiction depict not only girls from the traditionally patriarchal merchantry and peasantry, but also from supposedly Westernized gentry families being pressured by parents into loveless marriages.[4]

Most writers came from the poorer gentry and could not rely on having a secure lifelong home anywhere. All too often, the only alternative they saw to marriage was an equally problematic future caring for other people's children. Until the 1860s, women with the equivalent of secondary education could do little beyond serving as governesses or as teachers in state or private girls' schools. For those with talent and drive, writing increasingly offered an alternate way for a respectable woman to supplement the family income or gain some degree of personal independence. Not many, however, managed to eke out even a meager living entirely by their pen, and only a few late in the period began to earn substantial incomes with prolific writings and professional management—that is, not only publishing their works in journals, but keeping them in print as books for as many editions as they could sell.

Lack of mobility was another handicap for women writers: They could not pursue literary careers as men did by choosing to live in St. Petersburg, the center of cultural as well as of political power. Conservative Moscow seems to have offered the more comfortable milieu for women writers from the 1850s through the 1880s. The Moscow journal *Russian Herald* (*Russkii vestnik*) opened its pages to them in numbers in the late 1850s when the writer-critic who used the pseudonym Evgeniia Tur (Elizaveta Sailhas de Tournemire, 1815–1892, the sister of dramatist Aleksandr Sukhovo-Kobylin) served briefly as literary editor; from 1866, Mikhail Stasiulevich's moderate *Herald of Europe* (*Vestnik Evropy*) welcomed them as contributors.[5]

Avdotiia Panaeva (1819–1893) was the rare woman writer of those years who lived in Petersburg, and her career was furthered by personal connections: She was married to one editor of the famous radical journal *Contemporary (Sovremennik*) and lived for about fifteen years (1848–1863) with the other, the poet Nikolai Nekrasov. To help fill the journal's pages, she wrote bleak stories of women's mistreatment by men under the male pseudonym N. Stanitskii. An active group of women writers formed in Petersburg in the last quarter of the century to form a nucleus for the vibrant female culture of the Silver Age.[6] Throughout the age of Russian Realism, however, most women writers remained rooted in the provinces, cut off from day-to-day contact with editors and from the stimulation of interaction with other writers. They sent their manuscripts to the two capitals by mail.

Women writers faced conflicting demands peculiar to Russian society. Excluded from the public sphere, many women found depicting their immediate milieu within recognized ''feminine'' limits of subject and outlook natural and congenial. But that intimate focus was increasingly regarded by prescriptive critics as a retrograde clinging to Romantic egocentrism when the times called for scientifically based, objective—''masculine,'' ''realistic''—depictions of a broad cross-section of life. The censorship was equally sensitive to the ways in which women's expositions of private experience served as a semiotic code for the broader society and was quick to condemn less-than-rosy depictions of family life: In the tsarist government's eyes, women's first duty, even as fiction writers, was to uphold the sanctity of marriage and motherhood.[7]

Many women writers adopted pseudonyms—T.Ch., Kokhanovskaia, Shabel'skaia—to create a barrier between private identity and public discourse, a barrier that could ease the sting of captious criticism and censorship. As Nadezhda

Khvoshchinskaia (V. Krestovsky) wrote tersely to discourage a potential biographer: '' . . . pseudonyms don't have biographies at all. What is a pseudonym? Nobody. So what is there to say about it? That's logic.''[8] A passage, emphasized by its intrusive irrelevance, that the Moscow writer Sof'ia Engel'gardt (Ol'ga N.) inserted in her 1870 story ''In the Homeland'' (''Na rodine'') suggests the pressures women writers felt. A young man raised abroad who is trying to decipher life in Russia, asks his doctor why Russian women writers use pseudonyms. The doctor explains that if they do not, they are subject to attacks by critics:

We, so they say, wanted to spit on your blank powder; your works, they say, aren't even worthwhile for us clever people to glance at; so even if we do read them when we have nothing better to do, we'll make it hot for you.[9]

From the 1860s, the use of masculine, or gender-neutral, pseudonyms became common. The identity of these authors might be an open secret in literary circles, but the names gave them an official male viewpoint from which to treat the broader society without being accused of infringing on a sphere beyond their ken. The casual reader leafing through major Russian journals would be surprised to learn how much of the fiction signed by male names was actually written by women.[10]

   These sociological and psychological factors formed the subtext, and frequently the text, of women's fiction. Examples from the lives and writings of the authors discussed below—Anastasiia Marchenko (T.Ch.), Nadezhda Sokhanskaia (Kokhanovskaia), Sof'ia Engel'gardt (Ol'ga N.), Nadezhda Khvoshchinskaia (V. Krestovsky) and her sister Sof'ia Khvoshchinskaia (Iv. Vesen'ev), Aleksandra Montvid (Shabel'skaia), and Ol'ga Shapir—suggest facets of the rich contribution by women writers to the prose of Russian Realism. The most striking aspect of their art is their nuanced portrayal of their own sex. Younger women in the female fiction of Russian Realism are much more varied in character and fate than the Tat'ianas, Natashas, Ol'gas, and Elenas who are, as Barbara Heldt wrote in *Terrible Perfection*, ''used [by male authors] lavishly in a discourse of male self-definition.''[11] Far from being daunted, as Heldt suggests, by the example of those charming heroines who see the future only in terms of a riddle to be solved by a man's love, women writers resisted categorization fiercely to draw their own attractively individual female protagonists. In fiction no less than in autobiography and poetry, they created a gallery of gallant women who struggle to find spiritual and physical autonomy within the constrictive logic of patriarchal society. They wrote their own plots.

ANASTASIIA MARCHENKO (PSEUDONYMS: T.CH., A. TEMRIZOV, 1830–1880)

   The end of hyper-Romanticism in women's fiction was signaled in 1842 by Gan's death and Durova's disappearance from the literary scene. Of that generation only Mariia Zhukova, the most prolific author of the late 1830s, continued to write fiction into the mid 1850s, and her works, which featured female protagonists who were both plain and poor, deflated the Romantic pathos of the society tale [*svetskaia povest'*]. Marchenko followed Zhukova's lead: Female readers could readily identify with her young heroines of ordinary appearance and modest prospects as they moved through plots marked by the amorous intrigues that earlier authors had reserved for the leisured classes.

Marchenko grew up in a rich and outgoing Ukrainian-Polish family and began writing under the tutelage of a clever and innovative governess who was seeking ways to motivate the self-willed girl. After her father fell heavily in debt and became physically paralyzed, Marchenko worked as a music teacher in Odessa to support the family, a first-hand experience that, as her biographer Ekaterina Nekrasova pointed out, gave her a sober view of female emancipation.[12] Women's limited options in work as well as the necessity of maintaining dignity and joy of life in reduced circumstances are repeated themes of her fiction. In 1847 her stories, "The Governess" ("Guvernantka") and "Three Variations on an Old Theme" ("Tri variatsii na staroi teme"), came out under the blanket title *Travel Notes* (*Putevye zametki*) in Odessa. This new voice from the provinces created a sensation in St. Petersburg and Moscow. Surveying the year's literary output, the critic Vissarion Belinskii described the work as:

> . . . a beautifully printed little book. . . . That the author is a woman is clear from everything, especially the viewpoint on topics. There is much heartfelt warmth, much feeling and life, not always understood or understood too much in a woman's way [po zhenski], but never whitewashed or rouged over, not exaggerated or distorted, an absorbing story, fine language: that's the virtue of Mme. T.Ch.'s two stories.[13]

Belinskii's summary, like his praise, reflects the simplistic outlook on gender that permeates the radical criticism of the time.[14] The plot of Marchenko's "Three Variations . . . '' is a simple one: A widow, now free to revive past attachments, finds that the first love whose memory she has cherished is now a "married man and lives for ambition." Oblivious to the humorous title, jocular tone, and plot that suggests as much about the vagaries of fate as it does about love, Belinskii dumped a heavy weight of generalization on the slight tale by a novice author:

> Men have many interests in life, and therefore their memory retains histories that are more serious than a single kiss. Woman is another matter: she lives entirely for love, and the greater her inner emotions, the more she is obliged to conceal them. Women are particularly prone to love stories which have no serious consequences, in which nothing has to be risked and nothing sacrificed: she can betray her husband in her heart—and remain formally true to her vows; [she can] satisfy the need to love—and piously fulfill the obligations imposed by society.[15]

Marchenko's "Too Late!" ("Pozdno!," 1848) comes closest to observing the artificial conventions of the society tale. The poor but independent Aleksandrina is the inevitable odd-woman-out, losing to flightier but more prosperous competitors in the erotic *ronde*, for reasons that have as much to do with her superior intelligence and taste as with lack of money. The two men who pursue the three female protagonists are underdescribed and instantly forgettable. They confide their innermost feelings only to their dogs; Marchenko probably intended this as a humorous narrative ploy, but the unintentional effect is to rob them of much of the reader's sympathy.

The male protagonists of Marchenko's "A Near Miss" ("Vokrug da okolo," 1855) are more convincingly portrayed. She described the novella as an illustration of the "Gordian knots" of modern psychology.[16] The encounter between a man whose nature is "composite [*sostavnaia*], artificial, negative," and a woman who is "original [*samobytnaia*], natural, positive," reverses gender expectations.[17] Margarita [Rita] Torsina's widower father is a retired naval officer more interested in reliving the battle of Trafalgar than in supervising his spirited daughter. Left to her own devices, she spots an attractive young man at the Odessa opera who is obviously interested in her.[18] The two meet again at the post office and begin exchanging clandestine letters by slipping them under the cushion of Rita's theater seat. Valentin Kereutov's character is signified by his first name: Marchenko portrays him as a terminally idle and esthetic "porcelain doll." The frank and challenging stance Margarita presents in her letters is not at all what Valentin had envisioned in a romantic relationship, and he breaks with her. Grieving and confused, Rita turns to the family friend who has quietly watched over her upbringing, Ivan Petrovich, a sea captain in his mid thirties. Their discussion of her abortive love affair takes place on his ship, a setting that suggests his role as her moral pilot. Pressed for an opinion, he assures Rita that her flirtation with Valentin was not love but only "a near miss."

If the theater is a dangerously artificial venue for healthy minded provincial heroines, the drawing rooms of St. Petersburg are nearly fatal. In Marchenko's 1856 tale, "Hills" ("Gory"), the ice slopes that pleasure-loving city dwellers construct for winter sledding become a metaphor for society that a young gentry woman encounters in the capital. Ol'ga's emotional crisis is symbolized by a near-fatal bout of flu. Boris, the man-about-Petersburg who flirted with her on those treacherous hills, exudes Romantic desperation when he thinks she is dying; after her unexpected recovery, he sends his countess cousin to warn her not to expect anything from him. Chastened, but with ideals and morals intact, Ol'ga returns to her country estate and an independent life alone.

Marchenko's writing career petered out after her marriage in the mid 1850s. Her 1858 novel *Razluchniki* (a hard title to translate, but implying people who live apart), which appeared under the new masculine pseudonym A. Temrizov, is a transparent, sardonic portrait of her in-laws and life in Kherson province. As Belinskii suggested, love is, indeed, Marchenko's main theme, but she uses it as a framework within which to depict a cross-section of contemporary society. Her stories and novels are rich in secondary characters and observations of varied ways of life. They also share the common vices of the period: clumsy and artificial plots, loose ends, inconsistent use of narratorial voice, and flights of overblown rhetoric. Like their male peers, women were still learning to manipulate the complexities of Realist fiction and to tell a story resonating with the sense of lived experience.

NADEZHDA SOKHANSKAIA (PS. KOKHANOVSKAIA, 1823–1884)

Nadezhda Sokhanskaia's works were erased from the history of Russian literature precisely because of their strengths: Her subject matter and style—the contemporary life and historical lore of the minor gentry and merchants of Ukraine and south Russia portrayed in an idiom that reflected the exuberance of the culture—fit neither the stereotype of "feminine" writing nor the demand of Realist critics that literature serve social goals. No Russian woman writer ever made a more auspicious debut. Boris Almazov, a conservative "pure art" critic, granted her first major published work, "An After-Dinner Call" ("Posle obeda v gost'iakh," 1858), the highest of accolades—it could have been written by a *man*:

Judging from the subtle analysis of the feminine heart evident in the work, you will see that the author actually is a woman; but the rare power of observation of the life of people of the simple class, the rare fidelity and typicality of the language of the protagonists, the artistic tranquility of the story give one cause for doubt.[19]

The plot is simple: Two women meet at the house of a local magnate, and while more privileged guests linger over dinner, Liubov' Arkhipovna tells the narrator the story of how she came to love and appreciate the long-suffering merchant to whom she was married against her will.[20] Almazov praises the author's objectivity:

A mother forces her daughter to marry a man she detests only because he is well-off! What thunderous protests against the violation of personal rights another writer would release! . . . A mother beats her daughter![. . .] How à propos here would be an attack on the crudeness of family principles in people untamed by civilization![. . .] Nowhere does [the author] express either her own or the conventional views on the events she describes, and due to this what power there is in her depictions.[21]

The real tragedy of the tale—that the forced marriage separated Liubov' Arkhipovna from a man with a lively spirit that matched her own—emerges only slowly. A gentle question by the sympathetic frame-tale narrator leads her to tell the story of his untimely death. Sokhanskaia sets Liubov's and Sasha's emotional ordeal in the rhythm of the seasons and the Christian calendar: They part at Christmas; he drowns performing a heroic rescue the following Easter, and it is only after the year of ritual mourning that Liubov's frozen grief thaws the next spring.

It is not clear that critics grasped the archetypal overtones—Orpheus and Eurydice, Christian martyrdom—of these details, but they enjoyed the broad picture her heroine sketches of life in a small town in the Ukrainian-South Russian borderlands, the tale's colorful use of folklore and song (for instance, as Sasha and Liubov' exchange improvised farewells in verse on the night before her wedding), and the pathos of the protagonists' fate. The work was praised across the political spectrum. "The whole thing is astonishing," Turgenev wrote, "and more than once moved me, an old man [forty at the time] to tears. Tolstoi [. . .] is of the same opinion." (3: 242). The conservative Slavophiles, who sought to prove that Russia had a unique culture uncontaminated by Western values, were quick to claim Sokhanskaia as their own. Ivan Aksakov grandly informed her that "After-Dinner Call" was a worthy match to his father's *Family Chronicle* and *Childhood of Bagrov's Grandson*. In his brother Konstantin's article about it, he wrote, it is "called a 'Russian tale,' and this praise has not been bestowed by us on any author concocting tales in the Russian spirit, not Grigorovich or even Turgenev."[22]

In the turbulent 1860s, Sokhanskaia's fiction rapidly became a target of contention in the political split between Left and Right. She rejected the increasingly secular spirit of the time. Novellas like "After-Dinner Call" and "Kiril Petrov i Nastas'ia Dmitrova" (1861) depict heroines' spiritual accommodation to fates they cannot change. The comfort they find in religion comes in a slow process of spiritual growth that echoes Sokhanskaia's epiphany as she described it in her posthumously published *Autobiography*:

You'll guess that this feast of the Resurrection [Easter] brought my resurrection.[. . .] Around me nothing had substantially changed, but I was not the same—and nothing was the same. Making peace with myself, I was at peace with everything—with my life and with my lot. I came to love my steppes. Our little cottage became so dear and full of light. . . . I entered it as a church—in veneration.[23]

Among the critics of the Left, displeasure at what they saw as her retrograde views gradually displaced recognition of the integrity and complexity of her portrayal of her characters within the limits of their own world outlook. In Turgenev's *Smoke* (1867), the preachy Westernizer Potugin twice rails against Sokhanskaia's stylizations, calling them literature "en cuir de Russie."

Sokhanskaia, however, continued stubbornly to pursue her own line. In historical tales she attempted the creation of psychologically complex portraits of male characters stubbornly pursuing a goal: Mark Petrovich, the young hero of "From a Provincial Portrait Gallery" ("Iz provintsial'noi gallerei portretov," 1859), succeeds in carrying off Anna Gavrilovna after her father refuses him her hand;[24] the hero of "Swarm [the hero's nickname—he was born in a beeyard] Feodosii Savvich at Rest" ("Roi Feodosii Savvich na spokoe," 1862) dedicates his old age to building a church; and in "A Literary Breadcrumb" ("Krokha slovesnogo khleba," 1874), a Ukrainian landowner travels to St. Petersburg to obtain justice in a land dispute. All three tales are set in the late eighteenth century and reflect the rough ways of the frontier culture of the steppe. The love affair, the traditional framework for women writers' depiction of male characters, plays almost no role: It would have been an anachronistic element foreign to her determination to transmit the essence of the past and, at the same time, suggest the semilegendary aura of an oral tradition that remembers ancestors as larger than life. Critics still misread Sokhanskaia's stories as justifying the patriarchal mores they portray.[25] No such narrow standard has ever been applied to similar works by Nikolai Gogol' and Sergei Aksakov.

SOF'IA ENGEL'GARDT (PS. OL'GA N., 1828–1894)

From 1853 to 1892, more than thirty of Engel'gardt's long stories and novellas appeared in a number of major journals, most of them in *Russian Herald* (*Russkii vestnik*). A woman who moved in Moscow conservative circles, she is the rare example of a financially independent writer whose works fell into immediate obscurity because she never brought them out in separate editions. Her anecdotal early tales, which bore titles drawn from popular sayings (for example, "Morning Is Cleverer than Night" ["Utro vechera mudrenee"], 1853; "You Can't Please Everyone" ["Na ves' svet ne ugodish"], 1855; "Even with Four Legs a Steed Stumbles" ["Kon' i o chetyrekh nogakh spotykaetsia"], 1856) attracted critical attention—and some grumbles at their frothy inconsequence. Her rapid development into a serious writer who presages Chekhov's understated yet unsparing dissection of Russian society went unremarked. Her elder sister was the prolific popular historian Ekaterina Novosil'tseva (ps. T. Tolycheva, 1820–1885), and a deep historicism informs Engel'gardt's fiction as well. In quiet, apolitical tales firmly—in some cases, suffocatingly—under the control of an attractively humane, omniscient narrator, she describes clashes between generations and societal trends. One of her most persistent themes is men's failure to respect women's emotional and intellectual integrity, a trait that she perceives to be deeply rooted in Russian culture. She does not exercise Chekhovian economy, however: Her simple undramatic plots are cluttered with portraits of secondary characters and clumsily inserted tales intended to illustrate the main theme.

The strong-woman archetype, most commonly embodied as the domestic tyrant, has been delineated in Russian literature from medieval times.[26] Nineteenth-century women writers tended to identify strength of character with an autonomy that they defined as adulthood with a suitable income and indulgent or absent parents or husband. Young women with the masculine freedom to determine their own lives, however, are even less likely than their subordinate sisters to find happiness in the traditional framework of love, marriage, and motherhood. Throughout her works Engel'gardt asks "whether fate or the personal character of each of us plays the leading role in our life." In the long story that poses the question directly ("Fate or Character?" ["Sud'ba ili kharakter?"], 1861), Engel'gardt sketches case histories from the lives of three young women of independent means. The answer for two of them—that women of strong character are less likely to end up personally fulfilled in life—is clear from the story's epigraph: "They are not made for the world" (Lermontov).

Engel'gardt mentions that her first example, Mar'ia Keller, has been tutored in Russian literature by the critic Belinskii himself. His lessons transform her from social butterfly to liberated woman. (It is noteworthy that the story appeared two years before Nikolai Chernyshevskii's famous didactic novel *What Is to Be Done?* (*Chto delat'?*, 1863) put the "woman question" at the center of public debate.) Mar'ia marries a young artist for love. After two blissful years, he finds another muse, and she is tempted to take solace in an affair with a worldly rake, who respects her too much to take advantage of her vulnerable state. Visits to a sister who is absorbed in marriage and motherhood and an aunt who combines autocratic lifestyle and religiosity in monastic retreat offer Mar'ia no alternative model. Although she gradually develops a circle of interesting friends, Mar'ia Keller never manages to reconcile herself to her lonely fate, however, and at thirty-seven is a woman "tired, broken, asking only for peace and quiet."

Engel'gardt's second test case is Anna Belovodova. Not long before her wedding to an ambitious young government official, she fell in love with her cousin's husband. Radomskii returned her love, too, but his attachment to his three-year-old daughter overrides that passion. They part in great pain, and Anna calls off her marriage. Anna's mother never forgives her and her ex-fiancé's hostility wins her the opprobrium of society, but she remains serene in the virginal confidence that she has made the right choice.

Mar'ia and Anna, who have been lifelong friends, become the bemused witnesses of the quick attachment that springs up between two conventional young people. Polina Tumanskaia, who mindlessly adored her late husband and is equally prepared to worship a new one, has no trouble in attracting a "youth of thirty" who has been Mar'ia Keller's gallant cavalier. An encapsulated sketch of the elderly ex-tutor to all three, Mme de Saint-Maurr, a "typical personality" who, driven abroad by the French Revolution, has survived by her wits, suggests the contrast between ruthless Western pragmatism and ineffectual Russian idealism.

In "The Touchstone" ("Kamen' pretknoveniia," 1862), Engel'gardt contrasts the values of Westernized gentry and Slavophiles and finds them equally oppressive to women. The young widow Valentina Kolyvanova is reclaiming her independence after a marriage lived under her Francophile husband's despotic insistence that she blindly follow his empty and pretentious lifestyle. She is attracted to the Slavophile Tramonin, but repulsed by the pietistic atmosphere of the estate where he lives with his domineering mother and meek sister. (The depiction of the Tramonin family is a wicked, barely disguised satire on the life of the Aksakov clan.) Her doubts are resolved by a male confidant who points out how much Tramonin's arbitrary attitude toward women resembles that of Valentina's late Westernizer husband. Desperate to create a "last decisive meeting" in which she can make her independence of thought clear, Valentina lets

Tramonin catch her reading a novel by George Sand (the touchstone of the title), whose life and works played an important role in creating the Westernizers' ideas of liberated womanhood. The ploy succeeds brilliantly: Convinced at last that Valentina is not just a Slavophile lamb gone astray, but a woman deeply corrupted by European ideas, he rips up the book and renounces its reader. Like Mar'ia Keller before her, Valentina Kolyvanova is left to build an independent but lonely life.

NADEZHDA KHVOSHCHINSKAIA (PS. V. KRESTOVSKY, 1824–1889) AND SOF'IA KHVOSHCHINSKAIA (PS. IV. VESEN'EV, 1828–1865)

Nadezhda Khvoshchinskaia, who lived in Riazan', became one of the first women to support not only herself but an extended family as well by writing. Her forty-year career in literature began with poetry published under her own name. She adopted the male pseudonym V. Krestovsky for her first prose work in 1850 and stubbornly clung to it even after the historical novelist Vsevolod Krestovsky entered literature under his own name.[27] Under that mask, Kvoshchinskaia wrote over fifty works of fiction that tested the changing temper of her society.[28]

Contemporary critics appreciated her novel, *In Hope of Something Better* (*V ozhidanii luchshego*, 1860), as a depiction of the retrograde aristocracy who were offering stubborn resistance to the impending emancipation of the serfs. It drew direct comparison to Goncharov and Turgenev. Miliukov declared that "the novelty of the setting . . . and [the author's] delicate, ironically serene handling of his subject make Krestovsky's novel incomparably more significant than *Oblomov* or *On the Eve*."[29] More directly, it was an indictment both of domestic tyranny and of meek subjection to it. In works discussed above, Anastasia Marchenko and Sof'ia Engel'gardt depicted the limited options and broad dangers faced by independent younger women. Khvoshchinskaia's central protagonist is the more traditional type of "strong woman," a widow who holds the family financial reins after years of marriage in which she thoroughly absorbed oppressive patriarchal codes. A whole set of hangers-on cluster around the despotic Princess Desiatova, hoping for crumbs from her table or a share of her fortune. Khvoshchinskaia uses a running motif of handwork to define her characters' status. When the princess tires of the elaborate embroidery she is piously embroidering for the church on her estate, she can always order someone in her circle of sycophants to pick it up. By contrast, Anna Fëdorovna, a poor woman struggling to maintain a home for her idle husband and make a good match for the family's one viable asset, an attractive daughter, wages a desperate, clandestine battle with sewing and laundry to keep that asset dressed in style. A sad and eerie thread that runs through works like *In Hope* . . . , Karolina Pavlova's *A Double Life* (1848), and Engel'gardt's "Dream of a Greataunt and Greatniece" (1869) is the absence or irrelevance of men. In Khvoshchinskaia's novel, the princess's two grandsons are corrupt and spoiled, the object of female plots and aspirations; two positive male characters are mere bystanders, totally helpless to influence events in the society concentrated around the princess.

For Russian women, denied by law and custom the basic freedom to organize their life as they chose, setting and circumstance—the Bakhtinian chronotope—determined their fate.[30] Female confinement is the palimpsest under the "sleeping-beauty" plot of male fiction: Pushkin, Turgenev, Tolstoi, Dostoevskii, Goncharov, all depict female protagonists who have little occupation or goal in life beyond awaiting the appearance of men whose love will reward their "terrible perfection." In his 1863 novel *What Is to Be Done?*, Chernyshevskii, himself a prisoner in the Peter-Paul Fortress, created a pair of male angels to rescue his own terribly perfect heroine Vera Pavlovna—in his depiction, her only faults are a (curiously catlike) fondness for cream and lolling on a sofa—literally and spiritually from crass confines unworthy of her. Women saw no such easy happy endings for their heroines. Khvoshchinskaia's *In Hope* . . . symbolized women's constricted lives by the endless handwork they remain hunched over throughout long idyllic summer days on the Desiatov estate. In her dark-toned "Brother Dear" ("Bratets," 1858), the three Chirkin sisters fight a losing battle against the malevolent selfishness of the brother on whom their mother dotes; psychological duress is echoed in the women's physical confinement to their backwoods country house.

The provincial town is a frequent chronotope in Khvoshchinskaia's fiction. In novels and stories like "Anna Mikhailovna" (1849), "Boarding School Girl" ("Pansionerka," 1861), *Recent Times* (*Nedavnee*, 1865), and *Ursa Major* (*Bol'shaia medveditsa*, 1870), she describes spirited girls' struggle for autonomy, often in a provincial city (much like Riazan') that she calls "N." or "Ensk" (the equivalent of the generic "X" in English). It is distinguished by the cloud of smugness and desolation that hangs over it and, as one St. Petersburg critic described her cast of characters, a population of "family despots, incorrigible phrase-mongers, hard-hearted egoists of both sexes, ignoramuses frozen in their prejudices, weak-charactered creatures, in general the kind of rubbishy people who throng the provinces."[31]

In the city of N., Katerina Bagrianskaia, the heroine of *Ursa Major*, has to contend with the growing religious fanaticism of her father, the selfish careerism of her brother, and the fecklessness of the married man who courts her. Katerina's would-be lover Verkhovskoi is trapped in a marriage for money, a situation with which women were all too familiar. The critic A. M. Skabichevskii was not amused by the role reversal: He complained that Verkhovskoi just kept on whining ["vsë nyl, nyl, i ne iznyl'"]. Katerina has only the distant example of an independent older woman she never meets—Verkhovskoi's mother, the guiding constellation of the title—to guide her to a career as a village schoolteacher. Set in 1855–1858, *Ursa Major* was part of the continuing debate over the simplistic formula for women's liberation—via the loving efforts of men—a formula that Chernyshevskii had advanced in *What Is to Be Done?*; Skabichevskii reported that *Ursa Major* was "talked and quarreled about, it was a rare person who hadn't read it."[32]

Nadezhda Khvoshchinskaia's younger sister Sof'ia, under the male pseudonym and persona of Ivan Vesen'ev, wrote a series of talented long "sketches" [*ocherki*] musing on the temper of the times from the Crimean War through the emancipation of the serfs in 1861, as it was refracted in a provincial capital.[33] In "A Provincial's Plaint: December 1861" ("Plach' Provintsiiala: Dekabr'," 1861), ten months after the abolition of serfdom, Khvoshchinskaia-Vesen'ev grieved for the loss of the chance to catch

what the coming generation will need to know for a clear view of the past, just exactly what was our present society?

The precious moment when anyone who can combine two letters could have caught society alive under the pen—this minute has been irretrievably missed. Yes, there was a moment when the entire Russian world, from the peasant child, man, and woman, from the valet to the townsman and merchant, from the estate-owner with two serfs to his highness the thousand-serf prince, when all of us, all the Russian people, with a first irresistible impulse, a first exclamation, openly showed our true colors.[34]

Vesen'ev, reviewing the recent history of his town, reported that the enthusiasm and good will necessary to carry out Aleksander II's reforms had already given way to mute resistance and apathy.

Sof'ia Khvoshchinskaia is the extreme example of a woman who buried her identity under male pseudonym and voice in order to have her broad-brush portrait of society taken seriously, even going so far as asking the critic Dmitrii Pisarev not to publish an article about her works in *Dawn* (*Rassvet*), a magazine for young ladies.[35] After Sof'ia's early death, Nadezhda Khvoshchinskaia extended her own range of subject to take up her sister's challenge to catch "society live under the pen." In tales like "Happy People" ("Schastlivye liudi," 1874), "Among Friends" ("Mezhdu druz'iami," 1875), "The Meeting" ("Svidanie," 1879), and "The Snowstorm" ("V'iuga," 1889), she dealt more directly with the fates of radical activists of the 1860s who cling in lonely fidelity to the old ideals in a society full of former comrades for whom the "rational egotism" of Chernyshevskii's formulation has degenerated into egotism pure and simple.

ALEKSANDRA MONTVID (PS. SHABEL'SKAIA, B. 1845)

By the 1870s and 1880s, women had become an accepted part of the literary scene and were pushing at the boundaries of discourse, not always to the approbation of their male colleagues. In 1882, after the Russian satirist and editor Saltykov-Shchedrin had published in his journal *Notes of the Fatherland* (*Otechestvennye zapiski*) three tales signed by Aleksandra Shabel'skaia, Turgenev congratulated Saltykov "on obtaining a strong and fresh talent."[36] Saltykov replied:

I don't share . . . your pleasure and try to avoid corresponding with the lady. Her real name is Mon[t]vid-Monvizh (by her husband) and Tolochinova (by her lover) and she lives in Kiev. The *baba* (woman, denigrating) is apparently a brazen one and busy preparing to write a novel with an aborted fetus. She asked my advice, but I answered rather curtly that I am no specialist in the line of abortion [vytravlenie].[37]

Saltykov was probably referring to "The Master of Arts and Frosia: Their First Steps in Life" ("Magister i Frosia: Ikh pervye shagi v zhizni," 1883), in which suggesting an abortion indicates the hero's reluctance to deal with the consequences of his actions. Although in complexity and length we would call this depiction of a mismatch between an egotistical, married pedant and an idealistic girl a novella, Montvid included it among her *Pencil Sketches* (*Nabroski karandashom*, 1884), a rubric implying that a work was a quick study rather than a novella with a developed plot. The work begins with a sketch-like, leisurely travelog of the couple's honeymoon trip to Vienna, but overall the rubric seems to be feminine self-deprecation, a disguised plea to readers and critics to assess it kindly. Deformed by a scathing portrait of the male protagonist, "Magister" is Montvid's least successful tale, but Saltykov's reaction serves more as evidence of his puritanical streak than as an assessment of her fiction.

Sympathetic gentry-women authors saw the same factors of constraint and confinement that inhibited them "writ large" in the lives of peasants. Montvid's *Pencil Sketches* include a set of interesting tales devoted to the life of the Ukrainian villages of Upper and Lower Maliivka. All of the stories start with a leisurely and loving outline of the physical layout and history of the area. In "Paraska" (1882), Maliivka becomes a collective character in the conflict between a patriarchal peasant, long the respected pillar of the village, and his son's wife. In an ideal world, these two strong, determined people would be natural allies in promoting the interests of the family, but in Maliivka the clash between them ends fatally because the old man cannot bring himself to rise above his fellow villagers' jeers at him for failing to curb his daughter-in-law Paraska's blunt tongue.

The toponymic titles of Montvid's two tales set on the estate called Hilltop (*Nagornoe*—the title suggests its looming power over the village below) underline the horror of their plots. In the first, the new owner, a former tavern-keeper, offers his gentry predecessor's impoverished wife and daughter refuge in his now-deserted tavern, which bears the picturesque and cruelly apt name of "Naked Lady" ("Gola pani," 1883). Lelichka, the belle of her boarding-school, comes home to that rickety refuge with no advance warning that her father's dissolute life and untimely death have cost the family the estate. She locks herself in her room to sulk and contemplate suicide. On a melodramatically stormy night that threatens to demolish the tavern altogether, Lelichka finds her mother crumpled dead outside her door. Montvid leaves the girl's further fate to the reader's imagination. In the second tale ("Hilltop"), the tavern-keeper rapes a peasant girl in a summerhouse on the hilltop that still reeks with the moral stench of the previous landowner's debauchery.

OL'GA SHAPIR (1850–1916)

Ol'ga Shapir was one of the late Realist women writers who appeared in print under their own names.[38] From 1879 through the 1900s, Shapir published a flood of well-constructed fiction in which a frequent tinge of slightly pompous didacticism is balanced by the psychological complexity of her characters. Her major theme was the conflict in women's lives between the demands of love and fulfillment in motherhood and an equally natural need for social and intellectual accomplishment—a clash that became a major theme of Silver Age literature. One of the threads that runs through her works is "the innate, tragic trait of woman—to give herself into slavery even when fate itself sends her independence and freedom."[39]

In "Funeral Feast" ("Pominki," *Povesti i rasskazy*, 1889), the sudden death of just such a self-effacing spinster, Auntie Katia, who was her extended family's unfailing resource in the daily burden and major crises, leaves the family "at sea." Although they give her a splendid funeral, nobody seems to know much about her past and her actual relationship to them; even the fact that her real name is not Ekaterina but the more symbolic Konkordiia (Concord) comes as a shock. Shapir lets the black sheep of the Alazin family—as he describes himself, the opposite pole to Katia's quiet self-sacrifice—tell the story of her life in an increasingly drunken and self-loathing voice that recalls Dostoevskii's underground man. At the end, this continual recipient of Katia's unfailing charity calls into question the sense of all that meek self-sacrifice. He suggests that a proper epitaph for her would be "Everything for others":

A noble motto—but it is just because that woman made herself the property of the venerable Alazin family, of course, that not only nothing sublime but even anything worthy of notice could come of it. . . . What's worse, she raised egotists! She just simply corrupted my sister, beguiling her with the total prospect of living as a parasite and piling her responsibilities on somebody else's shoulders! She dragged out years as a martyr by the armchair of a decomposing old man who could and should have been satisfied with a simple nurse—it was the height of charity, but there wasn't a shred of human sense in it![40]

Shapir depicts another form of psychological slavery—to a cause rather than to family—in her novel *In the Stormy Years* (*V burnye gody*), written in the late 1880s but denied publication until 1907 because of its frank treatment of political trends. Shapir's young gentry heroine, Vera Baskina, throws herself into the populist [*narodnik*] movement and then, with its repression, into radical terrorism. Vera grows up, and remains, until she is thirty, in a home in which the family agenda is controlled by her mother's outbursts of hysteria. Shapir gradually makes clear that Vera's fear of that heredity underlies the dogged nature of her commitment to revolution. On the larger scale, the novel is a programmatic chronicle of St. Petersburg society and the revolutionary movement from 1866 to the Balkan War in the late 1870s. Vera's father was raised by a famous uncle, a Decembrist icon released after long years in exile. A liberal official and journalist, Baskin is bemused by his daughter's doctrinaire ideals and bitterly estranged from his brother Konstantin, who has married into a Slavophile family and has become a fanatic follower of their doctrine. Vera's tutors in political matters, the three Prosvetov sisters, are emblematic of the paths taken by liberal young women of the 1860s: Eva remains a dedicated revolutionary; Dasha deserts the movement to study medicine; and Son'ia, unabashedly blissful in her marriage to a fellow activist, serves as the humane but unappreciated focus of the group.

In later works, Shapir expresses more optimism about women's choices. Stories dedicated to women from the urban proletariat or demi-monde who take charge of their own fate are among her least doctrinaire and most charming. In "Avdot'ia's Daughters" ("Avdot'iny dochki," 1898), Arisha and Sasha, the two daughters of a cook in the family of a St. Petersburg official, are busy making a realistic assessment of their options and planning their future in the cramped cupboard downstairs that is their only home; upstairs the daughter of the house languishes in torpid self-pity.[41] In "The Upshot: An Incident in the Capital" ("Razviazka: Stolichnyi sluchai," 1901), Viktor Bezhaev's plans to treat his mistress, Mar'ia Arkadievna, to a "family outing" with a friend go awry. When the two men call for her, they find that she has mysteriously moved out of the apartment in which Bezhaev has been keeping her. She shows up late at the outdoor restaurant in a chic new gray suit to announce that she has taken a stenography course and plans a career as a court reporter. Walking away from the stunned men, Mar'ia Arkadievna is absorbed in anticipation of a "whole world of new relationships, emotions, and interests."

Realism was a mode of fiction that aimed to depict the "truth" of Russian society. These few works by a small number of the many female writers active in the last half of the nineteenth century clearly demonstrate women's continuing struggle to extend their rights and roles. The authors reflect what they saw as both the strengths and vulnerabilities of their sex. More important, they embodied their protagonists' dilemmas in competent and still enjoyable novels and stories. In our own contentious times, we seem to have forgotten that the literature considered important to read and inscribe in history—the "canon"—has never been a fixed and immutable body, but rather a rich and shifting dialog between past and present. To review the prose of Russian Realism from a feminist perspective that reintegrates the lost voices of women is not to challenge the established "great men" but to recover other interesting authors who speak to women's experience in a way their male peers could not, to see the works and lives of authors of both sexes against a broader understanding of the tensions and pulls of Russian society, and to gain both a more nuanced picture of the culture of their time and a clearer perspective on our own.

NOTES

1. For the Russian Realist period, see Hugh McLean, "Realism," in *Handbook of Russian Literature*, ed. Victor Terras (New Haven: Yale University Press, 1985), 363–67.

2. Fiction writers from non-gentry classes had begun to appear by the 1860s, but they were exceptional. Aleksandra Kobiakova (1823–1892) published bleak novels from the life of Volga merchantry; and a woman of peasant stock, Anna Kirpishchikova ("A. K-va," 1838–1927), wrote tales centered around factory life in Perm. From 1880 another peasant, Valentina Dmitrieva (1859–1947), educated as a doctor, produced extensive fiction depicting settings ranging from village life and provincial intelligentsia circles to the urban student milieu.

3. For a summary of women's social and juridical position in Imperial Russia, see Barbara Engel, *Mothers and Daughters: Women of the Intelligentsia in Nineteenth Century Russia* (Cambridge: Cambridge University Press, 1983) and William G. Wagner, "The Trojan Mare: Women's Rights and Civil Rights in Late Imperial Russia," in *Civil Rights in Imperial Russia*, ed. Olga Crisp and Linda Edmondson (Oxford: Clarendon Press, 1989), 65–84.

4. A real-life example of marriage under parental pressure is found in the reminiscences of Emiliia Pimenova, *Dni minuvshie: Vospominaniia* (Leningrad, 1929); it is the subject of a novella by Elena Sal'ianova [Ekaterina Starynkevich], "Ne oni vinovaty," in *Vestnik Evropy* 1 (1871): 133–66, 2: 667–704.

5. Other Muscovite writers included Karolina Pavlova, Sof'ia Engel'gardt, and Natal'ia Shalikova (1815–1878), who used the pseudonym E. Narskaia.

6. See both Charlotte Rosenthal, "Women's Silver Age Prose" and Jane Taubman, "Women Poets of the Silver Age" in this collection.

7. An extreme instance was the banning of Panaeva's autobiographical *povest' Semeistvo Tal'nikovykh* (*The Tal'nikov Family*, 1848) for "immorality and undermining of parental authority."

8. P. B. Bykov, *Siluèty dalekogo proshlogo* (Moscow, 1930), 187.

9. *Russkii vestnik* 8 (1870): 736.

10. In addition to those discussed here, the most productive include Mariia Markovich (1834–1907), who published her stories from Ukrainian folk life in Ukrainian and Russian as Marko Vovchok; Praskov'ia Lachinova (1829–1892) and her sister Anna (c. 1832–1914), who seem to have written sprightly popular fiction about contemporary fads and trends together and interchangeably under several male names, including P. Letnev (the most prolific), E. Blizhnev, and A. Vol'skii; Nadezhda Merder (1839–1906), who as N. Severin wrote over 100 prose works of increasingly conservative tendency from the mid 1870s on; and Varvara Komarova (1862–1942), who was the author of fiction in Russian and a four-volume biography of George Sand in French under the pseudonym Vladimir Karenin.

11. Barbara Heldt, *Terrible Perfection: Women and Russian Literature* (Bloomington: Indiana University Press, 1987), 2.

12. E. Nekrasova, "Anastasiia Iakovlevna Marchenko (T.Ch. ili A. Temrizov)," *Kievskaia starina* 11 (1889): 392–422.

13. Vissarion Belinskii, *Polnoe sobranie sochinenii*, vol. 10 of 13 vols. (Moscow, 1956), 351.

14. On the preoccupation of the first generations of the Russian intelligentsia with realizing the "feminine" side of their natures, consult Irina Paperno, *Chernyshevsky and the Age of Realism. A Study in the Semiotics of Behavior* (Stanford, CA: Stanford University Press, 1988), 60–91.

15. Belinskii, 352.

16. "Vokrug da okolo," *Otechestvennye Zapiski* 6 (1855): 357–416, 7: 5–70. The quotation is from 7: 41.

17. "Vokrug da okolo," 7: 20. Karolina Pavlova's story "At the Tea Table" ("Za chainym stolom," 1859) is a more sophisticated tale of role reversals that depicts "feminine" ploys used by poor men to attract a wealthy widowed princess.

18. The theater as a place where intrigue and romance are as rife in the loges as onstage is a Romantic trope that persists into Russian Realism. "Too Late!" also opens with a theater scene.

19. B. N. Almazov, *Utro* (1859), 78. Sokhanskaia's "Posle obeda v gost'iakh" appeared in *Russkii vestnik* 8 (1858): 641–96.

20. Aleksandra Kovalenskaia, "V sorochke rodilas' " ("Born Lucky"), *Russkaia mysl'* 2 (1880): 136–57, uses the same plot in a more conventional setting: whereas Liubov' Arkhipovna is from a poor gentry family, Kovalenskaia's heroine is a peasant. She too is in love with one man and forced to wed another, who overcomes her sullen resistance to the marriage with saintly patience.

21. Ibid., 82–83.

22. "Perepiska Aksakovykh s N. S. Sokhanskoi (Kokhanovskoi)," *Russkoe Obozrenie* 2 (1897): 569–70.

23. *Russkoi obozrenie* 8 (1896): 474. The autobiography was written in 1847–1848, when Sokhanskaia was twenty-four, at the behest of a SPb. editor who wanted to encourage her to write from what she knew rather than follow Sandian prototypes. The basic source of information about the rest of her life is a biography by N. N. Platonova, *Kokhanovskaia (N. S. Sokhanskaia) 1823–1884: Biograficheskii ocherk* (St. Petersburg, 1909).

24. An excerpt from "Iz provintsial'noi gallerei portretov" appeared in *Dacha na Petergofskoi doroge: Proza russkikh pisatel'nits pervoi poloviny XIX veka*, ed. V. V. Uchënova. (Moscow, 1986), 416–51.

25. As late as 1989, Vl. Viktorovich could still lament "the fading of [Sokhanskaia's] divine spark" due to her "doctrinaire views and fanaticism" ("Uroki odnoi sud'by," *Literaturnoe obozrenie* 3: 110–12.)

26. See: Vera Sandomirsky Dunham, "The Strong-Woman Motif," *The Transformation of Russian Society*. ed. Cyril Black (Cambridge, MA: Harvard Univ. Press, 1967), 459–83; and Antonnia Glasse, "The Formidable Woman: Portrait and Original," *Russian Literature Triquarterly* 9 (1974): 433–53.

27. She used several other male pseudonyms for literary criticism.

28. For a bibliography of Khvoshchinskaia's works and contemporary biography and criticism, see S. I. Ponomarev, "Nashi pisatel'nitsy," *Sbornik otdeleniia russkogo iazyka i slovesnosti Imperatorskoi Akademii nauk*, vol. 52, No. 7 (1891): 60–71. Arja Rosenholm addresses the question of how her works were received in a recent article, "Auf den Spuren des Vergessens: Zur Rezeptionsgeschichte der russischen Schriftstellerin N. D. Chvoscinskaja," *Studia Slavica Finlandensis*, vol. 4 (1989): 63–91.

29. A. Miliukov, "Mertvye dushi bol'shogo sveta," *Svetoch* 2 (1861): 44.

30. For a chronotope in recent fiction by Russian women, see Helena Goscilo, "Wom-

en's Wards and Wardens: The Hospital in Contemporary Russian Women's Fiction,"
Canadian Women's Studies, vol. 10, No. 4 (Winter 1989): 83–86.

31. From a review in *Sever* quoted in Vl. Zotov, "Nadezhda Dmitrievna Khvosh-chinskaia (Iz vospominaniia starogo zhurnalista)," *Istoricheskii vestnik*, 10 (1889): 105. Saltykov-Shchedrin, who served as vice-governor of Riazan' in 1858–1860, loathed the town's provincial smugness and found the Khvoshchinskaia home a hospitable refuge.

32. In the article by A. M. Skabichevskii, "Volny russkogo progressa," *Sochineniia*, 2 vols. (Moscow, 1903), vol. 1, 649–86.

33. Vesen'ev's sketches include "Prostye smertnye:" Ocherki iz provintsial'noi zhizni," 1858; "Plach provintsiala," 1861; "Zemnye radosti i radosti nashego perulka," 1862; "Koe-chto iz nashikh nravov," 1862; "Nasha gorodskaia zhizn'," 1864; "Provintsial'nyi Bon-genre i Mauvais-genre," 1864; and "Malen'kie bedy: Ocherki nastoiash-chego," 1865. A third sister, Praskov'ia Khvoshchinskaia (S. Zimarova, 1832–1916) published one volume of rather weak stories set in the domestic sphere.

34. *Russkii vestnik* 11 (1861): 366–92.

35. During Nadezhda Khvoshchinskaia's lifetime, she defended Sof'ia's posthumous privacy as zealously as she did her own reputation. The first article about Sof'ia's work appeared only in 1899: N. Demidov, "Khvoshchinskaia, S. (Vesen'ev, Iv.): Literaturnaia spravka," *Russkoe bogatstvo* 2 (1899): 99–112. For the sisters, see also, A. P. Mogilianskii, "N. D. i S. D. Khvoshchinskie," vol. 9.2 of *Istoriia russkoi literatury* (Moscow-Leningrad, 1956), 228–37.

36. Ivan Turgenev, *Polnoe sobranie sochinenii i pisem*, Pis'ma vol. 13.1 (Leningrad, 1968), 266.

37. M. E. Saltykov-Shchedrin, *Polnoe sobranie sochinenii*, vol. 19.2 (Moscow, 1977), 117–18.

38. Others include Valentina Dmitrieva, Ekaterina Dubrovina (1846–1913), Sof'ia Smirnova (1852–1921), and Ekaterina Letkova (1856–1937). Kapitolina Nazar'eva (1847–1900) used not only her name, but over fifteen pseudonyms as well.

39. Shapir's article outlining women's social bondage as an outgrowth of sexual slavery, "Zhenskoe bespravie" [Lack of Rights for Women], appeared in 1916. E. Chebysheva—Dmitrieva's memorial article, "Ol'ga Andreevna Shapir. Ee zhizn' i deiatel'nost'," *Viestnik Evropy* 10 (1916): 375–96, summarizes Shapir's works and philosophy. The quotation is from p. 389.

40. "Pominki," *Serdtsa chutkogo prozren'em . . . Povesti i rasskazy russkikh pisatel'-nits XIX v.* ed. N. Iakushin, (Moscow, 1991), 527–28.

41. "Avdot'iny dochki" was recently reprinted in: *Tol'ko chas: Proza russkikh pisatel'nits kontsa XIX—nachala XX veka*, ed. V. V. Uchënova (Moscow, 1988), 16–116.

6

Nineteenth-Century Women Poets: Critical Reception vs. Self-Definition

Diana Greene

Until recently women did not figure at all in discussions of nineteenth-century Russian poetry. They certainly were not included in the literary canon—the collection of writers and works considered central to the study of literature, as reflected in textbooks, course reading lists, anthologies, and scholarly research. According to D. S. Mirsky and other historians of Russian literature, the "tradition," or canon, of nineteenth-century Russian poetry up to the beginning of the Silver Age (1890) consisted of the following poets: Vasily Zhukovsky, Aleksandr Pushkin and his pleiad, the poets of the 1825 Decembrist uprising, Mikhail Lermontov, Aleksei Kol'tsov, Fedor Tiutchev, Nikolai Nekrasov, Lev Mei, Apollon Maikov, Semon Nadson, and Afanasy Fet.[1]

With the growth of feminist criticism in the West, however, scholarship on nineteenth-century Russian women poets has increased.[2] Perhaps in response, Russian scholars, too, have begun to write about Russian women writers, albeit somewhat condescendingly. Russian critics often refer to women writers by their first names (which they seldom do with male writers) and often focus as much on their looks, personalities, love lives, and interactions with male contemporaries as they do on their works.[3]

Like the other Russian women writers discussed in this collection, nineteenth-century Russian women poets have been excluded from the literary canon or lost to literary history. The causes are both general and specific to each century and genre.

For a woman in nineteenth-century Russia to define herself as a poet was not easy. The term "poetess" (*poetessa*) both described women poets and implied the inferiority of their poetry to that of men. Even the current term "woman poet" implies that writing poetry is somehow unnatural for women. After all, no one finds it necessary to talk of "men poets"; such a term sounds almost tautological.[4]

Women poets had to face an issue more basic than the term used to describe them; throughout the nineteenth century in Russia and Europe a debate raged over whether women should write at all.[5] In Russia, as we shall see, one of the most influential nineteenth-century critics, Vissarion Belinsky (1811–1848), often reviewed women's poetry negatively, but at least he found women's poetry worth reviewing. The weight of public opinion, however, seems to have opposed women writing altogether.[6] Even apparent praise of women's poetry often created a double-bind. In an article surveying North American women poets that appeared in a Russian journal in 1851, the reviewer praises them for treating poetry as an "accomplishment" rather than as an art. American women "don't write verse like European women writers, from empty vanity and love for shameful fame . . . they write as our young girls draw and sing." The critic praises their modesty and "pure and reproachless" morality.[7] The only feeling expressed, he notes approvingly, is that of mother love. The reviewer complacently continues that, of course, such poetry is monotonous, but this can be expected from those who have only three noteworthy events in their life: birth, marriage and death. "The rest consists in fulfilling the responsibilities laid on women by divine and human laws (126)." That is, women must be modest and obedient to men, which makes it impossible for them to be good poets. In such a social context women poets had to choose between being women and being poets.

The scholar Barbara Heldt describes other "cultural practices" inhospitable to women poets.[8] For men, a seemingly inevitable and continuous literary tradition grew out of poets' interactions with each other—at lyceums, gimnaziiums, and universities, as well as in public and private places off limits to women— interactions that made it comparatively easy for a young male poet to find mentors as well. Women, on the other hand, generally remained isolated in their homes, from male and female poets alike. Thus, they did not fit as easily into "schools" or have literary descendants. In addition, the publishing establishment—literary critics, publishers, editors—was male and often dismissed as trivial any poetry that reflected women's experience. In such a social context it is amazing that women wrote poetry at all.

In order to re-evaluate the nineteenth-century Russian poetic tradition, I shall consider five Russian women poets: Elisaveta Kul'man, Iuliia Zhadovskaia, Nadezhda Teplova, Evdokiia Rostopchina, and Karolina Pavlova.[9] The poets I have chosen range from the relatively well known (Pavlova, Rostopchina) to the obscure. My aim is not to argue that these writers belong in the present canon of Russian literature, nor to establish an alternative canon; a great deal of work needs to be done on these and other women poets. Rather, I would like to make some preliminary suggestions about the role gender played in their work and reputations, and to consider how these writers defined themselves and were received as women poets or as "poetesses." I suggest that the critical reputations of these poets have been shaped by the few cultural categories available for talking about women—the virgin-martyr, the passive victim, the invisible woman, the disreputable woman, and the masculine woman—and that we can read their lives and work differently and more accurately if we disregard these stereotypes.

ELISAVETA KUL'MAN

Elisaveta Kul'man (1808–1825) was of German extraction, lived in poverty, and died at the age of seventeen, having published nothing during her lifetime. She knew German, French, Italian, Latin, Greek, English, Spanish, and Portuguese. From the time Kul'man was five until she died, Karl Grossheinrikh, a family friend and doctor of law from Bavaria, tutored her in languages, supervised her translations of classical poetry into several languages, and critiqued the Russian poetry she wrote in imitation of classical models. After her death he wrote her biography, in which he explained and defended his teaching methods, and helped persuade the Russian Academy to publish some of her work. According to the Soviet scholar M. Sh. Fainshtein, more than 1,000 of Kul'man's poems and 400 letters have disappeared.[10]

Kul'man did not live long enough to develop into a mature poet. In any case, most Russian readers have found her work inaccessible both because she rejected rhyme,[11] and because she identified herself entirely with the Greek classical rather than the Russian literary tradition; there is no evidence that she knew of either Zhukovsky or Pushkin. Nonetheless, her work repays attention.

Several Russian critics have written about Kul'man, each one appropriating her life and work to his own concerns.[12] There are, however, recurring themes in this criticism. First, critics often seem uncomfortable with Kul'man's erudition, which is perceived to be inappropriate or even monstrous in a young woman. For Belinsky, Kul'man's learning made her a freak of nature, and he emphatically denied her the title of poet: "Elisaveta Kul'man without any doubt was an unusual phenomenon, not as a poet, not as an artist, but simply as some kind of marvel of nature. . . . Her verse is not only devoid of elasticity and plasticity, but it is crude, uneven, prosaic, and full of strains and mistakes in prosody."[13]

On the other hand, the censor and university professor Alexander Nikitenko heatedly defended Kul'man against charges of erudition, suggesting that rather than become learned, Kul'man quite properly arranged to die. "No! this was not a learned woman; perhaps she even had to die not to make herself one. . . . She was an angel on earth and died at age seventeen in order not to stop being one."[14] Fainshtein, too, indicates some discomfort with Kul'man's learning when he finds it necessary to argue that she is not a "cosmopolite."[15]

In a second recurring theme, critics usually recount Kul'man's biography as a kind of saint's life, placing great emphasis on her purity, modesty, and high moral character (qualities considered irrelevant when discussing male poets). In addition, they almost always portray her as a victim, albeit to different forces. Grossheinrikh wrote that Kul'man died of poverty; the critic Ekaterina Nekrasova considered Kul'man a victim of Grossheinrikh's misguided pedagogical theories;[16] and Aleksandr Druzhinin attributed her death to learning and intellectual ambition, apparently fatal qualities for girls and women.[17] Much of this writing suggests the stereotype of the dead virgin-martyr.[18]

The exaggerated purity attributed to the virgin-martyr is often viewed as an invitation to dominance or violation. One can see such attitudes in the writing of the Decembrist poet Vil'gel'm Kiukhel'beker, who complacently reduced Kul'man's life and work to material for a sexual fantasy. ''It's too bad I didn't know her,'' he wrote in a diary entry after reading Nikitenko's account of Kul'man. ''She herself is immeasurably better than her verses. . . . There is no doubt that I would have fallen in love with her, but that love would have been as beneficial to me as are harmful my little passions for petty, vain creatures. . . .''[19]

During the Soviet period Kul'man was ignored. In the one account of her, her evaluation as a poet simply reflected Soviet preoccupations with class affiliation, patriotism, nineteenth-century radical critics, Russian folklore, and xenophobia.[20] The basic elements of nineteenth-century Kul'man criticism remain, however: the discomfort with her erudition, the saint's life, the virgin-martyr.

If, however, we ignore the stories critics have told about Kul'man and look instead at the way she herself used gender in her work, a very different picture emerges: one in which Kul'man appears to have been anything but a passive victim. Although Kul'man knew no women writers, studied with men, and immersed herself in the male domain of classics, she was remarkably aware of herself as a female and a female writer. She daringly reversed traditional sex roles in one poem (''Narcissus'' [''Nartsiss'']), and wrote poems to such women poets of antiquity as Korinna (c. 500 B.C.) and Sappho, with whom she clearly identified.[21] Several of her poems attacked or challenged Apollo (the god of poetry), who for Kul'man embodied ancient Greek prejudices against women poets. Kul'man assigns Diana—Apollo's sister and rival, goddess of the moon, the hunt, and virginity—to be the champion of women and of women poets.

Apollo acts as the villain in Kul'man's unusual version of the Echo and Narcissus myth. In this poem, Kul'man casts the traditionally male Narcissus as a huntress who refuses to marry. Apollo lures her into a pool where she drowns and is mourned by Diana. Kul'man has reversed the Russian folk tradition of the *rusalka*, the dangerous female spirit who lures and then drowns men.[22]

Kul'man challenges Apollo and men's appropriation of high art even more explicitly in a narrative poem about Korinna, who is said to have defeated the famous Greek poet Pindar five times in poetry contests.[23] As the poem begins, we are told that Pindar has not appeared to defend his title of poet laureate for the last two Panhellenic Games at Delphi. Korinna, a young woman poet, presents herself as a competitor for the title. By coming forward as a contestant, Korinna challenges men's exclusion of women from the field of high poetry; in her song, she attacks the mythological basis of that exclusion.

According to myth, Apollo's temple at Delphi (the site of the poetry contests) stood on a sacred spot, once the domain of the earth goddess. Apollo killed the python who guarded the spot and built the temple to mark his possession of the source of poetry and prophecy. The myth could be seen as dethroning the female principle and enthroning the male as the source of poetry.

Korinna, unlike other contestants, does not glorify Apollo's victory over the python. Instead, she counters with another myth, that of Apollo's defeat by Daphne, a nymph who in Kul'man's version worships Apollo's sister, Diana. To avoid Apollo's advances, Daphne transforms herself into a laurel tree from whose branches Apollo fashions the poet's laurel crown of victory. At the conclusion of Korinna's song, Pindar appears "like a god of Olympus" to acclaim Korinna the winner of the poetry contest and crown her—and by extension, Kul'man—with the laurel. Thus, Kul'man re-establishes a feminine genealogy of poetry extending from the goddess Diana, to Daphne, to Korinna, to herself, one in which both the male god of poetry and a famous male poet are defeated by women.

Sappho—who is also supposed to have defeated a male poet, Alceus, in a poetry contest—was recognized in the early nineteenth century as a great poet, but not as homosexual. Kul'man's long poem about Sappho suggests that the world of heterosexual experience can destroy women poets. In the poem, Sappho, about to throw herself from the promontory of Leucas, recalls her victory over Alceus and her subsequent refusal of his love. The gods, she says, have punished her rejection of Alceus by having another man reject her, a situation that has driven her to suicide. Although Kul'man has Sappho—like Narcissus—destroyed by sexual attraction to a man, the poem more strongly emphasizes Sappho's glory and great stature as a poet. Apollo appears very strangely here, transformed through a trick of grammar into a female. Sappho first apostrophizes Apollo (who had a temple at Leucas) as "*vladyka*" ("ruler"), a feminine noun in Russian and, hence, in all subsequent references describes him with female pronouns and adjectives. These and other poems by Kul'man deserve further study from a feminist critical perspective.

IULIIA ZHADOVSKAIA

If most accounts of Kul'man evoke the image of the young, victimized virgin poet, those of Iuliia Zhadovskaia (1824–1883), who wrote prose as well as poetry, evoke the image of the helpless, frustrated woman in bondage. Biographies usually mention Zhadovskaia's physical limitations—she was born with no left arm and only a few fingers on the right—her legal impotence—her father refused to let her marry her tutor whom she loved—and her emotional bondage to this relationship, which, according to one account, "broke her health" (*Russkii biograficheskii slovar'* 1902, 7, 2).[24] The pornographic implications of this "bondage" motif were perhaps most fully realized in Aleksandr Skabichevskii's 1886 article, "Songs of Feminine Bondage":

On all of [her poetry] lies the seal of trampled happiness and of long years of heavy bondage. It is the groans of female slavery with all its tortures, its feelings of helplessness, loneliness, bitter humiliation, shame before its own impotence, and vain efforts to console itself and forget, now in religious paroxysms, now in contemplations of nature's beauty.[25]

A happy ending to Zhadovskaia's biography is usually implied in the fact that at the age of 38 she married a family friend. As in the case of Kul'man, much of Zhadovskaia's work has been lost; the poetry in the posthumous edition of her complete works edited by her brother is incomplete, arbitrarily edited, and very unreliable.[26]

As for Zhadovskaia's literary reputation, Russia's most famous critics have written about her, including those radical critics of the 1860s who claimed they wanted to free women from male domination. Yet at best (Pletnev, Dobroliubov), they condescendingly praised her work for its "sincerity" while dismissing it for its lack of artistry. Others (Maikov, Pisarev) used reviews of Zhadovskaia's poetry to show its inferiority to poetry written by men. Belinsky even compared Zhadovskaia's poetry unfavorably to a man's astronomical discovery! Zhadovskaia's work, Belinsky wrote was "poor in poetry" because as a woman her experience was limited. Real poetry, he said, concerns life on earth. Thus, Belinsky maintains, the astronomer Urbain Leverrier who discovered Uranus is more of a poet than Zhadovskaia, who merely writes poetry about the night sky. One wonders why so many of these famous critics felt the need to write about Zhadovskaia at all.

Unlike Kul'man, during the Soviet period, Zhadovskaia attracted some critical attention. A dissertation about her appeared (V. A. Blagovo), and her work was included in two anthologies. Following the prescriptions of socialist realism— the official Soviet approach to literature—Soviet critics highlighted the social and folk themes she supposedly added to her poetry during the 1850s, pronounced her a disciple of the canonized democratic poet Nikolai Nekrasov (1821–1878) an influence not mentioned before the Revolution, and emphasized the fact that she had been positively, if condescendingly, reviewed by the radical critics of the 1860s.[27] In Soviet criticism, too, condescension prevailed: Her love affair with her tutor was prominently featured,[28] and praise for her "revolutionary themes" was immediately followed by a comment about her "monotony and poverty of form."[29]

I suggest that other understandings of Zhadovskaia's life and work are possible besides that of languishing, frustrated (and titillating) victim of female bondage or boring but well-meaning disciple of Nekrasov. At the very least, her achievement in overcoming her physical disabilities to create a highly successful writing career suggests remarkable courage and faith in herself. A memoir by Zhadovskaia's niece and ward, N. Fedorova, presents an alternative view of Zhadovskaia as a very self-determined, effective woman whose most important relationships appear to have been with other women. Of course, Fedorova had her own axe to grind: she clearly disliked Zhadovskaia's brother and wished to be acknowledged as the most important person in Zhadovskaia's life. Nonetheless, her memoir puts the facts of Zhadovskaia's life into another perspective.

She describes Zhadovskaia as having been brought up by a group of loving and inspirational women. Zhadovskaia's mother, who graduated from the prestigious women's institute at Smolny and died when Zhadovskaia was three, felt particularly protective of Zhadovskaia because of her disability, and before dying she entrusted Zhadovskaia to her own mother's care. Zhadovskaia also lived and studied French with her aunt, the poet Anna Gotovtsova, who dared in an epigram to challenge Pushkin's depiction of women.[30] At the age of nineteen, Zhadovskaia adopted Gotovtsova's daughter, Fedorova, who became her amanuensis and fiercely loyal friend until Zhadovskaia died. Fedorova also suggests that Zhadovskaia's marriage at the age of 38 was not necessarily the "happy ending" to her life depicted by other biographers. Zhadovskaia wrote no more poetry from the time of her marriage until she died at the age of 59.

Zhadovskaia's poetry also deserves a fresh look. In short and deceptively simple poems about nature, love, folklore, and religion, Zhadovskaia creates a complex female persona, one who is isolated and wounded by love, yet spiritually self-sufficient; who finds consolation in nature, yet who cannot forget that nature is fundamentally other, alien to humanity; who appears to write with complete unself-consciousness, yet who is also aware of her obscurity as a poet while taking pride in her achievement. There is an eerie, glittery quality to the poems in which Zhadovskaia presents a *rusalka* (a female figure of Russian folklore) and a dead woman as sister selves ("Rusalka," and "You Asked Why I . . . " ["Ty sprosila, otchego ia"]). Her poems of despair ("A Difficult Hour," ["Tiazhelyi chas,"]; "Alas! I Also Like Prometheus," ["Uvy! i ia kak Prometei"]) are as compact, dense, and powerful as those of Gerard Manley Hopkins or Emily Dickinson.

Zhadovskaia's prosody also needs to be re-evaluated. Critics have repeatedly complained of Zhadovskaia's technical incompetence, awkwardness, unevenness, prosaicness, and bad rhymes, yet several of her poems were set to music: one by ten different composers, another by fourteen.[31] Clearly, Zhadovskaia could write smooth poetry when she chose. I suggest that her sophisticated experiments with prosody were interpreted as incompetence. Zhadovskaia withholds the final rhyme in "You will soon forget me" ("Ty skoro menia pozabudesh' "), very effectively uses half rhyme ("At Twilight" ["V sumerki"]; "Now It's Not the Same" ["Teper' ne to"]) and blank verse ("A Difficult Hour" ["Tiazhelyi chas"]), writes in meter of anything from two feet ("The Water Spirit" ["Vodianoi"]), to six feet ("Evening and Morning" ["Vecher i utro"]), to alternating four and three ("I Weep" ["Ia plachu"]), and in anything from five-line folk stanzas ("For Many Years My Bark Has Been Carried" ["Mnogo let lad'iu moiu nosilo"]) to an elegant Shakespearean sonnet ("Evening" ["Vecher"]).

NADEZHDA TEPLOVA

While the literary reputations of Kul'man and Zhadovskaia have been made to conform to potentially pornographic female stereotypes (the virgin, the woman in bondage), that of Nadezhda Teplova (1814–1848) resembles the invisible woman or wall flower, the woman who is ignored because she arouses no sexual interest. Critics wrote very little about her in the nineteenth century. In the Soviet period, she appeared neither in the standard Soviet bibliography for nineteenth-century Russian writers, K. D. Muratova's *Bibliographic Index* (*Bibliograficheskii ukazatel'*), nor in the *Short Literary Encyclopedia (Kratkaia literaturnaia entsiklopedia)* of 1964, although she did begin to attract some critical attention at the end of the period. Her poetry deserves closer study.

Teplova, who published under her married name of Teriukhina after 1837, came from a merchant family that encouraged her writing; she first appeared in print at the age of thirteen. A family friend, the Ukrainian historian Mikhail Maximovich, arranged for the appearance of her poetry in a wide range of journals and for three collections of her poetry, one posthumous.

Reviews of Teplova's work are few, short, and usually condescending. A short, anonymous review in the 1830s referred to her work as "sweet" (*milyi*) seven times; Belinsky chose "at random" one poem of hers—"To my sister," which he then pronounced "puerile." A third reviewer (Longinov) in the 1860s praised Teplova for her "modest" inspiration, for bringing her "mite, although small, to the general treasury of poetry" and for not burying "even a small talent."[32]

At the end of the Soviet period, Teplova appeared in one study and two anthologies, but she remained a shadowy figure. One critic conceded that "at times her verses attained a rather high level of technical mastery," but criticized her work as "purely romantic" (in socialist realist criticism, this indicates an unacceptable lack of class politics).[33] Another critic called her outlook "unduly pessimistic."

I suggest that Teplova has been ignored because of her woman-centered subject matter, which male critics may have considered uninteresting. The 1860 edition of her poetic works, *Stikhotvoreniia Nadezhdy Teplovoi* (Moscow, 1860), contains close to twenty poems addressed to women. These include three very moving poems to her sister (pp. 18, 25, 29), including the one Belinsky described as "puerile," several poetic tributes to women she admired (for example, "In Memory of M.A. L-oi" ["V pamiat' M.A. L-oi"]), and advice to a young woman not to write poetry because of the hostility she will encounter ("Advice" ["Sovet"]). One very passionate poem to a woman, "To E. O. Sh." (K E. O. Sh."), invokes in its first line ("No, I will not forget such happy moments"), Pushkin's famous and equally passionate lyric "I remember the wonderful moment." Like Pushkin, Teplova makes the subject of her poem represent poetic inspiration.

Besides writing many poems to women, Teplova also wrote about subjects seldom found in poetry by men: the death of a spouse ("A Dream" ["Son"]) and the desire to transcend the pain of life on earth (for example, "Regeneration" ["Pererozhdenie"]), a repeated theme. An elegiac mood predominates in much of Teplova's poetry, as it does in the poetry of other Russian woman (for example,

Zhadovskaia and Pavlova). While male critics often reacted to the sorrowful tone with impatience and irritation, I suggest that it might more usefully be seen to reflect both the realities of women's lives and the culmination of a woman's poetic tradition that started with women's lamentation for the dead.[34]

In any case, a great deal more research is needed on Teplova's life and work. It would be useful to know more about her life; how complete and accurate is the 1860 posthumous collection of her poetry edited by Mikhail Maximovich; if she wrote any prose; what became of her letters; and the identity of and her relationships with the various people to whom she wrote poems.

EVDOKIIA ROSTOPCHINA

Evdokiia Rostopchina (1811–1858) was an aristocrat who ran a famous literary salon, wrote novels, short stories, plays, and a novel in verse, in addition to poetry. If Teplova's critical reputation has suffered from a scarcity of critical attention, Rostopchina experienced the opposite problem: She attracted a great deal of attention, much of it hostile.[35]

In the late 1830s, at the height of her literary reputation, Belinsky, Vasily Zhukovsky, and Nikolai Iazykov compared her with Pushkin, while Pletnev called her "the first poet of Russia."[36]

By the 1850s and 1860s, however, the radical critics, Nikolai Chernyshevsky and Nikolai Dobroliubov, were attacking Rostopchina as a dissolute woman. Chernyshevsky was shocked that Rostopchina wrote about enjoying gypsy songs, and Dobroliubov was also shocked that she depicted a woman going around Moscow at midnight, accompanied only by another woman. These critics, who fought against the inequities of class politics, did not extend their analysis to gender politics; they wished to preserve male control of women's sexuality. Indeed, they could safely attack Rostopchina as a woman in order to covertly attack her as an aristocrat.

By 1916, the poet and critic Vladislav Khodasevich expressed embarrassment and incredulity over the praise Rostopchina had received from the poets and critics of the Golden Age. The Soviets rehabilitated her slightly; they anthologized her and even published a separate book of her poetry in which they praised her politically-correct acts (for example, writing a poem in support of the Decembrist uprising), and regretted her later conservatism. They, too, labeled her a "poetess."

This range of critical views says more about the history of literary politics than it does about Rostopchina. I suggest that if we look at Rostopchina in her own terms, we will see neither the first poet of Russia, nor a dissolute woman, nor a literary embarrassment, nor an apostate in the fight for the people's rights; rather, we will find a bright, ambitious woman with very few options, who used them all in the service of a literary career.

Women in early nineteenth-century Russia could attain social success by very few means: beauty, social position (by birth or marriage), or running a literary salon.[37] (It is no coincidence that the two best-known nineteenth-century woman poets—Rostopchina and Pavlova—both had salons.) Rostopchina, who agreed to a marriage of convenience with a count (although at great emotional cost), used beauty and the literary salon as well.

A Soviet critic writes approvingly that Rostopchina "strove to be a poetess, not a poet," citing the "feminine character" of her poetry.[38] In Western terms—which emphasize the cultural over the biological bases of femininity—Rostopchina was successful, because her writing inscribed contemporary gender roles. She instructed women in general and women writers in particular to defer to men in such poems as "To Russian Women" ("Russkim zhenshchinam"), "Pushkin's Notebook" ("Chernovaia kniga Pushkina"), and "How Women Should Write" ("Kak dolzhny pisat' zhenshchiny"). In other poems, her speakers act out feminine weakness, capriciousness, love of clothing, or a passion barely suppressed in the name of female modesty ("Putting on an Albanian costume" ["Nadevaia albanskii kostium"], "The Quarrel" ["Ssora"], "Temptation" ["Iskushenie"]). As the writer Alice Walker would say, Rostopchina was a female impersonator.

Men loved her work because it confirmed their beliefs about women. Women were grateful for any reflection of their experience in poetry. But with the gradual democratization of Russian literature, Rostopchina's poetry of upper-class women's lives became a target for hostile critics who, for example, never would have attacked the equally aristocratic and far more debauched Lermontov on the same grounds.

Rostopchina's work deserves a fresh consideration. There is a fascinating tension between her exhorting women to be modest and self-sacrificing, on the one hand, and her own very successful literary career, on the other. It would be interesting to look for those points in her work where her glorification of the female role breaks down. However, the attacks of the utilitarian critics suggest that she defined the female role less narrowly than they did. In addition, Rostopchina's novel in verse, *A Girl's Diary* (*Dnevnik devushki*)—an intensely written work embedded in citations from now-forgotten contemporary women writers—has been ignored. The work concerns the emotional cost to the heroine of a marriage of convenience, a theme that recurs in Rostopchina's work (for example, her novella "Rank and Money" ["Chiny i den'gi"]) and may have autobiographical overtones.

KAROLINA PAVLOVA

Like her contemporary, Rostopchina, Karolina Pavlova (1807–1893) ran a literary salon, attained social and literary prominence, and suffered sexual and political attacks from the left critics in the 1850s and 1860s.

But while the critics attacked Rostopchina for being dissolute, they attacked Pavlova as an unnatural, affected, insufficiently feminine woman. This may have been because her poetry did not lend itself to such adjectives as "sweet" and "sincere." Even at the height of her popularity, Belinsky praised her work for its "manly energy";[39] Heldt details how Ivan Panaev, D. V. Grigorovich, Ivan Aksakov, and others later attacked Pavlova as affected and unwomanly because she took herself seriously as a poet.[40] Pavlova was also attacked by such left critics as Saltykov-Shchedrin for being an unprogressive Slavophile and adherent of "art for art's sake."[41]

In 1853, Pavlova left Russia to spend the last forty years of her life near Dresden, where she died in poverty and obscurity. Some of the obituaries mentioned that she left a trunk of unpublished manuscripts, but nothing further was heard of them.

Pavlova differs from Rostopchina in that her reputation has continued to rise and fall. At the turn of the century, the Russian symbolists (believers in art for art's sake) rediscovered and rehabilitated her.[42] The well-known symbolist poet Valerii Briusov edited a two-volume edition of Pavlova's work (1915), which, in turn, inspired more biographical and critical writing about her. After the Revolution, however, the Soviets reconsigned her to oblivion since they, like the radical critics, considered her "unprogressive." The Soviets did publish her works twice (1939, 1964), the last time as a volume in the prestigious Poet's Library (Biblioteka poeta) series. In the introduction, however, Pavlova was described as "not first rate, but all the same somewhat noteworthy," and no other Soviet scholarship on Pavlova appeared.[43] Renewed Western interest in Pavlova starting with Sendich's work, led the Soviets to re-evaluate her in the 1970s.[44]

Russian women poets, however, have always held Pavlova in the highest regard. Cherubina de Gabriak cited Pavlova as an influence;[45] Sofiia Parnok wrote a poem to her; and Marina Tsevtaeva named a poetry collection *Craft* (*Remeslo*) after one of Pavlova's most famous poems in which she described poetry as her "sacred craft."[46] Anna Akhmatova cites the same Pavlova poem in "Nashe sviashchennoe remeslo" ("Our Holy Craft").

Pavlova's biggest contrast with Rostopchina consists of Pavlova's impatience with imposed female passivity, a characteristic that may have contributed both to her "unfeminine" reputation and to her popularity with other Russian women poets. While Rostopchina appeared to revel in the feminine role, Pavlova directly protested against the strictures that made it almost impossible for a woman to be strong and creative. She did so in a series of works spanning twenty years and in the name of ordinary as well as gifted women.

In "Jeanne d'Arc" (1839), a poem she wrote in French, she compares Joan of Arc, just before her execution, to a woman artist of genius for whom society has no use. In "Three Souls" ("Tri dushi," 1845), she depicts a sadistic God who plants the souls of three women poets (Maria Davidson, Delphine Gay, and herself) on hostile soil where they cannot develop their talents, and then commands them not to complain. In *A Double Life* (*Dvoinaia zhizh'*, 1848) she shows how an ordinary woman's creativity is destroyed by her stifling up-bringing.[47] In *Quadrille* (*Kvadril'*, 1859), she describes five women's power-lessness in their relationships with men.

Those critics who do not attack Pavlova as unwomanly often accept her as a minor, honorary male writer. Until Heldt's pioneering work, no one had con-sidered Pavlova's struggles as a woman poet, nor had anyone looked at *A Double Life* from a feminist perspective. Pavlova's other works on women's position in society—although only a small part of her oeuvre—also deserve more attention. In addition, while excellent scholarship traces the influences on Pavlova's life and work of male historical and literary figures (Mickiewicz, Nikolai Pavlov, Boris Utin, Humboldt, Novalis, Baratynsky, A. K. Tolstoy), very little has been written on the women she knew and the women writers who influenced her. Such scholarship might put Pavlova's work into a different perspective.

Despite the tremendous differences among these five poets, some common-alities exist: None belonged to any school of poetry; those who did not run salons needed a male protector or "agent"; much of their prosody is unconventional or experimental, perhaps because their outsider status in the literary establishment gave them more freedom; much of the work of four of them has been lost.

The most significant commonality, however, is in their treatment by male critics who seemed determined to relegate them to a separate and unequal sphere of literature. At best, they were condescendingly praised as "sincere" (that is, artless). Their innovations were labeled incompetence; their competence, when incontrovertible, was labeled monstrous or unwomanly; their protests against women's position in society were ignored, as were any works that did not deal with men. They were often punished for their presumption in writing poetry by being reduced to the sexual objects of domination fantasies.

Feminist critics have the opportunity to free these and other women writers from stereotypes that have distorted, obscured, and marginalized their work. Our reward is the recovery of a literature of great meaning: one that presents women as subject, women's experience as the norm, one in which all women can experience our humanity more intensely, because it combines the vast dif-ferences of time, place, and culture with shocks of recognition; strange worlds with resonances of our deepest feelings.

NOTES

1. My thanks to Mary Zirin for invaluable help. Mirsky, *A History of Russian Lit-erature from Its Beginnings to 1900* (New York: Vintage, 1958), mentions one nineteenth-century Russian woman poet; Soviet anthologies: A. Krakovskaia and S. Chulkov, eds., *Russkaia poeziia XIX veka* (Moscow, 1974), no women; S. M. Petrov, ed., *Istoriia russkoi literatury XIX veka* (Moscow, 1970), no women; Nikolai Bannikov, ed., Tri veka russkoi poezii (Moscow, 1968), no women; L. Ia Ginzberg, *Poety 1820–1830 godov* (Leningrad, 1972), 1, one woman, 2, no women; N. M. Gaidenkov, *Russkie poety XIX veka* (Moscow, 1974), three women out of forty-eight mentioned.

2. See Munir Sendich's fine series of articles on Karolina Pavlova; Barbara Heldt,

Terrible Perfection (Bloomington: Indiana University Press, 1987), (Bunina, Teplova, Pavlova); Heldt, "Karolina Pavlova: The Woman Poet and the Double Life," in *Pavlova, A Double Life* (Oakland, CA: Barbary Coast, 1978); Marina Ledkovsky, Charlotte Rosenthal, and Mary Zirin, *A Dictionary of Russian Women Writers* (Greenwood, forthcoming).

3. E. P. Rostopchina Talisman: *Izbranaia lirika*, ed., V. Afanas'ev (Moscow, 1987); N. V. Bannikov, *Russkie poetessy XIX veka* (Moscow, 1979); M. Sh. Fainshtein, *Pisatel'nitsy pushkinskoi pory* (Leningrad, 1989). P. A. Nikolaev's multivolume *Russkie pisateli*, 1800–1917 (Moscow, 1989), recovers many women writers, as does B. Ia Bukhshtab, *Russkie pisateli 1840–50 godov* (Leningrad, 1972). Fainshtein is particularly offensive, referring to Kul'man, Teplova, Rostopchina, and Pavlova by their first names and devoting a great deal of space to their physical appearances and relations with men. M. Sh. Fainshtein, *Pisatel'nitsy pushkinskoi pory* (Leningrad, 1989), 11, 91, 106, 110, 118.

4. On poetesses and women poets, see Svetlana Boym, *Death in Quotation Marks* (Cambridge, MA: Harvard University Press, 1991), 192–196, and Cora Kaplan, "Language and Gender," in *Sea Changes* (London: Verso, 1986), 89–93.

5. Sandra Gilbert and Susan Gubar, *The Madwoman in the Attic* (New Haven: Yale University Press, 1979). See Jane Costlow's chapter in this volume. For Russian women writers' adoption of George Sand as a role model, see Lesley Herrmann, "George Sand and the Nineteenth-Century Novel" (Ph.D. diss., Columbia University, 1979), and M. G., "Russkaia zhenshchina 30-x godov," *Russkaia mysl'* 32 (December 1911): 54–73.

6. Belinsky, for example, in his widely cited article, "Sochineniia Zeneidy R-voi (1843)," discussed several women writers, among them Zinaida Volkonskaia, Mar'ia Lisitsyna, and Anna Gotovtsova, whose poetry he condescendingly dismissed as "the poetic knitting of stockings, rhymed sewing." (*Sobranie sochinenii* [Moscow, 1955–59], 7, 654. All subsequent Belinsky citations are to this edition.) Negative images of women writers can be found in "Perepiska sestry s bratom," *Zvezdochka* 4 (October 1845): 27–48; M. Korsini, *Zhenshchina-Pisatel'nitsa: komediia v trekh deistviiakh* (St. Petersburg, 1849); "Zhenshchina-pisatel'nitsa: Fantasticheskii razskaz," *Syn otechestva* (April 8, 1856): 7–11.

7. Emil' Montegiu, "O zhenshchinakh poetakh v serernoi amerike," *Biblioteka dlia chteniia* 108 (1851): 124–33. This and all subsequent translations are mine.

8. Barbara Heldt, *Terrible Perfection* (Bloomington: Indiana University Press, 1987), 2, 105.

9. Many other significant nineteenth-century women poets have been neglected or forgotten, among them Zinaida Volkonskaia, Anna Bunina, Anna Gotovtsova, Nadezhda Khvoshchinskaia, and Mar'ia Lisitsyna. For bibliography, see K. D. Muratova, *Istoriia russkoi literatury XIX veka: Bibliograficheskii ukazatel'* (Leningrad, 1962); Katharina Wilson, *An Encyclopedia of Continental Women Writers* (New York: Garland, 1991); and Ledkovsky, Rosenthal, and Zirin.

10. M. Sh. Fainshtein, *Pisatel'nitsy pushkinskoi pory* (Leningrad, 1989), 23.

11. Grossheinrikh discusses his negative feelings about rhyme, which influenced Kul'man, in *Biblioteka dlia chteniia* 4 (1849): 112–13.

12. Kul'man scholarship cited: K. V. Grossheinrikh, "Elisaveta Kul'man i ee stikhotvoreniia," *Biblioteka dlia chteniia* 94:4 (April 1849) 3, 69–117, and 95:5 (May 1849) 3, 1–119; A. V. Nikitenko, "Zhizneopisanie devitsy Elisavety Kul'man," in *Piiticheskie opyty Elisavety Kul'man v trekh chastiakh*, (St. Petersburg, 1839), i–xxiv; A. B. Druzhinin, *Sobranie sochinenii* (St. Petersburg, 1865), 6, 131–37; E. S. Nekrasova, "Eli-

zaveta Kul'man,'' *Istoricheskii vestnik* 12 (1886): 551–79; ''Dnevnik Vil'g. Karl. Kiukhel'bekera,'' *Russkaia starina* 2 (1884): 351–55.

13. Belinsky, *Sobranie sochinenii*, II, 81; IV, 571.

14. A. V. Nikitenko, ''Zhizneopisanie devitsy Elisavety Kul'man,'' in *Piiticheskie opyty Elisavety Kul'man v trekh chastiakh* (St. Petersburg, 1839), xxi.

15. Fainshtein, *Pisatel'nitsy pushkinskoi pory*, 15.

16. E. S. Nekrasova, ''Elizaveta Kul'man,'' *Istoricheskii vestnik* no. 12 (1886), 575.

17. Aleksandr Druzhinin, *Sobranie sochinenii* (St. Petersburg, 1865), 134–36.

18. Interestingly, Druzhinin was considered an advocate for women because of his ''problem'' novel, *Polin'ka Saks* (1847). Dead virgin poets were popular in the United States as well. See Twain's parody in *Huckleberry Finn*, ch. 17, and, for the cult of Lucretia Maria Davidson, my ''Pavlova's 'Tri dushi','' *Proceedings of the Kentucky Foreign Language Conference* (Lexington, KY, 1984), 18.

19. ''Dnevnik Vil'g. Karl. Kiukhel'bekera,'' *Russkaia starina* no. 2 (1884), 352.

20. Fainshtein, *Pisatel'nitsy pushkinskoi pory*, 6–24.

21. ''Nartsiss,'' Piiticheskie opyty, 1, 27. ''Korinna,'' 2, 66–71; ''Safo,'' 84–88; see Jane Snyder, *The Woman and the Lyre: Women Writers in Classical Greece and Rome* (Carbondale, IL: Southern Illinois University Press, 1989), 1–37, 41–54.

22. See Natalie Moyle [Kononenko], ''Mermaids (Rusalki) and Russian Beliefs about Women,'' *New Studies in Russian Language and Literature*, ed. Anna Crone and Catherine Chvany (Columbus, OH: Slavica, 1986), 221–38.

23. K. V. Grossheinrikh, ''Elisaveta Kul'man i ee stikhotvoreniia,'' *Biblioteka dlia chteniia* 95:5 (May, 1849) III, 5, 18.

24. Zhadovskaia criticism cited: A. Skabichevskii, ''Pesni o zhenskoi nevole,'' *Sochineniia* (St. Petersburg, 1895), 2, 544–60; P. A. Pletnev, ''Stikhotvoreniia Iulii Zhadovskoi,'' *Sochineniia i perepiska* (St. Petersburg, 1885), 2, 542–46; N. A. Dobroliubov, ''Stitkhotvoreniia Iulii Zhadovskoi,'' *Sobranie sochinenii* (Moscow, 1962), 3, 133–47; V. N. Maikov, *Sochineniia* 1, 96–102, (Kiev, n.d.); D. I. Pisarev, ''Stikhotvoreniia Iulii Zhadovskoi,'' *Sochinenii* (St. Petersburg, 1909), 1, 4–6; V. A. Blagovo, ''Poeziia Iulii Zhadovskoi'' (Ph.D. diss., Hertzen Institute, Leningrad, 1975); N. Fedorova, ''Vospominanie ob Iu. V. Zhadovskoi,'' *Istoricheskii vestnik*, 8 (November 1887), 394–407. Poetry: Zhadovskaia, *Polnoe sobranie sochinenii* (St. Petersburg, 1894).

25. A. Skabichevskii, ''Pesni o zhenskoi nevole,'' *Sochineniia* (St. Petersburg, 1895), 2: 551.

26. Ia Bukhshtab, *Russkie pisateli 1840–50 godov* (Leningrad, 1972), 272.

27. N. V. Bannikov, *Russkie poetessy XIX veka* (Moscow, 1987), 120.

28. Ia Bukhshtab, *Russkie pisateli 1840–50 godov* (Leningrad, 1972), 271.

29. Bannikov, 119.

30. S. A. Vengerov, ed., *Pushkin* (St. Petersburg, 1911), 5, ix–x; Pushkin, *Sobranie sochinenii* (Leningrad, 1941), 14 (letters 388, 396): 27, 35.

31. Bukhshtab, *Russkie pisateli 1840–50 godov*, 495–96.

32. Teplova criticism cited: ''Stikhotvoreniia Nadezhdy Teplovoi,'' *Severnaia pchela* 175 (1834): 697–98; Belinsky, ''Sochineniia Zeneidy R-voi''; M. Longinov, ''Stikhotvoreniia Nadezhdy Teplovoi,'' *Russkii vestnik* 10 (February 1861): 917–19; Poems: ''Stikhotvoreniia Nadezhdy Teplovoi'' (Moscow, 1860).

33. Bukhshtab, *Russkie pisateli 1840–50 godov*, 81.

34. See Natalie Kononenko's chapter in this volume.

35. Rostopchina criticism cited: Chernyshevsky, ''Stikhotvorenie grafinii Rostopchi-

noi," *Sovremennik* 56 (1856): ot. 4, 1–18; Dobroliubov, "U pristani," *Sobranie sochi-nenii* 1, 423–39; Vladislav Khodasevich, "Grafina E. P. Rostopchina," *Russkaia mysl'* 11 (1916): 35–53. Works: Rostopchina, *Talisman* (Moscow, 1987); *Dnevnik devushki* (St. Petersburg, 1866).

36. E. Rostopchina, *Talisman* (Moscow, 1987), 7.

37. William Todd, *Fiction and Society in the Age of Pushkin* (Cambridge, MA: Harvard University Press, 1986), 55–72.

38. Viktor Afanas'ev, "Da zhenskaia dusha dolzhna v teni svetit'siia," *Talisman* (Moscow, 1987), 9.

39. Belinsky, *Sobranie sochinenii*, III, 191.

40. Barbara Heldt, "Karolina Pavlova," in *Karolina Pavlova: A Double Life* (Berkeley: Barbary Coast, 1986), iv–ix.

41. For an account of her salon, see Sendich, "Moscow Literary Salons," *Die Welt der Slaven* 17 (1972): 341–57; for attacks against her, Heldt, "Karolina Pavlova." Pavlova criticism cited: M. E. Saltykov-Shchedrin, "Stikhotvoreniia K. Pavlovoi," *Sovremennik* 94:6 (1863), 311–16; Sendich, "Karolina Pavlova: A Survey of her Poetry," *Russian Literature Triquaterly* 3 (1972): 229–48. P. Gromov, "Karolina Pavlova," *Polnoe sobranie stikhotvorenii*, (Moscow, Leningrad, 1964), 5–72.

42. Munir Sendich, "Karolina Pavlova: A Survey of her Poetry," *Russian Literature Triquarterly* 3 (1972), 229–48.

43. Pavel Gromov, "Karolina Pavlova," in *Polnoe sobranie stikhotvorenii* (Moscow, Leningrad, 1964), 72.

44. V. K. Zontikov, "Pishu ne smelo ia, ne chasto," in *Vstrechi s proshlym: sbornik materialov TsGALI* (Moscow, 1982), 35–39. E. Lebedev, "Poznan'ia rokovaia chasha," in *Karolina Pavlova: Stikhotvoreniia* (Moscow, 1985), 5–38.

45. Elisaveta Vasil'eva [Gabriak], "Dve veshchi," *Novyi mir* 12 (1988): 132–70.

46. Heldt, *Terrible Perfection*, 118–19.

47. *A Double Life* is a formally unique work in which prose and poetry alternate. "At the Tea Table" ("Za chainym stolom," 1859), although a prose work (it is Pavlova's only story), should be mentioned as part of this series as well; in it Pavlova shows the connection between class and gender oppression.

7

Women Physicians' Autobiography in the Nineteenth Century[1]

Toby W. Clyman

Since the mid 1970s we have witnessed a growing interest in the specificity and recovery of women's autobiographical writings. Scholars have shown that women autobiographers write differently from men but similarly to women of other nations, and that definitions of the genre have been based solely on men's autobiographies.[2] Such studies have prompted a re-evaluation of the genre and of the canon that excluded women's self-writings. Existing critical and theoretical works on women's autobiography, however, have focused mostly on Western and Third World texts. Except for Barbara Heldt's chapter on Russian women's autobiography, and the chapters in this collection,[3] to my knowledge there are no other studies that center on the specificity of Russian women's autobiographical writing.[4]

Russian literature abounds in autobiographical works by women. The five-volume bibliography of prerevolutionary Russian memoir literature is striking for the number of autobiographical texts by women it lists, variously titled "Reminiscences," "Recollections," "Notes," "Family Chronicles," "Diaries," "Autobiographies," and so on.[5] These designations do not demarcate formal distinctions of genre. The terms were used interchangeably, and "memoir" was the umbrella term that stressed the documentary nature of the reminiscences.

The first known autobiographies by women in Russia were written in the eighteenth century. Their numbers were few and were penned exclusively by women of the elite.[6] By contrast, the nineteenth century, especially the second half, produced a plethora of autobiographical writings by women from a broad segment of society. This phenomenon is largely the result of women's advance in education[7] and Russia's interest in the past manifested in the proliferation of journals publishing autobiographical writings.[8] Moreover, as one critic wrote, "memoirs made no great claim to higher artistic achievement; consequently, women could write in the genre without threatening male hegemony or offering claims to competition."[9]

A new kind of professional women's autobiography, other than that written by women authors, actresses, school teachers and governesses, appears in the second half of the nineteenth century—memoirs by women physicians. Alexander II (1855–1881) officially authorized medical courses for women in 1873. Ten years later, Russia graduated more women doctors than did France, England, and Germany combined.[10] Many of these graduate physicians left a rich and highly engaging memoir literature of the years they spent in medical school abroad and in Russia, and of their work as city (*duma*) and village (*zemstvo*) physicians.[11] In this chapter I focus on the memoirs of the city (*duma*) and village (*zemstvo*) women doctors: female physicians employed by self-governing city and village boards charged with the administration of hospitals ministering to the urban poor or village peasants, respectively.

These texts were published in widely read journals such as *European Messenger* (*Vestnik Evropy*), *Journal for Everyone* (*Journal dlia vsekh*), and *Russian Thought* (*Russkaia mysl'*). The second half of the century was a time of social consciousness, and the Russian reading public was anxious to learn from the physicians' first-hand experience with the less fortunate Russian populace. Of course, the women *duma* and *zemstvo* doctors were not the only ones to publish their accounts. Their male counterparts also wrote of their experiences with the poor and indigent. One sharp distinction, however, sets their recollections apart. The women writing their recollections were acutely conscious of how they were perceived as women and physicians. This awareness had a great impact on the memoirs they wrote.

Before turning to examine their recollections, we need to look at some relevant historical background. Russia first opened its university doors to all women auditors in 1861. Two years later, to the delight of those who opposed women's higher education, the women were categorically forbidden to attend, largely because of the growing student demonstrations and unrest. Barred from the universities at home, they went to Europe, mostly to Zurich, to study medicine.[12]

One lone female, Varvara Aleksandrovna Kashevarova (1842–1898), an orphan from a poor family and illiterate until the age of 13, managed, in an unprecedented move, to get official permission to stay on and complete her studies at the prestigious Medical-Surgical Academy in St. Petersburg. In 1868 she became the first woman in Russia to receive a medical degree. Dr. Kashevarova-Rudneva left a brief but fascinating autobiography that she wrote for her medical-school yearbook on the occasion of the twenty-fifth anniversary of her class graduation.[13] Because she had overstepped traditional boundaries and challenged deeply entrenched cultural values, she was attacked in the conservative press and made the butt of satire. Her abilities were questioned, and her private life was besmirched and brought under public scrutiny.[14] She uses the occasion of her autobiography to tell her own story and to validate her accomplishments.

Although Kashevarova graduated in 1868, medical courses for women in Russia did not officially open until 1873. The number of applicants far exceeded the available places. To be admitted, the woman had to be twenty years of age, have a gymnasium diploma, pass an entrance exam, and have the permission of a parent or husband. Many who could not get parental permission entered into fictitious marriages to overcome this stumbling block.[15]

A number of factors and social movements motivated individual women to seek a medical career. The Russian feminist movement in the 1850s and 1860s emphasized higher education and professional training in particular; women's magazines began to appear during that period championing higher education for women and professional training in medicine. The populist movement of the 1860s and 1870s advocated service "to the people," meaning the poor and downtrodden. Moreover, the intellectual atmosphere following the Crimean War (1853–1854) imbued medicine with special significance. Education and society looked to learning as the key to social progress. The younger generation exalted the sciences as the true source of knowledge and the panacea for Russia's social ills. The study of medicine offered a fortuitous combination of science and service to the people. There were also economic considerations. With the increase of government-supported public education, governess positions became scarce, and medicine was the only other socially acceptable avenue of support left for the impoverished gentry women. Initially, the applicants were mostly from the aristocracy. But by the end of the century, all classes were represented, although the gentry predominated.

The first women graduates could readily find positions where they could apply their skills.[16] With the abolition of serfdom in 1861 and the establishment of *zemstvo* and *duma* hospitals and clinics, the already-existing shortage of physicians was exacerbated. In the 1860s and 1870s, Russia had expanded its empire southeast into the Kirgiz region, where the population was mostly Moslem, and their religion forbade women to be treated medically by male personnel. The *zemstvo* and *duma* encouraged women graduate physicians to apply. As Jeanette Tuve noted, "a woman doctor was better than no doctor at all."[17]

The working conditions of the *zemstvo* and *duma* doctor were abysmal, and the pay was low. While the Petersburg public refused to accept the woman physician, the government offered special stipends to women to take their skills to those distant lands. By the end of the century, however, increasing competition for medical appointments had generated considerable antagonism toward women physicians from the lower ranks of the medical profession. Until 1883 women physicians had no legal status and could not practice independently. To write a prescription, they had to have a male doctor's signature, but the male doctors often challenged the women's medical qualifications and refused to sign their prescriptions.[18]

The autobiographical works I examine reflect these historical realities. I focus on four representative memoirs that I find especially interesting.[19] I note their literary characteristics, point out features these texts share, and, where applicable, indicate how they differ from the recollections of their male counterparts. I note also the memoirist's self-image as it emerges in her writings and show the extent to which her awareness of how she is viewed as female and physician shapes the content and form of her recollections.

E. V. SLANSKAIA

Dr. E. V. Slanskaia's memoir, "House Calls: A Day in the Work of a Woman Duma Doctor in St. Petersburg" ("Po vizitam: Den' dumskogo zhenshchiny-vracha v S. Peterburge"), was originally published in the journal *European Messenger* in 1894, and re-issued, posthumously, in 1904, in a separate, hard-cover edition, together with letters from grateful readers.[20] We have little information about Dr. Slanskaia's life, except what we glean from her memoir. Judging from this work, we can assume she was of the gentry class, was well educated, had completed medical school in the 1880s, and shortly thereafter, accepted a position as a *duma* doctor.

In her memoir, Slanskaia assumes the role of chronicler, physician, teacher, and, somewhat cautiously, of self-conscious artist. "I have focused on these house calls," she writes, "because they are more interesting."[21] Slanskaia takes as her literary model the physiological sketch used by the writers of the Russian Natural School of the 1840s.[22] Like these writers, she describes the slums of Petersburg and their inhabitants and depicts in minute detail, as in slow-motion cinematography, the dilapidated tenements with their dark stairways filled with debris and putrid odors and the dingy, crowded rooms where her patients and their families occupy small rented spaces. Like the characters in the physiological sketch, the people she encounters in her practice speak the language suited to their class and stations. She denigrates the "have's," the cultured class of the city, as do the writers of the Natural School. As in the physiological sketches, the structure of Slanskaia's memoir is episodic, composed of separate sketches, each describing her encounters with individuals or groups of people she met during the day's work.

Slanskaia's presentation of interactions between people merits attention. Like most *duma* and *zemstvo* women doctors, she relates to her patients and those she encounters in her practice in a connected, intimate manner. She shows special awareness of and sensitivity to the interplay between individuals: old and young, husband and wife, father and daughter, mother and her children, and groups of women. I cite one such example, a scene she paints of a mother interacting with her young children: In this portrait, Slanskaia captures with considerable economy the complex emotions of love, frustration, and solicitude the young mother experiences as she relates to her young. At the same time, Slanskaia lends a certain dignity to this world of women's experiences:

At a table in the corner sits a young woman, apparently the janitor's wife. Her face is sullen. She holds a baby in her arms and two more are on the floor. She uses a small spoon to scoop kasha out of a tiny pot on the table; she keeps the kasha in her mouth for a while, apparently to warm it and to moisten it with her saliva, then shoves it into the baby's mouth. The baby cries, makes swallowing movements, and spits it out. She scrapes it all from his cheeks and chin with her fingers and then shoves it back into his mouth. She does it all quickly and adroitly; all you see is the swiftly moving spoon. She is obviously an experienced hand at this. The woman is so absorbed in what she is doing that she does not notice when I walk in (212).

As a *duma* physician, Slanskaia performs the role of both healer and teacher. Her methods of teaching are noteworthy. Telling a young girl how to change her father's bandages, she says: "Here child, watch.... This is how you will do it later ... first you take a piece of clean gauze, then ... dip it in this water, and then place the gauze this way, on top ... " In another instance, she instructs a young husband how to care for his sick wife: "She needs to have a mustard plaster placed on her side, at first in one place, right here; then a bit lower; then to the side.... Now, can you do it?" (213–14). Dr. Slanskaia instructs by example: "Watch how I do it." This personal, connected way of teaching is characteristic of the women physicians as a group and sharply contrasts with the prescriptive and impersonal method of their male colleagues who distance themselves from their patients, as their memoirs show. Interestingly, Dr. L. M. Vasilevskii, in "Notes of a Zemstvo Physician" ("Zametki zemskogo vracha," 1904), suggesting how to improve the state of hygiene among the villagers, proposes that the *zemstvo* set up special courses for peasants where they will be taught about proper hygiene. "This," Dr. Vasilevskii adds, "would also give the villagers an opportunity to get acquainted with the physicians."[23] The method he proposes, unlike the women's hands-on instruction, is detached and hierarchical.

Slanskaia writes to share with the public what she has learned about the lives and ways of the city poor and, as the title of her memoir indicates, to show the work of a *duma* doctor in the course of a day. She has in mind both the general public and the medical student who aspires to practice among the city underprivileged but knows little about them. Taking the reader along with her, beginning with early morning at her home where she sees ambulatory patients and concluding with the last visit at a patient's home late in the day, Slanskaia describes the lives of the Petersburg underprivileged and notes how she treats their illnesses, teaches them hygiene, and deals with the many obstacles and frustrations she encounters in her practice. In the process, Slanskaia inscribes herself as a self-confident, effective, and caring physician who performs a valuable service to humanity. M. I. Pokrovskaia, in her fictional memoir "How I Was a City Doctor for the Poor" ("Kak ia byla gorodskim vrachem dlia bednykh"), notes: "Our public can not decide if women doctors are useful or bring harm to the profession."[24] Slanskaia, detailing her work with the Petersburg poor, subtly and unobtrusively attempts to set such public doubts to rest.

S. GRIN

Dr. S. Grin's account, "War with Bacilli: Recollections of a Woman Doctor" ("Voina s batsillami: Iz zapisok zhenshchiny vracha"), was published in 1900 in *European Messenger*, the journal that had also published Dr. Slanskaia's memoir.[25] As with Dr. Slanskaia, a bibliographical search revealed no other information about Dr. Grin. What we know about her we learn from the writings of this gifted memoirist and physician. "War with Bacilli," which details her experiences as an epidemiologist sent to contain an epidemic of diphtheria in the outlying villages, has all the earmarks of a good novel.

Its episodic structure is held together by an underlying plot line that recalls the archetypal hero adventure story. Like its hero, Dr. Grin sets out on a journey to unknown lands to accomplish an important mission.[26] On the road she must battle various obstacles to accomplish her task: to destroy the diphtheria virus and rescue the villagers from its deadly jaws. The uncertainty of the outcome adds to the suspense of this narrative. Grin overcomes the obstructions that stand in the way and conquers the dreaded virus. When her mission is accomplished, she leaves. On the way home, the village children climb up with her on the wagon and accompany her part of the way. The women wave to her and tell her how much she will be missed.

But writing about her success presents a problem for Dr. Grin. She faces a double bind. She wants her accomplishments known, but, as culture has it, nice girls do not boast. They are supposed to be humble and silent. Or, as Sidonie Smith, in her book *A Poetics of Women's Autobiography* writes, "If a woman seeks a place in the public arena, she transgresses patriarchal definition of female nature by enacting a scenario of male selfhood; she challenges cultural conceptions of the nature of women and invites public censure."[27] How then does Dr. Grin, who seeks a place in the public arena, avert public censure?

Several mothers come to see her to thank her for saving their children from death. They are grateful to her and want to know her name so they can include her in their prayers. "I told them," she writes, "they should not pray for me, but for those doctors who invented the new medicine," and told them the doctor's names.[28] Dr. Grin devalues her success and de-emphasizes her accomplishments, thereby diminishing the likelihood of public censure.

Consider one other telling example. Trying to persuade a mother to allow her to inject her child with the diphtheria serum, Dr. Grin tells her about all those other children she had cured. "There was no end to my boasting," Dr. Grin notes, "and may God forgive me, for it was meant for a good cause" (615). Showing that she is aware of the inappropriateness of such boasting, she circumvents public disapproval but also manages to make her accomplishments known.

But Grin's accomplishments are hard won. "The barriers *zemstvo* doctors—especially women *zemstvo* doctors—encounter can destroy the best of intentions," writes A. I. Veretennikova in "Notes of a Zemstvo Doctor" ("Zapiski zemskogo vracha").[29] The added difficulties women *zemstvo* physicians confront in their work is a recurrent theme in their memoirs and a focal motif in Grin's recollections. Grin speaks with anger and frustration of the difficulties she confronts "simply because she is a woman." The local administration treats her disrespectfully, they disregard her repeated requests for needed transportation and do not accord her the privileges due her as a physician. "I always have to be on my guard to be sure I get what is coming to me. My male colleagues (*tovarishchi*)," she notes somewhat sarcastically, "do not know of such concerns. But women doctors often tolerate all kinds of adversity because they are meek, because they are women, and not men." Striking out at her reading audience, Grin adds, "What can you expect of these simple folks? Why take offense at them, if even among the educated you constantly hear the familiar saying 'a chicken is not a bird. . . . ' " (601). She alludes to the often-repeated saying, "a woman is not a person and a chicken is not a bird."

Initially, the peasant populace equally fails to grant Dr. Grin the authority and the respect she must have if her mission is to be successful; because she is a woman, the villagers view her as just another peasant woman healer (*znakharka*); they push her around unceremoniously, and when, unlike their *znakharka*, Grin gives orders, makes demands, and travels to different locales to see patients, the village women sneer and mock her behind her back. "I had to be on my guard at all times," Grin writes, lest she lose her patient's respect, a problem her male colleagues would not understand.

"To voice authority a woman must disguise her sexuality," writes a feminist critic.[30] That is precisely what Grin tries to do, albeit unconsciously, in her choice of attire, as the following incident poignantly illustrates. A villager comes to her home one day for some reason and sees her dressed in "a brightly-colored skirt and colorful red blouse." The next day a woman from the same village tells Grin in a hurtful voice: "How come you don't dress nicely when you come to see us? You wear nothing but black. We thought you favor black, but yesterday Pet'ka saw you in a nice dress. Why don't you dress like that when you come to us?" Grin writes, "I told them it was not out of disrespect, but convenience" (649). Actually, Grin has made unconscious choices in her selection of dress. The black attire she wears to visit patients camouflages her sexuality, underplaying it. Were she to dress as she does in the privacy of her home, in the feminine attire that accentuates her sexuality, she would be viewed as a frivolous woman rather than a competent professional. But ultimately, Grin gains the peasants' trust and respect, not because she disguises her sexuality, but because of the concern she shows for her patients and the intimate, personal manner in which she relates to the people.

Grin's personal, "connected" manner of interacting with the populace is especially noteworthy. Like Dr. Slanskaia, Grin, try as she may to keep a distance from the people, becomes involved in their lives, asks personal questions, offers advice, and sympathizes with their plight. She gets angry with the people, scolds them, admonishes them, shows affection for some and disdain for others: Learning that her young driver, a boy of sixteen, plans to have some vodka when they arrive at the next station, she admonishes him, "You are too young to be drinking, you are still a boy." Undaunted by her rebuke, he answers, "Why I'm soon to be married." Hearing this Dr. Grin wants to know why his family is in such a hurry to marry him off. "What is the hurry?" she inquires (644). In response, the young man relates various details about his family and, in the process, evokes a vivid picture of the lives and customs of his peasant milieu.

In another instance, a woman patient confides that her husband sent her to clean the well, though she had been sick all winter. "Why couldn't he go himself?" Grin wants to know. "It isn't woman's work." When the woman informs her of the consequences she would have suffered had she not listened to him, the physician angrily retorts, "If I were in your place, I would have left such a bully" (622). Grin not only assumes the role of physician; she also communicates an incipient feminist consciousness. Moreover, these intimate conversations lend special interest and charm to her memoirs.

A. N. PAEVSKAIA/LUKANINA

Dr. A. N. Paevskaia (née Lukanina, 1843–1908) is known as a prose fiction writer, literary biographer, and memoirist.[31] In 1872 she left Russia to enroll in the medical school in Zurich. Before she completed her studies, the tsar issued an order recalling the women studying in Zurich. Afraid she would be arrested at home because of her associations with radical-political activities, she went to America. There she enrolled at the Women's Medical College in Philadelphia, where she received her medical degree in 1876. Her memoir, "A Year in America" ("God v Amerike"), offers a fascinating view of life in America and of the women's medical institutions from the perspective of this nineteenth-century Russian woman.[32] Back home, during the cholera epidemic in 1882, Dr. Paevskaia volunteered to go out into the rural areas to help contain the epidemic and was sent in charge of a medical team to villages along the Volga River. "A Mission Against Cholera" ("Komandirovka na kholeru"), published in 1902, records her experiences on this, her first professional assignment as a practicing physician.[33]

Traveling from one village locale to another, Paevskaia depicts in vivid detail the physical landscapes of each locale. She gives individualized portraits of the people she encounters on the way and of the medical personnel on her team. Describing the abysmal conditions under which the villagers lived and telling of the hardships and poverty they endured, Paevskaia readily displays her feelings, revealing a wide range and intensity. "When I saw it all . . . my heart stopped"; "On my way home I began to cry bitterly"; "I will never forget what I saw."[34] Such displays of emotions contrast sharply with the officious, arid tone that characterizes the memoirs of the male *zemstvo* physicians.

Structurally, her memoir recalls Dr. Grin's "War with Bacilli." Like the Grin text, the separate episodes that comprise Paevskaia's recollections are held together by a plot line analogous to the Hero Adventure Story with its set components: departure to the unknown land, encounters and battles with obstacles, and the victorious return. Her task accomplished, the epidemic contained, and the villagers freed of the disease, Paevskaia leaves. As in Dr. Grin's memoir, the peasants Paevskaia meets on her way home embrace her warmly and express their gratitude for all she has done for them.

Paevskaia's mission, moreover, is not just successful on a public level, but also on a personal plane. Setting out on her journey, she lacks confidence in her ability to treat cholera and is morbidly afraid of the dreaded disease. She is uncertain if she can gain the peasants' confidence. Nevertheless, Paevskaia confronts these barriers, both internal and external, that block her way. With each confrontation she gains greater strength and self-assurance. Like the hero adventure stories, on a psychological level, "A Mission Against Cholera" is the story of individuation, Paevskaia's journey from bondage to freedom. "Looking at my acquaintants," she writes, "I saw the change in me. I left . . . feeling somewhat ill, and emotionally drained. Now I look at life optimistically and with confidence. . . . I am no longer the same, I know that the surrounding vulgarity will not squelch me, will not draw me in like a bottomless morass. . . . I know that God is alive and my soul is alive as well" (8:93). The experiences on the mission had strengthened her in body and soul, and had empowered her to confront life's vicissitudes.

Unlike the archetypal hero, however, no trumpets greet Dr. Paevskaia on her return. Her accomplishments are not recognized publicly. She does not go back to rewards granted to the victorious hero. But then, her notions of success are different from those of the world in which she lives. Paevskaia knows she does not go back to promotions, public recognition, or material remuneration. Her reward is in knowing that she has helped to save lives and ease people's suffering.

Paevskaia presents herself as a compassionate, moral person with a boundless capacity for self-sacrifice. Describing her initial encounter with an ill patient, she writes: "I knew I had to do what had to be done." Despite her apprehension and dread of cholera, she throws herself into her work, conscious only of the "living human being" whom she "had to save at all cost." Having done "all I could and saved the patient, I stood up, took a deep breath, looked around and wondered where all the fear had gone. It seemed I had experienced such feeling a long, long time ago," she notes (7:132). Paevskaia shows that in exercising self-abnegation, in placing the interest of another before her own, she saves a life and conquers the fears and professional insecurities that blocked her way.

Noting how she interacts with subordinates and solves ethical problems, Paevskaia contrasts her ways of relating to people with those of her colleague, a fifth-year medical student who has joined her team. She tells her medical staff that she does not "wish to lord it over" them; she merely wants them to report to her and to consider her recommendations, for she is responsible for what happens. The medical student is taken aback at such interaction with subordinates. When Paevskaia asks him how he envisions working with the medical staff, he replies, "You and I will see patients and prescribe medication, and the medical assistant will distribute the medicine and administer it to the sick. The nurses will attend to the patients' needs, and the medical orderlies will take care of our needs." His way is hierarchical; hers is egalitarian.

Similarly, the medical student's conception of dealing with peasants differs sharply from hers. He insists they should give orders to the peasants. If they disobey, he tells Paevskaia that the authorities should be called. If necessary, he will use the revolver or send for the militia. The student asks to see the regulations outlining the physician's rights. "I would never think of using force," Paevskaia tells him. "Consider how it will affect the people!" (7:140). She takes into consideration the feelings of the people involved. Her attitude is humane, his is objective and impersonal.[35]

In her recollection, "Notes of a Zemstvo Doctor," A. I. Veretennikova remarks: "Women doctors bring to poorly run and badly equipped zemstvo medicine a sense of dedication, self-sacrifice, and profound empathy."[36] The qualities, Veretennikova notes, women doctors characteristically bring to *zemstvo* medicine, and Paevskaia shows she applies in her work, are religious ideals deeply ingrained in the Russian woman's psyche. They are attributes their culture has long valued and associated with the "good woman." Paevskaia and Veretennikova, as do most women *zemstvo* and urban doctors, show that they exercise these valued female qualities in the service of society. But what, we need ask, prompts these women physicians to emphasize this fact, to make a point of it? Dr. M. I. Pokrovskaia, in her memoir "How I Was a Doctor for City Poor," partly provides the answer. She writes: "I was constantly hearing that a woman can't be a good physician, that any decent 'feltsher' (doctor's assistant) can do the same a woman doctor can do. . . . I wanted to show that a woman physician is more dedicated, more conscientious than her male colleague, that she is not just good but better."[37] Considered less competent than the male, the women define themselves in relation to men. To compensate for the negative view the public holds of women physicians, they need to show that they are "not just good but better."

DORA APTEKMAN

Dora Aptekman (1852–1918) was born in Kharkov, in the Ukraine, to a petit bourgeois family. During her adolescence, she was influenced by her cousin, Osip Aptekman, who subsequently became a major populist leader. In 1872, like so many other idealistic young women, she went to Zurich to study medicine. In Zurich, like Paevskaia, she participated in radical-political activities. When the tsar decreed that the women should return home, Aptekman went to Berne, where she completed her medical degree.

Her memoir, "Recollections of a Zemstvo Physician" ("Zapiski zemskogo vracha") 1884, is an account of the three years she practiced medicine in the villages among the peasants.[38] Like most *zemstvo* physicians, she wrote her recollections to raise the public consciousness about the plight of the peasants. Aptekman divides the text into several sections. In the first section, she gives her curriculum vita. The information she provides, like the structure of her memoir, is revealing.

Aptekman notes that she had chosen medicine as a profession so she could help the people and that she had to make considerable sacrifices to complete her training. (Such personal information is uncommon in *zemstvo* memoirs.) Having described herself as a committed professional, she proceeds to tell what she encountered when she first arrived at her village station, and how she handled the many vicissitudes of *zemstvo* practice. The peasants, she notes, readily accepted her presence for they were accustomed to women healers, and the women actually told her they were pleased the administration had sent them a woman. It was easier, they said, to talk to a woman. Although her knowledge of country life was derived mostly from books and the reality in the villages did not always correspond to what she had read about it, Aptekman nevertheless had no difficulty adjusting. When she was told, soon after she arrived, that she was responsible for administrative and custodial matters at the clinic, in addition to treating patients in several localities under her supervision, she was not especially daunted, even though she knew nothing of such practical household needs, never having had to take care of such matters at home or at the university. She soon learned what she had to know. Nor was she upset by the many hazards she encountered on treacherous winter roads traveling from one locale to another to visit patients. "I am not one of those easily frightened," she tells the reader.[39]

Aptekman undercuts the public notion that the peasants would not accept a woman doctor, that women are flippant, and that women are incapable of applying themselves to the rigors of a medical profession.[40] In the first section, she debunks the public myths about women and physicians and establishes her own credentials. She then proceeds to tell about the lives and ways of the peasants, to comment about the state of *zemstvo* medicine, and to note factors society needs to change for *zemstvo* medicine to be more effective. Aptekman feels she must first establish herself as a credible adult and competent professional to ensure that her observations are taken seriously. Like Slanskaia, Grin, and Lukanina, Aptekman reveals her understanding of how she is being read as a woman and physician.

Working in a male profession, these physicians are ever-conscious of their femaleness. They use the occasion of writing their memoirs—telling what they learned and experienced in their work with the indigent and poor—to authenticate themselves. They shatter the distorted cultural hall of mirrors and construct an identity different from the one defined by their culture.

It might be appropriate now to ask how these women doctors were depicted in nineteenth-century canonical literature. By the end of the century, Russia had graduated a sizable number of women doctors. Many had made impressive contributions to science. Their work during the Russo-Turkish War (1878–1887) was well publicized and lauded in the newspapers. Their memoirs, as noted earlier, were published in widely read journals. The public was cognizant of women doctors and their work. Yet, with the exception of the writer Anton Chekhov, himself a physician, nineteenth-century Russian classical writers made few references to women doctors. How does Chekhov depict women physicians?

In "Good People" ("Khoroshie Liudi"), 1886, a story in which a woman doctor plays a focal role, Chekhov describes her as follows:

Having finished medical school, she got married. Practical medicine did not appeal to her; it did not satisfy her, it tired her. Besides, she did not give the impression of being knowledgeable. I never heard her say anything that relates to her studies. She left medicine and dispassionately waited for the years to pass. She was indifferent to everything except her brother, whom she loved dearly. When he was writing, she generally sat next to him watching the movements of his hand, not taking her eyes off him. At such times she looked like a large animal warming herself in the sun.[41]

The women physicians' accounts stand in sharp contrast to such negative literary depictions of the woman doctor. They wrote their memoirs against such deflation of their reputation, for they knew what the nineteenth-century English philosopher John Stuart Mill so elegantly wrote: "We may safely assert that the knowledge men acquire of women—even as they have been and are, without reference to what they might be—is wretchedly imperfect and superficial and will always be so until women themselves have told all they have to tell."[42]

NOTES

1. Autobiography does not readily lend itself to generic definition. I use the term "autobiography," in the sensible way Jelinek has defined it, "as a work each autobiographer writes with the intention of its being her life story, whatever form or content or style it takes. It includes works titled "recollections," "memoir," "family chronicles," "notes," and so on, but not "letters" and "diaries." See Estelle C. Jelinek, *Women's Autobiography* (Boston: Twayne Publishers, 1986), xii.

The term "autobiography" was first used in Russia in the early part of the nineteenth century. See Toby W. Clyman's entry, "Autobiography" in *Handbook of Russian Literature*, ed. Victor Terras (New Haven: Yale University Press, 1985).

2. Ibid., xiii. See also Estelle C. Jelinek, *Women's Autobiography: Essays in Criticism* (Bloomington: Indiana University Press, 1980), 1–20.

3. "Women's Autobiography in Russia" in Barbara Heldt, *Terrible Perfection: Women and Russian Literature* (Bloomington: Indiana University Press, 1987), 64–87. See also in this volume Beth Holmgren, "For the Good of the Cause: Russian Women's Autobiography in the Twentieth Century."

4. Concerning the reasons for the paucity of critical studies of Russian women's literature in general, both in Russia and in the West, see the "Introduction" in this volume.

5. *Istoriia do revoliutsionnoi Rossii v dnevnikakh i vospominaniiakh, annotirovnnyi ukazatel' knig i publikatsii v zhurnalakh*, 5 vols. (Moscow, 1976).

6. The two best-known eighteenth-century autobiographies by women in public life are the memoirs of Catherine II (1729–1796) and those of Princess Ekaterina Dashkova (1743–1810), president of the Academy of Sciences. The earliest written eighteenth-century woman's autobiography is the recollections of Princess Natalia Dolgorukaia (1714–1771). Another notable eighteenth-century woman's autobiography is G. I. Rzhevskaia, "Pamiatnye zapiski," tr. from Fr., *Russkii arkhiv* (1871): 1–52. Rzhevskaia (1758–

1826), in her autobiography, was among the first to write about the closed Smolnyi Institute where young women of the elite spent most of their formative years (ages 8–16) under strict supervision and in seclusion from the outside world. The memoirs of the *institutka* comprise a large and rich nineteenth-century women's memoir literature.

7. Prior to the great reforms of Alexander II (1856–1861) only one-tenth of one percent of the female population attended primary schools. The only institutions beyond primary education were the girls' boarding schools where the elite sent their daughters. In 1858, secondary schools for women of all estates were opened. By 1868, there were 125 with an enrollment of 1,000. See Christine Johanson, *Women's Struggle for Higher Education in Russia, 1855–1900* (Montreal: McGill-Queen's University Press, 1987), 29.

8. For a listing of journals that published memoir literature in the second half of the century, see *Entsiklopidecheskii slovar'*, vol. 7 (St. Petersburg, 1894), 64–65.

9. Jane Marcus, ''Invincible Mediocrity: The Private Selves of Public Women,'' in *The Private Self: Theory and Practice of Women's Autobiographical Writings*, ed. Shari Benstock (Chapel Hill: University of North Carolina Press, 1987), 120.

10. See Christine Johanson, 90.

11. Two highly fascinating autobiographies by Russian women physicians detailing their experiences as medical students abroad are A. N. Lukanina, ''A Year in America'' (''God'v Amerike''), *Vestnik Evropy*, 16, 8 (1881): 621–66; 16, 9 (1881): 31–78; 17, 4 (1881): 495–538; 17, 6 (1882): 503–45, also published in book form as *God v Amerike: Iz vospominanii zhenshchiny-medika* (St. Petersburg, 1892); A. N. Shabanova, ''Two Years at the University of Helsinki'' (''Dva goda v Gel'singforsskom universitete''), *Vestnik Evropy*, 2 (1888): 538–98.

12. See Christine Johanson, 81; Barbara Alpern Engel, *Mothers & Daughters: Women of the Intelligentsia in Nineteenth-Century Russia* (London: Cambridge University Press, 1985), 159.

13. Varvara Aleksandrovna Kashevarova, ''Avtobiografia'' in *Dvadtsati-piatiletie vrachei byvshikh studkentov imperatorskoi mediko-khirurgicheskoi akademii vypuska 9-go dekabria 1868 g* (St. Petersburg, 1892), 68–95.

14. See S. M. Dionesov, *V. A. Kashavarova-Rudneva, pervaia russkaia zhenshchina-vrach meditsiny* (Moscow, 1965). Also, E. E. Zabludovskaia, *V. A. Kashevarova-Rudneva* (Moscow, 1965).

15. Women found partners who were willing to enter into contractual marriages with the understanding that the marriage was contracted solely to enable each woman to get the permission she needed from a spouse to register for medical courses. For historical information about nineteenth-century Russian women physicians, I have consulted: Jeanette E. Tuve, *The First Russian Women Physicians* (Newtonville, MA: Oriental Research Partners, 1984); Christine Johanson, 52–86; Barbara Engle, 156–73; Nancy Mandelker Frieden, *Russian Physicians in an Era of Reform and Revolution, 1856–1905* (Princeton: Princeton University Press, 1981).

16. For a study of the first women physicians, see, especially, Jeanette Tuve, *The First Russian Women Physicians*.

17. Ibid., 7.

18. Until 1883, women doctors in Russia did not have legal status and were not listed in the medical directory. See Frieden, *Russian Physicians*, 89.

19. The number of *zemstvo* female doctors' memoirs is considerably larger than recollections by women *duma* doctors. It was a time of populism, and idealistic young

women were especially anxious to serve the peasants desperately in need of medical help. Fewer women were employed as city doctors.

20. Slanskaia, "Po visitam: Den' dumskogo zhenshchiny vracha v S. Peterburge," *Vestnik Evropy* 29, 3 (1894): 206–41; Slanskaia, *Den' dumskago zhenshchiny-vracha v S. Peterburge* (S. Petersburg: Amerikanskaia skoropechatnia, 1904). Among the letters enclosed in the reprinted, hard-cover edition, we read: "Your memoir serves as an example to entering medical students and those who are thinking of becoming doctors: doctors who would like to dedicate themselves to such work." Another reader notes, "We are trying to institute some new medical courses, and your brochure is very appropriate."

21. Slanskaia, "Po vizitam. Den' dumskogo zhenshchiny-vracha v S. Peterburge," 206. All subsequent page references to this text are given in the body of the work, following the citation.

22. The physiological sketch developed in the 1840s from the French feuilleton. In its Russian usage, the physiological sketch described the lower strata of St. Petersburg and Moscow. The Natural school received its name from the writer and journalist F. V. Bulgarin. In 1846, the influential critic Vissarion Belinsky adopted the term to designate that branch of Russian Realism that was associated with Gogol. See *A Handbook of Russian Literature*, ed. Victor Terras (New Haven: Yale University Press, 1985).

23. Vasilevskii, *Vestnik znaniia* 3 (1904): 147. As an example of the male-*zemstvo* physicians' characteristically detached and objective manner of narration in general, see also, K. Tolstoy, *Vospominania zemskogo vracha*, (Moscow, 1876), 1–97.

24. Pokrovskaia, (P. P. Soikin, St. Petersburg, 1903), 56; Pokrovskaia also wrote the memoir: "My Work as Duma Doctor" ("Moia dumskaia praktika,") *Mir bozhii* 3 (1898): 17–27.

25. Grin, "Voina s batsillami: Iz zapisok zhenshchiny vracha," *Vestnik Evropy* 5 (1900): 601–54.

26. For an excellent study of the hero adventure stories, see Joseph Campbell, *Hero with a Thousand Faces* (New York: Meridian Books, 1956).

27. *A Poetics of Women's Autobiography: Marginality and the Fiction of Self-Presentation* (Bloomington: Indiana University Press, 1987), 8.

28. Grin, "Voina s bacillami: Iz zapisok zhenshchiny vracha," 636. All subsequent page references to this text will be given in the body of the work following the quote.

29. Veretennikova, *Novyi mir*, 3 (1856): 205.

30. Susan Stanford Friedman, "Women's Autobiographical Selves: Theory–Practice," in *The Private Self, Theory and Practice of Women's Autobiographical Writing*, 54.

31. I an indebted for much of this biographical information to Mildred Davies. See her entry on Adelida Lukanina/Paevskaia in *Dictionary of Russian Women Writers*, ed. M. Astman, C. Rosenthal, M. Zirin (Greenwood Press, forthcoming).

32. Paevskaia, "God v Amerike: Iz vospominananii zhenshchiny-medika."

33. Paevskaia (née Lukanina), "Komandirovka na kholeru: Iz zapisok zhenshchiny-vracha," *Russkoe bogatstvo* 7 (1903): 121–69; 8 (1903): 49–93.

34. Paevskaia, "Komandirovka na kholeru," 7:125; 7:150. All subsequent page references to this text are given in the body of the work following the quote.

35. Interestingly, recent Western scholarship examining attitudinal distinctions between the sexes notes similar differences between male and female behavior as those Lukanina notes between herself and her male colleague, the fifth-year medical student. For example, Carol Gilligan, studying the differences in the way girls and boys solved ethical problems, found that girls, as a rule, considered the feelings of the person affected

by the decision, whereas the boys sought to solve problems more objectively and took into consideration the legalities involved. See Carol Gilligan, *In a Different Voice: Psychological Theory and Women's Development* (Cambridge: MA: Harvard University Press, 1982). In another, more recent study, Deborah Tannen, in *You Just Don't Understand: Women and Men in Conversation* (New York: Ballantine Books, 1990), finds that women expected decisions to be made by consensus. The girls mitigated conflicts by compromise and evasion. They placed relatively little weight on status, whereas the boys' group was hierarchical. See, especially, 24–27.

36. Veretennikova, 206.

37. Pokrovskaia (St. Petersburg, 1903), 57.

38. Aptekman, *Russkaia mysl* 12 (1884): 49–82.

39. Ibid., 54. All subsequent page references to this text are given in the body of the work following the quote.

40. See Pokrovskaia, "How I was a City Doctor for the Poor," 24, 53–57; Carolina de Maegd-Soep, *The Emancipation of Women in Russian Literature and Society* (Ghent, Belgium: Ghent State University, 1978), 63–64.

41. "Good People" ("Khoroshie liudi") in A. P. Chekhov, *Sobranie Sochinenii*, 4 (Moscow, 1963), 451. The translation is mine.

42. "Subjection of Women" in *Essays on Sex Equality by John Stuart Mill & Harriet Taylor Mill*, ed. Alice S. Rossi (Chicago: University of Chicago Press, 1970).

8

For the Good of the Cause: Russian Women's Autobiography in the Twentieth Century

Beth Holmgren

Over the last two decades, feminist scholars have been engaged in a massive project of recovering and reinterpreting the autobiographical writings of women.[1] Exposing the privileges and silences of patriarchal cultures, challenging traditional norms of genre and canon, they are outlining recurrent patterns in women's texts or, in the most ambitious cases, a poetics of women's autobiography. These critics tentatively conclude that women's autobiography (most often defined in contrast to men's autobiographical writing) exposes the marginalization and erasure of female subjects; delineates a self formed in relation to (rather than separation from) others; and explores fragmented, uncentered narratives and rhythmic, nonsense-language styles in order to liberate women's life stories from patriarchal modes of definition and relation.[2] Such conclusions have been drawn from a still rather limited selection of texts. The boldly entitled *A Poetics of Women's Autobiography*, as its author admits, is based mainly on Anglo-American examples.[3] Like so many critical movements, this autobiographical project originated among scholars of Western European and North American literatures—literatures of the prejudicially named "first world"—and has extended, in the main, to the texts of cultures colonized or otherwise marginalized by first-world groups. In principle, the analysis of women's autobiography is now expanding to register the differentiating impact of race, ethnicity, class, and sexuality on texts from all over the world; in fact, it has concentrated along lines of interaction and antagonism between first-world cultures and the cultures they deem colonial or oppressed. The texts of Russian and central European and formerly Soviet literatures, positioned outside this particular colonizer/colonized relationship, remain outside the mainstream of feminist scholarship. Where do these texts belong? Have they more in common with English, French, or Anglo-American models, or do they better fit among the writings of African-American or Latin American women? Or do they comprise a body of work too distinct for such comparisons?

These questions of difference and belonging certainly ring familiar to scholars
of Russian culture. As I began looking at the specific conditions and features of
Russian women's autobiography in the twentieth century, I found I was confronting the same problem of definition that perplexed nineteenth-century European critics.[4] Just as the nineteenth-century Russian novelists defied the norms
of European fiction, so these women writers seem to resist absorption into a
Western European body of work. However, I do not want to respond (as too
many have) by claiming Russian uniqueness and superiority, replacing pre-
sumptions of Western European universality with facile generalizations about a
more farsighted, transcendent Russian literature. Rather than attempt definitive
or exhaustive answers—a counterpoetics of Russian women's autobiography or
a detailed compendium of works—I propose to identify and analyze what I
consider to be important patterns of influence and response in the autobiographical
writings of twentieth-century Russian women and, most particularly, Soviet
Russian women.

It seems to me, then, that many of these writings can be located at an intersection of first-world and third-world texts and patterns, an intersection engendered by the specific political and socioeconomic conditions of twentieth-century
Russia. In place of the opposition between European colonizing power (with its
self-justifying cultural establishment) and colonized or marginalized people (with
its mandate of cultural protest), Russia and then Soviet Russia combined colonizer
and colonized within itself as its state not only subjugated non-Russians, but
exploited and in large part alienated a disenfranchised Russian society. On the
one hand, I contend that the autobiographies of Russian women frequently resemble those of the colonized in that they are called forth in protest, as the
testimony of oppositional lives. They are written for the good of often conflated
political and cultural causes: to expose and combat the injustice of a repressive
state and to perpetuate a high culture informed by moral action and concern for
the oppressed. In this essay I examine different representative sets of these
''cause-serving'' texts, grouping them roughly according to thematic emphasis
and mapping the relationship between the author's service and self-conception.
At the same time I argue that these different types of oppositional writing tend
to impose their own conformist positions: They either endorse a prescriptive,
male-oriented political or cultural model or project the ideal of the heterosexual
female *intelligent* (member of the intelligentsia) who upholds traditional notions
of high culture and proper social conduct. That is, Russian women autobiographers often articulate the position and standards of privileged women in the
first world, figuring themselves as the defenders of an ideology, morality, or
culture under siege. In conclusion, I consider how a few women radically depart
from these practices and risk the opprobrium of the state or its various oppositional movements in order to challenge approved notions of culture, conduct,
and the virtuous female self. Their example forecasts a productive alternative,
a potential outlet from the complex of causes and duties that has in great part
changed and constrained Russian women's autobiographical writings.

PRISONERS AND REVOLUTIONARIES

By the turn of the century, after several decades of improved educational and professional opportunities, a great many Russian women had committed their life stories to paper, proffering them as testimony to their new roles as doctors, lawyers, engineers, teachers, and revolutionaries and as a road map for the other women venturing into the public sphere. Of these many professional autobiographies, perhaps the most celebrated and influential were the memoirs written by female revolutionaries. Their life stories not only yielded important documents of party history, but extended the time-honored Russian tradition of oppositional autobiography: These women could claim the lofty status of political martyr on account of their rebellion against and punishment by the state.[5] The memoirs of Vera Figner (1852–1943), Eva Broido (1876–1941), Vera Zasulich (1849–1919), and Ekaterina Koval'skaia (1849?–1933), among many others, volunteer the instructive tales of conversion to and service for their particular versions of the revolutionary cause.[6] Indeed, their narratives of committed oppositional self-sacrifice established an inspirational model for an entire generation; they could use autobiography as secular saint's life, a pilgrim's testimonial to the true faith.[7] They, in effect, memorialized the image of the chaste, altruistic, utterly dedicated female revolutionary who had so impressed the revolutionaries themselves.[8]

Yet while their vision of autobiography as oppositional writing enabled their work, it also levied significant self-censorship. As Barbara Heldt notes in the case of Vera Figner (whose work she interestingly categorizes as "official" autobiography), the "public self" and "a clear sense of mission" conveniently simplify and schematize her life story.[9] Many of these memoirists may indicate (at least in the writing of their early years) that they stumbled into underground politics as they pursued a more personal, even explicitly feminist, emancipation. Vera Figner is proselytized as she fulfills her life dream of becoming a doctor; Vera Zasulich finds that "the distant specter of revolution" saves her from the fate of being a governess and makes her "equal to a boy." But as they progress in their conversion stories, they tend to edit their image according to the "generic" male model of a committed revolutionary, superimposing class conflict or concern for the "people" on their more intermittent account of gender discrimination. They either overlook sexual experience or displace it with images of chaste devotion.[10] Traditional family roles are generally renounced or, if presented, subordinated to revolutionary work. When Ol'ga Liubatovich (1854–1917) remembers her six-month-old daughter's death, she bitterly concludes that "it's a sin for revolutionaries to start a family. Men and women both must stand alone, like soldiers under a hail of bullets."[11] Even Eva Broido, a revolutionary who includes accounts of her marriage and family life, represents her wedding as politically approved, conducted in prison "to the accompaniment of clanking chains and with a ring borrowed from a convict" (27). The memoirists do celebrate the camaraderie and mutual support they found among other female students and prisoners, but they do not extrapolate any sort of woman-oriented agenda from these relationships, thereby echoing the ambivalent attitude most underground parties evinced toward feminism. In a sense, their narratives keep the stubborn silence Elizaveta Kovalskaia scenarizes in her memoir: When the revolutionaries Sofia Perovskaia and Elizaveta Kornilova are accused by other women of integrating with men's circles and so dismissing the special needs of women, they choose not to respond and leave the room.[12]

This tacit subordination is most painfully inscribed in the autobiography of Aleksandra Kollontai (1872–1952), the Bolshevik activist who succeeded these earlier generations of female revolutionaries and became, for a short while, the most prominent woman in the new Soviet government. Her case is at once representative and ironic, for Kollontai, more than any other female revolutionary, strove to link political revolution with personal and sexual liberation.[13] In her articles and fiction, Kollontai mapped out a vision in which "sexual honesty, erotic joy, and personal autonomy" were to be inculcated in Soviet life.[14] Yet by the time she penned her *Autobiography of a Sexually Emancipated Communist Woman* in 1926, she already had been demoted from her party posts on account of certain political mistakes and was effectively marginalized through her appointment to various diplomatic missions in Scandinavia. In her *Autobiography*, she seems to internalize and articulate this official judgment: She structures her life story according to a politically orthodox grid of early commitment, work in political exile, and fervent participation in the revolution and the new Soviet state. Fortunately, the English-language edition of the *Autobiography* preserves the various drafts of her text, exposing how she censored or muted many of her personal experiences and achievements.[15] Thus Kollontai excludes "the few words about [her] personal life" during World War I, when she admits that "the greater the demands life made upon me, the more responsible the work waiting to be tackled, the greater grew the longing to be enveloped by love, warmth, understanding" (22). She often simply replaces first-person singular assertions with the more self-effacing, party-conforming, first-person plural form. Even the chronological span of her text trains her autobiography on the years *before* her party censure; she declares she is unable to recover the "dark time" after her fall from grace, and she barely mentions the journalism and fiction that developed her own revolutionary theories (40). And she chooses to delete the ringing coda of her text:

No matter what further tasks I shall be carrying out, it is perfectly clear to me that the complete liberation of the working woman and the creation of the foundation of a new sexual morality will always remain the highest aim of my activity, and of my life (47–48).

Kollontai's *Autobiography* negatively enlarges on the women revolutionaries' pattern of self-censorship and overt political dedication. It also marks a decisive shift from subversive life story to officially sanctioned autobiography, from revolutionary subject to the figure of the public official, and, as such, it exacerbates the contradictory position assumed by almost all of these autobiographers. For even though these writers deliberately tailor (and sometimes mutilate) their life story to provide supporting testimony for the causes they serve, they write not merely to testify, but to prescribe. This contradiction emerges in clear contrast to the narration of other oppositional memoirs. If we compare their works with the Latin American *testimonio*—a first-person narrative relating the experience of a subjugated people or group—the Russian memoirists differ in projecting their mediating authority as party organizers and activists; they speak *for*, not *from* or *with* the people.[16] Supposedly renouncing the special interests of class (many of these women were raised in upper- or middle-class homes) and gender (avoiding the "bourgeois" trap of feminism), the memoirists testify and generalize from what they presume to be a non-nationalist, non-sexist, non-classist position, but this position in fact tends to privilege the viewpoint of a Russian intelligentsia distinct from and somewhat dismissive of the peasants and the working class.

This basic orientation underlies the texts of many Russian women revolutionaries who prepared the way for the February and October revolutions of 1917. Yet once the Soviet state settled into its own rigid, exclusionary orthodoxy in the 1930s, it produced a different sort of prison experience and a different set of memoirs by political victims. During the Stalinist period, when the purges swept the ranks of the political and cultural intelligentsia, countless women were either bereaved of their loved ones or themselves arrested, imprisoned, and exiled; with the intermittent thaw after Stalin's death, many felt compelled to write down their ordeals or bear witness to the persecution of their families and friends.[17] While these women also identified themselves with the Russian tradition of oppositional autobiography, their opposition mainly coalesced around their antipathy to Stalinist rule. There were memoirists like Evgeniia Ginzburg who at least initially pledged her work as a means of exorcising and revitalizing the Communist party, but in general these women wrote to chronicle the violation of human rights, not to advance a specific political program. The Stalinist government's random assignation of criminality forced them to a new evaluation of political opposition. As they were judged deviant and thrown into the prisons and camps, these writers encountered a host of other "criminals"—"nationalistic" non-Russians, practicing believers of different religions, lesbians and bisexuals, and political and common criminals from all classes.

Driven into a harrowing, bewildering diverse world, these Stalin-era memoirists often display a lively interest in the many female "others" incarcerated with them. Claiming that her suffering was eased by her curiosity "about these new sides of human nature," Evgeniia Ginzburg supplies numerous novelistic portraits of her cellmates and campmates (as well as her interrogators and wardens) in her two-volume memoir *Journey into the Whirlwind* and *Within the Whirlwind* (both volumes issued under the Russian title *Krutoi marshrut*) (1967). Nadezhda Ulanovskaia, the mother who testifies along with her daughter Maia in *A History of One Family (Istoriia odnoi sem'i)* (1982), dedicates separate stories to her campmates and asserts her extraordinary interest in the fates of others. In many instances, the women had to overcome two decades of indoctrination and, in the words of political prisoner Ol'ga Adamova-Sliozberg, "trust to [their] eyes and heart" (28).[18] Overall, their representation of the non-elite—the peasants and workers they can now observe up close and over time—seems less categorical and more knowledgeable than the random observations made by the nineteenth-century revolutionaries. Since they, too, were forced to perform the hard manual labor normally allotted (under less onerous conditions) to workers and peasants, they articulate an informed respect for the abilities and endurance of these women. Recalling one of her more manageable work assignments on a camp poultry farm in Elgen, Evgeniia Ginzburg remarks that she "had come to realize for the first time what a peasant's work is like" and she contemplates, albeit briefly, how she could make the system more humane with this new knowledge.[19]

They demonstrate the same sort of empathy in evaluating non-Russian prisoners. Listening to the stories of foreign communists caught in the purges and non-Russian Soviets arrested in phony campaigns against nationalist movements, these memoirists quickly discern the Russian chauvinism and xenophobia underlying Stalinist claims of inter-party and interethnic harmony. They admit the fallacy of their assumption (encouraged by the alarmist rhetoric of the Stalinist press) that every foreign communist is a spy; they confess a collective shame for Soviet mistreatment of other nationalities as well as Russian repatriates supposedly corrupted by foreign contact. In turn, the authors quite often depict themselves educating other prisoners to abandon their own ethnic prejudices. In one typical scene, Adamova-Sliozberg, herself a Jew, gives her young Ukrainian friend an effective lesson against anti-semitism.[20]

I would argue that these writers exhibit the other-directedness and sense of community so often noted in women's autobiographies, although a comprehensive comparison of the camp writings of women and men might reveal great similarity on this point. In any event, the women's recovery of other women's lives is a very significant venture. It not only indicates that women chose to assign inherent value to other members of their sex (regardless of their political utility), but it conveys, I think, a more fundamental shift in societal values. As their political goals become more generalized and focused on the issues of human rights, these women both reflect and help facilitate the movement of post-Stalin Soviet society away from public life and specific political commitment to the private sphere, personal attachments, and individual fulfillment.[21] They replace the icon of the dedicated revolutionary with a more capacious ideal; in the words of one camp victim, one is now "obliged to behave in such a way as to remain a human being."[22] So Evgeniia Ginzburg closes her two volumes of memoirs with a euphoric return to everyday humanity:

I remembered that while I was rummaging in my handbag, looking for my mislaid certificate, I had seen in the depths a square of chocolate. I ate it with relish and rose resolutely from the bench. I looked around me. The well-nourished Moscow pigeons, which had not yet gone out of fashion, were deep in conversation with one another. A little girl in a red dress was busily skipping. A constant stream of people was pouring into the subway. I was about to join them. I would merge with the general stream. Could I really do that? I was just like everyone else! (*Within the Whirlwind*, 415)

These memoirists, then, celebrate the humane treatment given them by individual and entire groups of women in the prisons and the camps. Many recount instances of generosity and caretaking (they value these gestures of female solidarity) and perceive their cells and barracks as a desperately improvised home, or, as memoirist Mariia Ioffe calls it, an "ark" (127). Their goal is to be released from prison and restored to their families and children, to be allowed to live "like everyone else." They revalue the domestic sphere—that prison house for earlier generations of female revolutionaries—as a locus of material pleasure, moral value, and freedom.[23] Their quest, however, signalled no simple retreat into domesticity; after all, once safe at home, they committed the oppositional act of writing their memoirs. Furthermore, their ordeal, along with their writing, inspired a new kind of dissident movement that aimed to respect and protect basic human rights in the Soviet Union and generated its own memoirs of the prisons and the camps. Thus, Irina Ratushinskaia (1951–), a poet and a human rights activist sentenced to a strict regime camp in 1983, produces a striking sequel to these Stalin-period memoirs. In *Grey Is the Color of Hope* (1988), she acknowledges the oppositional lessons of earlier *samizdat* texts and presents her life in the "Small Zone" for female political prisoners as a paragon of human dignity and community.[24] Here she discovers a miraculous home among dissident women who respect and support each other, sharing work quotas and domestic tasks, striving to make their meager circumstances livable, and sacrificing themselves to protest injustice to others. It is as if Ratushinskaia and her campmates have perfected the coping strategies and distilled the virtues and ideals that the previous generation of writers identified in women. Just as important, she testifies to the group's powerful influence as it wrings concessions from the camp authorities and wins sympathy and esteem among the common criminals.

On the other hand, Ratushinskaia's text distills attitudes that seemed to be understated and questioned in the earlier texts. I have noted how these Stalin-era texts inscribe and approve diversity and venture criticism of the politically orthodox. Yet if these memoirists resist a specific political orthodoxy, they still tend to maintain the vaunted position and many of the general attitudes of the Russian intelligentsia, whatever their class or ethnic background. In part, the regime condemned them to this position, punishing them as political enemies and thereby enforcing an antagonism between them and "less dangerous" common criminals. When conditions permit and they are not exhausted by hard labor, the "politicals" often portray themselves resuming, in some form, their old intellectual roles and activities—studying, teaching, debating, sometimes even proselytizing. Imprisoned under a relatively lenient regime at Solovki, Adamova-Sliozberg and her cellmates establish a daily curriculum of calisthenics and lessons in mathematics and foreign languages. Evgeniia Ginzburg devises a similar program with her cellmate in prison. Mariia Ioffe tells stories and informally lectures on Soviet history to her campmates. Nadezhda Ulanovskaia is nicknamed "Rabbi" and solicited for her political opinions. And Ratushinskaia, their legatee, is plied with requests for her poetry—by both her intellectual companions and common criminals outside the Zone.

Their superiority also breeds condescension, especially when the memoirists focus on the female criminals. While they no longer subscribe to Stalinist categories of political worth, they judge their companions according to implicit intelligentsia criteria of cultural literacy, altruism, industry, and sexual modesty; it is the latter two qualities that they most often sight and approve in peasant women. They revile the "blatnye" or common criminals, in turn, for their poor work ethic, unabashed materialism, and "immoral" behavior. Adamova-Sliozberg makes the distinction explicit: "work was the last thing that separated us from the mass of demoralized and cynical common criminals" (69). She remembers that, aside from "de-kulakized" peasants, "politicals" were the most sought-after workers on account of their conscientious attitude.

The "politicals" further elevate themselves by imposing standards for verbal and sexual conduct. In many of the narratives, the use of profanity marks a fallen soul—an uneducated common criminal or an educated woman who has become debauched. Although the authors lament their "loss of femininity" (their physical exhaustion by hard labor, premature aging) and their isolation from their families (especially their children), they construe many other manifestations of sexuality as immoral or unnatural. They note a few instances of "true love" among camp prisoners, but, as a rule, they record the erosion of sexuality from the effects of hunger, cold, and overwork or its eruption in debauchery, prostitution, and what they deem to be "unnatural" homosexual relationships. The memoirists almost invariably cast themselves as saddened, uncorrupted observers of these phenomena. When one of her educated campmates resorts to prostitution, Ginzburg relates the woman's story as a tragedy that opens up a Pandora's box of attendant vices—swearing, material indulgence, exploiting, and persecuting others.[25] As Ioffe comments, prostitution was an inevitable result of camp life, but the authors manage (often miraculously) to resist this fate.

Homosexuality, when noted at all, is judged to be another form of camp "contagion," at times a manifestation of lower-class influence. Even Maia Ulanovskaia, who declares her tolerance, surmises that most of the lesbians she encountered would never indulge in this "vice" if they lived under normal circumstances (389). She notes that among intellectuals, homosexuality was "hidden, veiled, ambiguous," whereas the common criminals flaunted and celebrated it in the "folklore" of their songs and poetry. Thirty years later, Ratushinskaia expresses almost identical prejudices against lesbianism in the criminal camps, presuming that gay women were "torn away from normal life" and "compensated by seeking substitute love and creating substitute families" (214). Ever the conscientious chronicler, Ratushinskaia offers a fascinating glimpse into the butch-femme culture of the common criminals in her camp, and she deplores their inhumane treatment by the authorities. But in her address to the ''poor'' lesbians, she clearly mixes compassion with a kind of politicized condescension:

All this in sum makes you want to shout with pity: you poor creatures, you poor creatures! To what have they reduced you? It's all very well to say that you lack self-control, have not known real love, that all your camp sufferings have only one outlet—aggression—and that ''culture'' is just another word for you. But are you the only ones to be blamed for that? Indeed, is it any of your fault? Or does the greater share of the blame fall on those who make you live in pigsty conditions, set you against one another, humiliate and debase you just to pass the time—in order that you will always feel their hand on the bridle? (217)

Thus, through their mode of relating, evaluating, and positioning themselves in the text, the women memoirists of the Stalinist terror and the post-Stalin era of stagnation not only protest injustice and celebrate their capacity for resistance (their ability to remain ''human''), but also present themselves as the arbiters of proper human—and especially female—behavior. Ironically enough, in the camps these educated, privileged, politically aware women come into closer proximity with peasants and workers and non-Russians than they would ever have done in Party or government positions. They discover there a criminal world that has been largely expunged from Stalinist society. In many important ways, these encounters condition them to understand and respect various kinds of ethnic and political difference. But their camp experience, particularly as it overlaps with the criminal world, repels them from other sorts of sexual and class difference and entrenches in them some of the traits and attitudes of the female intelligent—the use of ''proper'' language, chastity, or a modest heterosexuality, the roles of educator, spokesperson, and moral exemplar for the non-elite. Although they prove the special capacity of women to ''remain human'' under hellish circumstances (and, by extension, to ''humanize'' a post-Stalin society), they uphold a confining model of straitlaced, sentimentalized, heterosexual womanhood.

CULTURAL CONSERVATORS

As I noted in my introduction, we can draw no fast boundary between political and cultural causes in modern Russian society; since its beginnings in the eighteenth century, modern Russian culture has evolved in response to various political agendas—as a means of nation and empire building or as a forum for expressing political and moral opposition. And as we review the memoirs of women involved in Russian culture, it is important to note that this conflation has had much the same impact on their gendered self-conception as was evident in the case of female prisoners and revolutionaries. Perhaps because of its political importance, modern Russian culture has constituted a generically male preserve somewhat resembling the nineteenth-century underground political movements. To achieve a primary rank in this culture, a woman had to assume the role of honorary man—to project her image as a poet or author, not as a derivative, less-talented poetess or authoress.[26] To be sure, work that focused on women's experience or was in some way marked as women's writing was published by this establishment, but very often was judged to be second-rate and deemed adjunct to the "central" concerns of Russian society and literature.

In the first few decades of the twentieth century, this preserve of Russian culture underwent a diversification that encouraged and valued more contributions from women writers. This is the period of definite, if isolated, achievements for women, when poets like Zinaida Gippius, Anna Akhmatova, and Marina Tsvetaeva were accepted as anomalous female classics. But this diversification, barely under way, was soon arrested by the Stalinist literary establishment as it proceeded to impose its own man-centered conformity on Russian culture, promulgating a socialist realist literature in which power and heroism were invested in the supposedly generic figures of "fathers" and "sons."[27] For the most part, then, twentieth-century Russian culture remained a patriarchal establishment well into the post-Stalin era and is even today ambivalent about recognizing the abilities and importance of women writers.

Yet women gained an unexpected power outside this system. I have remarked how the Stalinist and post-Stalin camp narratives emphasized the values of home, family, and the caretaking, humanizing role of women. These values also became essential in the sphere of unofficial Russian culture under Stalin; the Stalinist system maimed and destroyed texts as well as lives. As proportionately more men were repressed by the purges, many women assumed the important task of preserving the unofficial texts left behind—either those older works that had fallen into disfavor or new texts produced in secret. In effect, they were specially empowered as the conservators and defenders of an unofficial Russian culture under state siege.

A large number of women's memoirs emerged in response to the Stalinist cultural holocaust and were devoted to recovering and sanctioning outlawed figures and works. Written or finally circulated after Stalin's death, their texts were pledged to resurrect, not revise, a patriarchal canon; from their vantage-point, the political victimization of these writers morally overwhelmed any other kind of critical evaluation. For most of them, this process resembled nothing so much as fulfilling a family obligation, the more so since they were often the wives and daughters of the repressed. Many of them qualify as the "literary widows of Russia," a category coined by the late Carl Proffer and illustrated in his portraits of women like Nadezhda Mandelstam, Elena Bulgakova, Liubov' Belozerskaia-Bulgakova, Lily Brik, and Tamara Ivanova.[28] Involved with important male artists, they clearly inherited both the duties and powers of cultural conservator, whether or not the government permitted them this title. The literary widows labored to safeguard the writer's archive, publish his work once this became possible, and promote his reputation. And very often their memoirs originated as an immediate essay to set the record straight: They dispatched their reconstruction of the past to refute all the other stories that, for them, distorted the writer's true image. In the process they frequently figured themselves in the supporting roles of companion, secretary, sometime muse, and chronicler. Elena Bulgakova (third wife of the famous playwright and novelist Mikhail Bulgakov) even acknowledges her "assignment" to start a journal: "Misha insists that I keep a diary. After his diaries were confiscated during a search in 1926, he promised himself that he would never keep a diary" (34).

In many instances, the literary widows performed the duties of conservator with intelligence and persistence, but without professional training. Yet even when the women writers possessed that training and presumed their right to write, their autobiographical work dutifully responded to the traumas of Soviet history and at least explicitly perpetuated the male-dominated structures of Russian and Soviet Russian culture. One of the most interesting examples of this sort of professional stewardship appears in the work of Lidiia Chukovskaia (1907–), a literary critic, editor, novelist, and dissident who conscientiously maintained the images of a number of artists, including that of her famous father, the critic and children's writer Kornei Chukovskii (1882–1969). Her *To the Memory of Childhood (Pamiati detstva)*, written after her father's death and focused on her childhood in the 1910s, represents the extended canon of Russian literature (both realist and modernist) as endangered family, or more particularly, paternal legacy. In a curious twist, Chukovskaia's text was spurred by her own persecution. She had been deliberately excluded from her father's official Literary Heritage Commission (she was already known as a dissident) and she discovered, after several heavily censored and then aborted attempts to publish her memoirs, that "it's been decided—I'm not to reminisce about him."[29] Chukovskaia is therefore galvanized into recollecting what she feels she knows best: "my childhood and [my father's] youthful friendship with children."

What obtains is a text that, while claiming to be about Chukovskaia's childhood, actually foregrounds Kornei Chukovskii as its "creator" (121). The daughter displays and endorses her father's "creator" model on a number of different levels. She not only analyzes and celebrates Chukovskii as the author of her childhood and the founder of her lifelong values, but she utilizes his technique of biographical criticism to achieve her own portrait of the artist. Her criticism, however, is more ambitious, for she defines his creative output more broadly— as his actual texts, his informal salon for visiting artists, and most vitally, his culturally enlightened parenting of Lidiia and her brothers Kolia and Boba. Her vision of her father's "creation" develops a marvelously integrated conception of art grounded in daily rituals, physical enjoyment, and emotional fulfillment. Through her biocritical interpretation, she amply demonstrates how her father equipped her with a valuable poetic education and early training for a literary career.[30]

Unfortunately, however, Chukovskaia's glorious portrait of her father tends to control and obscure her self-portrait. As her text highlights Chukovskii as a self-made intellectual enforcing a cult of high art in his household, we can sense the awestruck Lidiia on the sidelines, eagerly embracing a paternally approved canon and her father's own deferential, self-denigrating approach. And her awe and deference imply an insidious self-censorship, for she seems to accept her father's model as truly heterogeneous, universal, and absolute, encompassing both sexes and all classes, and she dismisses what lies outside it. She reports longing to be one of the "we" that he commands (10), an inclusion that preludes markedly "girlish" traits: playing with dolls, reading "girlish books" like *Little Women* (97), performing the women's chores of cooking, cleaning, and unobtrusively maintaining a household. From the opening passage of the text, Chukovskii is figured as the measure of all things natural and cultural—"the tallest man on earth," "the commander of our games,"—and he alone wields the power to realize the creativity he assumes to be innate in all children. In consequence, Chukovskaia diminishes her girlhood by "aligning male selfhood with culturally valued stories" and sacrifices her autobiography for an informed tribute to her father-creator.[31]

Nonetheless, Chukovskaia's text delineates an interesting pattern in which explicit conformity (her tribute to the great man) is tempered and even somewhat subverted by her distinctive creative approach and vitally synthetic world view. Her other major memoir, the two-volume *Notes on Anna Akhmatova (Zapiski ob Anne Akhmatovoi)* (1976, 1980), represents an important variation on this pattern, for she chronicles her meetings with the famous poet Anna Akhmatova, one of the few female classics admitted into Russian literature (and approved by her father).[32] In the process of transcribing her evolving relationship with Akhmatova, Chukovskaia obliquely conveys a far more comprehensive self-portrait that underscores her own development as a writer. *Notes on Anna* marks, in a still very muted way, her rite of passage from paternal "creation" to a kind of collaborative creator.[33]

Chukovskaia's pattern of stated conformity and applied creativity unfolds in the writing of yet another female professional, the scholar Lidiia Ginzburg (1902–1990), who eventually achieved prominence in the post-Stalin era.[34] Lidiia Ginzburg was not compelled into family service and cannot be classified as a "literary widow." But her professional curiosity, combined with her emotional attachment to certain endangered communities (both professional and national), disposed her to write reminiscences, keep an extensive journal, and compose a piece of memoiristic fiction. *Notes on the Leningrad Blockade (Zapiski blokadnogo cheloveka)*, which relates the experience of Leningraders during the World War II siege.[35] Paralleling Chukovskaia's focus on a male-dominated "we," the early segments of Ginzburg's *Journal* highlight her *professional* formation among the largely male group of younger Formalist critics. Her characterization of this experience simply alternates between the pronouns "we" and "he":

A pupil of the *Opoiaz* group is certainly close to contemporary literature and in general is an intelligent of his time, in his aesthetic tastes and entire world view. He is a skeptic of the most inveterate kind because he doesn't notice his skepticism. All of us, it seems, combine skepticism with decency . . . this is also a kind of tradition. . . .[36]

In her *Journal*, critics from the first generation of Formalists—men like Boris Eikhenbaum, Viktor Shklovskii, and Iurii Tynianov—emerge as mentors; early on, Ginzburg establishes the practice of recording the *bon mots* and significant statements of the famous people she encounters. And while Ginzburg deems a number of women quotable (both Anna Akhmatova and Nadezhda Mandelstam resonate in her text), she tends to detach herself from any explicit identification with women—either by subjecting them to distancing analytical scrutiny or by using female-marked epithets in a pejorative way (for example, the "psychology of ladies" [13], "Soviet ladies' sentimentalism" [292]). In lieu of revealing a private life of sexual relations and family attachments, she most often articulates emotion in connection with her work. As Ginzburg represents herself, she seems wholly invested in and defined by her vocation as a de-feminized writer-critic.

But just as Chukovskaia subtly conveys her own creativity in her paternal tribute, so Lidiia Ginzburg develops her own distinctly creative and personalized critical practice. Chukovskaia elaborates on the methods of her father and inscribes a fusion between her family life and Russian culture; Ginzburg, in turn, systematically breaks down the boundaries between "aesthetically determined fiction" and "historically determined fact" and seeks an integration of life, literature, and literary studies.[37] Ginzburg may de-feminize her self-conception, but she fleshes out her professional experience with deep emotional and even physical sensations. A profession, she notes, "is most like love" (141); she minutely describes the physical act of writing, when one can "hear the blood pulsing in [one's] temples" (81). She explains that she entered her profession on account of her love of literature and her penchant for analyzing and elucidating whatever she experiences (33). Given free rein in the *Journal*, her analysis applies equitably to all forms of writing and living, however mundane—from the poetry and person of Osip Mandelstam to life in a communal apartment.

One could posit, therefore, that for all her explicit detachment from female-marked flaws, Lidiia Ginzburg evinces certain similarities to the position and function of women writing in other societies. Focusing on intermediary genres and the linkages between biography and text, moving outside any particular critical school or institutional association, she displays the resistance to abstract boundaries and the tendency toward mediation and unbounded "relatedness" that psychologists and sociologists have traced most systematically in the social and cultural development of American women.[38] In her work, Ginzburg demonstrates the "fluidity of genre" and the intricate connection between life and art to a much greater and more varied extent than any of her "brother"-Formalists. At the same time, however, Ginzburg does not especially assert her distinction from a "we" that encompasses, at various points, the Formalists, the Russian intelligentsia, and all Soviet citizens. Throughout her writing, she relies on this supposedly generalized position from which she can observe and analyze and exercise the intellectual authority her society attributes to men and only atypical women. Her work, like that of many cultural conservators, displays, but does not own, her complex difference.

REBELS WITHIN THE CAUSE

Given this sampling of memoirs by revolutionaries, political prisoners, and cultural conservators, it appears that the problematic status of female selfhood in Russian society—its secondary value, adjunct roles, conformist virtues, convention-bound sexuality—remains, for the most part, a muted or non-issue, a concern that many women writers sense and circumvent, but choose not to confront. They seem satisfied with the more established options: Service to various political and cultural causes empowers them to testify, commemorate, and be of use, even though they must write of themselves in carefully restricted, socially approved ways. A thorough, nuanced reevaluation of the female self, in all its possible variations, would entail a reevaluation of traditional Russian and Soviet Russian constructs of gender as well as the audacity to question and disobey the consensus (whether it be official or dissident). In short, Russian women have had to write through an insidious opposition of patriarchal structures—government practice *versus* dissident action linked with high Russian culture—and they have had to endure daunting guilt and disapproval if they dared to transgress these understood boundaries.

Although this reevaluation has yet to take place on a large scale, it is crucial that several women writers have ventured more rebellious life stories, what might serve as bases for an alternative autobiographical tradition. The autobiographical work of the poet Marina Tsvetaeva (1892–1941) affords, I think, the most flamboyant, far-reaching possibilities. Heldt boldly claims that Tsvetaeva's poetry "is the model for future Russian poetry by women" (143); I would make the tandem claim that Tsvetaeva's autobiographical prose establishes important patterns and strategies for projecting a supremely valued, protean female self. Svetlana Boym has aptly defined Tsvetaeva's oeuvre as "a nonconformist one-woman show" in which the poet "wished to keep her female identity, but stretch it, push it to the limit, deviating from and violating the established conventions of both literary femininity and literary masculinity" (217). Emphatically reversing the progression of male mentors and progenitors, Tsvetaeva names her mother the troubling, demanding source of her genius in her sketch, "Mother and Music" (1935):

Mother did not bring us up—she tried us out: she tested our strength of resistance: would our rib cages fall in? No they did not fall in, they filled out so much that later—now—you can't feed them full, you can't fill them full with anything. Mother gave us drink from the opened vein of Lyricism, just as we afterwards, mercilessly opening ours, tried to give our children drink from the blood of our own anguish. It was their good fortune—that it did not succeed, ours—that it did.

> After a mother like that I had only one alternative: to become a poet. To expurgate her gift to me, a gift that would have suffocated me or turned me into a transgressor of all human laws.[39]

Her writings identify and engage with many other important female figures (both familial and cultural), and while her attitudes toward these women are by no means unambiguously positive, they are almost never detached or conventional. Rather, Tsvetaeva develops new non-essentialist constructs of gender that frequently assign primary value to female characters and "second-rate" feminine traits. In the eyes of many Russian readers and critics, this radical reevaluation constituted nothing less than a breach of good taste—a passionate embrace of those inferior feminine qualities that so repelled a female intellectual like Lidiia Ginzburg, a passionate rejection of the conventional heroines and female cultural myths that the consensus sanctioned.[40]

In her autobiographical essay, "My Pushkin" (1937), Tsvetaeva extends this reevaluation to the preserve of Russian culture.[41] In Pushkin she encounters the ultimate progenitor of modern Russian poetry, a forefather whose model included his tragic death in a duel over his beautiful wife, and his creation of the heroine Tat'iana in the verse-novel *Evgenii Onegin*—a character "whose perfection was a constant model for Russian girls."[42] Writing about Pushkin's wife, Pushkin's Tat'iana, and Pushkin himself, Tsvetaeva reinterprets and personalizes those mythologies that bind her as a female writer and reader. She juxtaposes the wife Natal'ia Goncharova, an empty beauty, with a twentieth-century namesake, the artist Natal'ia Goncharova, a contemporary who has overcome the conventional woman within herself and has achieved the "pure" virility of the artist (Boym, 210–11). Tsvetaeva prefers a family version of Tat'iana's story: Instead of accepting "the virtuous married woman" who is duty-bound to reject her girlish love, she adheres to her mother's embodied reading in which her mother, like Tat'iana, forever renounces the man she loved and voluntarily languishes "in the enlightened circle of her own loneliness in love."[43] The model of the poet, which Tsvetaeva immediately personalizes with the title "My Pushkin," yields in her imaginative memory a series of unorthodox, de-sanctified, and liberating connections: blackness, gypsies, the rebel Pugachev, the free elements of the sea, and, of course, poetry. In place of a respectful, self-effacing portrait of a male mentor, "her" Pushkin is, above all, her idiosyncratic reading and perceiving of Pushkin and her creative reincarnation of his poetic power.

In her bold assertion and exploration of her female identity, Tsvetaeva distinguished herself from almost all the female poets who had established themselves in the early twentieth century.[44] She was one of a very few who seemed willing to violate codes of political and cultural good conduct, whether she lived in the new Soviet state or anti-Soviet émigré communities. As difficult as this must have been, she maintained her contrariness as a fundamental part of her poetic birthright; to a significant extent, her self-assertion was privileged by her position as poet. It is perhaps more incredible, then, that other pioneers of nonconforming autobiographies emerged from the ranks of the conservators, since for them the very act of writing was sanctioned as a performance of duty, a gesture of defensive reverence. Heldt has already detected the case of one such rebel conservator in the memoirs of Liubov' Blok (1881–1939), the wife and incarnated ideal of the famous poet Aleksandr Blok (93–98). Liubov' Blok clearly understood the expectations of her readers: "My autobiography is not needed; I am not asked for it. What is needed is the life of the poet's wife, the "function" (I beg the typesetter to make a misprint: the "fiction"!) which, I repeat, is perfectly well known to the reader."[45] Nevertheless, even as she expresses great love and tenderness for her husband, she is not deterred from relating her own experience of a life he had mythologized and, in her view, obscured. Refusing to keep silent as his creation, she violates yet another code by discussing her sexuality—her delight in her adolescent body, her irregular sexual relations with Blok—and attempts an amateur psychoanalytic analysis of herself and Blok's family. In effect, Liubov' Blok dares to secularize and liberate her autobiography from the mytho-biographical legend of the Russian poet and his "Beautiful Lady."

Less explicit and self-involved than Liubov' Blok's text, Nadezhda Mandelstam's two-volume memoirs (translated as *Hope Against Hope* and *Hope Abandoned*) gradually disclose yet another rebel conservator.[46] The wife of the great poet Osip Mandelstam, who was arrested, exiled, and destroyed under Stalin, Nadezhda Mandelstam (1899–1980) truly defined the type of the literary widow: She voluntarily shared her husband's persecution, survived in silence and fear after his death, preserved his work in memory and manuscript form, and saw to his post-Stalin rehabilitation through her work with literary scholars and the writing of her memoirs. She did not conceive of herself as a writer and composed her first volume of memoirs as "something in the nature of a letter telling of our fate."[47] Here and in the second volume she brilliantly embellishes on her widow's duties. Nadezhda Mandelstam not only recovers her husband's lost life and art, but corroborates her biography of him with the self-mythologies he developed in his work, and establishes him as a seer and moral authority of his age.[48] As Charles Isenberg remarks, she succeeds so well that her books have become "the enabling condition [and] virtual horizon" for her husband's work.[49]

Yet her memoirs extend well beyond these duties, much the same way her personality and experience overwhelmed her prescribed role as poet's wife. Analyzing the nature of her marriage in the second volume, Nadezhda Mandelstam concludes that she "balked" at being a "wife" and "tried to insist on being instead a happy-go-lucky girlfriend with no rights," but with a ready sense of her own worth and autonomy (139). This notion of the "girlfriend"—the irreverent, prosaic companion of the poet—clearly influences her writing; intensified over the twenty-odd years she spent coping and observing on her own, this self-styled role enables her to relate her own candid, anecdotal history of her times. Although her poet-husband's writing and conduct remain the touchstone for her historical analysis, Nadezhda Mandelstam does not confer this sanction on the Russian intelligentsia as a whole. Rather, she exposes what she considers to be the vices and false cults of its various groups and individuals (herself included). Her memoirs, therefore, attempt at once a commemoration and a cathartic critique, for she maintains that the victims of Stalinism were also complicit, to greater and lesser degrees, in allowing the system to exist.

It is intriguing, moreover, that as Nadezhda Mandelstam casts a critical eye on the culture repressed under Stalin, she also progressively defines herself as a woman among women. This focus really emerges in the second volume, after she has completed the "main task" of recalling her husband's last years and can now recover her "self." Her autobiographical project is a complex one. She still suffers the collective guilt of Stalinist times when the word "I" was made "shameful or taboo," and she admits that while she intends "to write about myself alone," she is "really concerned less with myself than with the scraps of experience I have stored up during my life" (11). But over the course of the second volume, she describes the tragic plight of all "widows" like herself; recognizes the special strength, endurance, and caretaking abilities of women under Stalinism; and distinguishes herself as a non-"wife" and a non-"beauty"—as an unconventional, unaffected "girlfriend" who seems tolerant of various kinds of sexual behavior and "improper" language.[50] Having matured from madcap "girlfriend" into "a crazy old woman," she does not confine herself to the role of uncritical conservator but, instead, conducts a reevaluation of her society and culture on her own terms.[51]

The scattered examples of Tsvetaeva, Blok, and Mandelstam do not yet constitute a countertradition to the dominant tendencies in twentieth-century women's autobiographies. Yet their bold ventures, marked by their positive recognition of various types of female experience and behavior, their assertion of their sexuality, and their (sometimes implicit) reevaluation of Russian culture and the Russian intelligentsia suggest a positive blueprint for future writers, strategies for releasing a more capacious, differentiated female self from the constricting uniforms of whatever cause. Of course, the question of their influence is still very much bound to the national, political, and social conditions developing in the former territories of the Soviet Union. Certainly women writers have grown more numerous and (in still isolated cases) more respected in Russian prose, and these developments would seem to augur a greater diversity in women's autobiographical writing. We see this promise partly realized in the fiction of contemporary writers like Liudmila Petrushevskaia, Iuliia Voznesenskaia, and Valeriia Narbikova, who experiment with unconventional heroines and deliberately break the taboo on exploring female sexuality. Indeed, we may be witnessing a very productive moment for the ascendancy of women writers as the old binary opposition of official versus dissident is crumbling into a multitude of political platforms and special interest groups. Russian society is open as never before to exchanges with Western societies, and the longstanding privilege of high Russian culture is waning with the emergence of a more commercially successful popular culture. On the other hand, the economic chaos accompanying this political and cultural fragmentation has exacerbated the double burden of career and housework for most Russian women and forced many of them into the ranks of the unemployed. Even if they no longer confront the same monolithic political and cultural restrictions, Russian women now have to contend with much more severe limits on time and finances.

In sum, I cannot predict how the writing of women's autobiography will evolve in Russia over the next century. But my utopian speculation is that Russian women will stop writing their life stories for the good of the cause if these grand causes become obsolete, if they are broken down into different partisan agendas and tailored for a society in which all kinds of difference—those of gender and sexuality as well as class and ethnicity—are politically, socially, and culturally valued. Such diversity cannot support one value-legislating center or a binary opposition of two such centers. In a more diverse and tolerant Russian society, women will feel less compelled to write for the good of a "generalized" cause and less empowered to impose a conformist model on their sisters. Freed to a richer array of possibilities, they will be able to produce life stories that create from and experiment with the many patterns of difference obtaining between men and women and, just as important, among women themselves. In fact, more Russian women might even undertake the writing of their lives as a cause in and of itself.

NOTES

1. I want to thank Justyna Fife for helping me in this recovery of Russian women's autobiographical writings.

2. Domna Stanton, "Autogynography: Is the Subject Different?" in *The Female Autograph: Theory and Practice of Autobiography from the Tenth to the Twentieth Century*, ed. Domna Stanton (Chicago and London: University of Chicago Press, 1984), 3–20. Mary G. Mason, "The Other Voice: Autobiographies of Women Writers," in *Life/Lines: Theorizing Women's Autobiography*, ed. Bella Brodzki and Celeste Schenck (Ithaca, NY and London: Cornell University Press, 1988), 19–44; originally published in *Autobiography: Essays Theoretical and Critical*, ed. James Olney (Princeton: Princeton University Press, 1980). See also Susan Stanford Friedman's "Women's Autobiographical Selves: Theory and Practice," in *The Private Self: Theory and Practice of Women's Autobiographical Writings*, ed. Shari Benstock (Chapel Hill, NC and London: The University of North Carolina Press, 1988), 34–62. Sidonie Smith, *A Poetics of Women's Autobiography* (Bloomington: Indiana University Press, 1987), 49–59.

3. Sidonie Smith, 19.

4. See Eugene Marie Melchior de Vogue's famous essay to define Russian literature—*Le Roman russe* (Paris: Plon-Nourrit et Cie, 1868, 1897).

5. One could argue that Archpriest Avvakum (1620–1682) produced the first such autobiography in exemplary protest against the official religious establishment. The first such text by a woman writer—the memoirs of exiled Princess Nataliia Dolgorukaia—appeared almost a century later (1767); in it she bears witness to her family's persecution.

6. For an excellent anthology of these writings in English translation, see *Five Sisters: Women Against the Tsar*, ed. and trans. Barbara Alpern Engel and Clifford N. Rosenthal

(New York: Alfred A. Knopf, 1975); it includes autobiographical narratives by Vera Figner, Vera Zasulich, Praskoviia Ivanovskaia, Olga Liubatovich, and Elizaveta Kovalskaia. My citations from their works refer to this anthology. A reprint of the 1927 translation of Vera Figner's complete text appears as *Memoirs of a Revolutionist*, introduction by Richard Stites (Dekalb, IL: Northern Illinois University Press, 1991). See also Eva Broido's *Memoirs*, ed. and trans. Vera Broido (London: Oxford University Press, 1967).

7. In her "Journal for the 1970s–1980s" ("Zapisi 1970–1980-kh godov"), in *Chelovek za pis'mennym stolom* (Leningrad, 1989), Lidiia Ginzburg remarks how her generation, coming of age in the 1910s, was attracted to the model of the female political terrorist, Sof'ia Perovskaia (298).

8. See chapters 7, 9, and 10 of Barbara Alpern Engel's book *Mothers and Daughters: Women of the Intelligentsia in Nineteenth-Century Russia* (Cambridge: Cambridge University Press, 1983).

9. Barbara Heldt, *Terrible Perfection: Women and Russian Literature* (Bloomington and Indianapolis: Indiana University Press, 1987), 68–69.

10. When Praskoviia Ivanovskaia is describing her agitation work, she contrasts the peasants' sexual liberties with her fiercely defended chastity (*Five Sisters*, 108–11).

11. *Five Sisters*, 196.

12. *Five Sisters*, 217.

13. For an excellent synopsis of Kollontai's views, see Richard Stites's *The Women's Liberation Movement in Russia: Feminism, Nihilism, and Bolshevism, 1860–1930* (Princeton: Princeton University Press, 1978), 346–358. See also Barbara Evans Clements's *Bolshevik Feminist: The Life of Aleksandra Kollontai* (Bloomington: Indiana University Press, 1979), Beatrice Farnworth's *Aleksandra Kollontai: Socialism, Feminism, and the Bolshevik Revolution* (Stanford, CA: Stanford University Press, 1980), and Cathy Porter's *Alexandra Kollontai: A Biography* (London: Virago, 1980).

14. Stites, 358.

15. All citations taken from Aleksandra Kollontai, *The Autobiography of a Sexually Emancipated Communist Woman*, edited with an afterword by Irving Fetscher, translated by Salvator Attanasio (New York: Herder and Herder, 1971).

16. For discussion of the *testimonio* in different national contexts, see Doris Sommer, " 'Not Just a Personal Story': Women's *Testimonios* and the Plural Self," in *Life/Lines*, 107–30; also John Beverley and Marc Zimmerman, *Literature and Politics in the Central American Revolutions* (Austin, TX: University of Texas Press, 1990), 172–211. Like these Russian texts, the *testimonio* is meant to function as a political document—"as one part of a general strategy to win political ground" (Sommer, 109). Yet in the case of the *testimonio*, intellectual writers volunteer to be scribes for "the people," and while the act of transcription may well imply their intervention as editors and interpreters, it also reflects their intent to heed and speak *with* rather than *for* the oppressed (Beverley and Zimmerman, 176–77).

17. See, for example, among many others, the memoirs of Evgeniia Ginzburg, *Journey into the Whirlwind*, trans. Paul Stevenson and Max Hayward (New York: Harcourt Brace & World, 1967) and *Within the Whirlwind*, translated by Ian Bolland with an introduction by Heinrich Boll (San Diego, CA: Harcourt Brace Jovanovich, 1981); Maria Ioffe, *Odna noch': Povest' o pravde (One Night: A True Story)* (New York: Izdatel'stvo "Khronika," 1978); and Nadezhda and Maiia Ulanovskie, *Istoriia odnoi sem'i (A History of One Family)* (New York: Chalidze Publications, 1982); as well as the anthology of some

twenty women writers, *Dodnes' tiagoteet (A Present Danger)*, vyp. 1, Zapiski vashei sovremmenitsy, comp. Semen Vilenskii (Moscow, 1989). For one striking example of the many memoirs written to commemorate victimized family members, cf. Anna 'Bukharina,' *Nezabyvaemoe* (Moscow, 1989).

18. Ol'ga Adamova-Sliozberg's memoir, "My journey" ("Put"), is included in the anthology *Dodnes' tiagoteet*, 6–123.

19. *Within the Whirlwind*, 68.

20. *Dodnes' tiagoteet*, 114–15.

21. See Vladimir Shlapentokh's sociological study *Public and Private Life of the Soviet People: Changing Values in Post-Stalin Russia* (New York and Oxford: Oxford University Press, 1989).

22. Maria Ioffe, 127.

23. Elena Bonner's memoir, *Mothers and Daughters*, trans. Antonina W. Bouis (New York: Alfred A. Knopf, 1992), records this fascinating transformation in her mother, a dedicated Party worker who spent years in the camps and then ended her life as a devoted grandmother and great-grandmother (89–90).

24. As represented in Ratushinskaia's text, *Grey Is the Color of Hope*, trans. Alyona Kojevnikov (New York: Alfred A. Knopf, 1988), the Small Zone resembles a religious or utopian community. Like latter-day Robinson Crusoes, the dissident women manage to improvise an efficient, harmonious community (complete with garden, workspace, communal meals, and rituals) under the most difficult conditions.

25. Ginzburg describes how one young woman exchanges her body for a loaf of black bread and then protests: "It's hell to be an intellectual! Absolute hell! After all, it's not as if it were a tragedy, is it?" (*Within the Whirlwind*, 42).

26. For a good discussion of the concept of the poetess (particularly in early twentieth-century Russia), see Svetlana Boym's *Death in Quotation Marks: Cultural Myths of the Modern Poet* (Cambridge, MA and London: Harvard University Press, 1991), 192–96.

27. For further elaboration of the male-dominated plots and casts of socialist realist fiction, see Katerina Clark's *The Soviet Novel: History as Ritual*, 2d ed. (Chicago and London: University of Chicago Press, 1985).

28. See Carl R. Proffer, *The Widows of Russia and Other Writings* (Ann Arbor, MI: Ardis, 1987). I will refer to the memoirs of Nadezhda Mandelstam in greater detail toward the end of this essay. See also *Dnevnik Eleny Bulgakovoi* (Moscow, 1990); Liubov' Belozerskaya-Bulgakova's *My Life with Mikhail Bulgakov* trans. Margareta Thompson (Ann Arbor, MI: Ardis, 1983); and Tamara Ivanova's *Moi sovremenniki, kakimi ia ikh znala: ocherki* (Moscow, 1987).

29. Lydia Chukovskaya, *To the Memory of Childhood*, trans. Eliza Kellogg Klose (Evanston, IL: Northwestern University Press, 1988), 149.

30. I argue elsewhere that Chukovskaia interprets her father's model in a way that enables her to value some female-marked traits and positions. This argument is developed in the second chapter of my forthcoming book, *Women's Works in Stalin's Time: On Lidiia Chukovskaia and Nadezhda Mandelstam* (Indiana University Press, forthcoming).

31. Sidonie Smith, 50.

32. Lidiia Chukovskaia, *Zapiski ob Anne Akhmatovoi*, 1, 1938–1941, 2d ed. (Paris: YMCA, 1984); 2, 1952–1962 (Paris: YMCA, 1980).

33. I elaborate on this analysis of *Notes on Anna Akhmatova* in the fourth chapter of *Women's Works in Stalin's Time*.

34. For a fine summation of Lidiia Ginzburg's life and work, see Jane Gary Harris's obituary essay in *Slavic Review*, 49, no. 4 (Winter 1990): 699–702.

35. It is intriguing to note that a number of professional women writers produced impressive memoirs of the Leningrad siege. In addition to Lidiia Ginzburg's text, see Vera Inber's *Pochti tri goda: Leningradskii dnevnik* (Moscow, 1946), translated as *Leningrad Diary* by Serge M. Wolff and Rachel Grieve, with an introduction by Edward Crankshaw (London: Hutchinson & Co., 1971); and Olga Berggol'ts' poetic diary *Leningradskaia tetrad'* (1942).

36. *Chelovek za pis'mennym stolom*, 22–23.

37. Sarah Pratt, "Lydia Ginzburg and the Fluidity of Genre," in *Autobiographical Statements in Russian Literature*, ed. Jane Gary Harris (Princeton: Princeton University Press, 1990), 209, 215.

38. For the most famous examples, see Nancy Chodorow, *The Reproduction of Mothering: Psychoanalysis and the Sociology of Gender* (Berkeley, CA: University of California Press, 1978); Carol Gilligan, *In a Different Voice: Psychological Theory and Women's Development* (Cambridge, MA: Harvard University Press, 1982); *Mapping the Moral Domain: A Contribution of Women's Thinking to Psychological Theory and Education*, ed. Carol Gilligan, Janie Victoria Ward, Jill McLean Taylor (Cambridge, MA: Center for the Study of Gender, Education and Human Development, 1988).

39. Cited from the English-language translation of Tsvetaeva's prose, *A Captive Spirit: Selected Prose*, ed. and trans. J. Marin King (Ann Arbor, MI: Ardis, 1980), 276.

40. For an extensive discussion of this process, see Boym, 200–40.

41. Cf. her three essays, "Natal'ia Goncharova," "My Pushkin" ("Moi Pushkin"), and "Pushkin and Pugachev" ("Pushkin i Pugachev").

42. Heldt, 102.

43. "My Pushkin," *A Captive Spirit*, 337.

44. It is interesting to speculate on the possible connection between Tsvetnaeva's bisexuality and her literary self-conception. For more information on this subject (and on other authors "who wrote openly and favourably of the same-sex love"), see Simon Karlinsky's fascinating monograph, *Marina Tsvetaeva: The Woman, Her World and Her Poetry* (Cambridge: Cambridge University Press, 1986), 50–58.

45. Liubov' Mendeleeva-Blok, "Facts and Myths about Blok and Myself" in *Blok: An Anthology of Essays and Memoirs*, ed. and trans. Lucy Vogel (Ann Arbor, MI: Ardis, 1982), 9.

46. Nadezhda Mandelstam, *Hope Against Hope*, translated by Max Hayward, with an introduction by Clarence Brown (New York: Atheneum, 1970); *Hope Abandoned*, trans. Max Hayward (New York: Atheneum, 1974).

47. *Hope Abandoned*, 183.

48. On her affirmation of Mandelstam's self-mythologies, see Gregory Freidin, *A Coat of Many Colors: Osip Mandelstam and His Mythologies of Self-Presentation* (Berkeley, CA and London: University of California Press, 1987), 270–71.

49. Charles Isenberg, "The Rhetoric of Nadezhda Mandelstam's *Hope Against Hope*," in *New Studies in Russian Language and Literature*, ed. Anna Lisa Crone and Catherine V. Chvany (Columbus, OH: Slavica Publishers, 1987), 168; also in his revised version of this essay, "The Rhetoric of *Hope Against Hope*," in *Autobiographical Statements in Twentieth-Century Russian Literature*, 193.

50. It is notable that Nadezhda Mandelstam expresses a kind of indebtedness to Tsve-

taeva in her second volume, as if she and the female poet share the same important characteristics of spontaneity and wildness. See, especially, *Hope Abandoned*, 467.

51. In consequence, Nadezhda Mandelstam's second volume of memoirs was denounced for its display of "a sick self-rapture" and "a vulgar familiarity" by Veniamin Kaverin in a famous open letter dated March 23, 1973, and published in *samizdat*. Kaverin's response was echoed by a great many people in Soviet dissident society. For an account of this reaction, see Proffer, 32–38.

9

Achievement and Obscurity: Women's Prose in the Silver Age[1]

Charlotte Rosenthal

And here too there are passages about beds, about body warmers, and countless other things, as it were the tales of crazy women.

Prince A. M. Kurbsky

In 1899 the literary critic A. Skabichevskii wrote in his newspaper column "Current Literature" that Russia was being "inundated" by women's prose fiction, and he predicted that the nineteenth century would go down in history as the century of *women's* belles lettres. He pointed out that Russia had almost as many female prose writers as male, citing the presence of at least one or two pieces by women in most of the "thick" journals.[2] The reasons for this notable increase in the number of women prose writers resulted from historical circumstances, economic necessity, increased levels of education, a growing self-confidence and ambition by women prose writers to become part of the Russian literary tradition, and a greater acceptance by the literary establishment of the kinds of writing that women favored. By the early twentieth century, their numbers and popularity grew even greater with the advent of a market for popular fiction. Women realized that they could earn very good money and garner even greater fame by writing for a less-exclusive audience.

If there is unanimity among contemporary critics and literary historians about the quantity of women's prose, there were quite sharp differences of opinion about the quality of this prose. Skabichevskii thought that some women had admirable and exceptional talent.[3] Typical of the naysayers is A. Izmailov: Writing in 1904 about "ladies' belles lettres," he says that their writing is tepid, imitative, and old-fashioned, for it "not only does not move art forward, but positively prevents its entry into the new century!"[4] The most common objection is that its focus is narrow, confined to subjects of the "hearth and the heart," that is, love and family relations.[5] Critics such as M. Protopopov expected prose to focus on characters in a sociohistorical context and to present models of a "useful," positive life. He objected to the concentration in women's writing on morality and individual psychology.[6] Skabichevskii praised S. I. Smirnova for the very reason that she tried "to reflect the spirit of the times."[7] Nevertheless, though women's prose received little unadulterated praise, their situation had noticeably changed, because it had reached a critical mass that, it seemed, could no longer be ignored.

One trait that is revealing of society's attitude toward the woman writer, and of the writer's attitude toward herself, is the use of a male pseudonym. They "could use a masculine name to represent everything in their personalities that transcended the cramping feminine ideal."[8] What is striking is the increasing *lack* of pseudonym use by this time, especially of masculine pseudonyms. This trend indicates a degree of acceptance that had not previously existed. At this point, masculine- and neuter-gender pseudonyms appear to have been used by two kinds of writers: those who were reluctant to reveal themselves because they were hesitant about their careers[9] and those, like Ol'nem, who wrote prose that deviated from what was expected of "ladies' " belles lettres and did not want their work to be pigeonholed as such.

"Serious" ("high-brow") women writers tended not to write novels. The Silver Age generally did not privilege the novel, but was, instead, a time of short prose forms.[10] Typically, women prose writers favored the short story and the novella, and to a lesser extent, the sketch and the feuilleton. Novel writing became the preferred activity of two groups of women: those who wrote popular fiction such as Verbitskaia, Nagrodskaia, Lappo-Danilevskaia, Kryzhanovskaia ("Rochester"), and Bebutova, and those who stayed in Russia after the Bolshevik Revolution in 1917 and adapted to the demands of the new literary system, in part by writing novels. The latter group includes Forsh and Shaginian.

Women's prose in the Silver Age, like men's, can be put under the rubrics of "realism" and "modernism," though, like the men's, the boundary lines are not always so clear: One can often find aspects of both literary movements in the content and form of women's prose.[11] Still, the majority of women prose writers would have to be labelled "realists." As such, they tended to favor the depiction of character within a recognizable social setting and, often, within a framework of contemporary history and ideas. One also finds naturalistic details in such writers as Krestovskaia, A. Krandievskaia, Militsyna, Ol'nem, Runova, and Verbitskaia. This naturalism sometimes foregrounds so much unselected detail that it verges on ethnographic survey rather than imaginative prose. The modernists tended to experiment with prose forms, departing from realism in areas such as point of view, narrative system, choice of subject matter, character depiction, imagery, and style. They experimented with mixed genres, deliberately blurring the lines between prose and poetry, autobiography and fiction, autobiography and essay. Yet what is striking in women's prose is the common ground: in theme, character, setting, tone, and even relation to the dominant male tradition. For example, the 1905 Revolution provoked a series of political novels by women such as Gippius and Verbitskaia. Both looked to models worked out by men. While the modernist Gippius looked to Dostoevsky for her model, the realist Verbitskaia found hers partly by returning to the Chernyshevskian tradition and partly by learning from Artsybashev's *Sanin*. At the same time, one finds modernist experiments in such realists as A. Krandievskaia with her philosophical "An Insomniac's Aphorisms" ("Aforizmy bessonitsy," 1915) and Militsyna's poems in prose in the third volume of her *Stories (Rasskazy,* 1913). To some extent, both groups turned inward and became more concerned with journeys of self-exploration and with the human psyche. Whereas the realists approached the psyche in terms of motivational causality, the modernists tended to depict it as the "soul," the internal battleground of metaphysical forces.

What is significant is the lack of earlier women prose writers' influence, the absence of a conscious continuity between women writers. Though women had been writing prose fiction during most of the nineteenth century, this heritage remained largely unknown or unembraced. One exception appears to have been Verbitskaia, who, in an autobiographical statement prepared for an anthology published in 1901, cited V. Krestovskii (pseudonym of N. D. Khvoshchinskaia) as a writer she avidly read in childhood. When she and her sister returned home after graduation from an institute, she remembered waiting impatiently for journals with the novels of Smirnova. And when the two sisters themselves began writing, they imitated Krestovskii.[12] But despite this assertion, it is difficult to find direct linkages. Undoubtedly, it was, to some extent, a lack of feeling part of a recognized and successful female tradition that made it so difficult for Russian women to find their own way in prose.

Important sources of their prose were also various confessional forms. Diary-keeping, chronicling family histories, memoir writing, and correspondence were accepted and popular activities for literate Russian women as early as the eighteenth century.[13] By the end of the nineteenth century, the appeal of autobiography and memoir appears to have reached a crescendo, as Russians felt the need to look back and take stock of who they were and as the modernists, fascinated by the individual—often eccentric—personality, encouraged dramatizations of self and explorations of psyche and soul.[14]

One finds a preponderance in women's writings of "diaries" and "memoirs," whether nonfictional or fictional.[15] The most famous diary of the day belonged to Mariia Bashkirtseva. It was first published in Russian translation in 1889, and showed Russian women a greatly expanded presentation of the female self. Practically every taboo that Russian women writers experienced in depicting female characters was broken by Bashkirtseva. The diary's importance for women was indicated by the interest they showed in it and by references to it in nonfiction and in fiction.[16]

Opposed to Bashkirtseva's "decadent" confession was the more typical kind of autobiographically based work by women which arose from their tradition of writing for children and thus were closer to moral instruction than to confessional form. Women writers who wrote such instructional autobiographical works include Charskaia, Kiseleva, and Lukhmanova.[17]

By the early twentieth century, the use of a diary form became commonplace in fiction by women.[18] However, readers tended to confuse this fiction with factual autobiography, which the publishers themselves sometimes encouraged. For example, in the foreword to Nadezhda Sanzhar's novella, *Anna's Notes (Zapiski Anny*, 1910), the publisher openly encourages the reader to interpret the book as autobiography, while Anastasiia Tsvetaeva, in the introduction to *Smoke, Smoke, and Smoke (Dym, dym, dym*, 1916)—a playful mixture of factual and fictional genres—fervantly denies that the book *is* her diary.

Another outstanding feature of Russian women's prose, whether realist or modernist, is its tendentiousness and, frequently, its tone of moral earnestness. There are several explanations for this quality in their work. First of all, Russian literature in general tends to be didactic.[19] But with the ascendency of the Chekhovian type of short story, and the attack on traditional intelligentsia morality by the modernists, the didactic certainty of earlier prose by men became more muted or more problematic. This was less true of women. Their prose betrays an acceptance of their role as the bearers of morality in society and as educators of the young.[20] Indeed, many women writers wrote stories for children, and the influence of this type of writing can be seen in their fiction for adults. Furthermore, since they still were ambivalent about being serious writers, the "wish to do good" would justify such endeavors. Writing was still viewed as a self-centered activity, unbecoming to the traditional woman. Real "woman's work" was directed toward helping others.[21] Finally, the presence of a narrator who acts as a moral guide also betrays a lack of faith in their own art to stand on its own and in their readers to infer the correct meaning.[22]

In keeping with their high moral aims and the critical realist tradition, much fiction by Russian women could be labelled "protest fiction."[23] Women writers tended to champion the powerless, the helpless, the victimized, the outcast, and the underdog. The protest could be against social and economic conditions, as in early works by Shchepkina-Kupernik and Avilova, in E. M. Militsyna, A. R. Krandievskaia, Annenkova-Bernar, some of Ol'nem's stories, in Zinov'eva-Annibal's *The Tragic Menagerie (Tragicheskii zverinets*, 1907), and even, to some extent, in early stories by Gippius, or against more personal forms of oppression as in Ol'nem's "Dynasty" ("Dinastiia," 1904) and Krestovskaia's "The Howl" ("Vopl'," 1900).

While Russian women writers were often accused of using only "love" plots, upon closer examination one finds many narratives that center on love or contain love episodes actually are structured as quests, especially the quest for happiness or "self-realization."[24] The word "happiness" itself appears with a striking frequency in women's titles, both in fiction and nonfiction. Lukhmanova wrote a whole book on the subject *On Happiness (O schast'e*, 1898) in which she defines it primarily in non-material terms: the happiness of contemplation, knowledge, labor, love, and suffering. She fulminates against sensual love as the basis for marriage as well as against women's desire for equal civil rights, their egotism, and isolation.

Happiness for Russian women in the nineteenth century had been defined as existing outside of the self, as work for others, whether within the domestic sphere in familial obligations or in the public sphere to help the less fortunate. In the Silver Age we begin to see challenges to these notions of happiness.[25] One new goal of work outside of the domestic sphere was aesthetic activity, and devotion to art and beauty became a new form of happiness. This was a goal that was not aimed directly at other people; it was not relational. It enabled women to define happiness for themselves in a self-contained way. Even more unconventionally, happiness was redefined in terms of the world within oneself— in self-exploration and self-assertion that might include sexuality. This new definition offended the conservatives who viewed women's happiness always in terms of self-denial for the sake of the family; it offended the radicals who viewed female virtue in terms of self-denial for the sake of the common people. Fictional works by women that touted autonomy and self-fulfillment in unconventional terms—neither through love for a man nor customary domestic pursuits—brought on the sharpest criticism.

Starting in 1887, with Verbitskaia's clarion call, the novella "First Signs" ("Pervye Lastochki"),[26] much of the quest centered around the exploration of women's roles within society and within the family. This is a ground-breaking story, because many of its motifs and relationships were to be repeated and varied by women prose writers over the next three decades. The work is a transitional one, mixing the ideals of the populist ideology of the preceding period and those of the Silver Age with its emphasis on aesthetic pursuit. Thus, Verbitskaia's heroine, Valentina Kameneva, first finds happiness in the stereotypical populist activity of ministering to the peasants in the countryside.

Kameneva is also married to a doctor and has three children. Characteristically, for Russian political activists, the marriage is not a passionate one, but one in which the couple is united by a common ideology. In women's fiction, sexual satisfaction is commonly denied to female political activists. After her doctor husband's death, however, Kameneva moves to Moscow and tries to make a career by writing. Temptation is embodied in the handsome, wealthy, and conservative landowner Chagin. He represents both financial security and sexual passion. But because of his conventional views of sex roles, he also represents a threat to Kameneva's independence and artistic ambitions. So she keeps him at bay. Unemployed and desperately poor, she dies from consumption before achieving success as a writer.

Verbitskaia's heroine, however, achieves some degree of immortality in her final "testament" to a young governess she meets in a park. The latter, a "future woman," listens to this testament and "unconsciously" inscribes it "in her heart." In her testament, Kameneva exhorts women to reject love and domesticity for independence and satisfying work for the public welfare. Her story advocates female fulfillment in work rather than through marriage and motherhood. It views sex as an activity that women should engage in only for their own pleasure. It equivocates on the nature and purpose of the work. It also contains emblematic relationships that reappear in women's fiction: a strong, mutually beneficial friendship between women; a mentorship between an older woman and a younger one that "liberates" the latter.

These factors in the quest for happiness—work and sexual satisfaction versus marriage and motherhood—are the central themes in much Silver Age fiction by women. With the passing of the 1880s and the coming of modernism, more and more heroines take up artistic pursuits, though such populist careers as doctoring and educating the disadvantaged continue to be depicted. In the novel *The Actress (Artistka*, 1891), Krestovskaia sets up the choice between love and career. Gipppius's heroine in the story "The Light Blue Sky" ("Goluboe nebo," 1896), in rejecting marriage to a conventionally acceptable man, expresses a yearning for something more fulfilling in her life—symbolized by the sky. Shchepkina-Kupernik, in her novel *Happiness (Schast'e*, 1897), sets her heroine on a quest: first she marries her gymnasium teacher who turns out to be a "false" mentor; then she begins to find the "right" path through an older female mentor-artist; she deviates from the "right path" again and is reunited with her husband; in the end, she leaves her husband to rejoin her "true" mentor, the artist, and finds happiness in devotion to art and single motherhood. Again, happiness and satisfaction are to be found in an all-female world. Ol'nem's actress-heroine, in "Without Illusions" ("Bez illiuzii," 1903), goes on a quest for a true mentor to counteract the influence of her false mentor—her actress-mother. She finds the mentor as well as a mother substitute in the person of an older actress who has devoted her life to serving art.

After 1905, women's depiction of the quest for happiness usually ends in disappointment. The optimism of Shchepkina-Kupernik's novel, Ol'nem's story, and the hope embodied in Verbitskaia's "First Signs" is rarely seen. Many quests even end in death, often suicide. Zinov'eva-Annibal tried to depict an ideal all-female world of beauty, sensuality, and art in the novella *Thirty-Three Freaks (Tridtsat' tri uroda)*. It is a story of two actresses involved in a lesbian relationship. In a variation on the Pygmalion and Galatea story, the older actress, Vera, fashions and mentors the younger. The destruction of their idyll occurs with the intrusion of men.

Verbitskaia returned to many of the earlier themes of "First Signs" in her extremely popular six-volume novel, *The Keys to Happiness (Kliuchi schast'ia*, 1909–1913).[27] Mania, her heroine, rejects domesticity and marriage to the man she loves in order to explore her sexual nature and artistic potential. Her mentor is a man who, in his saintly perfection, seems to have been plucked from Chernyshevskii's *What Is to Be Done?* Though Mania tries to live by his precepts, she ends up committing suicide. She failed to find satisfaction in her career as a modern dancer or in motherhood. In the end, sensual love proves fatal. In fact, love is fatal to almost all the characters in the novel. The only character who retains her sanity and remains unscathed is the chaste Sonia, who perseveres in medical school.

A clearer message of the necessity for choice between a career, on the one hand, and sex and motherhood, on the other, is depicted by Nagrodskaia in *The Wrath of Dionysus (Gnev Dionisa,* 1910). The cheerful message of this popular novel is that women "can have it all," not simultaneously, but serially. The heroine is forced to give up her career in painting in order to become a mother. But she expresses no regrets about her choice. The heroine's mentor is a homosexual friend; her sister-in-law, a self-denying populist, is depicted in unrelievedly negative terms.

Finally, a work that encompasses many of these themes is Runova's "Nothing Sacred" ("Bez zaveta," 1913). Set in a woman's health clinic, the story gathers together a group of women of different ages and classes who exchange opinions on motherhood, marriage, sex, and independence. The heroine is tempted to reject her passionless marriage and vacillates in her feelings about motherhood, though she generally views it positively. Women who have made different choices come and go in the clinic. There is no clear resolution in the end.

The conservative view is represented by such writers as Avilova, Veselkova-Kil'shtet, and Ek. In her story "Creativity" ("Tvorchestvo," 1914), Avilova opposes two sisters: one has chosen a career path and remained unmarried and childless; the other sister opted for marriage and motherhood. Though the former says she is satisfied with her choice, the reader is given to understand otherwise. Veselkova-Kil'shtet, in her novel *The Kolychevs' Patrimony (Kolychevskaia votchina,* 1911), depicts the virtues of wifely and motherly devotion and the misery of bad mothers and sexually adventurous women. The short-story writer Ek felt the need to publish *Letters of a Mother (Pis'ma materi,* 1915) in which she discusses her ideas on child rearing. She insists that a mother must always put duty to her child before all other concerns.

Because of the types of narratives that women preferred and because of the nature of their own experience, certain types of characters appear with a noticeable frequency. These include the artist-heroine, the vulnerable child, and the victimized lower-class woman. There are also frequent depictions of powerful attachments between women, whether that of a mother and child or female friends. The latter very frequently form the most positive emotional core of many fictional works. Some writers such as Shavrova and Shchepkina-Kupernik liked to depict "superfluous women," the female version of the literary type, the "superfluous man." What is generally absent is the "terribly perfect" (Heldt) positive heroine of nineteenth-century male fiction[28] or autonomous women characters. Russian women writers of this period do "not imagine women characters with even the autonomy they themselves have achieved," and "they cannot, or for the most part have not, imagined characters moving, as the authors themselves have moved, beyond that pain."[29] Of course, there are some exceptions, such as Shchepkina-Kupernik's heroines in the novel *Happiness* and Nagrodskaia's heroine in *The Wrath of Dionysus.* There are also positive heroines actively engaged in populist political activity by such writers as Militsyna, Krestovskaia, and Verbitskaia. There is also the saintly warrior heroine, modeled after Joan of Arc, but generally not in prose fiction intended for adults.[30]

The "new woman," independent, career-minded, and unconventional, especially with regard to her sexuality, was usually an artist of some sort. This character enabled women writers to present women characters whose lives could be believably presented as conducted outside conventional bounds and through whom they could deal with issues such as love versus vocation and commercial versus "true" art. An especially frequent character was the actress.[31]

A subcategory of the "new woman" was the "female decadent" or "tango" woman[32] through whom women depicted the extension of equality of the sexes to the sphere of morality. Many women writers depicted this type negatively, emphasizing their characters' capriciousness and egotism (for example, Krestovskaia, Shchepkina-Kupernik, Annenkova-Bernar, Shavrova, and, to some extent, Ol'nem). The most positive presentations occur in Verbitskaia's *Keys to Happiness* and in the work of Zinov'eva-Annibal. Yet here, too, this assertion is problematic. Though Verbitskaia depicted her heroine Mania El'tsova positively, it is not a realistic treatment, and the character is hardly an example of positive characteristics: For example, she does not live independently but through the strong men who guide her life and death, and, basically, she is self-destructive. In the cases of Zinov'eva-Annibal and Mar, the latter, especially in her short stories, comes closest to depicting this character without qualifications. But in Mar's longer narratives and in the work of Zinov'eva-Annibal, the female decadent characters' behavior is incorporated into a larger metaphysical drama.

Of all the range of characters that women writers focused on, it is the child who most often enabled them to combine the best aspects of their talent. Women depict the child with a wonderful delicacy and enormous range: Vulnerable, very young children first coming to grips with the adult world's injustice and cruelty whereby they begin to develop a moral sense (some fine examples can be found in Kiseleva's and Avilova's work, and in the work of Krestovskaia, Annenkova-Bernar, Zinov'eva-Annibal, Guro, and Tèffi). Women writers aired their moral concerns and "protests" in faithfully observed stories about children that were particularly effective, because they could provoke the reader's compassion without recourse to sentimentality. Not just the very young, but the mature child served this purpose as well. Krestovskaia used this age group especially well in her novel "Early Storms" ("Rannie grozy," 1886) and in her novella "Outside of Life" ("Vne zhizni," 1889). In them, she protested the emotionally disturbing effects on a young girl of her parents' divorce and the crippling of a young woman by the educational system at an institute.

Another often-repeated and well-drawn figure is that of "Poor Liza," the seduced and abandoned lower-class woman. She was particularly suitable for protest fiction because she was doubly vulnerable due to her sex and her class. She was also a literary challenge, because she had a long fictional history. Gippius featured this figure both in early and somewhat later fiction ("The Ill-Fated Girl"

["Zloschastnaia," 1890], "Two Hearts" ["Dva serdtsa," 1892], and her novel *The Devil's Doll (Chertova kukla*, 1911). Krestovskaia, like Gippius, drew such a figure in "Mytishchev's Confession" ("Ispoved' Mytishcheva," 1901) as part of an exposé of a destructive hero, and Ol'nem portrayed her in "Ivan Fedorovich" (1903) as a counterweight to the indecisive and timid "superfluous" hero.

Within this overview of women's writing at the turn of the century, seven authors stand out for having made contributions of differing kinds: their popularity and concentration on certain literary issues peculiar to women's writing within their work (Verbitskaia and Tèffi); their success in developing a distinctive voice and an original vision as well as creating literary works that have stood the test of time and remain compelling today (the early Krestovskaia, Ol'nem, Guro, Tèffi, and, to some extent, Gippius and Zinov'eva-Annibal); and their attempts at literary innovation in either content or form, which, even when unsuccessful, extended the terms in which women wrote (Zinov'eva-Annibal and Guro); their outstanding achievements in another literary form that makes the study of their prose a necessity (Gippius).

ANASTASIIA ALEKSEEVNA VERBITSKAIA (1861–1928)

Of the seven women listed above, none has been treated so harshly by critics and fellow writers as Verbitskaia.[33] Reading later evaluations of her work, it is easy to forget that in her early career, which began with the publication of "Discord" in 1887, Verbitskaia frequently published in serious "thick" journals of the day. From the first, Verbitskaia wrote stories built around ideas. The strongest part of her writing was satirical, such as the amusing picture of the world of journalism that she presents in "Discord." But her early work is very tendentious, notably sentimental, and rather crude in form. She did, however, work on her story-telling craft and improved. She eliminated the earlier sentimentality; introduced more sophisticated narrative techniques such as the frame story; and moved away from a single, simple point of view, so that the ideas that form the core of her stories are presented and commented upon with greater variety and complexity. Yet there were always certain aspects of popular fiction in Verbitskaia's work from the very beginning: stylistically a simple syntax and repetitive vocabulary; in characterization, a tendency toward externally presented idealized figures from romance fiction, and—for Russian literature—a fast-paced, well-constructed plot.[34]

In her middle period, Verbitskaia continued to hesitate between populist and modernist ideology. She presents a series of successful, positive heroines who represent either the populist idea of working for the people or the modernist emphasis on aesthetic activity as an equally meaningful endeavor (the play *Mirage [Mirazh*, 1896]; "The Awakening" ["Probuzhdenie," 1899]; "Aesthetics" ["Estetika," 1901]; "Happiness" ["Schastie," 1904]). Verbitskaia's greatest success was reached with the six-volume novel *The Keys to Happiness*;

yet in many ways it is a continuation of what came before: aspects of popular fiction combined with "serious" literary models.[35] Here, too, Verbitskaia tries to combine left-wing politics and modernist ideology, and the combination comes out muddled. As in her earlier works, the great danger to human happiness is the irrational sexual drive; it brings misery to all the main characters. The popular literary elements are even stronger in this novel than in earlier works: the travels to exotic places, the heroine's remarkable fame and courtship by the rich and powerful, and, finally, the strong affirmation of woman's ultimate need to define herself in relational terms.[36] Her weakness in character depiction—characters who are outer shells with no inner workings—is more glaring in his long novel than in the shorter, swiftly plotted fiction. Her best scenes revolve around exchanges of ideas: She embeds her characters' ideological stances in their psychological states and social positions.

Actually, Verbitskaia's best writing is to be found in the second volume of her autobiography, *My Reminiscences (Moi vospominaniia)*.[37] In it she takes us back to the critical time in her life when she was 15 or 16 years old, and upon graduation from boarding school, was faced with the narrow range of options open to her and her sister as young, upper-class women. In this work she ably traced the process of her own self-realization and depicted a family of strong women who helped to form her: her grandmother, her mother, and her sister, also a writer. This memoir also contains some of her best satire. Especially wonderful is the description of her first job interview for a governess's position with two sisters who are presented as a grotesque pair like Tweedle-dee and Tweedle-dum. It is time to assess this writer both in the context of Russian women's literature and the middle-brow popular fiction that gained a large readership just before the Revolution of 1917.

MARIIA VSEVOLODNA KRESTOVSKAIA (1862–1920)

Krestovskaia, whose first published story appeared in 1885, was in many ways Verbitskaia's opposite. She specialized in the long novella with a minimal plot that unfolds at a snail's pace. Usually selecting just two or three characters, she diagnoses their relationship at length, usually from the point of view of one main character, concentrating on their perceptions. Her favorite narrative mode was indirect discourse. There is little dialogue in Krestovskaia's writings; instead, the narrator almost always reports the characters' speech. Furthermore, her work lacks the kind of intellectual content that Verbitskaia often included in her work.

One of her best early works is "Outside Life" (1889), a searing indictment of the exclusive boarding school (*institut*), a combination of grammar and finishing schools for upper-class girls. The narrative follows the heroine from age three to thirty, from a popular, lively girl to a frustrated woman, crippled by institute life. Krestovskaia's slow pace and consistent presentation of events from the heroine's point of view subtly and convincingly depict the evolution of a personality.

The early work that brought Krestovskaia the greatest attention was the novel *The Actress* (published three times between 1891 and 1903).[38] In this novel, the heroine is forced to choose between her career and love. She chooses the former. Because of this devotion to art, Krestovskaia's heroine was compared to Bashkirtseva. A number of critics scolded Krestovskaia for a sympathetic portrayal of a woman who had engaged in "free" love and for the lack of any substantive cultural or intellectual "meat" in the novel.

Krestovskaia's work, however, was quite popular: By 1896 she had published four volumes of prose; a number of her works were republished several times. After almost a decade of great productivity, she appears to have experienced something of a creative crisis by the mid nineties. She tried different narrative approaches, for example, *A Woman's Life (Zhenskaia zhizn'*, 1894–1903) is an epistolary novel. In the last decade of her life, she published only two new stories, using another narrative strategy, that of the diary. Her final publication in her lifetime, *To the Sunshine! (K solntsu)*, appeared in 1905. It consisted of diary entries and travel notes, the latter including a description of a visit to Mariia Bashkirtseva's relatives in Paris.

ZINAIDA NIKOLAEVNA GIPPIUS (1869–1945)

Of all women writers, Gippius strove the most to write like an "honorary male."[39] She wrote poetry,[40] narrative prose, plays, criticism, and memoirs. Though she is acknowledged primarily for her innovative and influential poetry, her prose is not without interest.[41] Unfortunately, much of Gippius's renown stems from her personal iconoclasm, and her work, particularly her prose, has not been sufficiently examined.[42]

Her first published story, "The Ill-Fated Girl," is a tour-de-force of *skaz* narration, that is, a first-person narrator whose speech differs notably from standard literary Russian. The heroine is of peasant origin but has become an urban dweller and received some education. Gippius here is re-telling the story of Karamzin's "Poor Liza" (Bednaia Liza, 1792)—a lower-class girl seduced and abandoned by an upper-class cad—but from the girl's point of view with its tone of resignation and its inarticulateness. Gippius turns what could have been a maudlin tale into an unsentimental one by the distancing effect of distinctive speech and point of view.[43]

Gippius's subsequent stories are usually told by a third-person omniscient narrator, although in emigration, she returned to the first-person narrative in *The Memoirs of Martynov (Memuary Martynova,* 1927). The stories of the early nineties have a realistic, recognizable social background, but by the late nineties, they take on aspects of the fantastic, and her characterization became more abstract and symbolic. They also increasingly feature more dialogue or sometimes just monologues, as Gippius became more earnest about spelling out her message. After the 1905 Revolution, Gippius turned to political issues in her prose, especially the intelligentsia's wrong-headedness as an obstacle to real revolution (compare the story "The Shop Assistant" ["Prikazchik," 1910] and the novel *The Devil's Doll* [1911].

From the beginning, Gippius's prose deals with intimations of immortality and the revolt against all forms of determinism, whether social conventions or biology. Her characters demand the impossible and are often overwhelmed by the mundane and the rational. A number of her heroines remain unmarried by happy choice (compare "Miss May" ["Miss Mai," 1895] and "The Blue Sky" [1896]). Yet rarely did Gippius find a really suitable narrative vehicle for her ideas. One of the best is "Outside Time" ("Vne vremeni," 1906). Here, she situates a story about time on an isolated estate—there are only three characters— and she finds convincing means to add confusion about the age of an older heroine, such as the Oscar Wildean device of a portrait that plays an active role in the hero's perception. Gippius's greatest strength in prose, like Verbitskaia's, was in satire: She has marvelous send-ups of the literary world, both in the provinces ("The Blue Sky") and in the capital of St. Petersburg (*The Devil's Doll*). Gippius's attempts to deal with philosophical and political ideas in her prose did not prevent her from being pigeonholed as a woman writer. Because she generally avoided writing about hearth and home, she was castigated as "insincere" and, even worse, as "hysterical."

'OL'NEM' (VARVARA NIKOLAEVNA TSEKHOVSKAIA, 1872–1941)

Arguably the best realist prose writer among women of the Silver Age, for an all-too-brief period of time (1895–1914), Varvara Tsekhovskaia (penname 'O. N. Ol'nem') produced one fine story after another.[44] Like Verbitskaia and Tèffi, Ol'nem began working for a newspaper, and this experience undoubtedly helped her hone a sober, straightforward style and gave her a lot of "material" for fictional treatment.[45]

Contemporary critics noted her thematic closeness to Chekhov, but one should also include Bunin: the economic and spiritual downfall of the old aristocracy that is also accompanied in some cases by physical degeneration. One finds this theme in her first story, "Warum?" (1895), and in several of her last stories such as "Dynasty" (1910) and "Quagmire" ("Triasina," 1914).[46] A moralist, Tsekhovskaia structured her stories around the tension between good and evil, the good included indifference to material well-being and devotion to a higher calling or genuineness of feeling. Yet her fascination was with human nature whether virtuous or not, so that the moral basis of the fiction is subdued. A number of her stories tell of the triumph of the human spirit over unhappy situations through the characters' resourcefulness and refusal to betray their central set of values. However, an equal number of stories deal with the entrapment of people by one another. It is not so much the workings of fate that she shows—nor social relations, though both are present in her fiction—as the positive and liberating or confining and destructive relations that people establish.

Frequently, the triumphant characters are women who are contrasted with "superfluous" men. She depicted some of the most colorful and memorable female characters in fiction by Russian women, such as the two brassy actresses in "Without Illusion" (1904).

Though Tsekhovskaia has some stories that consist primarily of internal monologue, such as "Without a Residence Permit" ("Bez prava na zhitel'stvo," 1901), she mostly used a third-person, objective narrator who comments little. Her narrative is lean, for she confines her descriptions primarily to the physical appearance of her main characters. As Tsekhovskaia gained experience and self-assurance, her stories grew in size as well as in the range of characterization and setting. Her early stories have only a few characters, while her last stories, "The Carefree Ones" ("Bezzabotnye," 1912) and "Quagmire" feature a much larger scale of both character and scene. But the most outstanding feature of her narrative is the use of dialogue. Tsekhovskaia had a wonderful ear for individualized speech, and she mostly depicts and reveals characters by how they speak and what they say and write. Many of them have such individualized speech that they can be readily identified by it.

While Tsekhovskaia generally received positive reviews, her work on the whole was ignored. This lack of acknowledgment was decried by a critic writing in 1911 for the bulletin of M. O. Vol'f's bookstores. Unfortunately, she published her last piece of serious fiction in 1914.

TÈFFI (1872–1952)

'Tèffi' is the pen name of Nadezhda Aleksandrovna Buchinskaia.[47] She is difficult to discuss in a limited amount of space, because she was prolific and published more than thirty books in her lifetime. She wrote prose—fictional and nonfictional, poetry, plays, and one book of memoirs. With the exception of one novel, her prose fiction consists of short feuilletons and stories. Like Ol'nem, Tèffi "cut her teeth" in journalism and developed a laconic style. But unlike Ol'nem, she was enormously popular, both in prerevolutionary Russia and in emigration after 1919.[48] There was even a candy named after her.

Tèffi was generally known for her short, humorous works. She was undoubtedly the finest wit and parodist among women writers of that era. This was a particular accomplishment, because women were not generally expected to write in this vein and were even discouraged from trying.[49] But Tèffi wrote a great deal that was quite serious. Given her productivity, her work was bound to be uneven. Yet one can find gems in every period of her writing and in each category.

In her verbal wit and word play, use of an obtuse, illogical, unreliable "skaz" narrator,[50] and the themes of "dead souls" and life's absurdity, Tèffi has much in common with Gogol'. She likes to use some of the same comic devices, such as absurd lists that combine the serious with the petty, ridiculous names, hilarious food details, and the grotesque, the cumulative effect of which is "laughter through tears." But Tèffi also invented a number of humorous devices of her own, such as play with common phrases where she substitutes an inanimate object where an animate usually occurs and puns using foreign languages, particularly the French surrounding the Russian émigré colony in Paris. She shares with Chekhov some of the same thematic concerns such as the impossibility of true communication between people, humanity's hopelessly divergent perspectives on the same phenomenon, and human illusions and self-deceptions. With Sologub she shares the view of childhood as the only time of innocence and adulthood as inevitably leading to corruption; with Gippius she shares an interest in time and a protest against the biologically determined aging process.

Many of Tèffi's stories display binary structures of various kinds. Some begin with the "skaz" narrator's "monologue" on some topic followed by a story to illustrate this monologue—or, more frequently, to contradict it. Another frequent opposition is between characters: male-female, old-young, opposite personalities, and human-animal. There is much parody of other texts in Tèffi and much meta-literary commentary, such as in the stories "How I Wrote a Novel" ("Kak ia pisala roman," in *Drug chelovechestva*, 1911), "The Demonic Woman" ("Demonicheskaia zhenshchina," in *Dym bez ognia*, 1914), "Two Diaries," and "Iago" ("Dva dnevnika" and "Iago," in *All About Love*, 1946). She has superb stories that contain a great deal of realistically observed detail, such as "Time" ("Vremia"), but there are also stories that she spins out of other texts of all sorts, such as "The Nanny's Tale About the Mare's Head" ("Nian'kina skazka pro kobyl'iu golovu")—a parody of the folktale, "The Translator" ("Perevodchitsa"), "The French Novel" ("Frantsyzskii roman")—also a literary parody, and "Advertisements" ("Reklamy," all from the first two volumes of *Humorous Stories [Iumoristicheskie rasskazy]*, 1910–1911). The ability to invent is a positive value in Tèffi, as highlighted in the delightful story "A Bright Life" ("Iarkaia zhizn'," *All About Love*). Though she is more widely discussed than most women writers, Tèffi still has not been given her rightful place in the "serious" canon of Russian literature.

LIDIIA DMITRIEVNA ZINOV'EVA-ANNIBAL (1866–1907)

Zinov'eva-Annibal came to writing late in her life: Only at the beginning of the twentieth century did she take it up seriously. She was the quintessential rebel and is the only writer of this group to deal with philosophical, feminist, and sociopolitical revolt. Her first few works bear the strong imprint of the ideas of her husband, Viacheslav Ivanov, as well as the search for a proper form in which to express them. She started with a novel, *Torches (Plamenniki,* unpublished), which dealt with the myth of Dionysus.[51] She then wrote a three-act play, *Rings (Kol'tsa,* 1904), also based on Ivanov's ideas about the "Dionysiac Eros."[52] She then wrote a novella, *Thirty-Three Freaks (Tridtsat' tri uroda,* 1907), which, like *Rings,* deals with the idea that love should not be exclusive but shared, though this may involve self-sacrifice and suffering. However, because Zinov'eva-Annibal depicted an overt lesbian love between the two heroines, the novella caused an uproar. Perhaps the reaction to the story was also so strong because *Thirty-Three Freaks* is an assault on many expectations about writing by women: It is not only very forthright about the female body, but it also presents lesbian sexuality and female narcissism positively. Critics overlooked Zinov'eva-Annibal's attempt at an all-female idyl based on physical and artistic beauty that is destroyed by the intrusion of male outsiders.

In her final major work, *The Tragic Menagerie* (1907), Zinov'eva-Annibal has freed herself from dependence on Ivanov's ideas[53] and has not only changed her style, but has also tapped a source of creativity that has served so many other women writers well. *The Tragic Menagerie* is a series of stories about the heroine Vera that follow her development from childhood to the age of eighteen. The style is one of psychological realism, with an emphasis on the child's developing consciousness, though some pieces are a hybrid, as Zinov'eva-Annibal included modernist lyrical flourishes. The book forms a spiritual journey in which the child's moral self evolves on both social and religious planes. This development is presented—especially in the early stories—through her adventures with various animals that she comes into contact with on the family's country estate.

Zinov'eva-Annibal uses an adult narrator who remembers these events, but they are filtered through the child's consciousness. One of her most effective devices is to switch from a past-tense narrative to the present tense to create a sense of immediacy in the child's world. Though there is also a ''Dionysian'' presence in the eternally interlocking cycle of death and life, there is much else in these stories including psychological realism, the depiction of the mother figure's powerful moral force, a consciousness of social and gender inequities, and a flexible prose style that encompasses an efficient narrative, richly idiomatic dialogue and suggestive symbolism. The book won high praise from Gippius, Aleksandr Blok, and Marina Tsvetaeva, among others. Unfortunately, shortly after this book appeared, Zinov'eva-Annibal died unexpectedly. Her husband, Viacheslav Ivanov, was able to publish one more book of her work, *No!* (*Nyet*, 1918), mostly short prose pieces that had been published during his wife's lifetime.

ELENA GENRIKHOVNA GURO (1877–1913)

Of the seven women selected for special attention, Guro was the most radical in literary terms and the least noted in her lifetime.[54] She also had very little time to develop as a writer: Her first prose piece appeared in 1905, and in 1913, not yet 36, she died. Her prose was radical in theme, form, and style. As she herself said in her prose: ''I will not sing about love'' (from ''Evening'' [''Vechernee''] in *Little Camels of the Sky* [*Nebesnye verbliuzhata*]). And she did not. Perhaps because she was a trained and practicing artist,[55] she ''sang'' about perception, and this perception—often imitative of a naive child's—was unique: She selected particular angles of vision such as in ''Arrival in the Country''

(''Priezd v derevniu''), where the child describes the landscape and objects as she moves away from them in a wagon (in *Hurdy-Gurdy* [*Sharmanka*]). Her narrator and characters dwell in a fluid, fragmentary fictional world in which people, nature, things, gestures, feelings, and ideas are all levelled to the same ontological status. They are animated with feelings and capable of action. Frequently she inverts the ''normal'' relationship between a subject and an object; in Guro, it is often the object that acts rather than being acted upon.

Her themes include art as salvation and the poet's central role as a ''doctor'' of souls, spiritual—at times specifically theosophical yearnings—and immortality. Guro was close to Tèffi thematically, in identifying the artist with the child, in seeing moral goodness in children and animals, and in emphasizing the importance of the imagination. She also shared with other women writers empathy with the disenfranchised and powerless.

Elsewhere she wrote, ''I do not want to know the chance happenings of unreal life'' (''An Impulse'' [Poryv] from *The Hurdy-Gurdy*), and she defied the conventions of nineteenth-century realism. She blurred genre lines, incorporating poetic and dramatic forms into prose.[56] She dispensed with a clearly defined narrator and characters. The narrator may start out as a third person and switch to first person and then back again without any reason. The narrative line proper has been reduced to a bare minimum, and it disappears entirely in some later prose pieces. She also moved in the direction of parable, such as in ''The Tale of Olaf the Towheaded'' (''Skazanie ob Olafe Belobrysom,'' 1911), but even here, she refuses to ''end'' the narrative properly. Instead of a story, we get a very vivid sense of immediacy, of a world alive with sentient forces, of word play and creation, and the repetition of key expressions. Her style is unique: It has unusual noun-epithet, noun-verb combinations often predicated on a universal animism. Her descriptions resemble modern painting by combining snippets of a concrete identifiable world with abstractions. The surrounding world is never neutrally or objectively presented. The perceiver's feelings determine the description. Guro likes to use ''subjectless'' verbs or phrases in which the subject is implied or omitted altogether. She avoids transitive verbs where there is a clear agent of action. These stylistic devices result in a unique vision of a world without logic or cause and effect.

Almost universally ignored by critics and the public, Guro was appreciated by some other writers, especially certain of the Russian Futurists.[57] She anticipates Olesha and Nabokov in playing with angles of perception, light, shadows, and reflections and in her hostility to philistinism and championing of artistic creativity.

What is striking in this survey of seven women writers is the fact that, although we see a great variety in women's fiction, on the one hand, on the other, there are some common themes and concerns; nevertheless, their work as a whole did not cohere into a tradition. Each woman writes as though she were the first woman writer: There is no evidence that they felt part of a vital continuum. This separateness contrasts starkly with Russian women poets, who, by the early twentieth century, had created an outstanding body of work to which other women poets felt a connection. While the work of women poets has survived into the late twentieth century, women's prose has largely been lost or marginalized.

NOTES

1. Research for this article was supported in part by a grant from the International Research & Exchanges Board (IREX), with funds provided by the National Endowment for the Humanities, the U.S. Information Agency, and the U.S. Dept. of State, which administers the Soviet and East European Training Act of 1983 (Title VIII).

2. A. Skabichevskii, "Tekushchaia literatura," *Syn otechestva* 224 (1899): 2.

3. Ibid., 2.

4. A. A. Izmailov, "Literaturnye zametki," *Birzhevye vedomosti*, No. 488 (1904).

5. Nine years later, Izmailov's negative views had not changed. Writing about Gippius's prose, he faults her for having the same weaknesses as all women writers, most grievous among them is a horizon confined to family life. Though this is a highly inaccurate claim about Gippius's prose, it is not surprising, given Izmailov's statement that "ladies' prose" cannot be spoken about with any profound respect at this point (1913). He was especially indignant that Gippius chose to write from a male point of view. See A. A. Izmailov, *Pestrye znamena: literaturnye portrety bezvremen'ia* (Moscow, 1913), 152–53.

6. M. Protopopov, "Zhenskoe tvorchestvo," *Russkaia mysl'* 4 (1891): 123.

7. A. M. Skabicheskii, *Istorii noveishei russkoi literatury*, 5th ed. (St. Petersburg, 1903), 400.

8. Elaine Showalter, *A Literature of Their Own: British Women Novelists from Bronte to Lessing*, 2d ed. (Princeton: Princeton University Press, 1982), 58.

9. For example, Shavrova ('E. Shavrov' and 'E. Shastunov'), Kiseleva ('Pince-nez' for fiction and 'Ego' for translations and book reviews in the mystical journal *Rebus*, but under her real name for children's stories), and Kurch ('Èk').

10. See Victor Terras, *A History of Russian Literature* (New Haven: Yale University Press, 1991), 450. In contrast to their male counterparts such as Belyi, Briusov, Kuzmin, Sologub, Remizov, and Gor'kii, the best women prose writers tended to avoid the novel form. Tèffi, whose work is littered with meta-literary commentary, suggests, jokingly, a hesitancy before the prestigious novel form and her fictional narrator's preference for the more congenial short story in "Kak ia pisala roman" (1911).

11. See the discussion on this point in Edith W. Clowes, *The Revolution of Moral Consciousness: Nietzsche in Russian Literature, 1890–1914* (De Kalb: Northern Illinois University Press, 1988), 40.

12. "Anastasiia Alekseevna Verbitskaia," *Sbornik na pomoshch' uchashchimsia zhenshchinam* (Moscow, 1901), 85–86. Interestingly, Khvoshchinskaia and Smirnova (along with Tur) were precisely the three Russian authoresses cited by Chekhov as possessing a special quality—"strong and noble in spirit"—a quality that he also found in Kiseleva's writing.

13. Barbara Heldt, *Terrible Perfection: Women and Russian Literature* (Bloomington: Indiana University Press, 1987), 64–102.

14. Frederick R. Karl has discussed what he calls "spiritual autobiography" and modernism, specifically the shift from the focus on the individual and society in the novel

"to matters of spirit, soul, and self." What he says about novels also holds true for other prose genres. See Chapter 4 of his book *Modern and Modernism: The Sovereignty of the Artist 1885–1925* (New York: Atheneum, 1985). Russia was no different in this regard: Fiction was becoming more focused on the individual, but so, too, was nonfiction. In the late nineteenth and early twentieth century, one can find numerous diaries, autobiographies, and memoirs published on the pages of "thick" journals and in separate book editions. Many autobiographical manuscripts from the past were now being published for the very first time. These include several very important autobiographies, "pseudo-autobiographies," and memoirs by Russian women. The historian E. N. Shchepkina discusses many of these works as well as others in the article "Vospominaniia i dnevniki russkikh zhenshchin," *Istoricheskii vestnik* 8 (1914): 536–55.

15. According to Tanya Nikolskaya, in the early twentieth century, men called on women writers "to reveal [their] intimate selves resulting in a large number of autobiographical stories and novellas often in diary form. See "The 'Contemporary Woman' in Early Twentieth-Century Russian Literature," *Irish Slavonic Studies* 8 (1987): 109.

16. For example, Liubov' Gurevich wrote an article on Bashkirtseva, "M. K. Bashkirtseva (Biografiko-psikhologicheskii etiud)," *Russkoe bogatstvo* 2 (1988): 73–122, and then published her translation of the diary in *Severnyi vestnik* in 1892; Zinaida Vengerova referred to Bashkirtseva in an introduction to her translation of Annie Besant's "Confession" [*Severnyi vestnik*, No. 1 (1895)]; Annenkova-Bernar's heroine in "Ona" (1901) says that the diary is her "gospel"; when E. A. D'iakonova's diary, *Dnevnik Elizavety D'iakonovoi (1886–1902)*, was first published posthumously in 1904–1905, critics consistently compared it to Bashkirtseva's. In the book of travel notes, *To the Sun!*, published by Mariia Krestovskaia in 1905, she writes of Bashkirtseva, whose family she visited in Paris: "Who has not read Mariia Bashkirtseva's diary or at least heard her name?" (127) and points out that interest in Bashkirtseva has not slackened since her death in 1884 (129). Laura Engelstein postulates Bashkirtseva as a model for Verbitskaia's heroine in *Keys to Happiness* (417n).

17. These types of autobiographical writing were extremely popular. They include Lidiia Charskaia's four fictionalized autobiographies beginning with *For What?* (1909); Mariia Kiseleva's *Morning of Life* (1893); Nadezhda Lukhmanova's *Twenty Years Ago* (later retitled *Girls: Memoirs from Life in an Institute*, published six times between 1893 and 1912. The most frequent setting of these works was a woman's educational institution. Prose fiction with this setting includes Krestovskaia's "Outside Life" (1889), and a part of Gippius's early story "The Ill-Fated Girl" (1890), Shchepkina-Kupernik's novel *Happiness* (1897), Ol'nem's "On the Threshold of Life" (1900), and Verbitskaia's novel *The Keys to Happiness* (1908–1913).

18. Examples include Krestovskaia's last two fictional works, Shchepkina-Kupernik's "From the Diary of a Superfluous Woman" (1903), Ol'nem's "Joy" (1904), Zinov'eva-Annibal's "Thirty-Three Freaks" (1907), Nagrodskaia's *The Wrath of Dionysus* (1910), Nadezhda Sanzhar's *Anna's Notes* (1910), A. Miré's "Pages from a Diary" (1912), Elena Guro's *Little Camels in the Sky* (1914), and Anastasiia Tsvetaeva, *Smoke, Smoke, and Smoke* (1916).

19. Donald Fanger and Gordon Cohen, "Abram Tertz: Dissidence, Diffidence, and Russian Literary Tradition," in *Soviet Society and Culture: Essays in Honor of Vera S. Dunham* (Boulder, CO: Westview Press, 1988), 168.

20. Jessica Tovrov, "Mother-Child Relationships among the Russian Nobility," in

The Family in Imperial Russia, ed. David L. Ransel (Urbana: University of Illinois Press, 1978), 24, 35.

21. Showalter, *A Literature of Their Own*, 52–57, and Rosalind Miles, *The Female Form: Women Writers and the Conquest of the Novel* (London: Routledge and Kegan Paul, 1987), 11, 48.

22. One can trace the inroads that modernism and the women's movement were making on the acceptance by women of such roles. Their fiction betrays conflicts between women and within women themselves about this very issue. While the presence of a moral purpose in women's prose was not in itself a problem, the expectation of it by readers and critics could be constricting. Their fiction was supposed to express clearly a conventional morality. Women whose fiction did not conform to this expectation were excoriated by critics who often paid no attention to the serious artistic aims of the works that they dismissed. Anna Mar addressed this pressure on women writers in a short prose work (she called it a "post card") entitled "Notes personnelles" (1916), in which the female narrator, a writer, argues with her readers who demand moral and "useful" literary works from her.

23. Such fiction, as Elaine Showalter has already pointed out (28) "represented a projection of female experience onto another group; it translated the felt pain and oppression of women into the championship of millworkers, child laborers, prostitutes, and slaves. Women were aware that protest fiction converted anger and frustration into an acceptable form of feminine and Christian expression."

24. See Clowes, 97. See the excellent discussion of "quest" and "love plots" in American and English women's fiction by Rachel Blau DuPlessis, *Writing Beyond the Ending: Narrative Strategies of Twentieth-Century Women Writers* (Bloomington: Indiana University Press, 1985), especially 6–7, 14–15.

25. Through both necessity and choice, late nineteenth-century Russia presented women with more possibilities of how they could lead their lives. This greater choice brought with it conscious debate and inner conflict, which was explored in fictional terms.

26. "Razlad," *Russkaia mysl'*, No. 6 and 7 (1887). Retitled "Pervye lastochki," it was republished in a separate book edition six times between 1900 and 1917.

27. See Laura Engelstein's discussion of this novel in *Keys to Happiness*.

28. Rufus W. Mathewson, Jr., *The Positive Hero in Russian Literature*, 2d ed. (Stanford, CA: Stanford University Press, 1975), 13–16.

29. Carolyn G. Heilbrun, *Reinventing Womanhood* (New York: Norton, 1970), 71–72.

30. See, for example, Annenkova-Bernar's play, *Daughter of the People* (1903) about Joan of Arc, Charskaia's fictionalized biography for juveniles, *A Bold Life* (1905) about Nadezhda Durova, and Stolitsa's novel in verse, *Elena Deeva* (1914), about a woman who eventually becomes a soldier.

31. Actresses are heroines in Krestovskaia's earliest fiction, "A Nook in the Theatrical World" (1885) and the novel, *The Actress*; Ol'nem's "Without Illusions," several short stories by Annenkova-Bernar such as "She"; Chiumina's short story "For the Sake of a Career" (1898); and Zinov'eva-Annibal's scandalous story "Thirty-Three Freaks" (1907). Other types of creative women include writers, musicians, dancers, and painters.

32. Nikolskaya, " 'The Contemporary Woman,' " 108, and "Novaia Eva," *Iskusstvo Leningrada* 8 (1991): 89–93.

33. See, for example, the rather negative view of her presented by Jeffrey Brooks, in *When Russia Learned to Read: Literacy and Popular Literature, 1861–1917* (Princeton:

Princeton University Press, 1985), 158–60 and 278–92 passim, and Clowes, 7–9, 11, 98–111, 226–27, though Terras calls her a "writer of talent" deserving to be anthologized alongside "Korolenko, Hippius, Sologub, and Andreev" (*A History of Russian Literature*, 463).

34. On hallmarks of popular romance fiction and Verbitskaia, see Janice A. Redway, *Reading the Romance* (Chapel Hill: University of North Carolina, 1984), 187–202 and Tatjana Antolovsky, *Der russische Frauenroman (1890–1917)* (Munich: Verlag Otto Sagner, 1987), 126–52.

35. The number of copies of this novel sold was truly staggering for the times: By 1915 she had sold 280,000. See A. M. Gracheva, "Verbitskaia," in *Biograficheskii slovar' russkikh pisatelei*, 1 (Moscow, 1989), 419. See also the perceptive discussion of the novel by Laura Engelstein in *Keys to Happiness: Sex and the Search for Modernity in Fin-de-Siècle Russia* (Ithaca, NY: Cornell University Press, 1992), 400–14.

36. See Redway, 84. Though it can be argued that this "message" is offset, on the one hand, by the triumphant portrayal of Mania's best friend Son'ia, who remains independent and committed to her career; on the other hand, by the conventional female characters such as Son'ia's mother and Nelidov's wife, who are hardly depicted as happy with their lot. And while Mania's sympathies with the Left are only a very minor aspect of her character, she is the first Russian heroine to combine sexual liberation with Left-wing sympathies. This combination is later picked up by women writers in the 1920s: Barkova, Seifullina, and Kollontai.

37. The first volume, *To My Reader*, was first published in 1908 and covered her childhood and years in school. The second volume was published in 1911 and covers little more than a year in her life after graduation from an institute.

38. See the discussion of this novel in Peter Ulf Moller, *Postlude to "The Kreutzer Sonata": Tolstoj and the Debate on Sexual Morality in Russian Literature in the 1890s*, trans. John Kendal (Leiden, Netherlands-New York: E. J. Brill, 1988), 231–32.

39. As used by Rosalind Miles about George Eliot, this phrase describes a woman author who writes "largely assuming the values and processes of the male-created and -dominated society of her time." See *The Female Form*, 38.

40. On Gippius's poetry, see Taubman's chapter in this book and my chapter, "The Silver Age: Highpoint for Women?" in *Women and Society in Russia and the Soviet Union*, ed. Linda Edmondson (Cambridge, England: Cambridge University Press, 1992): 38–40.

41. If Irina Odoevtseva is correct, that Gippius was unable to publish her novels in emigration—she says that there were as many as seventeen—then the published texts fall far short of offering us a full picture of her prose fiction. See *Na beregakh Seny* (Paris: La Presse libre, 1983), 97. In addition, a number of stories and one novel are scattered throughout émigré journals and should be republished in book form to make them more accessible.

42. For a general introduction to Gippius, see Simon Karlinsky, Introduction to "Who Was Zinaida Gippius?" in Vladimir Zlodin, *A Difficult Soul: Zinaida Gippius* (Berkeley: University of California Press, 1980). A fine thematic study of her poetry was written by Olga Matich, *Paradox in the Religious Poetry of Zinaida Gippius* (Munich: W. Fink, 1972). There are several books about her ideas and translations of her work by Temira Pachmuss.

43. Moller, translating the title "An Unfortunate Woman," makes the astute point that "this choice of narrator contributed largely to its effect of understated pathos. The poor woman lacks words in which to express her grief or in which to consider the moral and social implications of her fate. The reader cannot refrain from doing so on her behalf" (261).

44. By 1912 she had published three collections of stories, one in two editions. From 1915 to 1916, she edited the "thick" journal *Russian Annals (Russkie zapiski,* the renamed *Russkoe bogatstvo)* under her real name. After the Revolution, she brought out a fourth collection of stories (Moscow, 1919) and published a journal article on the writer Elizaveta Vodovozova (1923). After that, Tsekhovskaia disappeared from print.

45. For a discussion of her journalistic career, see Louise McReynolds, "Female Journalists in Prerevolutionary Russia," *Journalism History* 4 (1987): 104–110.

46. Tsekhovskaia wrote a play based on "Dynasty," which was staged in 1913.

47. Her pen name is the Russian version of the English Taffy, which she borrowed from Rudyard Kipling. Tèffi's maiden name was Lokhvitskaia, and she was the younger sister of the poet Mirra Lokhvitskaia, who was already quite famous when Tèffi began publishing.

48. On Tèffi's popularity, see Irina Odoevtseva, *Na beregakh Seny* (Paris, 1983), 79, and Edythe Haber, "Nadezhda Tèffi," *Russian Literature Triquarterly* 9 (1974): 457 and 471, n. 14. For a good summary of Tèffi's literary themes, see Haber, op. cit. The most detailed biography and bibliography of Tèffi are to be found in Elizabeth B. Neatrour, "Miniatures of Russian Life at Home and in Emigration: The Life and Works of N. A. Tèffi" Ph.D. diss., Indiana University, 1972.

49. Thus, Leikin wrote to Chekhov in 1886, returning a story by the latter's "protégé" Mariia Kiseleva: " 'Don't invite dames [baby] to write for *Oskol'ki,*' he requested, 'They don't know how to write humorous things.' " See Anton Chekhov, *Polnoe sobranie sochinenii i pisem,* 30 vols. (Moscow, 1974–1983), *Pis'ma,* 1, 456.

50. For an excellent brief discussion of this type of narrator, see Hugh McLean, "Skaz," in *Handbook of Russian Literature,* ed. Victor Terras (New Haven: Yale University Press, 1985), 420.

51. See Pamela Davidson's description of this novel in *The Poetic Imagination of Vyacheslav Ivanov: A Russian Symbolist's Perception of Dante* (New York: Cambridge University Press, 1889), 293, n. 7.

52. Ibid., 130–34, for a detailed discussion of the play's meaning.

53. That she felt the pressing need to do so is recorded in Ivanov's diary in June 1906: "She is desperately struggling for the final inner emancipation from the influence of my ideas." See Viacheslav Ivanov, *Sobranie sochinenii,* vol. 2 (Brussels: Foyer Oriental Chretien, 1974), 748.

54. For a general introduction to Guro and her work, see Milica Banjanin, "The Prose and Poetry of Elena Guro," *Russian Literature Triquarterly* 9 (1974): 303–16 and "Looking Out, Looking In: Elena Guro's Windows," in *Festschrift fur Nikola R. Pribic* (Neuried: Hieronymus, 1983), 5–17; Nils Ake Nilsson, "Introduction" to: Elena Guro, *Selected Prose and Poetry,* ed. A. Ljunggren and Nils Ake Nilsson (Stockholm, 1988).

55. Banjanin also posits the probability of the influence of cinematography on her work. See "Looking Out, Looking In," 8.

56. In a diary entry quoted by Banjanin in "Looking Out, Looking In," Guro wrote:

''Free rhythms. Prose into verse, verse into prose. Prose that is almost verse . . . Sections of stories taken as color and as leitmotifs . . . ! The story's concentrating on two or three words . . . To speak the words, as if they did not coincide with the meaning, but are provoking certain images, about which nothing at all has been said . . . '' (7).

57. Such as Vadim Shershenevich who, in 1914, called her the most talented woman poet and predicted that her name would not be forgotten, for she had created her own language and form. See his article, ''Poetessy,'' *Sovremennaia zhenshchina* 4 (18 May 1914): 74, 76.

10

Women Poets of the Silver Age

Jane A. Taubman

Russian poetry, eclipsed by the realist novel since the mid nineteenth century, returned to center stage in the years 1890 to 1922, usually called the Silver Age. The term "Silver" implicitly compares the period to the Golden Age of Russian poetry: the 1820s and 1830s, dominated by Alexander Pushkin and his pleiad. Many literary historians feel Second Golden Age is a more accurate term for the period 1890 to 1922, which far exceeded the earlier period not only in the sheer number of its strong poets, but also in the quality and diversity of their voices. The Silver Age produced a number of minor women poets and several major ones, two of whom, Anna Akhmatova and Marina Tsvetaeva, stand among the giants of twentieth-century world literature.

It was a period of rapid economic and social change. Russia was industrializing belatedly, bur frenetically. A new class of industrial entrepreneurs emerged, comparable in some ways to the American robber barons such as Mellon and Carnegie, whose wealth enabled them to rival the declining aristocracy as patrons of the arts. The reforms of the 1860s encouraged the development of a professional middle class: doctors, lawyers, engineers, teachers. Cultural ties with Western Europe intensified, and, by the end of the century, Russia was taking part, with hardly any time lag, in contemporary European artistic movements; by 1917, she had taken the lead in several movements, particularly ballet, music, and painting. But political change was held in check by the reactionary Russian monarchy, until it came suddenly and violently in the epochal revolutions of 1917. The disastrous World War I brought on the collapse of the monarchy and the end of an age. The pivotal year 1914 began what Akhmatova, in her "Poem Without a Hero," christened "the *real* 20th century." These social and economic changes affected the status of women. More women began to receive higher education either in Russia or in Europe and move beyond traditional domestic roles. Inevitably, the "woman question" involved issues of sexual freedom and the erotic. The Golden Age poets had all been male aristocrats, but the biographies of the Silver Age poets reflect the social changes since mid century. Many were the sons of the new middle class, and, for the first time in any numbers, they were also daughters.

The years 1890 to 1910 were dominated by Russian symbolism, a movement with roots in the European symbolist and aesthetic movements. After 1910, symbolism lost its cohesiveness as a school, and a variety of "post-symbolist" poets appeared, some associated with a movement now called Acmeism, some with Russian Futurism. For a variety of reasons, including isolation, independence, or downright discrimination, the women poets were less likely to be closely associated with any school.

Symbolism was itself divided into two generations. In the 1890s, the first symbolist poets, often called "decadents" by their contemporaries, played a crucial role in translating the culture of the European (particularly French) symbolist movement onto Russian soil. These symbolist poets aimed to retrieve for Russian poetic culture the technical sophistication lost during the age of the novel. They also reasserted, in their themes and often in their lifestyles, the claims of the individual and the erotic, disdained by the earnest "progressive" critics of mid century (Vissarion Belinsky, Nikolai Chernyshevsky, Nikolai Dobroliubov), who saw the social and political fate of the peasant and the Russian nation as their main concerns. For the second wave of symbolists, which formed at the beginning of the new century, mystical-religious searchings were more central. Between the revolutions of 1905 and 1917, apocalyptic presentiments of Russia's national catastrophe sounded in their writings with increasing frequency.

Symbolist poetics, which cast the poet in the role of priest, seer, or prophet, left little room for the distinctly female voice or experience. The women poets associated with symbolism, still uncertain about their standing in this largely masculine club, generally avoided specifically female themes and sought a neutral voice. This was made particularly problematic by the Russian language, which, in its past tense verb and adjectival endings, requires the speaker to specify her/his gender. While the masculine lyric "I" was usual and, therefore, neutral, feminine endings marked the speaker as "different" and marginal. Several women poets of the symbolist school used a male persona almost exclusively. The most important of them, Zinaida Nikolaevna Gippius (1869–1945), explained that she used the masculine persona (she also wrote criticism under male pseudonyms) because she wanted to write "as a *human being* and not just as a woman." (Kak chelovek, a ne tol'ko kak zhenshchina). Her phrase "not just as a woman" reveals the extent to which Gippius understood (and internalized) the values of her time: The female voice was not considered sufficiently authoritative for the weighty philosophical and religious questions she addressed in her poetry.[1]

There were other reasons, too, for the frequency of "verbal cross-dressing" in this first generation of women symbolists. A number of Silver Age poets were homosexual or bisexual, a fact well known to their contemporaries but passed over in silence by most Russian émigrés and, of course, all Soviet writing on the subject.[2] Homosexuality was even fashionable among the decadents, as in the *fin de siècle* cultures of London and Paris; these writers were contemporaries of Gertrude Stein, Natalie Clifford Barney and Renee Vivien, of Aubrey Beardsley, Algernon Charles Swinburne, and Oscar Wilde. For some lesbian poets, the masculine "lyric I" camouflaged the orientation of their love lyrics.

Though Jane Austen, George Eliot, George Sand, and others had established a tradition of women's writing (primarily novels) in Western Europe, in Russia the woman writer, let alone the woman poet, was still the rare exception. For some Russian women writers of this generation, a male mentor figure, often her husband, provided essential help in breaking into the closed world of literary circles, journals, and publishing houses. But moral support from other women was equally important. Many of Russia's pioneering women poets (Gippius, Mirra Lokhvitskaia, Marina Tsvetaeva, Adelaida Gertsyk, Natalia Krandievskaia) had an artist or writer sister to whom they were extremely close. The pioneering editor and owner of the Petersburg journal *Northern Herald*, Liubov' Gurevich, published and encouraged women poets in the late 1880s and early 1890s. She also translated (from the original French) the diary of Mariia Bashkirtseva (Marie Bashkirtseff), a Russian painter who lived, worked, and died young in emigration in Paris. Bashkirtseva was an important model for *fin de siècle* women throughout Europe who hoped for careers in the male-dominated creative professions.[3] Much research remains to be done about wider patterns of friendship and support networks among women writers and artists.

Mirra Aleksandrovna Lokhvitskaia (1869–1905) was extremely popular with readers and critics in the 1890s, though she is nearly forgotten today. She won the prestigious Pushkin Prize for poetry twice, the second time, posthumously. Lokhvitskaia typifies the new middle class: She was the daughter of a prominent lawyer and the wife of an architect. Lokhvitskaia managed to publish five volumes of verse before her early death from tuberculosis in 1905. She was dubbed "The Russian Sappho," a reference to Sappho's talent and gender, not her sexual orientation, which was only then becoming generally known in Western Europe.[4] The mere fact of her gender made Lokhvitskaia a curiosity, and the forthright passion of her love lyrics, which Russian Victorians did not expect from a woman, gave them an added *frisson*. She was fond of flower imagery, often with barely concealed erotic symbolism:

My soul, like a pure lotus
In the languor of watery silence,
Unfolds its silvery crown
To the humble secret of the moon.

Your love, like a ray of mist
Flows with a mute enchantment.
And my fragrant flower
Is bewitched by a strange sadness,
Pierced by its chill.[5]

(Between 1896 and 1898)

Lokhvitskaia's love of bright colors, exotic settings, and grace of line find their visual equivalent in the contemporary European "art nouveau": the drawings of Beardsley or the paintings of Burne-Jones. She was adept at manipulating the traditional meters of Russian verse; her lines flow smoothly and rhythmically. There is considerable variety in the subjects and vocabulary of her verse. But there is little to gladden the heart of the feminist in the willingness with which Lokhvitskaia's persona usually submits not only to the claims of passion, but to the dominance of her male lover. The insistent use of her married name and the fulsome dedication of her 1896 *Poems* "To my husband" may have been intended as a defense against imputations of impropriety.[6]

Zinaida Gippius was married to Dmitrii Merezhkovskii, novelist, critic, and theoretician of symbolism. Though Merezhkovskii was better known in his day, Gippius is now seen as the more important figure, both for her pioneering efforts in the renovation of Russian verse language and for her contributions to the religious-mystical revival at the turn of the century. She was a prolific writer who published five volumes of verse and seventeen books of prose (stories, novels, plays, criticism, and memoirs). Gippius's reputation still suffers from two generations of critical distortion that paid more attention to her admittedly and often intentionally scandalous personal behavior[7] than to her poetry and its philosophical underpinnings. Gippius's sharp tongue, both in private and in her critical articles (a favorite pseudonym was Anton Krainii, or "Anton the Extreme") made her many enemies in émigré circles. Her total rejection of the October Revolution and her emigration in 1919 made her a "nonperson" to Soviet critics, who would scarcely have been sympathetic, in any case, to the religious and personal quests of her poems.[8]

Gippius is unique in that she really belongs to both the first, "decadent" wave of symbolism and to the second, "mystical-prophetic" one as well.[9] Her poetry of the 1890s is notable for its technical mastery, but its themes are typical of the decade—spiritual exhaustion, a fascination with death, night, and autumnal nature. By the time these poems were reprinted in her first collection (1904), she was already striking new notes in the introduction. She lamented the "excessive individualism" of her age, but thought it unavoidable. "The inevitable solitary path, perhaps, will lead us, even in the realm of poetry, to a new and fuller intercourse." Poetry, she felt, would play the important role of prayer. "Poetry in general, versification in particular, verbal music—that is only one of the forms that prayer assumes in our soul." Gippius never abandoned her effort to link the musicality of "decadent" verse to the music of prayer and her spiritual yearnings. Though new themes arose throughout her long poetic career, the essential sound of her voice would change little. From the very beginning, it shared with liturgical poetry a simplicity of syntax and intentionally limited vocabulary, but her totally modern vocabulary was entirely different from the archaic Slavonic lexicon of Orthodox prayer.

The oft-quoted poem, "A Song" ("Pesnia") (1893), which opens her first collection, broke important new ground in its metrical and rhyme scheme; it was one of the first uses of the *dol'nik*, a line based only on stress rather than on the syllabo-tonic system of classical Russian metrics:[10]

> No plachu bez slioz o nevernom obete,
>> O nevernom obete . . .
> Mne nuzhno to, chego net na svete . . .
>> Chego net na svete . . .

> But I weep without tears at the faithless vow,
>> The faithless vow . . .
> What I need does not exist on this earth,
>> Not on this earth.

Typical of Gippius is the poem's total lack of imagery and restricted vocabulary: either simple terms from nature (sky, sunset, earth) or basic words for emotion (heart, sorrow, take pity, empty, poor, seek, die, desire, want, beg, weep tears). In this pared-down abstraction, many readers saw only Gippius's "coldness." But there is passion here, as in all her poetry, the passion of the desperate search for faith. This God seeking is familiar to readers of Dostoevski; not surprisingly, the great novelist was one of Gippius's favorite authors.

After her father's early death, Gippius grew up in a large and exclusively female provincial household, an experience that probably delayed, and thus intensified, the shock of confrontation with patriarchal Russian reality. A 1907 poem titled "The Feminine" ("Zhenskoe") is subtitled "Doesn't exist" ("Netu"). The (male) persona encounters a girl on the edge of an abyss, crying as she weaves a wreath. When he asks who has insulted her, she replies, "The Creator . . . I'm crying because I don't exist." The poem could well represent the young Gippius's first traumatic realization of the status of woman in Russian society of the 1870s and 1880s. Gippius's poetry often played with gender ambiguity: her 1905 poem "She" ("Ona") describes a repulsive female, "in her shamelessness and despicable vileness, grey as dust," who is revealed only in the last two words to be "my soul," a word grammatically feminine in Russian.

In 1901, Gippius and Merezhkovskii moved away from a symbolism that was largely aesthetic in orientation and launched an ambitious attempt at a rapprochement of the intelligentsia and the Orthodox Church, which they pursued through the meetings of their Religious-Philosophical society. From 1903 to 1904, they published the important journal *New Path (Novyi Put')*, which attracted symbolists like Aleksandr Blok and religious thinkers like Nikolai Berdiaev. But there was a wide and, ultimately, unbridgeable gap between the Russian Church and the Merezhkovskiis' cult of the Third Testament, which attempted to synthesize paganism and Christianity in a religion of the "consecrated flesh."[11]

Several other women poets associated with the symbolist movement still await rediscovery. Like Gippius, the lesbian poet Poliksena Sergeevna Solovyova (1867–1924) who used the grammatically neuter pen name "Allegro," almost always adopted a male persona. Solovyova was the daughter of a Moscow University historian and sister of Vladimir Solovyov, the religious philosopher and poet from whom the symbolist poets Aleksandr Blok and Andrei Bely drew their cult of Sophia, the idealized "Beautiful Lady." Between 1899 and 1923, she published nineteen books of poetry, verse plays, and stories for children. Solovyova was an artist as well as a poet, and the books often included her own artistic "vignettes." From 1907 to 1913 she and her companion, Natalia Manasseina, edited a successful children's journal, *The Path (Put')*, which attracted contributions from major contemporary poets.[12]

A characteristic melancholy, as well as the *fin de siècle* fascination with death, are typical of Solovyova's poetry. She often used natural settings, autumnal or evening, to develop her ideas on love and death, as did her close friend Gippius, to whom this poem is dedicated:

> The closer and colder we feel death's icy breath,
> The hotter the scarlet of a kiss,
> And death moans "alleluia" as an epitaph.
> The vernal flower would not smell so passionately,
> So sweetly, did not death's sting
> Threaten the autumn fruits:
> Without the shadow of death—there is no passion.

Though many of Solovyova's poems too clearly bear the mark of their time, they have a melodiousness and quiet charm that deserve a closer look.[13]

Lesbian themes were also important in the poems of Liudmila Vil'kina-Minskaia (1873—1920).[14] The cover illustration of her 1906 collection *Moi sad (My Garden)* is a Beardsley-esque drawing of two young women in decollete embracing in a garden.[15] Vil'kina-Minskaia's poems, even more than Solovyova's, now seem dated by their "decadent" cliches:

> Like ice water on a sweltering day
>   Like slow, sharp kisses
> My suffering, joy of my life,
>   Oh, if I could suffer forever!

Though Marietta Sergeevna Shaginian (1888–1963) was closer in age to the post-symbolist generation, she began her career as a symbolist poet with ties to the Gippius-Merezhkovskii circle. The daughter of a well-known doctor who died young, Shaginian began writing for newspapers at the age of fifteen to help support her family. Her early poems, often about nature, are written with impressive technique and a clarity unusual among the symbolists. In her second volume, *Orientalia* (1912), which brought her fame and popularity, Shaginian turned to her Armenian and Caucasian heritage for exotic and often erotic themes:

> Whoever you may be—come in, stranger.
> Gloomy is the evening, sweet is the scent of spikenard
>> The couch, laid with a golden leopard skin,
>> Has long awaited you. (1911)

Shaginian also wrote criticism, and her favorable reviews helped launch the careers of other women poets, such as Tsvetaeva. After the Revolution, Shaginian became a prolific, prizewinning, and largely conformist Soviet novelist (for example, *Hydrocentral, The Ulyanov Family*).

Around 1910, a new generation of poets began to react against symbolism's vagueness and otherworldly mysticism. Though their poetic voices differed among themselves, they shared a respect for clarity of expression and the heritage of world culture. These citizens of the world were essentially Russian Europeans who adopted the name "Acmeism," from the Greek "acme" to describe their movement. Acmeism's two greatest poets were Anna Andreevna Akhmatova (1889–1966)[16] and Osip Mandelstam; its theoretician was the poet Nikolai Gumilev, to whom Akhmatova was married from 1910–1918.

In contrast to the essentially romantic poetics of symbolism, Akhmatova's poetics are basically classical. Mandelstam and others since have identified the roots of her art in the realistic fiction of the nineteenth century. Indeed, a typical early Akhmatova poem is a highly compressed narrative, whose outline is sketched with precise physical details of her surroundings and a phrase or two about the persona's attitude to the situation. She gives just the most essential snatches of dialogue, leaving the reader to sketch in the rest:

> I pressed my hands together under cover
>> of my veil. "Why are you so pale today?"
> —Because I intoxicated my lover
> With numbing anguish, and drove him away.
>
> How could I forget? He went out, reeling.
>> His mouth dreadful—twisted, grim . . .
>> I ran down the stairs, not touching the railing,
>> At the gate I caught up with him.
>
> I shouted hoarsely—"It was just a joke.
> You mustn't leave me—I'd rather be dead."
> He smiled calmly, terribly, then he spoke:
> "Don't stand out here in the wind," he said. (1911)
>
>> (Trans. Lyn Coffin)

In contrast to the symbolist women poets who sought a neutral voice, Akhmatova took the opposite approach and went out of her way to mark her persona's gender. In this poem, for example, the very first word, a past-tense verb ("zhala"), alerts the reader that the speaker is a woman. These miniatures seem so artless that contemporary readers were convinced they were reading real-life confessions of the Akhmatova-Gumilev marriage. In fact this was far from true. Akhmatova was a profoundly private person, and her poems are poor sources for the biographer. The seeming intimacy of the lyrics is in fact the result of her consummate art.

Akhmatova's first collection of poems, *Evening (Vecher)*, appeared in 1912 in an edition of 300 copies. Her second collection, *Rosary (Chetki)*, published in 1914, assured her fame. It went through many editions over the following ten years; serious critical studies of her poetry began to appear. Yet the national tragedy she had long foreseen was about to begin: the war that overtook Europe in August 1914 is a frequent presence in the poems of her third collection, *White Flock (Belaia staia)* (1917). In a 1918 poem, Akhmatova consciously rejected the temptation to emigrate, choosing instead to share the fate of her nation:

> I am not one of those who left the land
>> To the mercy of its enemies.
>> Their flattery leaves me cold,
>> my songs are not for them to praise.

(Trans. Stanley Kunitz)

This poem marks the beginning of a new, national theme in her verse.

The tiny collection *Plantain (Podorozhnik)* appeared in 1921 and was incorporated into the somewhat larger volume *Anno Domini MCMXXI*, which would be her last published book for eighteen years. She wrote little and published nothing at all in the 1920s and early 1930s. In August 1921, Gumilev was executed for alleged participation in an anti-Bolshevik plot. As his ex-wife and the mother of his son, Akhmatova would remain under a cloud of fear and threat from the Soviet regime for the rest of her days. The tragic pathos of the late Akhmatova was that the elegant analyst of intimate relationships, the "carefree sinner of Tsarskoe Selo,"[17] by the will of history became, in the 1930s and 1940s, the chronicler of her nation's grim fate, particularly the fate of its women.

Marina Ivanovna Tsvetaeva (1892–1941) was the daughter of a classics professor at Moscow University who founded Moscow's first museum of European art, known today as the Pushkin Museum of Fine Arts. Her mother, Maria Mein, was a talented pianist, who died when Marina was fourteen. The loss of her talented and demanding mother at the crucial stage of early adolescence left a deep mark on Tsvetaeva's psyche; for the rest of her life, she sought out friendships with older women. Tsvetaeva began to write verse while still a child; she had a natural talent for versification and, as she developed as a poet, an extraordinary sense for the varied rhythms of Russian speech. But the Russian tradition provided the young Tsvetaeva with few models of an authoritative, yet female, poetic voice. Unlike Gippius or Solovyova, Tsvetaeva never referred to herself using masculine grammatical forms. Nor did she choose Akhmatova's path of using verbal and adjectival endings to underline her femininity. In her first two collections, *Evening Album (Vechernii al'bom*, 1910) and *Magic Lantern* (Volshebnyi fonar', 1912), Tsvetaeva adopted various strategies to avoid marking the gender of the poetic voice. She often wrote about the world of childhood, which allowed her to adapt the viewpoint of narrator ("they," "she," and "he" instead of "I"). Or she used the plural (not gender-marked) "we," usually referring to herself and her sister Anastasia (Asya). Marina and Asya made joint public appearances in those early years, reading Marina's verse in unison. It was as if Marina sought to increase the weight of her "merely female" voice by doubling it.[18]

From 1913 to 1915, Tsvetaeva rapidly matured as a poet. Beginning in 1913, she carefully dated her poems and, in most of her collections, arranged them chronologically to create a "lyric diary," a created spiritual autobiography that Tsvetaeva called a "diary of her soul." She ingeniously adapted the intimate diary, a favorite nineteenth-century female genre, to her own creative purposes. The poems of these years often contrast Tsvetaeva's external appearance, the way others see her, with the reality of her inner life. These concerns, so typical of adolescence, are perhaps one reason she titled the collection *Juvenilia (Iunosheskie stikhi)*. It was never published in her lifetime; war and then revolution intervened. Though she kept writing, usually every day, it would be ten years before Tsvetaeva, then a fully mature poet of genius, published another book. One of the strongest cycles in *Juvenilia* remained unpublished for over fifty years because of its lesbian theme. *The Girl Friend (Podruga)*, originally titled "The Mistake," is the testimony of Tsvetaeva's first serious marital infidelity, her tempestuous affair with the poet Sofiia Parnok. The romance may have been, in part, an attempt to fill a void of insufficient mother-love, as her farewell poem to Parnok strongly hints:

> In days of yore you were like a mother to me,
> I could call to you in the night ... (1916)

For Tsvetaeva, poetry was a way of reaching out, of attempting a kind of disembodied communication she often found impossible face to face; she often addressed her poems to a specific person. At first, it was her family and close friends; in the later, lonelier years of emigration, it was more often someone she had met seldom (Boris Pasternak) or never (Rainer Maria Rilke). Tsvetaeva's husband Sergei Efron was the first of several younger, or seemingly younger, men, often with Jewish blood, to whom she addressed some of her strongest and most ardent poems; others were Osip Mandelstam and Pasternak. Efron, or rather Tsvetaeva's idealized image of him, is an important figure in his wife's poetry.[19] Equally important was her daughter Ariadna (born in 1912). Like Akhmatova, Tsvetaeva was not the best or most traditional mother. She adored Ariadna as a second self, as a friend and companion rather than as a daughter.

A new maturity is evident in Tsvetaeva's poems of 1916, which she collected in *Mileposts (Versts, published 1922)*. Here, she tried out her newly honed voice in tribute to her greatest poetic contemporaries: At the heart of the book are cycles addressed to Aleksandr Blok, Osip Mandelstam, and Akhmatova. Tsvetaeva felt the need to find a poetic "space" for herself among the wealth of strong Silver Age voices. With the genre of the female love lyric dominated by Akhmatova, Tsvetaeva found the impetus to develop the magnificent chorus of diverse voices that characterizes her mature poetry. In *Mileposts*, Tsvetaeva first began to adopt a variety of literary masks. She mimicked the voices of the poets she praised and explored the rich dialect of the Moscow townswoman, then the rhythmic spells and charms of gypsy women, in which she found a female equivalent to the prophetic male voices of the symbolist school.

Tsvetaeva, unlike many of her contemporaries, did not greet the February Revolution of 1917 with enthusiasm. She was wary of revolution's anti-individualistic tendencies, and, always on the side of the underdog, she pitied the frail young tsarevich. The October Revolution left her alone in Moscow, in poverty and near starvation with her two daughters; Efron had joined the White Army fighting against the Bolsheviks in the south of Russia. For the first year or so, Tsvetaeva seemed oblivious to the new reality and her new responsibilities. Much of her time was spent with a group of young actors for whom she wrote romantic verse plays set in eighteenth-century Europe and revolutionary France. There was also a flood of lyrics whose electricity of rhythm and meter and mercurial force capture the music and spirit of the revolutionary age, despite Tsvetaeva's own political opposition. In the winter of 1919 to 1920, she was forced to put her daughters into a children's home, where Irina, not yet three, died of starvation. This tragedy brought a new sobriety to Tsvetaeva's persona and a new solemn majesty to her poetic voice.

The end of the Civil War in 1920 made it possible to think of earning money by publishing her poetry. She chose her strongest poems from 1917 to 1920 for the slim collection *Mileposts II* (1921), which she dedicated to Akhmatova. Its two sections reflect conflicting aspects of Tsvetaeva's life, the sexually and spiritually liberated woman:

> My path does not lead past your house.
> My path doesn't lead past anyone's house.

And the penitent, awaiting holy judgment for her sins:

> With upraised head and downcast eyes,
> Before the face of the Lord and all his saints—I stand.

The first section often draws on gypsy life for its imagery; the second, on the Orthodox liturgy. She collected her reactions to the two revolutions and poems in praise of the White Army, which she knew could never be published in Soviet Russia, in *The Swans' Encampment (Lebedinyi stan)*.[20] Two slim books, *Poems to Blok (Stikhi k Bloku)* and *Separation (Razluka)*, appeared in Berlin before she arrived there in May 1922, to begin seventeen years of emigration. *Psyche: Romanticism (Psikheia: Romantika*, Berlin 1923) was a thematically linked collection of poems from the revolutionary years. The achievement of the ten years when she had been able to publish little or nothing stunned poetry readers both in Russia and abroad. But her popularity was to be short-lived. The dense, hermetic poems of 1921 and 1922, collected in *Craft (Remeslo*, 1923), mark a new turn in Tsvetaeva's poetics, a turn that put her years ahead of most of her readers and of most critics as well. Like Tolstoi and Dostoevski in the nineteenth century, Akhmatova and Tsvetaeva represent a polar opposition of genius, a triumphant demonstration of the diversity within women's writing. If the classical impulse dominated in Akhmatova, Tsvetaeva was at heart a romantic. The themes and style of Akhmatova's early verse are essentially of a piece; Tsvetaeva's poems are far more varied, in quality as well as voice. While Akhmatova's life and work are intimately wedded to Petersburg, Tsvetaeva's roots are in Moscow and the Russian countryside. And while Akhmatova chose to remain in Soviet Russia, Tsvetaeva spent seventeen years in emigration before returning home on the eve of World War II.

Adelaida Kazimirovna Gertsyk (1874?–1925)[21] was an important link between the second-generation symbolists, particularly the Petersburg circle of Viacheslav Ivanov, and the Moscow post-symbolist poetic and philosophical circles. Gertsyk's first and only collection of verse, *Poems (Stikhotvoreniia*, 1910), shows Ivanov's influence, but there are original features that point forward to the post-symbolist generation. From Ivanov's fascination with classical Greek culture and religion, Gertsyk moved to native Russian folklore and beliefs in which female sorceresses played a central role. She also explored the female elements in Greek religion and prophecy; at least two reviewers referred to her as ''the Russian Sibyl.''

In 1910 Tsvetaeva's mentor, the critic Maximilian Voloshin,[22] introduced Gertsyk to Tsvetaeva, commenting, ''you need each other.'' Gertsyk's influence on Tsvetaeva's poetic development has not been fully appreciated; it was undoubtedly she who introduced Tsvetaeva to the native Russian incantations and spells (*zaklinaniia, zaplachki*) that became such central rhythmic and thematic elements in her work. After the 1917 Revolution, Gertsyk and her family remained in White-occupied Sudak, in the Crimea, where living conditions became increasingly difficult, bordering at times on starvation; Gertsyk died there in 1925. The spare and somber late poems that have surfaced in recent years[23] testify to her growing poetic mastery and strength of spirit:

ECHO
   Difficult is our path, and our night's rest is still far off
Must man go on like this for long?
An age.
What awaits him, if he retreats?
Hell.

> If he goes forward, will it be easier then?
> Yes.
> Who awaits us at the end of existence?
> I.
> And who art thou, who calls from all sides?
> Fate.

The image of the aged Sibyl, so important in Tsvetaeva's poetry of 1922 to 1923, may be a tribute to Gertsyk, who was then living in poverty in the "Greek" Crimean landscape.[24]

Sofiia Parnok (1885–1933) was Russia's first openly lesbian poet. Though she was briefly married to her close friend and mentor, the writer V. M. Volkenstein, all of Parnok's loves, from adolescence on, were women, whom she addressed and celebrated in unusually frank love poems. Like many other Silver Age poets, Parnok came from the provincial bourgeoisie: her father was a prosperous Jewish pharmacist in Taganrog. Her mother, a doctor, died giving birth to Parnok's twin sister and brother. As it did for Tsvetaeva, the tragic loss of a beloved, strong, intelligent mother left its mark in Parnok's poetry and in her life:

> But I cherish the tempting dream
> That you would have loved me.[25]
>
> ("To the Memory of My Mother")

Parnok's poetic talent matured slowly. A few poems appeared in periodicals as early as 1906, but her first collection, *Poems (Stikhotvoreniia)*, was published only in 1916, the year her "creativity competitive"[26] affair with Tsvetaeva broke off. Poems inspired by Tsvetaeva and their sojourn together with the Voloshins in Koktebel' pepper the collection:

> Oh, lead me away from my death,
> You, whose hands are sunburnt and fresh,
> You, who passed by, exciting me!
> Is it not in your desperate name
> I hear the wind of stormtossed coasts,
> O, Marina, namesake of the sea!
>
> (August 5, 1915)[27]

Parnok found refuge during the Civil War years with the Gertsyks in Sudak. The harsh, sun-drenched Crimean landscape inspired recollections of Greece and of Sappho, which fill her next volume, *Roses of Pieria (Rozy Pierii)*, 1922. Viacheslav Ivanov's translation of the complete Sapphic fragments in 1914 was an important revelation for Russian poets, particularly for the women, who generally knew no Greek.[28] Sappho was an important legitimizing model for Parnok, and the Crimean exile only intensified her impact, already felt in the 1916 collection. The unusually long line and spare diction Parnok uses in many of these poems imitate the Greek hexameter. Three other slim volumes followed Parnok's return to Moscow in 1922: *Vine (Loza)*, 1923; *Music (Muzyka)*, 1926; *Under my Breath (Vpolgolosa)*, 1928. Music was a lifelong love of Parnok's, a career she almost pursued. The 1926 collection is a rare attempt to capture in verse not simply the "musicality" of language, as the symbolists did, but the experience of great music in performance. The roar of an organ at a Catholic mass (Russian Orthodox services allow only vocal music) brought on a poetic epiphany Parnok recalled in one of her poems.[29] Parnok's own deep, throaty voice is both a subject and a presence in her verse. Her strength of character and clear-eyed, often ironic vision of self are a refreshing contrast to the self-indulgent symbolists. Parnok's voice fully matured in two cycles, *Ursa major (Bol' shaia medveditsa)* and *Unneeded Goods (Nenuzhnoe dobro)*, written in the two years before her death. Inspired by the last, great love of Parnok's life, Moscow University physics professor Nina Evgenyevna Vedeneeva, these poems have a classic simplicity and eloquence akin to the later work of her younger contemporaries Akhmatova, Tsvetaeva, Mandelstam, and Pasternak, who all, like Parnok, underwent creative crises in the mid 1920s that profoundly altered their poetic voices.[30]

Cherubina de Gabriak was the fictitious creation of Maksimilian Voloshin, the poet and critic who served as midwife to the careers of Tsvetaeva, Gertsyk, and Parnok. Behind her exotic foreign name and the tragic biography (orphaned French Catholic aristocratic émigré) Voloshin invented for her, hid a lame, young schoolteacher, Elisaveta Ivanovna Dmitrieva (1887–1928). Dmitrieva had submitted some poems to the new journal *Apollo (Apollon)* whose editor, Sergei Makovskii, summarily rejected them. Voloshin collaborated with Dmitrieva on the invention of "de Gabriak," under whose name they submitted more of her poems on elegant paper, with a tamarisk leaf inserted. These were immediately accepted by Makovskii, who conceived a passion for the unseen and mysterious Cherubina. The hoax was intended to unmask the arrogance of the *Apollon* editors, who expected women poets to be decorative as well as talented. At the same time, "Cherubina's" poems subtly parodied the petrified conventions and vocabulary of Russian symbolism.[31] Scholars still debate the extent of Voloshin's involvement in writing "Cherubina's" poems; Dmitrieva published a few more poems as "Cherubina" after her identity was revealed. During the early 1920s she published plays for children and a novella.[32]

Nadezhda Grigor'evna L'vova (1891–1913) managed to publish only one collection of verse, *The Old Fairy Tale (Staraia skazka*, 1913). A few months after it appeared, L'vova was driven to suicide by the callous behavior of her lover, the symbolist poet Valerii Briusov.[33] L'vova's "scandalous" death attracted the attention of readers, and a second, enlarged, edition of the book was promptly issued. The poet Vladislav Khodasevich, one of the few reviewers to notice and praise the first edition, called it "a woman's book in the best sense of the word. Its lyricism is involuntary: a series of intense and complex emotions find their resolution there."[34] Despite the strong influence of Briusov on her early work, and attempts by the Futurists to claim her as their own, Khodasevich astutely noted L'vova's "striving to compress the greatest quantity of content into the smallest quantity of words."[35]

> I'm already glad that I'll lie to you.
> I'll tell you about a fictive betrayal.
> I'll laugh in your face, as in an enemy's
> With silent contempt.
>
> And when you cower like a beaten dog
> Stroking your greying temples
> I'll not confess how I cried at night
> Contemplating my revenge under the syringe of depression.[36]

This and other L'vova poems recall the work of Akhmatova, but in a stronger key. Had she lived, the talented L'vova might also have developed into a major poet.

Elena Guro (pseudonym of Elenora Genrikhovna Notenberg, 1877–1913) published three books of verse, prose, and plays before her death from leukemia in the same fateful year of 1913. Guro published her work in Futurist anthologies and was married to Mikhail Matiushin, a painter, musician, and publisher who was an important figure in the Futurist avant-garde. Despite Guro's ties to the Futurist movement, her verse, as Khodasevich noted,[37] has many affinities with the later symbolists. Yet her poetry sometimes experiments with "trans-sense" ("zaum") language in the Futurist manner, attempting to break language down to its basic sound units, as cubism broke down visual forms. One such poem, "Words of Love and Warmth," evolves into nonsense words as the speaker fondles a cat:

> Zhil-byl
>   Botik-zhivotik
> Vorkotik
>   Duratik
> Kotik pushatik,
>   Pushonchik,
>
> Belovatik,
>   Koshuratik—
> Potasik . . .

Her best-known work is the posthumous *Little Camels of the Sky (Nebesnye verbliuzhata*, 1913). Like many Futurists, Guro painted as well as wrote; in fact, her cultural importance is probably greater as a visual artist.[38]

It is not coincidental that the years 1909 to 1913, which saw the "death" of symbolism, saw the debuts of so many talented women poets. The post-symbolist aesthetic, particularly in its acmeist version, was oriented toward a human reality of emotion and action quite different from that of the symbolists. The shift of focus from abstract figures like Blok's idealized "Beautiful Lady" or hypostases of Russia to real human beings and their interrelations created a space for the voices and experiences of contemporary women to be heard. The new women poets were noticed but often lumped together, even by sympathetic reviewers, into collective surveys of "women's poetry," which indicated some unease with this novelty. Voloshin reviewed Tsvetaeva's first book while surveying the entire phenomenon of women's poetry, comparing its sudden flowering in Russia to the pleiad of female poets in France who immediately followed the symbolists:

This female poetry is different both in its variety of content and in its strongly expressed temperament, and its marked frankness. In several respects, this female lyric is more interesting than the male. It is less burdened with ideas, but deeper, less bashful (bashfulness, of course, is an exclusively masculine trait). Woman has a deeper and more detailed sense of herself than man, and this tells in her poetry.[39]

Writing in the same newspaper six years later, the critic Vladislav Khodasevich, while sympathetically reviewing Parnok's first book, still felt the need to generalize about "women's poetry":

The so-called "poetry of the female soul" has attracted the general attention of poetry lovers. The specific "femininity" of poems has begun to be valued much more highly than heretofore. And demand has called forth supply, and to meet it, either in whole books, or in individual poems on the pages of journals and almanacs, there have glistened not only feminine, but even characteristically "ladylike" ("damskoe") poems. A rash of mannerisms, psychological crises, caprices, affectations has rained upon us—everything with which these young pupils of Sappho have tried to display and underline to each other the "femininity" of their poetry. Through the thicket of silks, rouge, necklaces and feathers, which have become the necessary accessories of this poetry, it has become hard to make anything out except the desire to be original. (*Utro Rossii*, 1916/274 Oct. 1)

Akhmatova's triumph with *Rosary* should have demonstrated that, at last, one could be a major poet who happened to be a woman, and whose gender was but one element of her genius. But the very "femaleness" of the voice in her early poetry misled not only critics like Khodasevich, but also female imitators who realized too late (or not at all) exactly how much lay behind the simple perfection of her lyrics. Akhmatova was jealous of her own fame, and not charitable to imitators; she complained in a 1960 epigram:

> Could Beatrice have written like Dante,
> Or Laura have glorified love's pain?
> I taught women how to speak
> God help me shut them up again!
>
> (Trans. Stanley Kunitz, adapted by JT)

Fortunately, her half-jesting plea went unanswered. The twentieth century brought new generations of women poets who could see themselves as part of a female tradition in Russian poetry, a tradition enriched, if not actually begun, by Gippius, Akhmatova, Tsvetaeva, Parnok, and their sister poets of the Silver Age.

NOTES

1. See Antonina Filonov Gove, "Gender as a Poetic Feature in the Verse of Zinaida Gippius," in *American Contributions to the Eighth International Congress of Slavists* (Columbus, OH: Slavica Publishers, 1978), 379–407, for a detailed discussion of Gippius's use of grammatical gender.

2. Homosexual relations between males were a criminal offense in the Soviet Union; lesbianism was such an "indelicate" issue that the Soviet legal code tried to wish it out of existence by not even mentioning it.

3. I am indebted for information about Gurevich to Stanley Rabinowitz, who is writing a monograph about Gurevich and her journal.

4. Joan de Jean, *Fictions of Sappho 1546–1937* (Chicago: University of Chicago Press, 1989). I thank Diana Burgin for calling my attention to this fact and to de Jean's book.

5. M. A. Lokhvitskaia (Zhiber), *Stikhotvoreniia* 2 (St. Petersburg, 1900), 66. Translations are mine unless otherwise indicated.

6. She styled herself "Lokhvitskaia (Zhiber)" on the title page of all her books. For more on Lokhvitskaia's verse, particularly her erotic verse, see Sam Cioran, "Mirra Lokhvitskaya: The Russian Sappho," *Russian Literature Triquarterly* 9 (1974): 317–35 and *Women Writers in Russian Modernism: An Anthology*, ed. Temira Pachmuss (Urbana: University of Illinois Press, 1978), 85–113.

7. There has been much speculation about Gippius's sexual orientation. She herself confessed that she was attracted to homosexual men, like Merezhkovskii, or their long-time disciple Dmitry Filosofov. Her 52-year marriage, she let it be known, was never consummated. The memoirist Sergei Makovskii recalled that, after ten years of marriage, she pointedly wore her long hair in the traditional maiden's braid. Simon Karlinsky suggests that "she was an androgyne. Though apparently not totally female physically, she felt herself to be a male intellectually and spiritually." ("Introduction: Who Was Zinaida Gippius?" in Vladimir Zlobin, *A Difficult Soul: Zinaida Gippius* [Berkeley: University of California Press, 1980], 10). But after Stanley Rabinowitz's recent publication of her passionate letters to Akim Volynskii, co-editor of the journal *Northern Herald*, it is difficult to deny that, in at least this case, there was certainly more than flirtation at issue. ("A 'Fairy Tale of Love'?: The Relationship of Zinaida Gippius and Akim Volynsky," *Oxford Slavonic Papers* 24 (Oxford: Clarendon Press, 1991). The dedications to her poems reveal at least one lesbian love affair. (See N. A. Bogomolova's annotations to the 1991 Soviet edition of Gippius, 417–18.) Rather than trying, as her contemporaries did, to pigeonhole Gippius in terms of sexual orientation, a feminist biographer can see, instead, an independent woman trying to explore and define love and interpersonal relationships on her own terms.

8. The first Soviet edition of Gippius's poetry (Z. N. Gippius, *Stikhotvoreniia. Zhivye litsa* [Moscow, 1991]) appeared, with fitting irony, in the Soviet Union's final year.

9. I am indebted for this insight to Olga Matich's illuminating study, *Paradox in The Religious Poetry of Zinaida Gippius* (Munich: W. Fink, 1972).

10. For more on Gippius's metrical innovations, see Oleg A. Maslennikov, "Disruption of Canonical Verse Norms in the Poetry of Zinaida Gippius," in *Studies in Slavic Linguistics and Poetics in Honor of Boris O. Unbegaun* (New York: New York University Press, 1968), 89–96. The *dol'nik* became a favorite meter of Anna Akhmatova, who used it to bring the cadences of private conversation, particularly female speech, into the poetic canon.

11. The fullest study of Gippius's life and career is still Temira Pachmuss, *Zinaida Gippius: An Intellectual Profile* (Carbondale, IL: University of Illinois Press, 1971). Pachmuss also edited and translated a volume of her prose, *Selected Works of Zinaida Gippius* (Urbana: University of Illinois Press, 1972).

12. Prerevolutionary children's literature in general, and Solovyova's contributions to it, have been little studied. See Elena Sokol, *Russian Poetry for Children* (Knoxville: University of Tennessee Press, 1984), 51–52. In its sentimentality and religiosity, early twentieth-century Russian children's literature had much in common with late Victorian British children's literature.

13. For more information on Solovyova, and translations of some of her poems, see Pachmuss, *Women Writers*, 175–90.

14. She was married to the symbolist critic and theoretician Nikolai Minskii.

15. The cover is reproduced in Diana Burgin, "Laid out in Lavender: Perceptions of Lesbian Love in Russian Literature and Criticism of the Silver Age 1893–1917," in *Sexuality and the Body in Russian Culture*, ed. Jane Costlow, Stephanie Sandler, and Judith Vowles (Stanford University Press, forthcoming). I am indebted to Diana Burgin for providing me with an advance copy of the article, the best source to date for information on lesbian writing in the Silver Age and its critical reception.

16. Akhmatova was born Anna Gorenko. Her family was not in the least literary, and when she began to publish her poems, her father, a naval officer, asked her to not bring shame upon his name. She chose as a pseudonym the name of her Tatar great-grandmother.

For a discussion of Akhmatova's impact on women poets of the Soviet period, see Carol Ueland's chapter in this volume.

17. Akhmatova's ironic description of her prewar self in her magnificent long poem "Requiem" (1935–1940).

18. In a poem that serves as the preface to *Magic Lantern*, Tsvetaeva ironically, and ambiguously, assured her "dear reader" that "Of course a woman's book/Is only a magic lantern."

19. The marriage would be clouded by infidelities on both sides, and during the 1930s in emigration in Paris, when Efron had been recruited by Soviet intelligence, the two lived essentially separate lives. But in her own strange way, Tsvetaeva remained loyal until the end and followed Efron when he fled back to the Soviet Union in 1939.

20. The book was first published in Munich in 1957.

21. The few biographical sources on Gertsyk give conflicting dates for her birth, ranging from 1870 to 1877. This seems to me the most reliable.

22. Voloshin and his formidable mother owned a rambling stone house on the rocky shore of Koktebel', in the Crimea, that, along with their Moscow apartment, became the center of a literary and artistic circle similar in its importance to Bloomsbury. Like Bloomsbury, it was a *milieu* in which female talent was nurtured and recognized, in

which androgyny and alternative modes of sexuality were tolerated. Voloshin introduced the professor's daughter to a whole new circle of friends, including her future husband Sergei Efron, as well as Gertsyk and Sofia Parnok.

23. See Evgenia Gertsyk, *Vospominaniia* (Paris: YMCA Press, 1973), 187–91; and *V mire knig* 9 (1987): 84; and *Nashe nasledie* 3 (1991): 123–29.

24. Tsvetaeva pays Gertsyk a warm tribute in *A Living Word about a Living Man* (1932) her memoir of Voloshin (translated in Marina Tsvetaeva, *A Captive Spirit: Selected Prose*, trans. J. M. King (Ann Arbor, MI: Ardis, 1980), but she never wrote the more detailed memoir she promised. For more information on Gertsyk, and translations of some poems, see Pachmuss, *Women Writers*, 314–34; and Diana Burgin, "The Life of Adelaida Gertsyk," *Russian Literature Triquarterly* 23 (1990): 357–67.

25. Sofia Parnok, *Sobranie stikhotvoreniia*, ed., anno., and intro. Sofia Poliakova (Ann Arbor, MI: Ardis Press, 1979), 117.

26. The phrase is Diana Burgin's.

27. Parnok, 114. I have adapted Diana Burgin's translation of the penultimate line.

28. In Russia, as in Western Europe, the study of Greek was part of the classical curriculum, which defined the "educated man" and was seldom available to women.

29. Parnok, 152–53.

30. For more on Parnok in English, and the complicated question of her influence on Tsvetaeva, see three articles by Diana Burgin, "After the Ball Is Over: Sophia Parnok's Creative Relationship with Marina Tsvetaeva," *Russian Review* 47, 4 (1988): 425–44; "Signs of a Response: Two Possible Parnok Replies to her 'Podruga,' " *SEEJ* 35, 2 (1991): 214–27, and "Sophia Parnok and the Writing of a Lesbian Poet's Life" *Slavic Review* 51, 2 (Summer, 1992): 214–31. Burgin's book-length study of Parnok's life and work, the first in any language, is nearing completion.

31. V. P. Kupchenko, V. A. Manuilov, and N. Ia. Rykova, "M. A. Voloshin–literaturnyi kritik," in Maksimilian Voloshin, *Liki tvorchestva* (Leningrad, 1988), 573.

32. For texts and translations of some of "Cherubina's" poems, see Pachmuss, *Women Writers*, 243–60. For a slightly romanticized reminiscence, see Tsvetaeva's memoir of Voloshin in Marina Tsvetaeva, "A Living Word About a Living Man," in *A Captive Spirit*, 36–43. The most informative account of Dmitrieva's career in English is by Vadim Kreyd in vol. 8 of *The Modern Encyclopedia of Russian and Soviet Literature*, ed. Harry Weber (Gulf Breeze, FL: Academic International Press, 1987), 80–84. In Russian, see Cherubina de Gabriak, *Autobiografiia, Izbrannye Stikhotvoreniia* (Moscow, 1989).

33. Briusov liked to fancy himself a mentor of women poets (he published the first posthumous edition of Karolina Pavlova in 1916). But it was he who rejected Tsvetaeva's *Juvenilia* at the State Publishing House. Tsvetaeva gives a scathing account of an "Evening of Poetesses" Briusov sponsored in Moscow in 1921 in her memoir "A Hero of Labor."

34. V. Khodasevich, *Sobranie sochinenii* (Ann Arbor, MI: Ardis Publishers, 1990), 129.

35. Khodasevich, 142.

36. Khodasevich, 142–43.

37. Khodasevich, 205.

38. For more on Guro in English, see Milica Banjanin, "The Prose and Poetry of Eleno Guro," *Russian Literature Triquarterly* 9 (1974): 303–61, and Banjanin's entry on Guro in vol. 9 of *The Modern Encyclopedia of Russian and Soviet Literature*, 169–78.

39. Maksimilian Voloshin, "Zhenskaia poeziia (Marina Tsvetaeva. *Vechernii al'bom)*" *Utro Rossii* 11 (Dec. 1910): 6.

11

Waiting in the Wings: Russian Women Playwrights in the Twentieth Century

Melissa T. Smith

Although it has commonly been noted that "the Russian votes with his theater ticket," little attention has been paid to the fact that dramaturgy is mostly a one-party system that seldom elects women. While there has been no dearth of women writing plays, their legacy is scant. The designation of "playwright" is provisional, for playwriting tends to be a phase in a woman's career rather than an area of her major emphasis, even among the most prolific female writers for the stage. This is not an exclusively Russian phenomenon. The phrase "and also wrote plays" is a common bibliographical appendage.[1]

The influential Soviet playwright Aleksei Arbuzov has offered the following view on women and drama:

In *The Passion According to Barbara* [*Strasti po Varvare*], Olga Pavlova-Kuchkina has decided on a fairly brave move—only women act in the play. Is this not paradoxical? Indeed. But it is even more paradoxical that a woman has chosen as her craft dramaturgy— the most merciless, most "masculine" form of literature. Here, besides talent, the dramatist must have a strong will, unyielding character, a defensive reaction against literary failures and life's misfortunes.[2]

Arbuzov's article operates on paradoxes inherent in certain traditional assumptions and linkages: 1) drama, which according to Aristotelian poetics depicts *action*, seldom has truck with the "passive sex"; 2) the "weaker" sex produces weaker writing, and, therefore, 3) women demurely sit back and avoid entering the literary battleground, of which theater is the most public arena.

Women playwrights face a "double burden" unknown to their nondramatist sisters: Their works must ultimately stand both as works of literature and as material for stage production. Not only must a play find its reader, but also its director, actors, and theater collective. Playwrights yearn not only for "rooms of their own," where they can commit ideas to paper, but theaters of their own, where they can see their plays staged.

The dramatic text is rooted in the linguistic medium of dialogue and is normally oriented toward public performance rather than reading. While studies of dramaturgy commonly enough ignore the performance aspect of drama, the tendency in current scholarship is to take into account the specifics of the genre. In the Russian/Soviet context, this dual nature of drama has been marked by the existence of dual censorship. It has not been uncommon in either the prerevolutionary or Soviet period for a play to be allowed for publication or distribution, but not for staging, or to restrict a work's public exposure to performance in a limited number of theaters. Such lack of consistent archival record and review complicates the process of recovery and evaluation of dramatic works by women.

In her book, *Feminist Theories for Dramatic Criticism*, Gayle Austin identifies three phases of feminist criticism:[3]

1. Working within the canon: examining images of women.
2. Expanding the canon: focusing on women writers.
3. Exploding the canon: questioning underlying assumptions of an entire field of study, including canon formation.

Unfortunately, due to the traditional neglect of both women's studies and the drama and theater in American Slavic studies, neither phase one nor phase two has been accomplished. ''Phase three,'' challenging the canon, is not a theoretical construct in Russian literature; it is, rather, an objective political phenomenon. During the *glasnost* era, women playwrights have actively contributed to the canon. Although women are still underrepresented in theater, their plays are increasingly published and staged (*Sovetskii teatr* in 1988 announced that a ''genuine women's crusade'' was occurring).[4]

This chapter focuses on eight twentieth-century women playwrights with established positions in both the Russian literary and theatrical canons. Since so little work has been done in the study of women as playwrights, we can only hypothesize as to why the term ''women playwright'' has achieved some measure of creative equality only in the contemporary period.

Harold Segel's 1979 study *Twentieth-Century Russian Drama* eloquently illustrates the omission of women playwrights from the Russian dramaturgical canon: The entire volume mentions only two women dramatists, Zinaida Gippius and Marina Tsvetaeva, both of whom owe their celebrity to their work as poets rather than as playwrights.[5] Soviet drama and theater histories add more women's names, but only Vera Panova, best known as a prose writer, is given a separate entry in *The History of Soviet and Russian Dramaturgy (Ocherki istorii russkoi sovetskoi dramaturgii).*[6] The lack of a lasting women's dramaturgical legacy can be explained in part by the theater/literature dichotomy: Often, plays of considerable popularity in their own time become quickly dated and of minor historical interest to successive generations. Even so, three names out of a century is an extreme measure of inequality. The list of women playwrights begins to grow if the definition of theatrical creativity is expanded to include popular and provincial theaters, children's theaters, "national theatre" ("narodny teatr") and the one-act play. When political authorities have mandated that attention be paid to these normally marginal theatrical endeavors, women playwrights have emerged, if not into the canon, at least into theater histories and mainstream theatrical publications.[7]

The confluence of literature and the stage, or "women writing women's roles," offers a unique area of women's self-definition, seldom exploited in the history of Russian and Soviet theater. When performance is taken into account, the relative invisibility of women playwrights contrasts with the relative visibility of women in theater as actresses.[8] While women playwrights do not write exclusively on women's themes, I have chosen to focus on the development of female characters in the works of the authors treated.

ZINAIDA GIPPIUS: FROM METAPHYSICS TO REVOLUTION

Zinaida Gippius (1869–1945) owes her place in the theatrical canon to the confluence of theatrical and literary innovators at the turn of the century. Gippius's three plays—*Holy Blood* [*Sviataia krov'*, 1900], *The Red Poppy* [*Makov tsvet*, 1912], and *The Green Ring* [*Zelenoe kol'tso*, 1914]—which evolve in content and style from metaphysical symbolism to topical realism, explore issues of self-definition of the human spirit.[9]

The first two decades of the twentieth century saw a burgeoning of creativity unparalleled in the development of Russian culture, and theater, the syncretic medium drawing on all the arts, became a major focus for artistic endeavor. Dramaturgy, at the turn of the century, was a battleground for the conflict between the "old" *bytovaia* dramaturgy with its preoccupation with everyday life and the new ideas of Russian modernists.[10] Chekhov, Ibsen, Gorky, and Leonid Andreev dominated the playwriting canons. Simultaneously, the rise of the director as creative controller of stage production influenced the course of dramaturgy away from the "well-made play." Although censorship placed certain limitations on plays with strongly religious, sexual, or political-revolutionary themes, works hinting at such thematics were extremely popular. The "woman question" figured prominently in works by both men and women.

Although by her own accounts an "antifeminist," Gippius introduces active female protagonists whose choices determine the course of the dramatic action in her plays. In *Holy Blood*, Gippius chooses a "rusalka" (a feminine pagan spirit most often associated with luring men to their deaths) as a protagonist to enact eternal salvation through Christian self-sacrifice. This play, therefore, operates on many levels of mythic conflict, including traditional associations of masculine/feminine.[11] While the overt religious themes made *Holy Blood* unstageable under the prevailing censorship laws, contemporary critics have noted the play's centrality in the dramaturgical canon of its day. According to Harold Segel, *Holy Blood* "anticipates a folkloric current in Neoromantic drama" while it "dramatizes the transfigurative power of mystical Christianity with which much Symbolist thought was informed" and "distantly echoes Gerhardt Hauptman's *Sunken Bell*.[12] George Kalbouss, on the other hand, expresses the intriguing hypothesis that *Holy Blood* is a metaphor for *A Doll's House* by Henrik Ibsen.[13]

Gippius's later plays, *The Red Poppy* [*Makov tsvet*, 1912] and *The Green Ring* [*Zelenoe kol'tso*], abandon some of the symbolist's dramatic innovations to deal in a more conventional way with political and social themes of the day. *The Green Ring* was staged by Meyerhold in the Imperial Aleksandrinskii Theater in 1914 and later in the First Studio of the Moscow Art Theater in 1916. At first judged "immoral" by the literary censors, *The Green Ring* owed its first performance to the willful Maria Savina, *prima donna* of the Aleksandrinski. While *The Green Ring*'s topical interest lay primarily in its presentation of the conflicting values of parents and children, it also presents an interesting cross-section of relations between the sexes. Like *Holy Blood, The Green Ring* centers on a young woman's struggle for self-definition in a world where a vice-ridden old way of life is gradually ceding its place to purer younger forces. The protagonist Finnochka fails to reunite her estranged parents, but finds a spiritual and intellectual family in "the Green Ring," a society of revolutionary-minded youth. "The Green Ring's" protector, Uncle Mika, finally agrees to an arranged marriage with Finnochka in order to provide the young woman with the security she sought in vain from her own parents. Marriage as social convention is opposed to relations built on love; the "ideal" is embodied in the future alliance of a young couple, Serezha and Rusia, in the society of the Green Ring.[14] Gippius's last play, *The Green Ring*, successfully captured the prerevolutionary mood of the Russian intelligentsia; its author's emigration from Russia no doubt contributed to keeping the work from becoming a fixture of the Russian repertory.

MARINA TSVETAEVA: REWRITING ROMANCE AND TRAGEDY

Another poet spurred to dramaturgy by a need for "dialogue" with the revolutionary was Marina Tsvetaeva (1892–1941). As was the case with Gippius's theatrical works, the combination of idiosyncratic dramatic form with inauspicious historical circumstance have denied Tsvetaeva's works a place in the Russian repertory up to the contemporary period.

In 1919, Tsvetaeva wrote in her notebook: "I began writing plays—it was inevitable—my voice simply grew into verse. The breath in my breast was too much for the flute . . . I write, really without protecting myself, without remembering."[15] During this period, Tsvetaeva came into close association with the director Evgenii Vakhtangov and his theater-studio and developed strong attractions to several members of the troupe.[16] She read her play *The Snowstorm* [*Metel*] to the theater in 1919 in the hope of getting it staged; her departure from the Soviet Union in 1922 prevented the staging of her later works in the Soviet Union until their rediscovery in the more liberal atmosphere of the 1980s.[17]

Marina Tsvetaeva's *Theater* can be seen as variations on the eternal romantic dialogue between male and female. Reversing traditional dramatic roles, her plays (which have been grouped into two categories: *Romances* [*Romantika*] and *Tragedies)* privilege the female's romantic yearnings and cast the male as object. Her early female protagonists in such plays as *Jack of Hearts* [*Chervonnyi valet*] and *The Snowstorm* are feminine wanderers [*skitaltsy*], escaping from the imperfect love of their marriages. Her full-length romantic plays, set in the eighteenth century, center on male characters famous for their amorous escapades. *An Adventure* [*Prikliuchenie*] and *Phoenix* [*Feniks*] focus on the legendary Giamcomo Casanova, in two of his least typical romantic situations. The first concerns his relationship with the sexually ambiguous figure "Henri-Henriette." The second finds Casanova well past his prime resisting the attentions of the forest warden's young daughter at the castle of his patron-in-exile, Count Waldstein.[18] *Fortuna* follows the turning wheel of the fortunes of the French aristocrat, Armand-Louis de Gontaut-Biron, Duc de Lauzun, whose real-life role in the French Revolution provided Tsvetaeva with a distant parallel to the contemporary political situation. (Tsvetaeva reports that reading Lauzun's final monologue before his death on the guillotine in front of Lunacharsky, the Director of Culture, counted as her most responsible political act prior to emigration.)[19]

Tsvetaeva's tragedies, *Ariadne* and *Phaedra*, are also connected by a central male character, Theseus, and deal with the theme of unhappy love in its mythic dimensions—as the original subtitle of her intended trilogy, "the wrath of Aphrodite," indicates. As she wrote in a letter to Anna Teskova:

My Theseus is conceived as a trilogy: Ariadne-Phaedra-Helen; but out of superstition I haven't announced it yet—I need to finish at least two parts first. Did you know that all the women of all time befell Theseus? Ariadne (the soul), Antiope (the Amazon), Phaedra (passion), and Helen (beauty). Yes, the famous Helen of Troy. Theseus at the age of seventy abducted her as a seven-year-old girl, and perished as a result. So many loves and all of them unhappy.[20]

Tsvetaeva's notes during the writing of *Phaedra* reveal the author's preoccupation with discovering real psychological motivation in the ancient myth.[21] Tsvetaeva enhances the active role of Phaedra's nurse in the developing tragedy and creates a vigorous and dramatic tension in the rhythms of her verse.

Verse tragedy as a genre has seldom found favor on the Russian stage, and Tsvetaeva's works were no exception. A recent production of Tsvetaeva's *Phaedra*, however, is worthy of note. Actress Alla Demidova of the Taganka Theater used the play to present the tragic fate of Tsvetaeva herself.[22] Although Tsvetaeva's *Theater* has had little exposure in the repertory, *Sovremennia Dramaturgiia* reports that Tsvetaeva's poetry has long been the favorite material for both male and female students auditioning for admission to theatrical institutes.[23]

LIDIA SEIFULLINA: IN SEARCH OF A REVOLUTIONARY HEROINE

If Gippius and Tsvetaeva internalized the spirit of the revolution in their dramaturgy and ultimately rejected it by emigrating, Lidia Seifullina (1889–1954) probably best illustrates the fate of a woman playwright who attempts to collaborate with the new age. Seifullina's stage adaptation (together with V. Pravdukhin) of her novella *Virineia* is the first work by a woman author to capture the general attention of theater historians. Under the direction of Aleksei Popov at the Vakhtangov Studio in 1925, *Virineia* was acclaimed as one of the first native successes of the new Soviet theater. In the words of the influential critic B. Alpers, "this production, perhaps, most completely reflected the turning point in the life of the contemporary theater, a turning point that has been demonstrated with greater or lesser acuity in almost all the productions this year."[24]

Virineia (subtitled "scenes from the life of the people in five acts and ten scenes") traces the emotional and political growth of a willful, independent young woman, Virineia, in a Siberian village from the eve of World War I through the Civil War. Virineia submits to no man's authority—until she encounters sex appeal and political perspicacity combined in a widowed young soldier. While Virineia's rebellious nature leads her to political activism, her husband Pavel, not she, is the ideological center of the work. This perhaps explains why, despite the play's illustrious stage history (revived as recently as 1977[25]), Virineia is much less familiar today as a prototype for the Soviet "positive heroine" than Trenev's contemporaneous *Liubov' Yarova*, the Commissar in Vishnevsky's *Optimistic Tragedy* (1932) or Afinogenv's later *Mashenka* (1940).[26]

Although Seifullina remained an influential cultural figure throughout the Stalinist period, her later experience with the theater was considerably less happy than her dramaturgical debut. *Fellow-Travelers* [*Poputchiki*, 1932], according to a reviewer of the time, only "confirmed the Central Committee's analysis of the need to restructure literary organizations" (I. Kruti, quoted in *Ocherki*, 1,375). *Natasha* (1937) presents a latter-day Virineia who works her way from village orphan to kolkhoz director and government official, eventually finding Soviet feminine happiness with a top-notch tractor driver. The then out-of-favor theatrical revolutionary, Meyerhold, seized upon *Natasha* in a last-ditch attempt to bring his theater into line with official expectations. Unfortunately, the play was purged from the repertory at the rehearsal stage. Official criticism of *The Son* (1946–1950, published in 1959), Seifullina's last play set in World War II, irrevocably poisoned the author's relations with the stage.

OL'GA FORSH AND THE "NEW SOVIET WOMAN"

Although dramatized variations of the "New Soviet Woman" abound in the late 1920s and 1930s,[27] the "failures" of novelist Ol'ga Forsh (1873–1961) in this genre represent an interesting chapter in the history of women's playwriting. Writing to Maksim Gorky in 1929, Forsh states:

For a long time I have been preparing to speak about woman. All the best about her for the time being has been said by men, but their experience is nonetheless different. The woman question is decided fundamentally not by legal equality, which is, without question, an elementary necessity, but by a very complex self-liberation . . . Woman is not at all poorer than man in talent and will, but one rarely encounters in her an internal biography, which is needed if one is to be called a human being.[28]

Forsh, therefore, strikes at a fundamental issue of women's images on stage: Most often, women are depicted in a state of "being" (a passive role) rather than "becoming"—the main attribute of an active character. Turning to the drama, Forsh made various attempts to conceive a play with a positive heroine who participates in public life but retains her specific "feminine interests." Her final solution, *The One Hundred Twenty Second* (1937), derives its title from the article in the new Soviet Constitution guaranteeing equal rights to women. The play, in keeping with the political demands of the day, loosely fits into the genre of "industrial play" and climaxes with the reading of the article at the Eighth Congress of Soviets. The idea of growth of women's consciousness toward equality is best embodied in Zina, the wife of the head construction engineer. Zina, early in the play, argues that her professional engineering talents are equal to those of any man, and she later demonstrates them during a crisis at the construction site in her husband's absence. Yet she finds her greatest personal challenge in overcoming her grief at the death of her first child and her inability to bear more children. The play's myriad of other female characters represent variations on the theme of balancing love, motherhood, and social responsibility.

Although Forsh did not totally abandon drama after *The One Hundred Twenty Second*, she apparently did not return to the "woman question." Thus, the positive heroines of the Stalinist stage remained primarily the creations of male authors. For example, probably the most enduring portrait of a woman transcending her domestic drive in the spirit of socialism has been the young doctor Tania in Arbuzov's *Tania* (1939), a role created for the actress Maria Babanova.

VERA PANOVA "DESCRIBING LIFE AS IT IS"

Prose writer Vera Panova (1905–1973) began her career as a dramatist before the outbreak of World War II, although only her children's play, *Girls* [*Devochki*, 1945], saw the footlights before the mid 1950s. Her first play, *In Old Moscow* (1940, published in 1957), set on the eve of the Russian Revolution, showed her to be an apt student of Ostrovskian and Gorkian realism, but it foreshadowed the diffuseness of plot that characterizes most of her later drama. In a more complex work, *The Snowstorm* [*Metelitsa*, 1945],[29] a surrogate for the author observes the misfortunes of Soviet prisoners of war, eventually aiding them in their escape from captivity in German-occupied Estonia. *Insomnia* [*Bessonitsa*, 1944], Panova's wartime domestic drama about a pianist who loses a hand, remained unpublished until 1985.[30]

In the 1950s, as Soviet drama dispelled the doldrums of postwar "conflictlessness" (the alleged impossibility of conflict in a "classless" society), playwrights turned increasingly to the problems of young people, whose moral and spiritual formation was of renewed concern during the ideological re-evaluation of Stalin's legacy. The emergence of Panova into the dramaturgical canon (although on not-quite-equal terms with Aleksei Arbuzov, Victor Rozov, and Alexander Volodin) is thus fully consistent with the mainstream development of the theater in the 1950s and 1960s.[31]

In the 1960s, Panova became increasingly adept at portraying the problems of her contemporaries while remaining within the bounds of permissible themes. Ninka, the heroine of Panova's exceedingly popular *Farewell to the White Nights* [*Provody belykh nochei*, 1961], falls victim to the romancing of a modish young *stiliaga*, Valerik, on the eve of Ninka's departure to virgin lands with her fellow Komsomol activists. Gradually nursed back to social conscience by her younger-but-wiser brother, Ninka heads off again (with baby), accompanied by Valerik's former buddy Herman, whose intentions toward Ninka are fully consistent with the ideals of Communist youth.[32]

Cautiously experimental in form, Panova's later plays also vary the theme of wisdom-gained-through-painful-experience of romantic love. Panova's heroines, while interesting as characters, do not seem capable of self-definition without the intervention of wiser and more courageous male partners. Reversing the romantic conflict of *White Nights*, the hero of *How are You, Kid?* [*Kak pozhivaesh', paren'*, 1962] is enthralled by a mysterious "Nameless Woman"; *Not Yet Evening* [*Eshche ne vecher*, 1967] features a strong woman character (a nurse) as savior of an alcoholic man; *It's Been Ages!* [*Skol'ko let, skol'ko zim*, 1967][33] uses the setting of an airport during a snowstorm to bring together a cross-section of society, including two former lovers now married to others; *A Wedding Like Any Other* [*Svad'ba kak svad'ba*, 1973] deftly interweaves wedding parties of several generations. Also chronicling the romantic fate of a central heroine is *Nadezhda Milovanova* (also produced as *Fidelity* [*Vernost'*] and as *Let's Talk of the Peculiarities of Love* [*Pogovorim o strannost'akh liubvi*, 1967]).

PETRUSHEVSKAIA AND THE "WOMEN'S CRUSADE"

By the late 1970s and 1980s, Soviet theater once again presented a varied landscape characterized, on the one hand, by the revival of theatricalism by such directors as Anatolii Efros and Yuri Liubimov at the Taganka, and on the other, by the widespread experimentation with smaller, more intimate theatrical forms in amateur and studio theaters. Along with differing theatrical styles, a demand arose for various forms of playwriting. Plays by women in the 1970s and 1980s attest to this diversity and surpass most of their Soviet-era predecessors in both craft and influence, illuminating contemporary life from a variety of angles.

Masters of the "thaw" generation nurtured the younger new wave, or "shes-tidesiatniki."[34] Ol'ga Pavlova-Kuchkina, Anna Rodionova, and Liudmila Pe-trushevskaia emerged from Arbuzov's studio in Moscow; Alla Sokolova and Liudmila Razumovskaia benefited from the tutelage of Ignatii Dvoretsky in Leningrad. These studios, however, forced no artistic credo on their members, who used the studios as a means to challenge each other critically and sharpen their individual creative voices.

The thorny path to critical acclaim and official recognition for Liudmila Pe-trushevskaia (b. 1938) spanned the Brezhnev era. Petrushevskaia began writing in the late 1960s and turned to drama under the inspiration of Alexander Vam-pilov, whose name is associated with an entire generation of playwrights of the so-called period of stagnation under Brezhnev. Petrushevskaia came to prose and playwriting from a brief career in radio journalism. She brought to literature and the stage an ear for the vernacular of the urban semi-intelligentsia and an uncompromising moral sense, which expresses itself in her plays, not overtly but through dramatic irony. Official critics long dismissed the works of Petrush-evskaia and "new wave" contemporaries as "kitchen drama" [*"kukhonnaia dramaturgiia"*], defined as drama devoted to "superficial thematics" [*"mel-kotemia"*].[35] Such plays as the dramatic diptych *Cinzano* (1973) and *Smirnova's Birthday* [*Den' rozhdenie Smirnovoi*, 1977] captured the spirit of moral dilemmas unfolding in drunken discussions around the kitchen table, while her *Music Lessons* [*Uroki muzyki*, 1973] and *Three Girls in Blue* [*Tri devushki v golubom*, 1980] developed the tragicomic dimensions of everyday family conflicts in full-length drama.

The title characters of *Three Girls*—the play that finally won her widespread acknowledgment by the theatrical establishment in 1985—are all, ironically, mothers of little boys. In the absence of adult males, children serve as the sole objects of their mothers' somewhat immoderate affections. While the author denies any intention of parodying Chekhov's *Three Sisters*, Petrushevskaia's young women similarly seek flight from their unrelieved, humdrum existences. Petrushevskaia's central protagonist, Irina (as in Chekhov), finds no salvation in her work with exotic foreign languages or in pursuing the inadequate love objects who come her way. By the end of the play, Irina accepts the need for reconciliation (temporarily) under one (leaky) roof with mothers, cousins, children, and stray cats.

Petrushevskaia's characters complain ad nauseum about women's condition in the contemporary Soviet Union. Yet Petrushevskaia herself, when asked by an editor, "Which side are you on, the women's or the men's?" responded, "I'm on the side of children." This response is not purely flippant.[36] If her women often appear victimized in their relationships with men, Petrushevskaia does not minimize her women's collusion in their own victimization.

An undercurrent of the absurd and grotesque runs throughout Petrushevskaia's works. This becomes most overt in the nonsensical language of *Andante* (1974) and the use of *commedia dell'arte* characters in *Columbine's Apartment* [*Kvartira Kolumbiny*, 1975]. Self-revelatory monologues veer toward the pathological in Petrushevskaia's later one-act plays, such as *A Glass of Water* [*Stakan vody*, 1978], featuring a rather one-sided dialogue between rivals, an older and younger woman, labelled mysteriously "M" and "A." Use of initials, stock characters, or other unusual appellations (such as the name "Au" in *Andante*) indicates that it is not individual character but the *process* of self-exposure that interests the author. While presenting a devastatingly bleak spectacle of human nature, one that moves the audience to the classical responses of pity and terror, Petrushevskaia nevertheless offers a minimal optimism, through a symbolically redemptive "glass of water."

LIUDMILA RAZUMOVSKAIA

The body of work Liudmila Razumovskaia (b. 1946) has produced is perhaps the most evident attempt by a woman playwright to rewrite the dramaturgical canon to include women's roles written by women. Razumovskaia has taken the subjects of her plays from mythology, history, and contemporary life. Her titles alone are sufficient evidence of her preoccupation with the canon of women's roles. *Under One Roof* [*Pod odnoi kryshi*, 1978] investigates the psychologically complex relations of grandmother, mother, and daughter forced to coexist under one roof with no exit in sight. The title character in *Dear Elena Sergeevna* [*Dorogaia Elena Sergeievna*, 1980], a schoolteacher, confronts her society's (and her own) failure to instill ethical values in the next generation. *Sisters*, or *Garden Without Soil* [*Sestry, Sad bez zemli*, 1982], depicts two sisters' futile quests for love, home, and family. The sequel, *Maia* (1984), after the Greek goddess, focuses on two "thirty-something" women, an actress and a writer, who attempt, unsuccessfully and tragically, to create a life independent of men. In *Medea* (1981), Razumovskaia substantially rewrites Euripides's classical tragedy. In *My Sister the Mermaid* [*Sestra moia rusalochka*, 1985], she uses Hans Christian Andersen's tale as an archetype of unrequited love. Razumovskaia's most recent publication, *Your Sister and Prisoner* [*Vasha sestra i plennitsa*, 1991], enacts the historical conflict between England's Elizabeth I and Scotland's Mary Stuart, presenting their fates as parallel, nonintersecting, yet irrevocably conflicting in psychological, political, and spiritual values.

In a decade and a half of writing for the stage, Razumovskaia has moved from multilayered depiction of the spiritual bankruptcy of her contemporaries to an ever-deepening search for eternal moral and religious roots. This search culminates in her *End of the Eighties* [*Konets vos'midesiatykh*] (originally titled *My Sons-Cains* [*Synovia moi—Kainy*, 1990]), which constructs a parallel between a contemporary Soviet family (whose patriarch, Bogoliubov, is "exactly the same age as the revolution") and the family expelled from paradise in the Book of Genesis. Expulsion from Soviet Socialist paradise in the contemporary plot takes the varying forms of alcoholism, emigration, exile, and imprisonment. The old man's name, Bogoliubov (lover of God), is an ironic linking of the two story lines, as the old man's intransigent adherence to his principles forces the disintegration of the family.

Although women figure less prominently in *End of the Eighties*, Razumovskaia unwittingly presents a powerful spokesperson for a "feminist" rewriting of Judaeo-Christian civilization and its history in her character Eve. Attempting to make sense of their expulsion from paradise, Eve challenges Adam to accept co-responsibility for succumbing to the temptation to eat from the tree of knowledge. She wonders why God the Father creates life and then denies His creatures the right to celebrate their love for it.

NINA SADUR

If Razumovskaia gradually unfolds the everyday and mythic aspects of her creative imagination, Nina Sadur (b. 1950), a leading representative of the "new drama" in post-*glasnost* Russia, accomplishes the leap from the mundane to the supernatural in a single instant, looking not backward toward Genesis, but forward, toward apocalypse. Sadur combines the classic Russian concern for the "cursed questions" of human existence with an urgent contemporary alarm at the disintegration of culture.

Sadur's imaginative flights from the real to "the other" emerge more from language than from plot and utilize devices of grotesque and absurd. Her plays explore the ancient roots of contemporary folklore. Women characters frequently appear possessed of diabolical supernatural powers and heightened sensitivity to the psychology of their victims, ordinary people whom these women figures manipulate to catastrophic ends. It is not surprising that one of her most successfully staged works (at the Theater-Studio "Chelovek," 1988) is *Pannochka*, Sadur's adaptation of Gogol's horrific tale, *Vii*, which depicts a female demon haunting a seminarian.

The Marvelous Old Woman [*Chudniai Baba*, 1982], Sadur's best-known work,[37] interpolates dream with reality in a fateful encounter between two female representatives of opposing worlds. Lida, an employee of a research institute in Moscow, is sent to the countryside (a yearly ritual in Soviet society) to help with the potato harvest. She meets an old peasant woman [*baba*] by the name of "Ubienko" ["Murderson"] who claims to embody the evil of the world. The importunate old woman challenges Lida to a game of "tag": "Catch me, there's paradise, you don't catch me, it's the end of the whole world." Lida's half-hearted engagement in the game causes a worldwide cataclysm. The surface of the earth and all that is on it slips into the sea, leaving only the old woman and Lida alive. So that Lida "will not be bored" with the barrenness of the newborn world, however, Baba offers to create "simulants" of everything and everyone who formerly existed, exactly as before. In the second part of the play, Lida returns to Moscow and to dissipate the old woman's apparent spell, challenges the "simulants" of her friends and colleagues to prove that they are real. They cannot. The play, like most of Sadur's works, ends in disquieting ambiguity.

Sadur's works draw on turn-of-the-century modernism and the experimentalist writers of the 1920s and satisfy the contemporary impulse to reclaim Russia's lost legacy of the avant-garde. The highly stylized *Red Paradise* [*Krasnyi Paradis*, 1988] might be described as a Russian answer to *Raiders of the Lost Ark* and *Ubu Roi*. The play was inspired by Sudak, an ancient Black Sea fortress on a site occupied over the centuries by various invading cultures: Tatars, Genovese, Russians under Suvorov, and, finally, the Soviets, under whom Sudak became a cultural preserve. The young Soviet visitors to the fortress in Sadur's play suffer all the violent fates imaginable, from hanging to shooting to cannibalism, and each time they rebound from certain death only to end their search for lost treasure by literally drowning in blood. This absurdist bloodbath represents an alternative vision of apocalypse. Thus, Sadur warns, contemporary attempts to escape grim reality end in even grimmer fantasy.

Russian women have been writing plays in virtually all genres throughout the twentieth century. While contemporary women playwrights resist attempts to regard their work from a Western feminist perspective,[38] some patterns emerge in the recovery of women's writing in twentieth-century Russia and constitute a certain legacy in the contemporary period:

1. Women playwrights seem to have achieved greater prominence in "marginal" theatrical enterprises such as verse drama, children's and amateur theater (not to mention theater criticism).

2. Women playwrights, whether or not they see their own craft as informed by their gender, tend to subscribe to the idea that a woman's experience of the world is essentially different from a man's.

3. Periods that have validated investigation in the sphere of private rather than public life (turn-of-the-century, Thaw, *glasnost*) have opened opportunities for women writers who have found in women's roles a prism for an original vision of the human experience.

While attempts to "write women's experience" for the stage have not always been successful, with the breakdown of communist ideology, there seems to be a greater interest on the part of audiences and the theatrical establishment in women's experience. Perhaps, as Liudmila Petrushevskaia has suggested, Eve is sitting in judgment in the theater audience.[39]

NOTES

1. . . . *And Also Wrote Plays* is the title of a forthcoming women playwrights' sourcebook. (Susan Croft, ed. " . . . *And Also Wrote Plays*": *Women Playwrights Sourcebook* (New York: Methuen, 1993).

2. Aleksei Arbuzov, "Paradoksy remesla," in Olga Pavlova-Kuchkina, *Strasti po Varvare* (Moscow, 6 [1982]), 3.

3. Gayle Austin, *Feminist Theories for Dramatic Criticism*. (Ann Arbor: University of Michigan Press, 1990), 17.

4. *Sovetskii teatr* lists as established contemporary playwrights Liudmila Petrushevskaia, Liudmila Razumovskaia, Valentina Vrublevskaia, Viktoria Tokareva, Anna Rodionova, and Sofia Prokofieva; as "rising stars" Maria Arbatova, Nina Sadur, and Elena Gremina (Galina Guseva, "Dramaturgiia—muzhskoe zaniatie?" *Sovetskii teatr* 2 [1988]: 28). This list excludes prominent names such as journalists Zoia Boguslavskaia and Nina Pavlova, "village prose" writer Nina Semenovna, and non-Russian writers such as Georgian Lali Raseba, and Latvians Mara Zalite and Lela Stumbre. Writers from earlier eras whose plays have recently appeared in print include poet Ol'ga Berggol'ts and writers with careers in emigration, Tsvetaeva, Tèffi, Mother Maria (Elizaveta Iur'evna Kuz'mina-Karavaeva), and Nina Berberova.

5. Harold B. Segel, *Twentieth Century Russian Drama* (New York: Columbia University Press, 1979).

6. *Ocherki istorii russkoi sovetskoi dramaturgii*, 3 vols. (Leningrad, 1963–1968) . . .

7. Playwrights who owe their theatrical fame to memoirs and children's theater include Tatiana Schepkina-Kupernik and Aleksandra Brushstein, who began their careers in theater before the Revolution. For recent writers in amateur theater, see *Bibliotechka v pomosch khudozhestvennoi samodeiatel'nosti*, which cites 1959 as the official beginning of *narodnye teatry*. In the 1860s, the journal *Teatr* also published a number of women authors in its section designated "Narodnyi teatr." Most of these plays are one act. Among the most prolific women writers in this genre were Maria Storozheva and Estonian Mai Talvest.

8. Actresses have their own "double burden" connected with available roles for women. The practice of Soviet theater institutes to admit ten men and five women to each acting class indicates that women at best have a thirty-three percent chance of representation in Soviet theatres.

9. The title page of *The Red Poppy* lists Gippius's husband, Dmitri Merezhkovskii and D. V. Filosofov as coauthors. Temira Pachmuss asserts that a careful analysis of *The Red Poppy* indicated that in all probability Gippius was the sole writer of the drama. See Tamira Pachmuss's introduction in Z. N. Hippius, *P'esy* (Collected Dramatic Works), vol. 1 and 4 (Munchen: Wilhelm Fink Verlag, 1972).

10. The "play-within-a-play" in the first act of Chekhov's *Seagull*, for example, parodies the "new drama," while the reactions of the play's actress, Arkadina, demonstrate her adherence to the "old" school.

11. Catherine Schuler offers a detailed feminist analysis of *Holy Blood* in "Zinaida Gippius: An Unwilling and Unwitting Feminist," in *Theater and Feminist Aesthetics*, ed. Karen Laughlin and Catherine Schuler, forthcoming.

12. Segel, *Twentieth-Century Russian Drama*, 59–60.

13. George Kalbouss, "The Plays of the Russian Symbolists." (East Lansing, MI: *Russian Language Journal*, 1982), 42.

14. The two young female protagonists' names are symbolic: "Finnochka" is a nickname for "Sophina," a variant of "Sophia," meaning "wisdom"; "Rusia" evidently comes from "Rus'."

15. Marina Tsvetaeva, *Teatr* (Moscow, 1988), 342. This and all subsequent translations are mine.

16. Simon Karlinsky mentions the connection in *Marina Tsvetaeva: Her Life and Art* (Berkeley: University of California Press, 1966), 237. Additional evidence of Tsvetaeva's

links with the Vakhtangov theater is given by E. P. Simonov in "Dva stixotvoreniia Mariny Tsvetaevoi," *Novy Mir* 3 (March 1988): 169–70.

17. At least, *Phaedra*, one of the later plays, was staged in emigration, but it received very negative reviews in the émigré community.

18. These two plays were staged together under the title *Tri vozrasta Kasanovyat*, in 1984, at the Vakhtangov Theater. See Inna Vishnevskaia's review, "Vosrast liubvi," in *Sovetskii teatr* 2 (1986), 41.

19. Marina Tsvetaeva, "Moi sluzhby," *Izbrannaia proza v dyukh tomakh, 1917–1939* (New York: Russica Publications, Inc., 1979), 70.

20. R.D.B. Thomson, "Tsvetaeva's Play *Fedra*: An Interpretation." *Slavonic and East European Review* 67, No. 3 (July 1989): 340.

21. Tsvetaeva, *Teatr*, 375–79.

22. In "The Theater Must Heal Souls," *Soviet Literature* 3 (1987): 178–81, Demidova describes her experience in the role of *Phaedra* at the Taganka Theater, directed by Roman Viktiuk.

23. See Evgenii Simonov's article "V put' . . . " *Sovremennaia dramaturgiia* 3 (1988): 214.

24. B. Alpers, "*Virineia* Vakhtangovskoi studii" in *Teatralnye ocherki* 2 (Moscow, 1977), 115.

25. Reviewed by O. Dziubinskaia, "V nachale vesny," *Teatr* 4 (1978): 33–35.

26. For a discussion of the term "positive hero" as a central tenet in the literature of socialist realism, see Rufus Matthewson, *The Positive Hero in Russian Literature* (Stanford, CA: Stanford University Press, 1975). Interestingly, in its 1954 retrospective portrait gallery entitled "Geroi nashego vremeni," the journal *Teatr* includes roughly twice as many women as men among its gallery of "heroes" (twelve of eighteen). Only two of these roles, however, were written by women playwrights: The character of Virineia in *Virineia* and the heroine in Margarite Aliger's war saga, *Tale of Truth* (*Skazka o pravde*, 1943). See *Teatr*, 11 (1954): 171–89.

27. For plot descriptions of numerous comedies by and about Soviet women of this period, see Peter Yershov, *Comedy in Soviet Russia* (New York: Frederick Praeger, 1956), 30–31, 72–73, 106–108, 156, 200–201. A note in Vera Inber's diary of the period provides further evidence of official interest in the portrayal of women: "20 June 1934. Was at the Comintern. They requested I write about women. Here's the theme: New Soviet Femininity." Inber, *Stranitsy dnei perebiraia* (Moscow, 1977), 31. Inber responded by writing the play *The Mothers' Union* [*Soiuz materei*] (Moscow, 1935).

28. Quoted by Anna Tamarchenko in "Rasskazy, ocherki, p'esy O. Forsh." Forsh, *Sobraniie Sochinenii* 6 (Moscow, 1964), 633. The translation is mine.

29. See M. Korallov's review, "Ob odnoi staroi p'ese," *Teatr* 7 (1957): 96–107.

30. The title of Diana Tvekelyan's article, "You Describe Life As It Is," which accompanies the translation of this play, shows that its publication is a form of "recovery" of Panova as a *bytovoi* (everyday) realist.

31. Other women writing plays on the ethical development of young people during this period include V. Liubomova, V. Geraskina, L. Vepritskaia, and V. Ketlinskaia. These writers have all merited entries in *Teatral'naia entsiklopedia*.

32. Cognoscenti of Soviet cinema will recognize a certain similarity with the action of the first half of the 1980 film *Moscow Doesn't Believe in Tears*.

33. This play was translated into English as *It's Been Ages!* in *Contemporary Russian Drama*, ed. Franklin D. Reeve (New York: Pegasus, 1968).

34. The term "shestidesiatniki" is used in a recent critical article to cover the careers of playwrights whose formative experience was in the 1960s, but whose stage success was delayed until the late 1970s to early 1980s. See Natalia Brzhovskaia, "Repertuarnaia politika i 'Novaia drama,' " *Sovremennaia dramaturgiia* 2 (1991): 191–95.

35. For a summary of these attacks against Petrushevskaia, see Konstantin Rudnitskii, "O krupnom i melkom (kontseptsiia cheloveka v sovremennom teatral'nom iskusstve") *Teatr* 11 (1986): 127.

36. See M. Zonina's interview, "Bessmertnaia liubov'," *Literaturnaia gazeta* 23 (November 1983): 6.

37. To date, English-language translations of Sadur's work have been performed in this country and in Canada, but have not been published. *The Marvelous Old Woman* has been staged at Trinity College in Hartford, Connecticut, and the one-act play *Drive On* (*Ekhai*) at Yale University. For an account of Soviet productions of these plays, see Iniakhin's review, "Ston skvoz' zhizn' ": in *Teatr* 9 (1988): 65–72. A volume of her works has appeared in Russian as *Chudnaya Baba* (Moscow, 1989).

38. In my interviews with Soviet women delegates to the First and Second International Women's Playwrights Conference, I have encountered the same resistance to Western feminism prevalent among Russian women in general.

39. See Petrushevskaia commentary "Eva v zritel'nom zale," in *Sovetskii Teatr* 2 (1986): 2.

12

Paradigm Lost? Contemporary Women's Fiction

Helena Goscilo

"Yes, a woman's soul ought to shine in the shade."

Evdokiia Rostopchina
("How women ought to write," 1840)

"I taught women how to talk . . . "

Anna Akhmatova (1960)

TAXONOMY AND GENDER

The vexing issue of *how* an author's gender inscribes itself in a literary text, which Western feminists continue to debate in increasingly complex terms, obviously presupposes such an inscription and, accordingly, focuses instead on the nuances of its diverse manifestations. Contemporary Soviet discussions, by contrast, still query *whether* a text evidences its author's gender; and the self-contradictory opinions on this score volunteered by Russian women writers disclose the problematics of self-perception within female creativity in the Soviet Union.

The now controversial but earlier largely unexamined categories of "women's literature" and "woman's talent" were invoked regularly in reviews of Evdokiia Rostopchina's published poems throughout the 1830s.[1] Symptomatic of the times is her admirer Petr Viazemskii's letter to Aleksandr Turgenev, which caps an enthusiastic response to her lyric "The Last Flower" ("Poslednii tsvetok") with the somewhat enigmatic exclamation "skol'ko zhenskogo!" ("how much of the womanly there is in it!").[2] What exactly constituted "womanliness" may be deduced from the correspondence of the period and the then popular genre of the society tale, with its embryonic feminist impulse,[3] which illuminate the degree to which early nineteenth-century Russian society embraced the gendered binarism that Hélène Cixous outlines in "Sorties." In this essentialist polarization, which equates the masculine (normative, ideal) with activity, culture, light, intellect, and Logos, woman, as the deviant (lesser, Other) becomes synonymous with passivity, nature, darkness or reflected light, emotion, and Pathos.[4] Indeed, Rostopchina's own programmatic verses, cited above, with their "feminine" images of veils, marble, and moon, valorize modesty, suppression, mystery, propriety, dreaminess, and tears *qua* supplementary discourse as the desiderata of specifically women's poetic (self-)expression.[5] Biology, rigid social customs, and the conditions of everyday life during this period seemed to reinforce the "identity by antithesis" that separated women from men in both private and public spheres.[6] Few skeptics challenged the essentialist binary paradigm formalizing differences purportedly legitimated by Nature.

A convergence of historical developments at the turn of the century, however, urged a radical reassessment of woman's role in society, and, consequently, of her nature. These included rapid modernization, with its industrial boom and technological advances; the accession to power of the Soviets, with their agenda of enforced uniformity; and a rapid succession of wars, which compelled Russian women to undertake traditionally male functions in addition to their own. As women joined the labor force, fought in battle, and supported families single-handedly, the inculcated image of woman as a decorative vessel of emotion, a fragile repository of tender ideals, became increasingly difficult to sustain. Faced with the novelty of strong, resilient women capable of shouldering the double burden of professional and domestic responsibilities, Russian society persisted in conflating femaleness with gentle femininity, even though empirical circumstances called upon women, who far outnumbered the war-decimated male population, to be resourceful, aggressive, physically tough, and decisive.[7] Meanwhile, in the cultural arena, the familiar phrases "women's literature" and "woman writer" acquired pejorative or, at best, ambiguous connotations that were intuitively grasped by everyone, if unarticulated. Anna Akhmatova, while claiming to have taught women poets to speak in their own voice, nonetheless vigorously repudiated the rubric "woman poet" (*poetessa*). Female authors instinctively disavowed such labels, correctly construing them as dismissive, thinly coded signals for inferiority within their culture.

The patent incongruity between the drastic transformations in women's activities in the Soviet Union, on the one hand, and the country's retrograde adherence to immemorial gender stereotypes, on the other, renders the woman writer a paradoxical creature. Although Soviet society proselytizes sexual distinctions in all other walks of life, it makes a unique exception for literature. Writers themselves, while participating in the entrenched habit of touting women's inherent "femininity," simultaneously discount the relevance of gender to creative processes. According to their untenable scenario, the instant a woman starts to write, she miraculously jettisons the "inherent" feminine traits that she unavoidably displays elsewhere. This willful exclusion of gender from artistic creation in the face of its reinforcement everywhere else may be explained by the Soviets' sense of what constitutes "women's literature." Comments by three of the most successful contemporary women prosaists—Liudmila Petrushevskaia, Viktoriia Tokareva, and Tat'iana Tolstaia—as well as by the prolific, influential critic Natal'lia Ivanova, betray the irrationality of this disjunctive reasoning. While denying the validity and usefulness of a gendered literary category, on the one hand, they do not hesitate, on the other, to derogate it as superficial, trivial, decorative, excessively descriptive, philistine in outlook, saccharine in tone, and overly preoccupied with romance.[8] Yet Tolstaia's revelatory statement that men also produce "women's prose" leaves unanswered the crucial question why hack work of this sort merits a gendered label.[9] The assertion of all four writers that there is actually only good and bad prose, irrespective of gender, makes clear that the negative epithet, for reasons anchored in the gender disposition of Russian society, is interchangeable with "women's." In short, female authors dissociate themselves from "women's" writing chiefly because the ostensibly innocent term does duty for evaluative modifiers.

CONTEMPORARY WOMEN'S FICTION

Given the sizable corpus of Russian women's fiction published during the last quarter century, a thorough survey would warrant a book-length study.[10] Setting aside the volatile issue of literary quality, even a cursory overview would require discussion, minimally, of four generations of women, separated, to an extent, by key historical events in Russia's history: those born (1) before the Bolshevik Revolution: I. Grekova (b. 1907) and Natal'ia Baranskaia (b. 1908); (2) between the two world wars: Liudmila Uvarova (1918–1990), Irina Velembovskaia (1922–1989), Inna Varlamova (1922–1990), Maiia Ganina (b. 1927), Natal'ia Sukhanova (b. 1931), Galina Shcherbakova (b. 1932), Nina Katerli (b. 1934), Anna Mass (b. 1935), Viktoriia Tokareva (b. 1937) and Liudmila Petrushevskaia (b. 1938); (3) in the post-World War II period: Tat'iana Nabatnikova (b. 1948), Nadezhda Kozhevnikova (b. 1949), Tat'iana Tolstaia (b. 1951), Elena Makarova (b. 1951), Irina Polianskaia (b. 1952), and Dina Rubina (b. 1953); and (4) in the post-Stalin era: Svetlana Vasilenko (b. 1956) and Valeriia Narbikova (b. 1960). Such demarcations, of course, inevitably smack of arbitrariness, particularly since the correlation between age and professional debut varies enormously; some individuals (for example, Dina Rubina) began writing in their early youth, whereas others embarked on a literary career only at retirement age (for example, Baranskaia and Grekova, at fifty-five and fifty, respectively). Still others encountered resistance from censorship, which occasioned extraordinary delays in their access to print (for example, Petrushevskaia, who waited approximately two decades before having her stories from the 1960s accepted). Finally, one could make a persuasive argument for expanding the proposed roster to encompass Vera Panova, Natal'ia Sukhanova, Natal'ia Il'ina, Liubov' Iunina, Larisa Fedorova, Irina Raksha, Alla Kalinina, Inna Goff, Nina Gorlanova, Larisa Vaneeva, Nina Sadur, Valentina Sidorenko, Marina Palei, and dozens more. Considerations of space rather than the subjective preferences that invariably govern any selection oblige me to exclude them here so as to concentrate on only a handful of the above-named writers.

Despite the reductive consequences of any generalization, which applies falsely universalizing measures and downplays those individual aspects on which any concept of authorship depends, it is possible to isolate certain typical features of contemporary women's prose. The single most distinctive common denominator, which generates a series of corollary commonalities, is, not surprisingly, an intense focus on women's experience and psychology. Women of all ages, social backgrounds, professions, and temperaments not only hold center stage in women's fiction, but most frequently also provide the prism through which events are refracted. In feminist parlance, Russian women's fiction is gynocentric. Women's search for self-actualization (usually played out in the context of a modern urban environment) spawns many of the recurrent themes in this literature: love, marriage, familial relations, single parenting, abortion, maternity, infidelity, divorce, conflicting pressures of home and career, and generational antagonism. Through these personal (and highly personalized) concerns, such perennial human preoccupations as integrity, materialism, compromise, self-delusion, loneliness, and so forth, come under analysis, as does a wide range of social problems: male alcoholism, widespread institutional corruption, disaffection of youth, men's involvement in multiple "marriages," parental irresponsibility, and lack of adequate living space, products, and medical care. Stylistic hallmarks of women's fiction, which favors the short story and *povest'* novella over the novel, include a subordination of plot to a preponderance of description; an exploration of levels and modes of consciousness; a style that eschews modernist techniques; and a stable perspective conveyed through quasi-direct discourse—a limited (most frequently female) viewpoint in which boundaries between author, narrator, and protagonist often dissolve.[11]

To counter the anticipated objection that such an account applies equally to contemporary male fiction, one need only appreciate how substantially a portrayal of women from within—with its nuanced tracing of mental and psychological processes—differs from a mainly external depiction. In addition, the direct, focal treatment of political issues and the immanent impulse to universalize that mark male prose are largely alien to women's writing, just as vividly particularized insights into the anguished atmosphere of a maternity ward or an abortion clinic rarely, if ever, find their way into male prose.[12] Moreover, since many real-life husbands and fathers hold themselves aloof from household and parental duties, domestic and familial obligations in the former Soviet Union have become almost exclusively women's realm. When accurately reflected in literature, that situation yields correspondingly different emphases. Because women's disproportionately more numerous responsibilities entail intimate familiarity with kindergartens, schools, clinics, hospitals, stores, teachers, children, nurses and doctors, pensioners, and so on, it stands to reason that these figure much more prominently in works by authors with first-hand knowledge of them (the correlation is especially notable *"literatura byta"* ["literature of everyday life"]).[13] Furthermore, while both sexes essentialize through ascribing irrationality, emotionalism, love of domesticity, and inordinate absorption with clothes and physical appearance to "the gentle sex" (supposedly destined for maternity and self-sacrifice), women tend to "problematize" these hackneyed formulations, which malestream fiction (above all, the village prose contingent) takes for granted and therefore relegates to the invisible status of natural givens and immutable truths sedimented in the nation's psyche.

If women's fiction contrasts in thought-provoking ways with men's, it also demonstrates shifts and permutations within the corpus along a chronological continuum. Under the impact of changing sociopolitical, psychological, and artistic conditions, that fiction has evolved over the last quarter century, gradually moving away from an adoption of the gender paradigms imposed by official orthodoxy (internalized in the work of the older generation), through ambivalent revisionism (among those of the middle generations), to relative autonomy (of the younger generation). While few writers seem to grasp the politics of gender formation whereby institutionalized ideology propagates an essentialist "norm" of womanhood in order to consolidate its own political or economic power,[14] the coercive exemplar of "femininity" has perceptibly weakened its hold over women's self-conceptualization within the last decade.[15] Nowadays female authors ironize or impugn gender stereotypes, adduce alternatives to sanctioned models, or write as though the latter did not exist.

ORTHODOXY WITH A WOMAN'S FACE

The oeuvre of Natal'ia Baranskaia and I. Grekova, the undisputed doyennes of contemporary Russian women's fiction, testifies to the inseparability of the particular historical moment from the psychological development of a writer. Born within a year of each other, widowed by war, and drawn into literature after successful careers in other professions, both underwent hardships during the country's successive upheavals that indelibly stamped their psyche and, by extension, their prose. That prose instantly identifies them as members of a generation bound by a sense of personal accountability, an admiration for and commitment to ideals, and an awareness of the apparently limitless reserves of human fortitude and self-sacrifice, notably on the part of women. Their gynocentric prose focuses above all on ethical problems,[16] dramatized through pivotal decisions and behavior in Grekova's case (from "On Maneuvers" ["Na ispytaniiakh," 1967] to "No Smiles" ["Bez ulybok," 1986]) and in Baranskaia's case, through the less visible medium of perception and judgment. For example, Grekova's novella *The Department* (*Kafedra*, 1978), with its dizzyingly tangled web of heterosexual relationships, grapples with professional and personal integrity in scientific research, the story "One Summer in the City" ("Letom v gorode," 1965), with the moral choice of abortion. Baranskaia's more understated narratives caution against prejudice, simplistic readings, and impatient conclusions in our assessment of others (for example, "Woman with an Um-

brella'' [''Zhenshchina s zontikom''], ''The Thief'' [''Vorovka''], ''Partners''
[''Partnery'']). Curiously, both writers seem to share their female protagonists'
optimistic faith in the power of love, even though the specific romantic pursuits,
liaisons, and marriages proliferating in their fiction emphasize the pain and
humiliation of love relationships, which ultimately end in failure. The lyric haze
of personal desire patently beclouds the clarity of dispassionate authorial observation. This general affirmation in the teeth of circumstantiated misery and gloom
allies Baranskaia and Grekova with socialist realism and the optimism it man-
dates, no matter how grim the circumstances. And this brand of optimism is
license to conceive women as impermeable.[17] Indeed, the conservative strain
that surfaces in their female characters' obligatory cheerfulness, self-denial, and
reconciliation to the status quo also accounts for the cult of maternity that resides
at the core of their fiction and coincides with official campaigns for enlarging
the country's labor force. Furthermore, their lackluster style, whereby the prose
occasionally slides into an anemic, generic flatness that verges on journalese,
by default ''foregrounds'' the thematic content of their works, consolidating their
value more as social documents than as artistically crafted texts.[18]

Baranskaia's reputation as a specifically female author will ultimately rest on
the two narratives that frame her career: *A Week Like any Other* (*Nedelia kak
nedelia*, 1969) and *Remembrance Day (Den' pominoveniia*, 1989).[19] Its status
as the first piece of fiction to chronicle women's way of life in the Soviet Union
virtually guaranteed *A Week Like any Other* the sensation it caused in Russia
and abroad. The steady accumulation of data through the first-person narration
of Ol'ga Voronkova, a technical research assistant at an institute laboratory,
coheres into a poignant account of the educated Russian woman's insoluble
dilemma: how to juggle the relentless barrage of duties that attach to her multiple
roles of loving wife, nurturing mother, conscientious housekeeper, and full-time
skilled employee. This ''mission impossible'' transforms Ol'ga into Alice in
Wonderland, desperately racing just to stay in the same place. Baranskaia's
skillful handling of time and space as Ol'ga's twin enemies conveys the un-
bearable pressure under which she struggles to meet superhuman demands, while
harboring guilt for her quite understandable failure to do so.

Permeated with compassionate understanding, *A Week Like any Other* established a model for subsequent forays in depicting the plight of women laboring
under the burden of Soviet icons of womanhood. The avalanche of mail provoked
by the story evidenced that, in Soviet eyes, Baranskaia admirably fulfilled her
stated intention to portray the hardships of women's lives.[20] Abroad, Baranskaia
exceeded that intention, insofar as the West interpreted *A Week Like any Other*
as a feminist protest against male oppression exercised on a personal as well as
social level. The divergence in reception suggests how fundamentally sociopolitical forces affect reading strategies. What impressed Western readers, initiated
into the debates on gender, as an unambiguously feminist text was conceived
by its decidedly unfeminist author as a story affirming the triumph of love! After
all, Ol'ga's spouse Dima is ''a wonderful husband,'' Baranskaia insists (echoing

Ol'ga's coworker Dark Liusia), for he "still" loves her after five years of marriage, helps her with the children, and neither drinks nor commits adultery.[21] This defense of Dima illustrates the startlingly minimal expectations the majority of Russian woman have of men, by contrast with what their society has trained them to exact from themselves. In fact, *A Week Like Any Other* embraces the gendered myths premised on the conviction that Nature, through biological differences, scripted dissimilar lives for men and women, entrusting them with functions and responsibilities determined by their contrasting physical (hence character) traits. Those absolutes buttress the cult of motherhood (Dima "helps Ol'ga" with the children, as if they were not equally his, and Ol'ga alone misses work repeatedly on account of the children's various ailments, even though her professional qualifications parallel Dima's); the identification of women with domesticity (both Ol'ga and Dima view cooking, cleaning, washing, ironing, and sewing as her domain, because of which she can never read the technical materials that Dima has time to enjoy); and the coercive yoking of love to women's self-abnegation (significantly, all of the women at work "cannot but admire [seventy-year-old Mariia Matveevna] for her life of sacrifice"). Here, as elsewhere, Baranskaia glorifies love as the primary motivation for her female protagonist's basic accommodation to both the imbalanced division of domestic labor and, more comprehensively, the treadmill that comprises her hectic, frustrated existence. Although the narrative broaches the issue of gender inequity through Ol'ga's case, as well as through her female coworkers' thwarted biographies, it ultimately shies away from drawing conclusions that would rock the boat of Soviet misogyny. Baranskaia's reluctance to pursue such problems beyond a certain point stems not from any compelling narrative short-circuiting, but from the inconsistency in her own thinking, grounded in an internalized sexism that confuses femaleness with femininity.[22]

Remembrance Day, the novel Baranskaia considers the culmination of her literary career, confirms in less mediated fashion the values implicit in *A Week Like any Other*. A memorial to her husband, who perished in 1943, this highly retrospective autobiographical work follows seven women's journeys on the twenty-fifth anniversary of World War II to the graves of their husbands, all killed in the war. Despite the diversity of the women's backgrounds, education, and temperaments, their ruminations and reminiscences intersect on several major gender-related points: Women live not as independent beings, but primarily through men and above all through children, who constitute the *raison d'être* of existence; intrinsically different from men, women are more religious, instinctual, and in closer communion with nature; women's preordained mission (epitomized in motherhood) is that of nurturing, support, stoic acceptance, and self-denial. On a universal scale these largely passive qualities translate into procreation and the promotion of a pacifist ethic through example. In this sluggish novel, which Baranskaia values as the summary of her life's thoughts, she practically eliminates the irony and ambiguity that infuse her best short stories, in order to obviate uncertainties about her position on issues she deems crucial.

The work exemplifies the concept of women's niche in culture advanced by
Boris Eikhenbaum: to effect the link between generations by preserving and
transmitting memory.

Grekova, a renowned mathematician with scholarly publications on the theory
of probability under her real name of Elena Ventsel, is a more prolific prosaist
than Baranskaia, and more uneven in quality. Although she is bold in tackling
delicate subjects (the need for scientists to confront the long-range consequences
of their research ["Beyond the Checkpoint" ("Za prokhodnoi," 1962)], the
dismal conditions of Red Army military life ["On Maneuvers"], self-seeking
opportunism among academics [*The Department*], bribery and incompetence in
the medical profession ["The Break" ("Perelom," 1987)]), her proclivity to
sentimentalize, schematize characters, and provide somewhat facile solutions
undermines her weakest works. While Grekova conveys the intellectual and
emotional experiences of her educated, mature female protagonists with verve
and sensitivity (for example, in *Ladies' Hairdresser* [*Damskii master*, 1963])
and etches moving, persuasive portraits of female bonding, she nonetheless
persists in elevating men as figures of unassailable authority drawn along mythic
lines. Women's repeated disappointments and unhappiness at men's hands do
not deter them from yearning for "Mr. Right"—who has the irritating habit of
materializing in a halo of superhuman attributes at some juncture in the narrative.
In *The Hotel Manager* (*Khoziaika gostinitsy*, 1976), true to the formula of
fairytales, Vera Platonovna (whose name nakedly adverts to her idealism and
faith) outlives the military tyrant of a husband who turns her into a willing slave
and sheds the alcoholic live-in lover who discovers a safe berth in her home, to
find "true happiness" ("her first real love," Grekova tells us) on her third
attempt. Her "prince" of a sea captain sails into her life bathed in an imagery
of gold, silver, lofty height, health, and—saddled with a crippled wife, whom
he nobly refuses to abandon. Instead, he embarks on a (lifelong?) liaison with
Vera, moralized by Grekova's relentlessly lyricized domestication of their meetings (presided over by "some ancient god of the family hearth"). In *The Department*, the smitten widow Lidiia Mikhailovna can conceive of no greater bliss
than the security of marriage with the aged professor Zavalishin, a paragon of
wisdom and integrity. The supernaturally omniscient "eagle" Dr. Chagin in
"The Break" not only restores the middle-aged heroine to health and marries
her, but also transforms her values, foresees his own death and her consequent
loneliness, and ensures their adoption of an unwanted child to fill that anticipated
gap. Chagin's mythic proportions make him less a doctor than the ultimate
dispenser of infallible prescriptions for life.

According to Grekova, the peak of achievement for women involves the
creation of cozy domesticity: catering to men's and children's needs, adminis-
tering hefty doses of sympathy along with lovingly prepared food, and staying
energetic, industrious, and cheerful. Uncontrollable passions and raw sexuality
have no place in such a bourgeois environment. As *The Hotel Manager* illustrates,
they represent a temporary stage to be surmounted rather than prolonged, for

the ideal woman is neither the hedonist nor the successful professional, but the beaming, dedicated housekeeper. It is no accident that Vera Platonovna actualizes her dream and her natural potential by managing a hotel. A "home" on an extended scale, it provides the perfect venue for showcasing her "feminine talent" of arch-nurturer, just as her surrogate mothering of Vika (her best friend's daughter) allows her to channel her ample maternal instincts. Pangs of remorse trouble any woman in Grekova incapable of building such a "nest" for her family, even an intellectual with an advanced degree and specialized training whose commitment to her job borders on the fanatical (Kira Petrovna, the therapist in "The Break").

Grekova's most memorable work is the novella that brought her back into the public spotlight in the Soviet Union, sparked impassioned debates, and was adapted for the stage: *The Ship of Widows* (*Vdovii parokhod*, 1981). A close-up of five widows in a Moscow communal apartment during and immediately following World War II, this microcosm of Soviet society comprises a world, primarily of women, struggling to cope with the degradations, losses, and invisible wounds inflicted on survivors both by the war and the mechanisms holding the country in place. The five women, representing different social strata, are the religious peasant Kapa; Ol'ga Flerova, a former concert pianist, and Ada, a retired operetta singer, who belongs to the intelligentsia; the proletarian Panka; and the working woman Anfisa, with whose funeral the novella opens. The retrospective narrative, which emanates largely from Ol'ga's viewpoint but intermittently yields to an omniscient narrative voice, traces the birth, adolescence, and early adulthood of Anfisa's illegitimate son Vadim. His development into a callous, self-absorbed egotist interweaves with the affecting group portrayal of intolerable human suffering, both mitigated and exacerbated by the relationships that arise solely from people's enforced cohabitation in a limited space.

The Ship of Widows is a woman's version of *Crime and Punishment* that dramatizes inconclusively the conundrum frequently posed in the former Soviet Union: What accounts for the self-seeking superciliousness and indifference of postwar children born to a generation noted for its communal spirit and self-sacrifice? While wisely withholding final or even tentative answers to that query, Grekova nonetheless mounts several of her favorite hobby horses regarding gender distinctions, love, and the sanctity of motherhood. Women meekly acquiesce not only to men's intemperate drinking and violence (although Anfisa's husband Fedor drinks and beats her, he is "like her child," just as the soldiers fighting at the front "need comforting like babies") but also to their dictating of terms. Because her alcoholic husband does not want children, Panka has three abortions, and when her unofficial second husband tires of her, he leaves without a word; Kapa contracts two loveless marriages for her family's sake, is widowed each time, and takes a married lover, who also later abandons her. "Love," we learn, "is a rare talent," possessed, it seems, primarily, if not exclusively, by women, who, with their "women's tears" and eagerness to please, "suffocate" men (claimed by Fedor and Vadim about Anfisa). Grekova resorts to the sadomasochistic vocabulary of enslavement to define Anfisa's relations with Vadim and, by implication, two of the three men in her life: "Anfisa fed her son. She overflowed into him, her master. No one had ever mastered her like this, neither Fedor nor Grigorii. No one but Vadim." The lexicon echoes Anfisa's, who believes that "A man's his own master" (whereas woman, presumably, is not her own mistress). Ada refers to her "weak feminine character" and declares that "stoutness doesn't hurt a man, it's women who have to watch their figure"; Ol'ga wonders whether inside her lives "a woman begging for charity" and pays Vadim the ultimate compliment on his nursing/housekeeping abilities by feminizing them ("it looked as though a woman's hands had made [. . . Anfisa's] bed"). When repeated by diverse characters, these solidify into a chorus of code-confirming sentiments to which Grekova herself subscribes.[23]

RURAL IR/RECONCILIATIONS

Although they were more than a decade younger than Baranskaia and Grekova, the late Irina Velembovskaia and Inna Varlamova began writing at an earlier age, so their literary debut roughly coincided with Baranskaia's and Grekova's. Whereas most female authors opt for urban locales, both Velembovskaia and Varlamova set a number of their works from the 1960s and 1970s in the rural or peripheral regions of the Soviet Union (the countryside in Velembovskaia's "Family Matters" ["Dela semeinye," 1966] and a village in her "Through Hard Times" ["V trudnuiu minutu," 1965], a Ukrainian kolkhoz in Varlamova's "Threesome" ["Troe," 1968] and western Siberia in her "A Ladle for Pure Water" ["Kovshik dlia chistoi vody," 1969]). They have the vision and subtlety not to dismiss uneducated and even somewhat stupid women from their spectrum of female protagonists; they have the skill to endow them with psychological complexity despite their rudimentary intellect (for example, Pania in "Through Hard Times," Ania in *A Sweet Woman* [*Sladkaia zhenshchina*, 1973], and Khatanzeeva in "Ladle"). Instead of schematizing along gender lines that produce predictable heroines and villains, they treat strengths and weaknesses in both sexes even-handedly and do not make a fetish of maternity. Unlike their unusually prolific contemporary Liudmila Uvarova, Velembovskaia and Varlamova wrote comparatively little, that small output showing their flair for reproducing regional dialects in a prose that is somewhat old-fashioned, straightforward, and, regrettably, often anonymous in style.

The gynocentrism of Velembovskaia's fiction is attested by her declarative titles: *Women* (*Zhenshchiny*, 1964), *A Sweet Woman*—both adapted into films—and *Marisha Ogon'kova*. In her most popular and best work, ironically called *A Sweet Woman*, Velembovskaia creates a rounded portrait of a vain pragmatist whose machinations alienate her husband and lover, leading finally to middle-aged solitude relieved only by the undeserved compassion of the son she neglected and never loved. Devoid of sentimentalism and unflinchingly consistent in its exfoliation of Ania's psychology and its ramifications, Velembovskaia's finely shaded novella shatters clichés about femininity and frees men from the two-dimensionality of pure Otherness. In creating an unlikable woman without resorting to misogynistic formulae, Velembovskaia prepared the ground for such subsequent works as Galina Shcherbakova's "The Wall" ("Stena," 1979), Nadezhda Kozhevnikova's "Vera Perova" (1983), and Viktoriia Tokareva's *Trial Run* (*Pervaia popytka*, 1989).

Varlamova, likewise, does not "absolutize" femininity, maternity, or family as sacrosanct entities, though her most ambitious narrative, *A Counterfeit Life* (*Mnimaia zhizn'*, 1978), intermittently drifts into "purple prose" during overly lyricized love scenes. For a feminist, the autobiographical novel's chief interest lies in its moving, courageous exploration of how women cope with the trauma of mastectomy, an intimate dilemma embedded in the larger context of the intelligentsia's crisis of conscience during the 1960s in Moscow.

REVISIONISM

The stylistic affinities with journalism in Velembovskaia's and Varlamova's prose also mark Galina Shcherbakova's and Maiia Ganina's fiction. While Shcherbakova's novella *You Never Dreamed of It* (*Vam i ne snilos'*, 1977) credits the possibility of noble impulses in the young, her predilection in such narratives as "The Wall" and "The Kuz'menko Incident" ("Sluchai s Kuz'menko") is to expose the almost imperceptible inner corruption of self-deluded careerists driven by utilitarian motives. Accordingly, in analyzing the dynamics of marriage—tracing the disillusionments, betrayals, and grievances that accrue over the years—she "rhetoricizes" its disintegration as a metonymy for social decay. With dispassionate candidness she documents how the degrading conditions of Soviet reality, with its mendacity, shoddiness, and bleak deprivation, gradually erode people's sensitivity, kindness, and integrity, fostering pragmatism at the price of humane values. Shcherbakova firmly rejects her countrywomen's biologism (which extrapolates an immutable female identity from a set of bodily features)[24] and either writes across gendered binarism (for example, "The Wall" and her latest work, signally titled *Anatomy of a Divorce* [*Anatomiia razvoda*, 1990]) or implicitly invokes it only to ironize its untenability. "Uncle Khlor and Koriakin" ("Diadia Khlor i Koriakin," 1988), for instance, mocks a number of stereotypes through its tongue-in-cheek account of the fight over a little girl by two misogynistic middle-aged men (the natural father and her stepfather) to whose lives she unexpectedly brings meaning. The conflict is resolved through their living together as an unlikely reconstituted family, the two fathers exhibiting all the emotional attachment, tenderness, and anxiety that gendered clichés impute to maternity alone.

The quest for self-realization by strong, talented women propels Ganina's fiction. Prone to merciless self-analysis and skeptical about others' motives, the typical Ganina protagonist seeks an appropriate outlet for her artistic and, secondarily, her romantic yearnings. Although many Ganina heroines do not fear solitude, and, indeed, prefer it (for example, "Notes of an Unknown Poetess" ["Zapiski neizvestnoi poetessy," 1966], "Golden Solitude" ["Zolotoe odino- chestvo," 1970]), disappointments in love (affairs peter out, marriages end in divorce) can lend a compensatory dimension to their professional successes. These, in turn, cost dearly; painfully attained through discipline, struggle, and impartial self-criticism, they often require forfeiting colleagues' affection. Be- cause in Ganina's moral universe the facile seduction of compromise and re- assuring fictions is omnipresent, gifted individuals (Agrippina in "Stage Actress" ["Teatral'naia aktrisa," 1971]) subject themselves and those around them to constant scrutiny. This tendency to monitor oneself incessantly, to judge every- one according to stringent criteria, and to find them and oneself wanting obtains in both professional and personal spheres. A Freudian in her understanding of psychological drives, Ganina harbors few illusions about human nature, ac- knowledges the crippling tenacity of early formative experiences, and detects egotism, fear, and pride in ostensibly innocuous and noble actions.

Particularly fearless in this regard is Ganina's novella *Hear Your Hour Strike (Uslysh' svoi chas*, 1975). An achronological first-person account by a middle- aged film actress, Mariia Kovaleva, of representative moments in her biography, it shifts back and forth in time to intertwine several plot lines involving Mariia's knotty interactions with her father, husband, lover, daughter, friends, and former and current coworkers. Through Mariia's educated, weak-willed old father, Gan- ina ruthlessly spotlights the degradation of sexual enslavement and the urge to whitewash our motives so as not to confront or divulge our baser instincts. The ambivalence Mariia feels toward him—contempt, impatience, irritated resent- ment, alternating with guilt, love, and compassion—likewise shades her relations with her daughter Sasha, an actress whose self-confident youth and beauty heighten Mariia's melancholy awareness of aging without having contributed anything really durable to life. Mariia's readily admitted bouts of jealously, moodiness, and vanity, her sexual susceptibility, and her refusal to conform to prefabricated models of behavior are a departure from the touted Soviet ideal of daughter, wife, and mother. She emerges, consequently, as a credible, if not always admirable, human being. Although she is stylistically unmemorable, Ganina's transgressive narrative constructs an important bridge between the ret- icence of the older generation and the uninhibited outspokenness of recent wom- en's prose by integrating what formerly was deemed reprehensible into a basically decent personality. *Hear Your Hour Strike* humanizes instead of stigmatizes woman's sexual appetite, rationality, independence, and greed for life.[25]

Nina Katerli, one of the few women writers of the interwar generation to experiment with the fantastic, parallel plot lines and male viewpoint in her prose (for example, in the collections *Window* [*Okno*, 1981] and *Color Postcards* [*Tsvetnye otkrytki*, 1986]), not only challenges the conventional paradigm of femininity, but in *Polina* (1984), posits a subversive alternative to the exemplary family extolled for decades by the Soviet establishment (as does Tolstaia in "Fire and Dust" ["Ogon' i pyl'," 1986]). Katerli contrasts the anomalous, freewheeling life of Polina, a successful senior engineer involved with an impotent poet on the social fringe, and the regularized domesticity of her friend Maiia, a responsible wife to the influential director Igor', a caring mother to their spoiled daughter Larisa, and an immaculate housekeeper. While the prodigal Polina follows the unpredictable zigzags of instincts and feeling that lead her into diverse friendships and a series of amorous entanglements, Maiia's meticulously organized existence is ruled "by the iron principle of doing everything as it should be done" around the immovable hearth of home. Juxtaposing the centrifugal and the centripetal,[26] the story is structured on the seesaw effect: as Polina's approach to life, which originally seems catacombed with every possible risk, becomes increasingly attractive in that it proves capable of absorbing and dealing with every change, the ostensibly secure stability of the familial Maiia disintegrates because of its imperviousness to the unforeseen and unforeseeable. When Maiia's jealousy upon inadvertently glimpsing her husband in an apparent tryst with another woman culminates in a nervous breakdown, the fabric of their family unit unravels with devastating speed. As in many of Katerli's stories, which examine how the shocking, irrational, and fantastic can erupt without warning and invade the most tranquil and stolid regimen, so here Katerli implies that the superimposition of social form on human relations offers no guarantees. In *Polina* Katerli makes a compelling case against repressive uniformity through cultural mandate.

If fantasy distinguishes some of Katerli's stories from the enervated rhythms of her colleagues' rather nondescript style, Viktoriia Tokareva's distinctive authorial signature is humor. Irony, lightness of touch, and irrepressible hope in the midst of desolation tend to distract the reader from the unsettling frequency with which infidelity, disillusionment, mutual abuse, and partings surround Tokareva's major theme of love, from her first collection, *About That Which Wasn't (O tom chego ne bylo*, 1969), to her sixth and last, *The Flying Swing. Nothing Special (Letaiushchie kacheli. Nichego osobennogo*, 1987). Tokareva's heroines have grown older along with their creator, but the scenarios of mutability they enact and witness have not altered substantially over the last quarter century: friendships cool, passions wither, affairs end, and marriages collapse. Change is inexorable and inevitably for the worse, and Tokareva's defensive strategy of humor masks both her own and her protagonists' vulnerability to this painful process. Discrepancy is Tokareva's dominant perception and her chief structuring device: Her characters tend to reside in limbo, shuttled back and forth between imagination and reality, hopes and results, beginnings and endings, youth and age. In one of her best stories, "Between Heaven and Earth" ("Mezhdu nebom i zemlei," 1985), both the title and the airplane setting metaphorically capture the suspension between the ideal and the concretely accessible that defines the human condition; tellingly, the plane lands before story's end. The chasm yawning between expectations and fulfillment is metaphorized or made explicit in numerous stories (see "The Flying Swing" ["Letaiushchie kacheli"] and "Nothing Special'' [''Nichego osobennogo,'' 1981], in which habit and weakness devour dreams. What imparts to Tokareva's prose its characteristic tone is, similarly, the disjunction between matter and manner, whereby the potentially tragic is soft-pedaled by a comically breezy formulation, while aggrandizing similes and pseudosyllogisms elevate the incidental to significance.

Until the mid 1980s, Tokareva's narrators functioned as bittersweet rueful observers. *Glasnost* suddenly inspired her to start injecting doses of moralizing into her increasingly longer narratives, with infelicitous results. Social issues, earlier submerged in an inconspicuous but plausible background, now obtruded. And the foregrounding of alcoholism, systemic corruption, paralyzing bureaucratism, and so on, in such works as *A Long Day* (*Dlinnyi den'*, 1986), *Five Figures on a Pedestal* (*Piat' figur na postamente*, 1987), and *Pasha i Pavlushka* (1987) did not mesh with Tokareva's sardonic style.[27] The regrettable effects of this metamorphosis on the representation of womanhood are most evident in *Trial Run*, an allegory of moral punishment visited upon a woman's body for her ''unwomanly'' conduct. Approximating Katerli's and Tolstaia's technique of presenting a female protagonist through the eyes of her ''closest friend,''[28] Tokareva filters Mara's series of monstrous acts through the reactions—awe, revulsion, embarrassed envy—of a contrasting personality. Hence, Mara's manipulation, flamboyant consumerism, infidelities, and terminal selfishness cohere into a way of life that becomes a counter-example to the narrator's quiet, sometimes dull, modest but steady, family existence. This recuperation of the traditional domestic paradigm lacks, however, the complexity of Katerli's *Polina*, for Tokareva paints Mara in such unrelievedly dark colors that she verges on caricature. A woman who destroys marriages and careers, wantonly despoils nature, and dehumanizes everyone around her as merely a means to her own ends so patently violates the whole range of unwritten laws overseeing decency that she can hardly present a legitimate alternative to any model. By default, then, the narrator's way of life in this specious, overdetermined ''either/or'' acquires a positive aura, particularly since she addresses precisely those moral problems that never trouble Mara.

The most profoundly disquieting aspect of *Trial Run* is Tokareva's apparent conviction that Mara's ''punishment'' ultimately fits her ''crimes'': Justice is presumably served when a woman who uses her sexuality ''illegitimately'' for self-empowerment gets a breast cancer that necessitates a radical mastectomy and eventually destroys her sinful body. A moralized concept of disease, which interprets fatal illness as divine retribution, carries disturbing implications (which have surfaced in American fundamentalists' response to the AIDS epidemic). As Susan Sontag has remarked, cancer, as the most radical of disease metaphors, is particularly tendentious and therefore appealing to paranoid, fatalistic, and totalitarian minds.[29] If sexualized in its gender-specific manifestation, breast cancer as metaphor joins that legion of misogynistic moves calculated to reduce women's flesh to trope or collapsed identity—a primitive summation that precludes authentic physical being. One need only compare *Trial Run* to Varlamova's *Counterfeit Life* to realize what a harsh disservice Tokareva's conclusion performs to fictional representations of womanhood.[30]

SUPERBLY OUT OF SYNC

Of the female authors born between the two world wars, Liudmila Petrushevskaia stands supreme by virtue of her stylistic sophistication and her formidable originality as prosaist and playwright. These two factors, in light of the unrelieved somberness of her vision, doutbless account for the insuperable obstacles that blocked her route to regular publication for almost twenty years. For Petrushevskaia's controversial talent overturns the one-dimensional expectations of women's writing on several fronts through her grim pessimism (optimism is women's duty); her violation of decorum through physiological detail (only men may advert explicitly and crudely to the body and its functions); her broaching of such taboo topics as nymphomania and incest (interdicted for men and women alike); and the gnarled, aggressive poetry of her synthetic yet unique language (Logos/linguistic imperialism is a male prerogative).

Petrushevskaia's compressed short stories, of which only one collection (*Immortal Love* [*Bessmertmaia liubov'*, 1989]) has appeared to date, portray a nightmarish world on the psychological edge of existence. Suffused with morbid humor and grotesquerie, her harshly unidealizing narratives record the underbelly of human relations—the nasty traffic in desires and fears where everything carries a literal and metaphorical price. Condemned to life, the inhabitants of her grim universe invariably find themselves cut adrift from reliable moorings; are ruled by appetite and self-interest; fall into seemingly irreversible patterns of (self-) destructive behavior; abrogate moral responsibility; inflict and suffer pain in an unbroken chain of universal abuse. Suicide, alcoholism, prostitution, one-night stands, fictitious marriages, unwanted pregnancies and abortions, neglected children, crushing poverty, theft, and physical and psychological violence constitute the "norm" of Petrushevskaia's fiction.

Like her plays,[31] Petrushevskaia's overtly gynocentric stories concentrate on the middle class, chiefly the urban technical intelligentsia. Most of her protagonists lead lives irremediably maimed through personal weakness, uncontrollable circumstances, male mistreatment, and relatives' interference or overbearing demands: All too often Petrushevskaia's women must tend simultaneously to dependent children and needy, typically hospitalized, mothers. Alienation, irretrievable loss, dereliction, and demeaning hardships comprise the lot of these beasts of burden (and unreliability) mainly because in Petrushevskaia's instrumentalized world, coldblooded selfishness governs the relations between family members, spouses, lovers, and friends (for example, in "Mania" [1973], "Nets and Traps" ["Seti i lovushki," 1974], "The Overlook" ["Smotrovaia ploshchadka," 1982], "A Gloomy Fate" ["Temnaia sud'ba," 1988], "Country" ["Strana," 1988], "That Kind of Girl," ["Takaia devochka," 1988]). Women traffic in sexual favors, get impregnated by men they barely know, miscarry, have abortions, and foist their children onto others or bring them up only to utilize them as objects of vented frustrations or unreasonable pressures. Maternity in Petrushevskaia's work, as in Grekova's, is the most telling moral test but one her heroines appear doomed to fail. Men, in turn, drink, engage in multiple infidelities, and express themselves most eloquently with their fists. Romantic love, the staple of much women's fiction, is a luxury to which Petrushevskaia's characters rarely aspire as they battle for temporary shelter ("The Violin" ["Skripka," 1989]); clothes, food, and sex ("Ksenia's Daughter" ["Doch' Kseni,"]); and alcohol ("Ali-Baba" [1988]). Ethical considerations fall by the wayside in this Darwinian struggle, painted in flauntedly physiological hues. Since the violation of the psyche, which is Petrushevskaia's ruling obsession, carries the taboo of ultimate sin, it cannot be represented directly and therefore is displaced onto the body.[32]

Devoid of nature, sparse in dialogue and psychological analysis, and stripped of imagery, Petrushevskaia's prose relies for its effects on the distinctive language of its ambiguous narrators. That language, like the lives it records, is a triumph of incongruities, synthesizing urban slang, professional jargon, cultural clichés, malapropisms, racy colloquialism, and solecisms. These cascade in a relentless monologic stream that seems random but, in fact, strives to camouflage or to defer confrontation with what is most crucial and, usually, most painful (Petrushevskaia obviously has learned a great deal from Dostoevskii and Freud). Revelation, not action, is the pivot on which her narratives turn, yet the impulse to withhold constantly puts brakes on the desire to divulge. That is why omission, hints, and unclarified allusions define Petrushevskaia's narrative mode. The seamy catastrophes of abandonments, beatings, scandals, and hysterical suicide attempts in which Petrushevskaia's plots abound are conveyed in a monstrously calm narrative voice whose digressive, casual chatter is a stratagem of deflection, transference, and avoidance. The most chilling aspect of the narration is precisely the discrepancy between the horrors that implacably multiply and the flat, offhand tone of reportage that diminishes everything to the same level of banality. Although Petrushevskaia divides her prose into stories (*istorii*) and monologues (*monologi*), they differ stylistically only in the use of free indirect discourse versus first-person narration, respectively.

"Our Crowd" ("Svoi krug," wr. 1979, pd. 1990), Petrushevskaia's longest and best narrative, offers a vivid, multifaceted illustration of how the moral underpinnings of contemporary Russian society have eroded. Her recent stories, "The New Family Robinson" ("Novye Robinsony," 1989) and "Hygiene" ("Gigiena," 1990), belong to the flood of apocalyptic visions inundating current Soviet fiction, and with one of her latest publications ("Fairy Tales for Adults" ["Skazki dlia vzroslykh," 1990], Petrushevskaia has made a transition to a new genre: that of gnomic allegory and Kafkaesque parable. In these, as in all her prose, Petrushevskaia's trenchant *sui generis* style sets her apart from writers of both the older and her own generation. It allies her with such practitioners of fiction as Tat'iana Tolstaia and Valeriia Narbikova, whose principal inspiration comes from language and their desire to exploit its potential. If the extended postponement of Petrushevskaia's full-fledged entrance into the literary community has synchronized readers' discovery of her oeuvre with the emergence of much younger writers, that belatedness, ironically, locates Petrushevskaia where she, in a sense, belongs—alongside authors with whom she enjoys the authentic kinship lacking with her contemporaries.[33]

LANGUAGE RULES

Women's prose of the 1980s evidences a perceptible shift whereby a fascination with language has displaced the primarily thematic preoccupations of earlier decades. The fiction of Elena Makarova, Larisa Vaneeva, and Nina Sadur, for example, heightens the reader's awareness of language as mediator through the elliptical, fragmented ordering of their story materials. With the "realistic surface" ruffled by such underlying forces as linguistic deformation and aesthetic logic, the interplay between "what" and "how" gains complexity and redistributes emphases. What occurs is, in Ortega y Gasset's memorable phrase, "the dehumanization of art," with metaphor as its most radical instrument of dehumanization.[34] The process, if not actually invalidating the seminal nineteenth-century trope of literature as the mirror of life, at the very least depotentiates it by distorting the mirror's reflective properties almost beyond recognition. This "estrangement" and self-assertion of style showcase language most rewardingly in the prose of Tat'iana Tolstaia and most ostentatiously in the prose of Valeriia Narbikova.

Language, imagination, and time are the reigning divinities of Tolstaia's fictional universe. With the aid of myth, folklore, and a plethora of intertexts, her maximally condensed narratives offer meditations on eternal universal concerns: the elusive significance of a given life (in "Sonia" [1984] and "Most Beloved" ["Samaia liubimaia," 1986]); the isolation of the individual personality ("Peters" [1986], "Sweet Dreams, Son" ["Spi spokoino, synok," 1986]); the conflicting claims of spirit and matter ("Hunting the Wooly Mammoth" ["Okhota na mamonta," 1985]); the subtle symbiosis of perception and language ("Fakir'" [1986] "Night ["Noch'," 1987]); and the transforming power of imagination and memory ("On the Golden Porch . . ." ["Na zolotom kryl'tse sideli . . . ," 1983], "Okkervil' River" ["Reka Okkervil'," 1985]). Yet, as Tolstaia herself acknowledges, throughout her oeuvre, style has primacy over thematic novelty and psychological insight, for the mainspring of Tolstaia's creativity is a love of the language into which, she declares, we are all born, and whose riches she mines through an epic array of devices.[35]

Combining minimal plots and scant dialogue with extravagant poetic description, Tolstaia's narratives surge at an irregular pace as they slip unobtrusively in and out of temporal frames and characters' thoughts through quasi-direct discourse. Critics with a characterological ax to grind have made much of Tolstaia's characters (often situated at the two extremes of the age spectrum), largely because Tolstaia's vividly grotesque depiction of their simultaneously risible and pitiable features renders them memorable: for example, the aged protagonists of "Dear Shura" ("Milaia Shura," 1985) and "Most Beloved," the little girl in "Loves Me, Loves Me Not" ("Liubish'—ne liubish'," 1987). A comparably synthetic technique for portraying hapless "losers" embroiled in amorous endeavors allows Tolstaia to demythologize romance (in "Peters" and "The Moon Came Out" ["Vyshel mesiats iz tumana," 1987]), just as shifting, even contradictory, impressions of a given individual destabilize a single, unilinear interpretation of character. Tolstaia's fiction teems with dreamers, eccentrics, self-abnegators, failures, pragmatists, and misanthropes tossed between unrealizable desires and brute reality. They bridge that gap by the transfiguring capacities of the imagination, which flourishes unchecked in childhood but dwindles with time's passage; hence, the melancholy sense of loss and helplessness that imbues Tolstaia's texts.

In compensation for her protagonists' deprivations, Tolstaia conjures up for the reader an Aladdin's cave of stylistic treasures. Scrambling temporal and spatial categories, alternating poetic flights with satiric irony, veering from one narrative perspective to another, leaping from colloquialisms and popular slogans to elevated diction and citations from "authoritative" sources, Tolstaia packs her kaleidoscopic narratives to the brim. Readers' attention is enticed away from the (as a rule remarkably simple) plot line by the bold originality of her metaphors, which sometimes swell to Homeric proportions; by her breathtakingly unconventional, subversive juxtapositions; by her idiosyncratic, garrulous Sternian narrator, who splinters into several voices; and by the dense palpability of a mood or atmosphere built through an accumulation of rhetorical devices. Tolstaia's irridescent, sumptuous prose—laden with colorful tropes, apostrophes, exclamations, and allusions—isolates her stylistically from the majority of con temporary Soviet authors and consociates her with stylistic innovators of the 1920s (Iurii Olesha, Izaak Babel', Ivan Bunin) and Andrei Belyi and Vladimir Nabokov.

Tolstaia's outspoken opposition to Western feminism has prompted readers to comb her fiction for gender biases and to locate them in her depiction of women, who typically appear as temptresses (Faina, Valia, and the peri in "Peters," Tamila in "Rendezvous with a Bird" ["Svidanie s ptitsei," 1983]), oversized, bossy termagants (Veronika in " 'On the Golden Porch . . . ,' " Peters's grandmother and wife in "Peters"), gargoylish hulks of decrepitude (Shura in "Dear Shura"), or empty-headed husband-hunters (Zoia in "Hunting the Woolly Mammoth"). Such a selective focus, however, ignores the equally bizarre images of masculinity in the same texts (Uncle Pasha, Peters, Simeonov, Filin). To varying degrees Tolstaia subjects all her personae to a modernist dehumanization through metaphor. If any of Tolstaia's texts lend themselves to a reading consonant with feminist principles, their status as anti-essentialist statements derives, not from Tolstaia's sympathy for the women's cause, but from her ironic debunking of clichés as cultural detritus. Language, not politics, fuels her inspiration. In fact, "Hunting the Woolly Mammoth," "The Poet and the Muse" ("Poet i muza," 1986), and "Fire and Ash" dethrone specifically gender stereotypes through ironic double-voicing, literalization of metaphor, and parodic interpolation of myth.[36] Paradoxically, then, Tolstaia—the antifeminist of countless interviews and conferences—in her fiction dismantles through parody precisely the kind of gendered formulae regarding physical attributes, idealized womanhood, domestic structures, and so on, that feminists battle. For, perhaps more than any writer since Nabokov, Tolstaia grasps what Bruno Schulz called "the terror and predatoriness of the platitude." Tolstaia's post-modernist authorial practices—decentering, irony and paradox, interrogation of institutionalized separations, simultaneous installation and subversion of prevailing norms[37]—and her self-assured seizure of language not only annex those prerogatives that traditional binarism has automatically assigned to "malekind," but unmakes the absolutist presuppositions that enable ideologies to "harden into objects and so sustain themselves as real presences in the world."[38]

With the publication of her first novella, *Equilibrium of Light of Diurnal and Nocturnal Stars (Ravnovesie sveta dnevykh i nochnykh zvezd*, 1988) Valeriia Narbikova earned the dubious sobriquet of the first female writer of erotica in the Soviet Union. Subsequent works, paronomastically entitled *Around Ecolo . . . (Okolo ekolo . . .* , 1990), *Running through the Run (Probeg—probeg*, 1990), and *Ad kak Da/aD kak dA* (1990), have confirmed some critics in their view of Narbikova as a proponent of sexual liberation. Certainly, Narbikova's avowed appreciation of the libidinal as a healthy respite from the unremitting stress of modern existence—an appreciation demonstrably shared by her heroines—plus the recurrence of love triangles and references to private bodily parts, underwear, and copulation in her texts seems to offer sufficient grounds for such a perception. Yet, despite her express wish to rehabilitate the body as a means of expressive communication,[39] what reigns supreme in her works is, in fact, language: In *Equilibrium* Sana becomes impregnated by an exchange not of fluids, but of words over the telephone; Pushkin's physical presence is conjured up by mere mention of the word "grasshopper" (*sverchok*)—his friends' nickname for him; literalization of metaphor causes materialization of entities. Narbikova's ludic antics with perverse syllogisms, her paronomastic exercises and irreverent recontextualization of phrases all privilege words at the expense of character, setting, plot, and so on. In *Running through the Run*, the entire episode of Gleb's visit to a dentist (*dantist*) hinges on the latter's homonymic coincidence with the name of Pushkin's killer, D'Anthès. Cultural resonances, evoked by mention of Aristotle, Boileau, Avvakum, Pushkin, and Lermontov, are either completely repressed (Avvakum) or confined to a single instance of a deflationary device (for example, Aristotle's unities for tragedy are applied to sex) and ultimately take a back seat to the verbal games that dominate Narbikova's literary manner.

Narbikova's works all deal with entrapment through cultural baggage, whether in the form of comprehensive cliché, ironclad hierarchies, paradigmatic situations, or words vitiated through overuse. The invariant motifs of her novellas—a love triangle, a journey (usually to the sea), a confrontation with nature, and a circular return—yield a chronotope in which time loses specificity while space receives extravagant elaboration. The extensive spatial movement reflects the genre of a utopian voyage, a search for authenticity. Narbikova essentially yearns to restore the world to a prelapsarian state, where the heuristic capacities of body and language are still intact and attuned to the Word and its Maker. To break out of the prison of inertness and rote repetition that immure bodies and words, Narbikova jettisons physical and verbal trappings (hence the shedding of clothes and traditional grammatical markers) by original reconfigurations of existent components that introduce the illicit into the conventional. Formerly taboo words like "blevat' " (to throw up) and "sisat' " (to pee) consort with a poetic lexicon, just as dirty underclothes witness the "sublime" conjoining of two lovers; a third party (Otmatfeian: redolent of the Biblical Matthew ["high" text] and of sperm ["low" body]) invades a marriage, and the ménage à trois of Sana-Avvakum-Otmatfeian becomes reconfigured by the substitution of the lover's linguistically illegitimate friend Chiashchiazhyshyn (illegitimate insofar as his name violates Russian spelling rules). This conflation of sexual and textual in *Equilibrium*, which creates the illusion of eroticism, reappears in *Running through the Run* and also marks her subsequent narratives.

PARADIGM SHIFT

One could argue, validly, that Narbikova's themes overlap with those traditional women's preoccupations that form the cornerstone of Grekova's and Baranskaia's oeuvre: nature (in its modern, politicized form of ecology), love, birthing, and personal fulfillment. Yet, as in Tolstaia's and Petrushevskaia's case, sophisticated techniques of mediation and a fascination with the powers and limitations of language not only alter the entire framework of (re)presentation, but they yield texts of such density that the reader must work hard to excavate those thematic links with the earlier generation. To equate modernist with revolutionary and realist with reactionary is to collude in a progressive notion of literary tradition cast in naive melioristic phrasing, though the specific politically-cultural conditions that prevailed in the Soviet Union (where modernist automatically signaled antiestablishment) invite such a collusion.

Meanwhile, Western feminists have queried the extent to which the postmodernist enterprise can accommodate feminist imperatives.[40] Through their shared deconstructive stance, both feminism and post modernism challenge the Western rationalist tradition of objective truths on the grounds, essentially, of bad faith, whereby specific political agendas have masqueraded as universals. Rejecting totalizing truths, both postulate humanistic disciplines (for example, philosophy, history, and literary criticism) as sites of competing ideologies that inevitably reflect individual or group biases. Consequently, both "celebrate liminality, the disruption of boundaries, the confounding of traditional markers of 'difference,' " and the decentered subject.[41] Skeptical of "eternal verities" and fixities, both opt for the provisional and contextually determined over the transcendent generalized. Hence, the irony, self-reflexiveness, and tendency to contest values while inscribing them are common to both.

For contemporary Soviet women's literature, the single greatest benefit of feminist and postmodernist decanonization is its antiessentialism. The falsification that results from rigidly gendering human qualities and treating them as immutable givens has not served Soviet literature well. Among other disservices, it has foisted on women writers a model of female talent at dramatic odds with their individual authorial inclinations. Through a systematic inculcation of sex differences within its society, it has also set too narrowly the compass of possible representations of womanhood in their fiction. Postmodernism, therefore, may offer a promising route to liberating innovations in these areas. Russia historically has made a cult of language even while grossly abusing it. It therefore makes sense that the female authors who have ruffled conservative feathers are precisely those whose ironic texts are implicated in a confident, highly self-conscious use of language: Petrushevskaia, Tolstaia, and Narbikova. Whatever the permutations in Russian women's prose over the last quarter century, one recent development gives cause for excitement: Women have finally seized the word.

NOTES

1. During the 1830s, Rostopchina's poetry met with enthusiastic encomium from Pushkin, Zhukovskii, Polevoi, Bulgarin, Grech, and others. References to the womanly cast of her verses may be found in Belinskii, Shevyrev, and Sergei Ernst, plus at least half a dozen reviewers.

2. See the recent volume of selections from Rostopchina's poetry, prose, and correspondence: E. P. Rostopchina, *Talisman* (Moscow, 1987), 6.

3. On the feminist element in society tales, see Helena Goscilo, "The First Pechorin En Route to *A Hero*," *Russian Literature* 11, No. 1 (Spring 1982): 129–62.

4. Hélène Cixous and Catherine Clément, *The Newly Born Woman* (Minneapolis: University of Minnesota Press, 1986), 63–64.

5. For the entire text of the poem, see Rostopchina, 74.

6. Exceptions to this rule consisted of those who joined the women's liberation movement. See Richard Stites, *The Women's Liberation Movement in Russia* (Princeton: Princeton University Press, 1978).

7. For the gradual formation (largely via superimposition) of gender roles in Soviet society, see Lynne Atwood, *The New Soviet Man and Woman: Sex-Role Socialization in the USSR* (Bloomington: Indiana University Press, 1990) and Mary Buckley, *Women and Ideology in the Soviet Union* (Ann Arbor: University of Michigan Press, 1989).

8. See Sigrid McLaughlin, "Contemporary Soviet Women Writers," *Canadian Woman Studies* 10, No. 4 (Winter 1989): 77; Sigrid McLaughlin, "An Interview with Viktoria Tokareva," *Canadian Woman Studies*, 10, No. 4 (Winter 1989): 75; Tatyana

Tolstaya, "A Little Man Is a Normal Man," *Moscow News* 8 (1987): 10; Natal'ia Ivanova, " 'Kogda by zhizn' domashnim krugom . . . ,' " *Literaturnaia gazeta* 4 (1986): 72–74.

9. Tolstaya, "A Little Man . . . ," 10. For an examination of women's self-perception during Gorbachev's tenure, see Helena Goscilo, "Perestroika or Domostroika?: The Construction of Womanhood in Culture under Glasnost," *Late Soviet Culture*, ed. Thomas Lahusen (Durham: Duke University Press, 1991).

10. The choice of 1965 as the year marking the birth of contemporary women's fiction not only suffers from the kind of oversimplification that attaches to all cut-off dates but is also an approximation at best. It was dictated partially by the death of Anna Akhmatova in 1966, whose disappearance from Russian literature seemed to end an entire era and by the official or unacknowledged debut of those women authors whose names are synonymous with women's prose today: Baranskaia, Grekova, Ganina.

11. For a thumbnail sketch of current Russian women's fiction, see Helena Goscilo, "Introduction," in *Balancing Acts*, ed. Helena Goscilo (Bloomington: Indiana University Press, 1989), xiii–xxvii; Sigrid McLaughlin, "Contemporay Soviet Women Writers," *Canadian Woman Studies*, 10, No. 4: 77–82; Nicholas G. Zekulin, "Soviet Russian Women's Literature in the Early 1980s," *Fruit of her Plume*, ed. H. Goscilo (New York: M. E. Sharpe, forthcoming).

12. For female authors' exploration of the hospital ward as productive chronotope, see Helena Goscilo, "Women's Wards and Wardens: The Hospital in Contemporary Russian Women's Fiction," *Canadian Woman Studies* 10, No. 4: 83–86.

13. Soviet critics have chastized women's (and the late Iurii Trifonov's) prose for wallowing in *byt*—a strange rebuke in light of Russians' enduring devotion to the mimetic school of fiction. On this, see Zekulin.

14. See Atwood and Buckley, note 7.

15. Soviets have drawn the blueprint for womanhood in impossibly heroic proportions that synthesize at least four discrete, often conflicting, identities: the reliable, industrious worker; the loving, supportive wife; the nurturing mother-homemaker; the attractive, stylish woman (whose sexuality is unobtrusive and sublimated via one or more of the other three functions).

16. Grekova, who disclaims the concept of women's literature, nevertheless firmly believes in "the special emotional and nervous structure of a woman's personality, in her enslavement to problems of love, marriage and the family." She goes on to claim: "Complete equality between men and women is hardly possible. And [,] more importantly, is it desirable? There is not and cannot be equality in physiology, in the emotional sphere or in the raising of children." Interview with Nikolai Nazarov, "About I. Grekova's Work," *Soviet Literature* 5 (1986): 140–41.

17. On this phenomenon (in Daniel Defoe's *Moll Flanders*), see Gillian Beer, "Representing Women: Re-presenting the Past," *The Feminist Reader*, ed. Catherine Belsey and Jane Moore (New York: Basil Blackwell, 1989), 75.

18. On Baranskaia's stylistic limitations, see David Gillespie, "Whore or Madonna: Perceptions of Women in Modern Russian Literature," *Irish Slavonic Studies* 9 (1988): 96–97; on Grekova's, see Nancy Condee, "Irina Grekova," *Institute of Current World Affairs Newletter* 10 (1 September 1985): 9.

19. For a commonsensical survey of Baranskaia's stories, see Susan Kay, "A Woman's Work," *Irish Slavonic Studies* 8 (1987): 115–26.

No less sympathetic to women's lot in the 1830s than to their plight in the modern era, Baranskaia, in her fictional memoir *The Color of Dark Honey* (*Tsvet temnogo medu*,

1977), defends Pushkin's wife Natal'ia Goncharova from charges of self-promotion and frivolity by stressing her youth, modesty, shyness, insecurity, and repeated pregnancies. See the interview with Pieta Monks in *Writing Lives*, ed. Mary Chamberlain (London: Virago Press, 1988), 25–36.

20. Monks, 30.

21. During my interview with her (1988), Baranskaia waxed indignant over Western feminists' appropriation of *Nedelia kak nedelia*. Her dismay that the English translation had been brought out by a publisher called Virago duplicates Grekova's irritated sense that her *Ship of Fools* (*Vdovii parokhod*) was distorted by the mere fact that its English version appeared in a feminist press. On this, see Condee, 8; Goscilo, "Domostroika."

22. See Toril Moi, "Feminist, Female, Feminine," *The Feminist Reader*, 117–32.

23. A reader conversant with Western feminism and sharp-edged prosaists such as Fay Weldon and Margaret Atwood receives mixed messages from the softened-and-blurred gynocentrism of Baranskaia and Grekova, with its essentialist notions of maternity, femininity, and so on, and its addiction to powerful male figures.

24. Soviets reject out of hand the basic conviction on which the scholarship of psychoanalytically inclined feminists like Nancy Chodorow and Dorothy Dinnerstein rests: namely, that bodies are culturally as well as physiologically produced. See Beer, 64–65.

25. The original prototypical woman with appetite in Western culture, of course, was Eve—a figure stigmatized for illicit desires that have continued to be condemned in women. Feminist criticism has suggested different readings of the lapsarian myth and its implications for womanhood. See, for instance, Sandra W. Gilbert and Susan Gubar, *The Madwoman in the Attic* (New Haven: Yale University Press, 1979), 53–59.

26. The antipodes reproduce the myriad binary oppositions in E. Zamiatin's *We* (*My*), subsumed under the governing dualism of Energy (freedom, revolution, the irrational and haphazard) and Entropy (control, totalitarianism, the logical and ordered). Seeing such connections enables one to detect the politically repressive aspects of certain ostensibly personal structures.

27. For an overview of Tokareva's work, emphasizing its latest phase, see Richard Chapple, "Happy Never After: The Work of Viktoriia Tokareva and Glasnost," *The Fruit of her Plume*.

28. Katerli, with her penchant for multiple points of view, makes rich use of both Polina's and Maiia's perspectives as mutual correctives and sources of self-revelation. Tolstaia's method invariably filters the more likable or enigmatic character, who remains distanced and ambiguous, through the consciousness of the more crass and vulgar foil (in "Ogon' i pyl'" the reader's perception of Svetlana/Pipka is constantly mediated through Rimma's jealous disapprobation). Katerli and Tokareva flesh out their narrating personae sufficiently to convey their subjectivity and thus to dissociate them from any authorial judgment. Tokareva's failure to do so virtually turns her narrator into her mouthpiece.

29. Susan Sontag, *Illness as Metaphor* (New York: Vintage, 1977–1979), 79–82. Although Sontag's study of punitive fantasies flourishing around disease, especially tuberculosis and cancer, may first strike the reader as extreme, the evidence she marshals to expose the political nature of its tropological abuse is persuasive. See also her recent study, *AIDS and Its Metaphors* (New York: Farrar, Straus & Giroux, 1988–1989).

30. Tokareva's latest story opts for a different reductionism in its equally unsatisfactory conclusion: "But right then I pressed my girl to me as if I were holding my regained life in my arms. And that's the way it is, for LIFE and WOMAN are one and the same

thing.'' Viktoriia Tokareva, ''Kak ia ob' iavlial voinu Iaponii'' (How I Declared War on Japan), *Krokodil* 12 (April 1991): 9.

31. Petrushevskaia's other book-length publications include three collections of drama: *Plays (P'esy*, 1983), *Songs of the Twentieth Century (Pesni XX veka*, 1988), and *Three Girls in Blue (Tri devushki v golubom*, 1989). For a good introduction to Petrushevskaia's works, see Nancy Condee, ''Liudmila Petrushevskaia: How the 'Lost People' Live,'' *Institute of Current World Affairs Newsletter*, No. 14 (1 Feburary 1986).

32. For a discussion of Petrushevskaia's euphemistic displacement and the stylistic consequences of that transferral, see Helena Goscilo, ''Body Talk in Current Fiction: Speaking Parts and (W)holes,'' *Stanford Slavic Studies* 7 (1993):145–77.

33. This does not mean to suggest that younger writers without exception are blessed with or cultivate an original style. In the fiction of Nadezhda Kozhevnikova and Tat'iana Nabatnikova, for example, thematics not only far outweigh aesthetic interest, but also reveal both writers' proximity to Velembovskaia, Shcherbakova, and Uvarova. For a list of Kozhevnikova's collections, see *Balancing Acts*, 328; see Tat'iana Nabatnikova, *Stories (Rasskazy*, 1982), *Home Upbringing (Domashnee vospitanie*, 1984), *Sitting on the Golden Porch (Na zolotom kryl'tse sideli*, 1987), *Pick a Wish (Zagadai zhelanie*, 1990), and *Izora's Gift (Dar Izory*, 1991).

34. Ortega y Gasset, *The Dehumanization of Art and Other Writings on Art and Culture* (Garden City, NY: Doubleday Anchor Books, 1956), 32. Soviet appraisals of Tolstaia's prose (as ''cold,'' ''inorganic,'' and ''aristocratic'') have corroborated Ortega y Gasset's thesis that aesthetic enjoyment is counter to the demotic requirement of readily recognizable human qualities in contemplated objects.

35. For Tolstaia's views on language, see the interview with Peter Barta, ''The Author, the Cultural Tradition and Glasnost: An Interview with Tatyana Tolstaya,'' *RLJ* 44, No. 147–149 (1990): 266–68. For more detailed analysis of her prose, see Helena Goscilo, ''Tat'iana Tolstaia's 'Dome of Many-Coloured Glass': The World Refracted through Multiple Perspective,'' *Slavic Review* 47, No. 2 (Summer 1988): 280–90; ''Tolstajan Love as Surface Text,'' *SEEJ* 34, No. 1 (1990): 40–52; ''Paradise, Purgatory, and Post-Mortems in the World of Tat'jana Tolstaja,'' *Indiana Slavic Studies* 5 (1990): 97–113. See also Adele Barker, ''Are Women Writing Women's Writing in the Soviet Union Today? Tolstaya and Grekova,'' *Studies in Comparative Communism* 21, No. 3 and 4 (Autumn-Winter 1988): 357–64.

36. In this connection, see Helena Goscilo, ''Monsters Monomaniacal, Marital, and Medical: Tat'iana Tolstaia's Regenerative use of Gender Stereotypes,'' *Sexuality and the Body in Russian Culture*, ed. S. Sandler, J. Costlow, and J. Vowles (Stanford, CA: Stanford University Press, forthcoming).

37. Linda Hutcheon, *A Poetics of Postmodernism: History, Theory, Fiction* (New York: Routledge, 1988), Preface and Chapter 1.

38. Beer, 64.

39. The concept of the Intentional Fallacy pioneered by K. Wimsatt (*The Verbal Icon*) remains unknown in the former Soviet Union. Russians not only equate authorial intention with textual realization, but they credit the authority of a single ''correct reading'' that (at least in the eyes of those I have interviewed) must coincide with authorial intention.

40. For a volume of essays devoted to the topic, see Linda J. Nicholson, *Feminism/Postmodernism* (New York: Routledge, 1990).

41. Patricia Waugh, *Feminine Fictions: Revisiting the Postmodern* (New York: Routledge, 1988–1989), 4.

13

Women's Poetry in the Soviet Union

Carol Ueland

The Soviet period of Russian literature, just ended, will now have to undergo an intense re-evaluation before it can be accurately assessed. The more than sixty-five years (1925–1991) in the development of Russian women's poetry to which this chapter speaks is replete with texts and figures yet to be discovered. Since the advent of *glasnost* in the mid 1980s,[1] and with increasing velocity since the collapse of the Soviet regime, new poetry by Russian women has been published that brings to light little-known figures, some of major stature. Also the publication of previously unknown works of established women poets calls for a reassessment of their oeuvres. No other genre or period of Russian literature is as ripe for the recovery of an important body of Russian women's literature.

The beginning of this period, the mid 1920s, offered great promise to many women poets. Poetry had been a vital component of Russian literature since before the Revolution that saw the emergence of a number of important women poets. The new Bolshevik regime sought to support and promote the growth of all aspects of culture, particularly among those segments of society, the workers and peasants, who were the Revolution's leading supporters. To this end, poetry workshops, often led by established poets who supported the Revolution, such as the prominent Symbolist poet Valerii Briusov, were organized to teach basic skills of prosody to the newly enfranchised group of aspiring poets. Many Soviet women poets got their start in these workshops. As Soviet culture developed, poetry, a highly valued genre, was increasingly ritualized and institutionalized. Public readings by poets at mass gatherings, already a popular event in the 1920s, by the 1950s became an annual "Day of Poetry" in major cities. *Day of Poetry (Den' poezii)* anthologies promoted the first works of young authors, many of them women, and provided a guide to those currently in official favor among established figures. Women's poetry was also regularly promoted in conjunction with another prerevolutionary ritual adopted by the Bolsheviks, the celebration of International Woman's Day on March 8. To date, the holiday has been marked by the publication of poetry by women in major journals and newspapers.

In the 1920s, many women poets enthusiastically embraced the new Soviet regime's espousal of women's rights and set out to explore new thematic possibilities in their verse. Some now envisioned themselves in active social and political roles. The poetry of Elizaveta Polonskaia (1890–1969), a member of the "Serapion Brothers" writers group,[2] provides an interesting example. In her poem "Carmen" ("Karmen") she transforms the sultry temptress of Bizet's opera into a gun-toting proletarian who leads a revolt against factory bosses outside Petrograd.[3] Freed from the puritanism of the tsarist censorship, some women poets focused on previously neglected aspects of female identity. The poetry of Mariia Shkapskaia (1891–1952) records her feelings with immediacy and frankness about sexuality, pregnancy, abortion, and the birth and death of her son.[4] Having published several outstanding books of verse, innovative in form as well as content, Shkapskaia abruptly stopped publishing her poetry after 1925 and became a journalist.[5] Shkapskaia was typical of a number of gifted women who abandoned their art, at least publicly, as the political climate became more repressive. For many women poets who had become established figures before the 1917 Revolution, such as Sofiia Parnok and Anna Akhmatova (until 1940), the 1920s marked the last time their works were published. As the Communist party sought increased control of the literary process in the late 1920s and early 1930s, many gifted women poets turned to careers in journalism, children's literature, or translation.

With the establishment of the Soviet Writers Union in 1932 and its first Congress in 1934, the Communist party set out to dictate both literary form and content in the doctrine of "socialist realism."[6] Since socialist realism favored larger forms—the novel in prose, the epic in poetry—lyric poetry was often disparaged as a genre of the individual poet cut off from the social concerns of the collective. But as Stalinism increasingly extended into literature, lyric poetry remained important for another reason. Because it could be memorized and transmitted orally, even in the most oppressive conditions, lyric poetry became the most subversive literary genre of the Soviet period. In official Soviet literature, lyric poetry remained an important genre whenever the party needed to mobilize emotional resources to respond to crisis or change, especially during World War II (1941–1945). After Stalin's death in 1953, lyric poetry tended to flourish during "thaw" periods, when party strictures were relaxed in favor of more "sincerity" in literature. In the mid 1980s, the final thaw of *glasnost* released a wealth of new poetic texts from the entire Soviet period.

The two outstanding women poets of the prerevolutionary period, Anna Akhmatova and Marina Tsvetaeva, are now regarded as the two great Russian women poets of the twentieth century. However, the full impact of their art, outside of their own literary circles, was not felt until the 1950s and later. Tsvetaeva left the Soviet Union in 1922, and her poetry written in emigration developed in radical new ways. When she returned to the Soviet Union in 1939, her poetry had profoundly changed and was now unfamiliar and less accessible to her earlier readers. The failure to be published or to find an audience for her art was one of the multiple causes of her suicide two years after her return. Although Anna Akhmatova remained in the Soviet Union, she, like Tsvetaeva, also had limited access to a wide readership in her homeland until the last years of her life. After 1922, only one book of verse, *From Six Books* (*Iz shesti knig*), was published in 1940, during the relative freedom of the war. From 1946–1956 her work was again repressed; Akhmatova was reduced to penning empty lines on the struggle for peace, hoping it would help her obtain the release of her imprisoned son, Lev Gumilev. After 1956, both Akhmatova and Tsvetaeva would have considerable impact on younger generations of Russian women poets.

The lives and works of Akhmatova and Tsvetaeva have received widespread critical attention. This chapter, therefore, concentrates on three of their lesser-known contemporaries—Ol'ga Berggol'ts, Anna Barkova, and Mariia Petrovykh—and then surveys a number of more recent women poets. Like Akhmatova's, the lives of these three women poets spanned most of the Soviet period, but their careers took entirely different courses: Berggol'ts was an "official poet," Barkova spent much of her adult life in prison because of writing poetry, and Petrovykh purposely avoided literary fame. Despite the dramatic contrasts in their biographies, their careers, and their current status in literary history, their works reveal many points of contact, reflecting the generational experience of women in the Soviet period.

OL'GA BERGGOL'TS

Ol'ga Berggol'ts (1910–1975) was one of the most honored women poets in the Soviet literary establishment.[7] Her books, including several collected editions, were published throughout her lifetime; she was a fixture at Writers Union Congresses and received a Stalin Prize in 1950. Although she was a doctor's daughter, Berggol'ts's sympathies lay with the Bolshevik cause, and as a young teen, she became an enthusiastic member of Communist youth groups. While still in high school, she frequented meetings of the proletarian literary group "Change" ("Smena"), and later was married, briefly, to one of its leading poets, Boris Kornilov. Her poetry of the 1920s and early 1930s in unimaginative in a formal sense (as is her later verse). It abounds with party slogans, symbols, and a naive and banal enthusiasm for the building of socialism.[8] Her other early work included forays into journalism, prose pieces such as a history of the Electrosila power plant, and children's literature.

Berggol'ts gradually emerged as a much more compelling poet in response to personal calamities during the purge trials of the 1930s and during World War II. Her husband, Kornilov, was expelled from the Writers Union in 1936 and was subsequently arrested. He died in prison, probably in 1938. Berggol'ts herself was expelled from the party and arrested in 1938. She suffered a miscarriage because of beatings she received while in prison but was released a year later and readmitted to the party in 1940. Her two young daughters both died in the late 1930s. In a poem of 1939, "To my homeland" ("Rodine") she fears her patriotism cannot withstand such trials as "the treachery of my friends/ . . . the deaths of my beloved children."[9] Her second husband, the literary scholar Nikolai Molchanov, died of ill health and starvation during the German blockade of Leningrad in the winter of 1942.

For Berggol'ts, World War II became an opportunity for personal resurrection. She remained in Leningrad for almost the entire 900-day siege, reading verse on the local radio that combined acutely realistic details of the city's suffering with a fierce belief in its eventual victory. In "Leningrad Poem" ("Leningradskaia poema"), a neighbor appeals to the poet to give up her day's ration of bread so she can use it to buy a coffin for her daughter who has lain unburied for ten days, reminding her that Berggol'ts, too, has buried a child.[10] The poet refuses, instead persuading her neighbor to eat the bread herself, to keep on living and struggling. One of Berggol'ts's contemporaries, Nikolai Tikhonov, noted about her,

Not one male poet had the right to express weariness or weakness, only women had the right to do so. In the most difficult days her verses sounded like the expectation of victory, like the justification of sacrifices carried out in the name of our truth and righteousness. By right, she became the voice of the hero-city.[11]

Tikhonov's comment, despite its patronizing tone, does offer some insight as to why the most memorable poetry of the war years was written by women poets such as Berggol'ts and her Leningrad compatriot, Vera Inber. In describing her own and her neighbors' grim struggle for existence—both material and psychological—Berggol'ts's verse avoided abstract rhetoric in favor of genuine details and precise and understated language.

When the relative liberalism of the war years ended and a new period of literary repression began, this wartime reputation gave Berggol'ts a certain protection. To her credit, she did what she could to help friends less favored by the party, such as Akhmatova.[12] In 1953, after Stalin's death, she was one of the first voices of the thaw after Stalin's death. On April 16, 1953, her article, "Conversation on Lyric Poetry" ("Razgovor o lirike"), published in *Literary Gazette* (*Literaturnaia Gazeta*), attacked the impersonal quality of Soviet poetry at that time, poetry that called itself lyrical but lacked any emotional engagement on the part of the poet. She argued that the "I" of the poet in lyric verse is always appropriated by the reader as his or her own when the poet successfully expresses the basic and best emotions of a given era. She went on to rebuke a number of prominent party poets for attacking the notion of "self-expression" as a return to prerevolutionary decadence.[13]

Toward the end of her life and after her death, a more complex picture of Berggol'ts, both as a person and a poet, emerged. The split between Beggol'ts's official persona and her private self grew wider. While she wrote autobiographical sketches, *Daytime Stars* (*Dnevnye zvezdy*), which was later made into a popular film, she also kept other diaries, which, when published abroad, showed for the first time the degree of her disillusionment with the Soviet regime.[14] After the advent of *glasnost*, her sister Mariia published poems that Berggol'ts had asked her to burn, because, "I wanted it understood, especially by young people, who sometimes throw out the reproach 'How could you then. . . .' "[15] One such poem, "I sat all day at the meeting" ("Na sobran'i tselyi den' sidela") was written in the late 1940s. It begins:

> I sat all day at the meeting—
> Sometimes voting, sometimes lying . . .
> Why didn't I go grey with grief?
> Why didn't I die of shame?
> For a long time I couldn't leave the street—
> Only there could I be myself with myself.[16]

In a memoir, the critic Vladimir Lakshin recalls, "It seemed Ol'ga Berggol'ts liked to speak least about the books which brought her the most recognition, prizes, and articles in newspapers. Reminding her of some of her publications simply wounded her: she wished that they didn't exist."[17] But the unpublished Berggol'ts did influence the further development of lyric poetry. Nina Koroleva, a young Leningrad poet of the 1960s, recalls that, for her generation, Berggol'ts was one of the poets who revealed the truth about Soviet life, "not with her blockade poems, but with her prison poems, with her confessional poems on fate, devastating to such a degree that a person no longer had the strength to hold on to love."[18] Even with "official" poets, the real transmission of poetic culture in the Soviet period more often took place at kitchen readings than at public functions. The gradual unfolding of the complex and difficult career of Berggol'ts should persuade scholars that other "official" women poets of the Soviet period deserve a second look.

ANNA BARKOVA

Anna Barkova (1901–1976), who came from an impeccably proletarian background and had an early commitment to the Revolution, would have seemed a likely candidate for a brilliant career in the Soviet period. She was born in Ivanovo-Voznesensk, the daughter of a guard at the local high school, which she later attended. Little is known of her childhood, except that it was evidently unhappy and that she lost her mother at an early age.[19] Barkova welcomed the Bolshevik Revolution as a liberating force that would wipe away the rigid social conventions of the past. From 1919 to 1922, she worked at the local newspaper *Workers' Land* (*Rabochii krai*), mainly writing reviews and editorials. Among her colleagues was a group of young proletarian poets with whom she began writing and publishing her verse, at first under the pseudonym "Wandering

Beggar-Bard'' (Kalika Perekhozhaia). Barkova's work in particular found a responsive reader in Anatolii Lunacharskii, the Commissar of Enlightenment, who was largely responsible for early Bolshevik cultural policy. In a December 16, 1921, letter to Barkova, Lunacharskii predicted that she had the potential to become ''*the* outstanding woman poet of Russian literature.''[20] He wrote the introduction to Barkova's first book of verse, *Woman* (*Zhenshchina*), published in 1922, saying that it was difficult to believe that this was the work of a twenty-year-old author, so varied was the experience it recorded.[21]

The early poems that comprise the collection, *Woman*, are immediately arresting both from a technical and a thematic point of view. The formal aspects of Barkova's verse are unique: She often violates metrical norms and prefers assonance to full rhyme. As Lunacharskii noted, her poetry has a ''deliberate slight crudeness.'' Despite her early literary affiliations, her work strays far from the standard themes of proletarian poetry, glorifying the working class.[22]

In some poems Barkova exhibits an affinity with symbolism, especially in its later stages. As in Blok's ''Night Violet'' (''Nochnaia fialka''), the persona in Barkova's poem ''I fell into a mysterious dream'' (''Ia upala v tainstvennyi son,'' 37) searches for a golden flower, an otherworldly realm that remains in the future: ''Another heaven, isn't it starting to shine in the distance?'' Her consistent use of color—gold is positive, grey negative—is consistent with symbolist practice. Like the symbolists and their Scythian offspring, she is fascinated by Russia's Mongol heritage and attributes to it her persona's wild, untamed spirit. In ''Russian Asian Woman'' (''Russkaia aziatka,'' 1921, 79–80) she sells her soul to the devil, taunting him, ''Don't be stingy or you'll yearn for my red hair.''

But Barkova's personae range far beyond symbolist prototypes. They are as disparate as an Amazon, Mother Earth asking the rain and dew to fill her breasts to nourish mankind, a devotee of Sappho[23] and a female Red Army soldier who playfully twirls a revolver while affirming her ''faith in the red star.'' However, her political sentiments are far from proletarian pieties and are ultimately rooted in an anarchic spirit: ''I am a criminal. I blow up churches/ And, in revolt, dance by the flames.'' Her sensibility has decidedly Dostoyevskian overtones, as she notes, ''How sweet is the moment of crime/ The liberating moment is sweet'' (29).[24]

However, many of Barkova's other poems reveal a less confident lyrical persona, one who sees herself only as the ''forerunner'' of the conquering Amazon warrior. While many poems are allegories of the self, the poet ultimately confesses, ''But my real face I sadly conceal/With a confident lying mask'' (63). Elsewhere she sees her soul as water that never stops moving, and asks, ''Is it true I will never know myself, will not stand still?'' (41). At times two sides of her lyrical persona are seen in opposition within the same poem, ''I the Amazon rebel,/ Speak with double words/ But the heart of the frightened child-woman, /Cries with secret tears'' (61). Evidently, it was largely the complexities of Barkova's self-portrait that fascinated Lunacharskii. He writes, ''What a rich connection there is in this daughter of the proletariat between the Amazon [in her] and the wounded girl in love."[25]

Barkova moved to Moscow, working first as Lunacharskii's secretary, living in his family's Kremlin apartment and studying for a short time in Briusov's literary institute. She then worked for *Pravda*, from 1924–1929, where some of her articles and poems appeared. In the late 1920s, Barkova's poetry acquires a sense of foreboding, "Are my verses really poetry?/ Death, rebellion and misfortune lie in them" (102). A Dantesque imagery of a coming hell and judgment day becomes a major motif from then on. Barkova's star dimmed: Outspokeness, sincerity, and revolutionary romanticism were increasingly less desirable traits in a writer for the party than conformity. By 1932 she questions her earlier visions: "Do stars and heavenly distances exist?/ I can no longer raise my snout./ They called me a person/ And someone lied, saying that this sounds proud" (109) and that she will soon believe in a god as hairy and simian as the beast she has herself become.[26] In the same year, her poem "Where is loyalty to some fatherland . . ." (Gde vernost' kakoi-to otchizne . . . ," 110) speaks of a fatal mistake in her homeland,

> In concerted effort with slavish obedience
> We bring our bloody ration
> In order to build an unnecessary
> Reinforced concrete paradise.
>
> Behind a fettered door
> In the darkness of our strange hearts
> Lives the priest of godless mysteries,
> The great sufferer and liar.

On December 26, 1934, Barkova was arrested, the first of three arrests that resulted in her spending almost a third of her life in the camps. She served from 1934–1939. During the war years, she was released, but in 1947, she was re-arrested and sentenced to ten years. During the Khrushchev "thaw" of 1956 she was freed again, only to be re-arrested a year later and sentenced to another ten years. Her poetry written in the camps is startling for its direct expression of forbidden political themes. In several poems she places her personal fate within a broad historical spectrum, often identifying with both victim and oppressor. In "Don't demand an unnecessary answer" ("Ne trebuite nenuzhnogo otveta," 1938), she is a victim of the Spanish Inquisitor and Queen Elizabeth, relishing the destruction of the Armada, a drunken participant in the Parisian mob and a "powdered, proud marquise" guillotined by the people.[27] In "Vera Figner" (1950, 117–19), she presents a revisionist history of the revolutionary movement, starting with the assassination of Alexander II in 1881.[28] In the poem's third section, the dead tsar confronts his assassin, saying his murder was a fatal mistake that has created "hordes of unprecedented new slaves." The venerated red stars of 1922 have become "bloody stars/ on the submissive Kremlin towers" now that "Soviet Rus' has colonized Dante's ninth circle of hell."

Other Barkova poems on camp life picture human nature in its bleakest aspects, with gritty, realistic detail. In "A pen for human cattle" ("Zagon dlia chelovecheskoi skotiny," 1955, 142), she describes two kinds of sexual encounters in the camps: furtive, accidental couplings, "without a word, without love," that "only a eunuch or monk would condemn" and those on a cot kept by the camp commandant where women prisoners could sleep with their lawful husbands, to the accompaniment of jeers and whistles. The poem ends with what one critic has justly termed one of the most tragic aphorisms of the twentieth century: "No, better, better the straightforward shot,/ So honestly piercing hearts."[29]

In 1965 Barkova was completely rehabilitated. Thanks to the efforts of several influential writers, including Aleksandr Tvardovskii, the editor of the leading journal *New World* (*Novyi mir*), she was able to return to Moscow in 1967. She spent the last nine years of her life in one room in a communal apartment, living on a small Writers Union literary fund pension, which she used mainly to buy books that she would shelve in an empty refrigerator. She died after a long, painful bout with cancer. Barkova did, however, continue writing poetry until the very end of her life. According to Irina Ugrimova and Nadezhda Zvezdochetova, fellow inmates who preserved some poems, many of Barkova's works were lost, "carried away by the Russian wind," but undoubtedly more remain to be published.[30] What is most striking about Barkova's late poetry is its fierceness: Unlike the oblique political allusions of even the most liberal poets published in the Soviet period, Barkova's poems, written in the harshest of times and circumstances, are vitriolic screams of defiance and rage against a perverse historical fate.

MARIIA PETROVYKH

Mariia Petrovykh (1908–1979) was born in Yaroslavl province but spent most of her life at the center of Moscow's intellectual circles. In 1925 she began attending a poetry workshop at Moscow University and immediately impressed her contemporaries with her talent.[31] Already in her earliest poems she reveals a polished classical style, honed since childhood. "Autumn at Boldino" ("Bol'dinskaia osen'," 201–203)—the poem's title refers to the time and place of Aleksandr Pushkin's most creative period—pays homage to her chief mentor's creative consciousness. By the late 1920s and early 1930s, the central guidelines of Petrovykh's poetic universe are already clear: a resignation to a harsh fate and the vagaries of history, tempered by a sense of consolation in the natural world.

Petrovykh's biography outwardly lacks the drama and personal tragedies that marked many of her contemporaries' lives, yet her poetry, especially works that have recently come to light, records many of the same emotions and experiences.[32] In 1939 she describes the sensation of not being able to take a step without a backward glance.[33] During the war years, she writes that more frightening than other human ills—sickness, plague, madness—is her sense of her homeland as a prison where even the instruments of suicide are unobtainable.[34] Later in life, as her numerous poems of the 1960s attest, Petrovykh suffered from a sense of guilt at having been a survivor of terrible times, "You say: 'I didn't create evil . . . '/But indeed did you save anyone?'' (132–33). In this and other poems she is aware of her own talent and of a sense of the enormous responsibility to truth-telling that is part of the Russian poetic tradition. She fears that she has squandered her gift:

> You hid yourself in a sealed shell,
> You mingled with the vacillating crowd,
> There you entered not like a ray of dawn—
> But became a cloud in line of clouds.
> Where is the word I put in your hands,
> So that the good would rejoice, and evil suffer?

In such self-accusatory verses, Petrovykh's lyrical persona evinces a painfully divided self.[35] Her use of the imperative mood—mainly for self-addressed admonitions—is unique in Russian verse. She constantly questions her own identity and worth, squarely facing the problem of defining her own contribution to poetry in light of her more celebrated contemporaries:[36]

> Not with Akhmatova's gentleness,
> Not with Tsvetaeva's fierceness,
> At first [I wrote] from timidity,
> And later from age.
> Haven't so many years been lived
> in vain in this locale?
> Who, then, for all that, are you?
> Respond from obscurity!

Petrovykh's answer, in "Not with Akhmatova's gentleness" ("Ne akhmatovskoi krotosti," 115), is a typically self-effacing metaphor from nature: a reed that sings and cries.

However, a more positive sense of self also emerges in the 1960s. In the 1964 poem "Never despair" ("Ne otchaivaisia nikogda," 96), Petrovykh writes of her renewed sense of calling and the further possibility of creative achievement:

> You're still alive. Begin anew,
> No, it's not too late: you're still alive.
> I have unmasked you more than once,
> And again you jingled your keys
> At the doors of enchantment's hiding place.

In 1971, toward the end of Petrovykh's career, "There's one thing I'd like to say to poets" ("Odno mne khochetsia skazat' poetam," 144) directs the imperative, at last, toward others:

> Know how to be silent until verses [do stikhov].
> Don't feel like writing? Think about it,
> Without excuses, without beating around the bush,
> But, inquiring into the cruel essence
> Of your own cruel silence,
> Don't forget about directness,
> And the main thing—don't fear anything.[37]

Here, the poet at last seems to find self-justification for the periodic lapses into silence that marked her own creative path.

THAW (1953–1966) AND STAGNATION (1967–1985)

Petrovykh's need to assert that she was not Akhmatova or Tsvetaeva points to a major problem for the next generation of women poets. The year 1956 marked the return of Akhmatova and Tsvetaeva to Soviet publications. *Literary Moscow* (*Literaturnaia Moskva*), a two-volume almanac published that year, included Ilya Ehrenburg's essay on Tsvetaeva and two of Akhmatova's poems.[38] Thereafter, their poetry spread to a wider and wider readership. Their literary reputations grew to such an extent that both were soon venerated as cultural icons. Because their works express such contrasts of personality, theme, and style between them, they seem to have covered the entire range of self-expression for women's poetry. Their "polar opposition of genius"[39] seemed so complete that critics identified new women poets as "a new Akhmatova" or "a new Tsvetaeva."

For women poets who were born in the Soviet era and began publishing in the 1950s and 1960s, the mythical proportions Akhmatova and Tsvetaeva had assumed made it difficult for them to establish their own identities. At the same time, for these poets Akhmatova and Tsvetaeva were the consciously chosen role models who defined their artistic responsibility and integrity.

Bella Akhmadulina (1937–   ), the best-known woman poet of her generation, in the poem "Night Before a Performance" ("Noch' pered vystupleniem"), expressed not only the blessing she felt at having such predecessors ("as if Marina and Anna are preserved/and literature and conscience are indissoluble"), but also the resulting loss of her own sense of self ("I in myself am worth only a little/I am an old word in a contemporary cover").[40]

Akhmadulina was hardly alone in this quandary and, as we shall now see, a similar concern with identity is at the center of much postwar women's poetry.

IUNNA MORITS

Iunna Morits (1937–   ) was born in Kiev. She wrote her first poems as a very young child. At four, during World War II, she was evacuated to the Ural Mountains, but the Germans bombed the train on which the family escaped. Such childhood experiences figure in some of Morits's most memorable poems, such as "After the War" ("Posle voiny").[41] When the war was over, the family returned to Kiev, where Morits completed her schooling.

In 1955 she moved to Moscow to attend the Gorky Literary Institute, a prestigious training ground for many young poets. At one point she was suspended for two years because of her participation in an expedition to the Arctic, but she eventually completed her studies in 1961. Her adventures there resulted in the book *Cape of Desire* (*Mys zhelaniia*), which records her exhilaration at living in extreme conditions and escaping from everyday life. Many early Morits poems are simple declarations of a thirst for new experiences and sensations.

Morits's outspokenness extended to political themes as well. "A Star Is Falling on Mtskheta" ("Na Mtskhetu padaet zvezda," 266), written in 1962 when censorship was at its most liberal during the period of thaw, attracted attention for its daring. It expresses outrage at Stalin's crimes, specifically alluding to the killing of the Georgian poet Titian Tabizde:

> A star is falling on Mtskheta!..
> Who allowed its execution,
> Who gave this right to a cretin
> To thrust a star under a guillotine?

The poem established Morits's reputation as a truth-teller—an often harsh observer of her homeland and its history.

Among those who admired "A Star . . ." was Anna Akhmatova, who asked to meet her. Morits relates that she refused the invitation because "her [Akhmatova's] verse meant so much to me that a meeting with her would have been a shock I would not physically survive." Such a visit, in fact, came about anyway, because Mariia Petrovykh asked her to an editing meeting and then revealed that it was a ruse so Akhmatova could meet her. In Morits's account she was terrified, because "I knew well who Akhmatova was, knew the value of her poetry and her fate, and precisely at this time was thinking a great deal about the fates of Akhmatova and Tsvetaeva, about what it is to be a woman poet in Russia . . ."[42] Morits's awe of these women, however, did not impede her from seeing the damage done to herself and her contemporaries by facile comparisons to their predecessors. In an article written in 1975, "To be a woman poet in Russia is more difficult than being a male poet" ("Byt' poetessoi v Rossii trudnee chem byt' poetom"), Morits complained that while Russian male poets are not compared with Tiutchev, Blok, Pushkin, or Lermontov, women poets are endlessly compared with Akhmatova and Tsvetaeva. The article was rejected by the leading journal for literary criticism, *Questions of Literature* (*Voprosy literatury*), and appeared only in Poland and Europe.[43] Morits expressed the same ideas in verse in a poem titled "Between Scylla and Charybdis" ("Mezhdu Stsilloi i Kharibdoi").[44]

In her verse, Morits views the vocation of poetry in decidely less exalted terms than do her predecessors. The 1966 poem "On the Death of Juliet" ("Na smert' Dzhul'etty," 77) is a plea to Juliet not to die passively, not "to trade youth for immortality." In contrast, speaking of herself, the persona declares,

> I want to be! Not afterwards, not in the ages,
> Not by heart, not twice and not again,
> Not in anecdotes or in diaries—
> But only in the full meaning of the word.

Morits often delights in puncturing conventional images of the poetic process. In "Birth of a Wing" ("Rozhdenie kryla," 23)—a traditional symbol of poetic inspiration—the process is supervised by a doctor who pronounces that it's nothing to cry about, no more painful than cutting a baby tooth. In the 1979 poem "I didn't drink vodka with geniuses" ("Ia s geniiami vodku ne pila," 99), Morits clearly prefers to be an outsider who refuses to play the role of an establishment poet:

> I didn't drink vodka with geniuses
> And didn't allow them to get close to me.
> I wasn't a young poet,
> Wasn't pleasing to the ear or to the eye.

The poem jabs at the celebrity status, particularly of the male poets of the thaw generation and their public posturing ("So God helped me not to fall into a retinue,/not to be one of the patriarchs of the Muse").

In the 1970s and 1980s Morits's poetry, which earlier relied heavily on sound repetitions, anaphora, and refrains in a songlike manner, became increasingly complex in both form and theme. The author of more than a dozen books of verse, including verse for children, Morits most recently published *Muscle of Water* (Muskul vody) where her lyrical voice exhibits even greater range.[45]

INNA LISNIANSKAIA

Inna Lisnianskaia (1928–   ), born in Baku, published her first book of verse in 1957, although some of her poems date back to the late 1940s. In the early 1960s, her poetry was generally well received, even by conservative critics. Her love poems, seen by one critic as "expressing the emotional weakness of a loving and suffering woman"[46] seemed to fall within the conventional concerns of "women's poetry." (For most of the Soviet period, the phrase "women's poetry" [zhenskaia poeziia] was used as a term of derision to denote sentimental, trivial, and clearly second-rate verse written by women.) By the early 1970s Lisnianskaia was already chafing under the constraints of being an official poet, sardonically expressed in "House of Creativity" ("Dom tvorchestva").[47]

Lisnianskaia's poetry of the 1970s and early 1980s reflects the general artistic trend of the period of stagnation in its retreat into an exploration of the self and its relationship to the natural rather than the social or historical world. Lisnianskaia often envisions herself as a prophetess whose source of authority is her subconscious. In the 1970 poem "And I let fall a vacant look" ("I vzor rasseiannyi roniaiu," 75), she states, "I don't create anything—I retell dreams . . . From the cradle to the grave, they define my life." Like other prophets, she often feels alienated from her society, but she knows the value of her utterances and predicts that her compatriots will eventually accept them, as in the 1972 poem "What a falling winter!" ("Kakaia zima paduchaia!" p. 62):

> Your poems, blood children,
> Will find, finally, a refuge,
> In a country where the speechless snows,
> Live more audibly than people.

For Lisnianskaia, poetry is a calling filled with pain and agonizing moral questions, yet one that she cannot abandon. In the 1971 poem "There, where oblivion is mixed with betrayal . . ." ("Siuda, gde zabven'e s izmenoiu . . . ," 121), the figure whose daily presence in her consciousness compels her to keep writing is Anna Akhmatova:

> There, where oblivion is mixed with betrayal
> And shame with conscience,
> the Simple One, the Haughty One arrives
> and awakens me in the mornings.

> And I badger her with questions:
> Where and why are we to go,
> For what purpose do we beat our breasts
> with scorched roses?

> After all, we've long known this is not feminine,
> More than that, it's a Shiite ritual.
> Why, then, from the cherished word,
> are my burns daily on fire?

Like other women poets of this generation she is absorbed with the question of identity, but in Lisnianskaia's case, it centers on her dual Russian-Jewish identity. In a poem of the late 1960s she asks, "Who am I in your creation?"

and answers herself, "An alien branch/On a native tree/The apple of paradise,/ But with hell's worm" (18). Many of her poems celebrate her Jewish heritage and its tragic history in Russia. Like many women poets in their struggle for self-realization, Lisnianskaia finds herself in confrontation with her father, a military doctor and wounded war veteran, who "raves for the second night/ about the gas oven/Don't sign yourself as a Jew, daughter—/he ordered me" (100).[48] In response she orders a fiddler to play "Israel's lament" over his grave. Elsewhere, however, she sees herself as formed by Russian nature and culture: "I grew into the Russian snow and Russian word/And there's no exit" (103). Lisnianskaia's poetry expresses the painful problem of emigration for Russian-Jewish artists of the 1970s and often expresses anguish over the loss of friends whom, at that time, she could only assume she would never see again. Although she herself remained in Russia, Lisnianskaia feels the accusation of divided loyalty, "No one will ever understand,/That I don't dream of another land/But my native one won't let me sleep" (211).

Lisnianskaia's career as a published poet within the Soviet Union came to an abrupt halt in 1979, when she allowed several poems, mostly of a religious nature, to be included in *Metropol*, an almanac compiled by leading liberal writers. They appealed to the Writers Union for permission to publish without state censorship. When permission was refused, the writers themselves printed the volume (such uncensored but illegal self-publishing ventures were known as *samizdat*) and it was later published by a Western press (*tamizdat*). Along with her husband, the poet Semen Lipkin, Lisnianskaia resigned from the Writers Union and was subsequently expelled from its literary fund. Thereafter, she was unable to publish again in the Soviet Union until the late 1980s; however, her poems were published by émigré presses abroad. Lisnianskaia's works continue to demonstrate her mastery of traditional poetic form.

Morits, Lisnianskaia, and other postwar women poets present a rich variety of lyrical voices. Each successfully confronted and resolved the dilemma of her relationship to Akhmatova and Tsvetaeva in her own work. However, critics, both Soviet and Western, have shown little imagination in describing the diversity of personalities and the thematic and formal range represented in their verse. To the present day, critics invariably compare these poets to Akhmatova or Tsvetaeva (or even both!). Joseph Brodsky, in a review of Lisnianskaia's *Rains and Mirrors* (*Dozhdi i zerkala*), writes, "A Russian poet, like any poet, is always a product of what is written before him, rejecting it, or echoing it. The only echo I distinctly discern in Lisnianskaia's verse, is Akhmatova's and thank God!"[49] Undoubtedly, Brodsky, Akhmatova's closest protégé, sincerely meant this as the highest praise, but the remark says nothing about Lisnianskaia's own unique voice. A brief survey of some recent major dictionaries and histories of Russian poetry shows that the practice of such comparisons continues unabated: on Akhmadulina, "In the simplicity of her style she resembled Akhmatova,"[50] or on Morits, "Morits consciously belongs to the tradition of M. Tsvetaeva."[51] Little wonder that a poet of the subsequent generation, Elena Ignatova (1947–   ), began in 1969 a poem with the sardonic opening line, "And what of Akhmatova? She's dead and annoys us from afar" ("A chto Akhmatova? Mertva/i razdrazhaet otdalenno").[52]

THE END OF THE SOVIET PERIOD

Lisnianskaia's career proved to be typical for many women poets born after World War II as well. Women poets who were outright political dissidents continued to be subjected to arrest and imprisonment,[53] but generally, the control mechanisms on culture were becoming more ineffectual. More daring themes and imaginative forms in poetry came to be written and circulated even before the onset of *glasnost*. In the 1970s and early 1980s, a Russian poet had, in effect, two possible career paths, although they were not always a matter of choice. One was to become a member of the Writers Union and have access to its literary journals and publishing houses and, through them, to a mass readership; however, the price was having one's work subjected to the vagaries of the censor. The alternative was to confine one's publications to *samizdat* or *tamizdat*.

Olesia Nikolaeva (1955-) is a leading contemporary poet who chose the first path. Now the author of three books of verse, Nikolaeva typifies her generation's urge to break from the great legacy of modern Russian poetry. Feeling the need to distance herself from such poets as Akhmatova, she has turned to sources outside the traditional canon, especially the Russian Orthodox liturgy and Biblical texts, such as *Ecclesiastes* and *The Song of Songs*.[54] In poems such as "A Party for Women," she exposes what she sees as the hypocrisy of the promise of equality for women as implemented by Soviet society.[55] While Nikolaeva's fundmentalist views on gender ("In the Christian view, the boundaries within which equality between men and women is realizable are located beyond earthly natural laws."[56]) will certainly not appeal to Western feminists, her views are not atypical of those of many contemporary Russian women. Her search for values based in traditional Russian culture represents an emerging trend in post-Soviet literature.

Other contemporary women poets took the second path. The poetry of Elena Shvarts (1948-) was highly regarded in literary circles long before its appearance in print in the Soviet Union. With the gradual easing of censorship in the last five years of the Soviet regime, the two career options were no longer mutually exclusive. Shvarts had published several collections abroad in the 1970s and 1980s before *Corners of the Earth* (*Storony sveta*) was published in the Soviet Union in 1989.[57] Shvarts works on the boundaries of formal verse, often employing elements of traditional metrics and rhymes. The density of metaphors in her verse purposely disorients the reader's quest for linkages. Her verse is culturally eclectic, visually imaginative, and visionary in its orientation. She draws heavily on the metaphysical tradition in Russian poetry, often in a highly stylized fashion, as in *The Works and Days of Lavinia, A Nun of the Order of*

the Circumcision of the Heart (*Trudy i dni Lavinii, monakhinii iz ordena obrezaniia serdtsa*).[58]

It is now clear that much of what had been going on in contemporary Russian
poetry in the seventies and eighties operated primarily outside of the cultural
establishment. For a long time, the more avant-garde strains of Russian poetry
were unacceptable to official outlets of publication on formal as well as thematic
grounds. Many underground poets felt that their task was to distance themselves
deliberately from the traditional canon and to form an alternative culture, exploring, in the process, new means of reaching an audience, such as performance
art. Like other postmodernist writers, the avant-garde poets of the 1970s and
1980s manipulated cultural codes in order to destabilize the conventional norms
of poetic language and free it from ideology. Nina Iskrenko (1951–   ) emerged
from such circles in the 1980s. Like her fellow members of the Moscow Poetry
Club, such as Ivan Zhdanov or Aleksandr Eremenko, Iskrenko playfully ma-
nipulates the linguistic "ready-mades" of her generation, juxtaposing lexical
extremes, such as banal Soviet slogans and famous lines by canonical poets.
Iskrenko's poem "A person—she is not a bird" ("Chelovek—ona ne ptitsa")
reconstructs the misogynistic proverb, "A chicken is not a bird, a woman is not
a person" and goes on to parody a series of traditional gender associations.
Iskrenko interweaves allusions to the classics of Russian verse with references
to Soviet popular culture, and in effect, de-"iconicizes" the poetic heritage on
which her generation was raised.[59]

The women discussed in this chapter present only a few examples of the
diversity and range of women's poetry in the Soviet period, particularly by the
end of the era when the boundary between "official" and "nonofficial" art had
virtually disappeared. As new texts from the whole period become available,
this diversity and range will surely continue to expand the notion of what constitutes "women's poetry" in twentieth-century Russian culture.

NOTES

1. *Glasnost*, usually translated as "openness," refers to the cultural policy initiated
by Mikhail Gorbachev in the mid 1980s calling for greater freedom of expression and
less party control.

2. The Serapion Brothers was a group of writers and poets, formed in 1921, that
advocated individual freedom for the artist rather than a fixed set of literary principles.
See Hongor Oulanoff, "Serapion Brothers," *Handbook of Russian Literature*, ed. Victor
Terras (New Haven: Yale University Press, 1985), 398.

3. Elizaveta Polonskaia, *Upriamyi kalendar'. Stikhi i poemy 1924–27* (Leningrad,
1929), 7–12. Polonskaia published three books of verse in the 1920s but then turned to
journalism and children's literature, although her poetry did appear infrequently into the
1960s.

4. Seven separate publications of Shkapskaia's verse appeared from 1920–1925. See
introductory essay by Boris Fillipov in Mariia Shkapskaia, *Stikhi* (London: Overseas
Publications Interchange, 1979). See also Fillipov's entry, "Shkapskaya Mariya Mik-

hailovna'' in Terras, 406–407; and Barbara Heldt's analysis of Shkapskaia's poetry in her book *Terrible Perfection. Women in Russian Literature*, (Bloomington: Indiana University Press, 1987), 121–24.

5. Barbara Heldt has succinctly commented on this change in her career, "Writing about the costs of being a woman in the new society never again became a permissible occupation," 121. Recent publications indicate that some women poets did continue to write but did not attempt to publish their works.

6. This term was defined by the Writers' Union as follows: "Socialist realism, being the basic method of Soviet literature and literary criticism, demands from the artist the truthful, historically concrete depiction of reality in its revolutionary development." See Herman Ermolaev's entry, "Socialist realism," in Terras, 429–31.

7. There are many studies of Berggol'ts's life and work in Russian, including book-length studies by D. Khrenkov, N. Bank, G. M. Tsurikova, and in German by Eva-Marie Fiedler-Stolz. A book of memoirs by her contemporaries, *Vspominaia Ol'gu Berggol'ts* (Leningrad, 1979), has also been published. Perhaps because of her "official" stature, American Slavists have given little attention to her work. There is a translation into English of Andrei Siniavskii's essay, "The Poetry and Prose of Olga Berggol'ts" in his *For Freedom of Imagination* (New York: Holt, Rinehart and Winston, 1971).

8. In the words of one biographer, Berggol'ts's poetry of this period exudes "publicistic pathos." See Dmitri Khrenkov, *Ot serdtsa k serdtsu. O zhizni i tvorchestve Ol'gi Berggol'ts* (Leningrad, 1982), 73.

9. This poem was published in *The Knot* (*Uzel*), (Leningrad, 1965), 19–20, a collection of poems that includes for the first time those written in the late 1930s and early 1940s. This and all subsequent translations are mine.

10. Ol'ga Berggol'ts, *Sobranie sochinenii v trekh tomakh*, (Leningrad, 1989), 2: 40–49.

11. Khrenkov, 138.

12. See Khrenkov, especially 224–27, 241–42.

13. Berggol'ts, 2:367–78. She continued to defend these views in the article "Protiv likvidatsii liriki" (October 1954), which rebuts attacks on her by conservative critics. See Berggol'ts, 2:378–90.

14. Some of these diary entires were published in *Vremia i my* 57, (1980).

15. M. F. Berggol'ts, "Vmesto predisloviia—sestre," *Ogoniok* 26 (June 1987): 15.

16. *Znamia* 3 (1987): 179.

17. V. Lakshin, "Stikhi i sud'ba, "*Znamia* 3 (1987): 187.

18. Nina Koroleva, "V gostiakh u Anny Akhmatovoi," *Knizhnoe obozrenie*, 24 (June 16, 1989): 8.

19. The biographical information on Barkova is still sparse. This account is based on several sources, especially Leonid Taganov, "Anna Barkova. Sud'ba i stikhi," the introduction to the first collected edition of Barkov's poetry, *Vozvrashchenie* (Ivanovo, 1990), 5–22. All further page references to poems in this edition are given in the text. See also: Lev Anninskii, "Krestnyi put' Anny Barkovoi," *Literaturnoe obozrenie* 8 (1991): 7–10; I. Verblovskaia, "Poet tragicheskoi sud'by," *Neva* 4 (1989): 206–207; Irina Ugrimova and Nadezhda Zvezdochetova, "Anna Barkova. Stikhotvoreniia. Ob avtore" in *Dodnes' tiagoteet* (Moscow, 1989), 335–37. Boris Pasternak's lover, Ol'ga Ivinskaia, met Barkova in the camps. Ivinskaia wrote a short and extremely hostile account of Barkova in her memoirs, *A Captive of Time*, trans. Max Hayward (New York: Doubleday, 1978), 356–57.

20. Cited in Taganov, 5.

21. Lunacharsky's foreword appears in Barkova, *Vozvrashchenie*, 23–24 together with the texts of *Woman*.

22. According to Taganov, Proletcult critics reacted negatively to *Woman* and accused Barkova of mysticism, aestheticism, individualism, and a complete alienation from proletarian ideology. Boris Pasternak was among the poets who defended her. See Taganov, 10.

23. Barkova's love poetry is addressed to both men and women—especially to the latter in her later works.

24. According to the unpublished memoirs of a classmate, A. P. Orlova, Barkova was a rebellious adolescent whose favorite authors included Dostoevskii; at fourteen, she kept notes titled "Diary of the Underground Man's Grandson." See Taganov, 6.

25. Lunacharskii, "Predislovie," in Barkova, *Vozvrashchenie*, 23–24.

26. "Someone lied, saying that this sounds proud," pointedly refutes Maksim Gorky, one of the party's leading authors and, specifically, Satan's famous monologue in Gorky's *The Lower Depths*, Act IV, "Only man exists, all the rest is the work of his hands and his brain! Man! This is magnificent! This sounds . . . proud!"

27. Barkova, *Vozvrashchenie*, 113.

28. Vera Figner (1852–1942) was a member of the Executive Committee of the People's Will party, that planned the tsar's assassination. The murder marked the end of attempts at liberal reform for Russia.

29. Taganov, 18.

30. *Dodnes' tiagoteet*, 337.

31. One of her fellow students was the poet Arsenii Tarkovskii, who noted, "Secretly, she was a great Russian poet." See his introductory essay, "Taina Marii Petrovykh," in Mariia Petrovykh, *Prednaznachen'e. Stikhi raznykh let* (Moscow, 1983), 3–6. All further page references to poems in this edition are given in the text. During her lifetime, Petrovykh was primarily known as an editor and gifted translator, particularly of Armenian poetry. Only one volume of her verse, *The Distant Tree* (Dal'nee derevo, 1968) appeared before her death and that was mainly compiled by the Armenian poets whom she had translated. Mariia Petrovykh, *Dal'nee derevo* (Erevan, Asiastan, 1968). In addition to *Prednaznachenie*, the other major posthumous collection of her work is *Cherta gorizonta. Stikhi i perevody. Vospominaniia o Marii Petrovykh* (Erevan, 1986).

32. For example, Mariia Petrovykh, "Stikhi iz arkhiva," *Znamia* 1 (1989): 90–95.

33. "Bez ogliadki ne stupit' ni shagu," *Znamia* 1 (1989): 91–92. The feeling of constantly being watched, the fear of unknown callers and footsteps, is a theme common to Berggol'ts, Barkova, and Petrovykh. See Berggol'ts's poem, "Ia ne liubliu za mnoi idushchikh sledom," from her "Triptyk 1949 goda," *Ogonek* 26 (June 1987): 15, and Barkova's "Dnem oni vse podobny porokhu" (1954), *Vozvrashchenie*, 132.

34. Especially the line "No uzhasy ty zatmevaesh' eti—/Prokliat'e rodiny moej—tiur'ma" from the poem "Est' ochen' mnogo strashnogo na svete," *Znamia* 1 (1989): 91.

35. This theme recurs throughout Petrovykh's career. For an earlier example, see "Kahoe uzh tut vdokhnovenie,—prosto" (1943), *Prednaznachenie*, 37.

36. At the same time, Petrovykh dedicated poems to both Akhmatova and Tsvetaeva. Her poems to Akhmatova testify to their friendship and mutual support. "Den' izo dnia i god iz goda," (1962) and "Ty sama sebe derzhava" (1963) are dedicated to Akhmatova while the poems "Ni akhmatovskooi krotosti" (1967), "Bolezn' " (1970) and "Pustynia

...Zamelo sledy" (1971) take Akhmatova as their subject. These, along with other poems by male and female poets written to or about Akhmatova, appear in Pamela Davidson and Isia Tlusti, *Posviashchaetsia Akhmatovoi* (Tenafly, NJ: Hermitage Press, 1991), 90–94. In 1975, Petrovykh wrote a moving poem to the memory of Marina Tsvetaeva, empathizing with her loneliness and the lack of response that Tsvetaeva experienced even from those she loved most: "even your son in his short span/how mercilessly cruel he was." "Pamiat M. Ts.," *Znamia*, 1 (1989): 94.

37. This poem had particular resonances for other women poets. Sara Pogreb (1921–   ), who did not begin to publish until after *glasnost*, titled her first collection *I Was Silent Until Verses* (*Ia domolchalas' do stikhov*) (Moscow, 1990). Inna Lisnianskaia wrote three poems to Petrovykh, one of which, "Mariia Sergeevna! Ia domolchalas'," (1987) is a direct response to "There's one thing I'd like to say to poets." See Inna Lisnianskaia, *Stikhotvoreniia* (Moscow, 1991), 122. Lisnianskaia's poem and her relationship to Petrovykh were discussed by Stefanie Sandler in a paper, "The Canon and the Backward Glance: Akhmatova, Nikolaeva, Lisianskaia, Petrovykh," at the "Glasnost in Two Cultures" Conference, at New York University, March 1991.

38. *Literaturnaia Moskva* (Moscow, 1956), vol. 1 includes Ilya Ehrenburg's article, "Poeziia Mariny Tsvetaevy" and seven of her poems, while vol. 2 includes two of Akhmatova's poems.

39. This phrase is from Jane Taubman's chapter in this volume that discusses both poets in detail and contrasts various aspects of their works.

40. Bella Akhmadulina, *Svecha* (Moscow, 1977), 112–13. The topic of Akhmadulina's relations to these poets is quite extensive, as she has written at least a dozen poems relating to Akhmatova and/or Tsvetaeva. For an interesting recent assessment of Akhmadulina's career in the context of the thaw generation, see Viktor Erofeev, "Novoe i staroe. Zametki o tvorchestve Belly Akhmadulinoi," *Oktiabr'*, 5 (1987): 190–94.

41. Iunna Morits, *Izbrannoe* (Moscow, 1982), 25. All further page references to this edition are given in the text.

42. See Elena Mikhailova's interview with Morits, "Iunna Morits: 'Vse korni tianutsia k svobode . . . ' ", *Daugava* 7 (1987): 79.

43. *Daugava* 7 (1987): 79.

44. *Daugava* 9 (1986): 60–61.

45. Iunna Morits, *Muskul vody* (Moscow, 1990).

46. This remark comes from Aleksandr Dymshits's review of Lisnianskaia's third book, "Ne prosto liubov'," (1963), "Vzyskatel'nost'," *Znamia* 7 (1963): 223–24.

47. Inna Lisnianskaia, *Dozhdi i zerkala* (Paris: YMCA Press, 1983), 41. All further page references to poems in this edition are given in the text. The most recent collected edition of Lisnianskaia's poetry is *Stikhotvoreniia* (Moscow, 1991).

48. On Soviet passports, Jews were identified as a separate nationality.

49. Joseph Brodsky, quoted in *Russkaia mysl'* (Paris) February 3, 1983.

50. Evelyn Bristol, *A History of Russian Poetry* (Oxford: Oxford University Press, 1991), 292. Sonia Ketchian's article, "Poetic Creation in Bella Axmadulina," *Slavic and East European Journal*, 28.1 (1984): 42–57, is devoted largely to the ways in which Akhmadulina's self-presentation and concept of the creative process differ from Akhmatova's.

51. Wolfgang Kasack, *Dictionary of Russian Literature Since 1917* (New York: Columbia University Press, 1988), 256.

52. The poem was never published, but it was circulated widely. The author wishes

to thank Marina Temkina for bringing the poem to her attention, and Elena Ignatova for supplying a complete text of the poem.

53. The best known are the cases of Natalia Gorbanevskaia (1936–) and Irina Ratushinskaia (1954–).

54. Nikolaieva's books of poetry are *Sad chudes* (1980); *Na korable zimy* (1986); *Smokovnitsa* (1990); and *Zdes'* (1990). She is also the author of a book of short stories, *Invalid detstva* (1990). On her relations with Akhmatova, see Sandler, fn. 34.

55. Olesia Nikolaeva, "Devichnik," *Zdes'* (Moscow, 1990), 15.

56. Olesia Nikolaeva, "Woman Against Woman: The Russian Religious Tradition and the Problems of Feminism," an unpublished paper presented at the "Glasnost in Two Cultures" Conference at New York University, March 1991.

57. Elena Shvarts, *Storony sveta* (Leningrad, 1989). For information about Shvarts's earlier career, see Kasack, 375–76 and Heldt, 158–60. Several poems in English translation appear in *The Third Wave. The New Russian Poetry*, ed. Kent Johnson and Stephen Ashby (Ann Arbor: The University of Michigan Press, 1992). The book also contains translations of other fine contemporary women poets such as Ol'ga Sedakova, Tat'iana Shcherbina, Nina Iskrenko, and Nadezhda Kondakova.

58. Elena Shvart, *Trudy i dni Lavinii, monakhini iz ordena obrezaniia serdtsa* (Ann Arbor, MI: Ardis, 1987).

59. Nina Iskrenko, *Ili* (Moscow, 1991), 31.

14

Russian Women Writers in Émigré Literature

Marina Ledkovsky

The subject of Russian women writers in emigration has not yet been seriously discussed by literary critics. I hope the following discussion, the first of its kind, will at least stimulate curiosity and, eventually, interest in this significant phenomenon.

The cataclysms in twentieth-century Russia[1] have forced many talented Russian women writers to flee from their homeland and seek asylum in many countries and on all continents. The motivation for this incomparable exodus of millions of Russians[2] was not just avoidance of annihilation by a ruthless new regime; it was primarily and distinctly moral and ideological for those belonging to the first "two waves" and for many of the most recent "third wave."[3] They wholeheartedly rejected Bolshevik/Soviet tyranny in exchange for independence and spiritual freedom beyond their homeland's borders. They followed the dictum so aptly worded by Pythagoras of Samos, one of European civilization's most ancient exiles: "For a reasoning man it is immoral to remain under the authority of a tyrant."[4]

Soon after the massive exodus of 1918–1925, cultural centers emerged in the entire diaspora, with the most significant in Paris, Berlin, Prague, Riga and Revel' (Tallinn), Sofia and Warsaw, Belgrade, and the Far East—Harbin and Shanghai.[5] The participation of women in the émigré literary process throughout the geographical dispersion and the seven decades that have elapsed since 1920 has been impressive from the beginning. They contributed to Russian literature in all existing genres from poetry, fiction, and drama to literary criticism, journalism publicistic prose, philosophic-religious treatises. Yet, among American Slavists little is known about most of those women. "Big" names like Zinaida Gippius, Nadezhda Tèffi, and Marina Tsvetaeva have received due attention in American scholarship, but only a handful of émigré women writers is included in scholarly anthologies and the available literary handbooks and/or dictionaries,[6] a lacuna that will be corrected to an extent by the forthcoming publication of

Dictionary of Russian Women Writers.[7] The general neglect of Russian émigré literature, not to speak of its women contributors, by American Slavists is a deplorable fact that needs revision and is beginning to be corrected. It seems that Russian émigré women writers are subject to double discrimination in Western, specifically American Slavic, studies: first as émigrés and then as women. Even the first serious volume dedicated to women in Russian literature, *Russian Literary Triquarterly*, No. 9, Spring 1974, features only two émigrés, already established writers in pre-1917 Russia: Tèffi and Tsvetaeva. With the exception of a few American scholars, themselves notably of émigré background,[8] who deal sparingly with isolated prominent émigré female authors, for American Slavicists, most names of émigré women contributors to Russian literature remain obscure.

   In contrast, the reception of women's writings by émigré literary critics has been regular and fair, a continuation of the Silver Age, when women writers increasingly gained ground in professional ranks. Throughout the seven decades of Russia abroad, women writers have had equal access to publication of their writings and have been reviewed by their peers, female and male, with genuine interest and respect. They have participated in diverse publishing enterprises, frequently becoming co-editors or editors-in-chief, a practice still continued in the present.[9] Likewise, European Slavicists have duly recognized émigré women's writings and have produced respectable works dedicated to their literary talents.[10] Most gratifying since the middle sixties has been the renewed and ever increasing interest in émigré literature—women representatives included—in the Metropolis, that is, the Russian homeland. Many émigré works, specifically writings by remarkable women, have been published recently and are scheduled for distribution in the near future.[11]

   In the United States, as a rule, prominent women writers of prerevolutionary Russia have been given the recognition they deserve. Major works have been written about Gippius, Tsvetaeva, and scattered critical essays about Berberova, Odoevtseva, and Tèffi. However, women authors whose careers started in emigration have been ignored and passed over in silence. For this reason, the ''big names'' will be left out in the following discussion and attention will focus on lesser-known poets and prose writers, on those seldom discussed in existing accounts of émigré literature. This chapter is intended to bring to light a few unfamiliar names and works and is designed as an introductory assessment of émigré women's contribution to Russian letters. Its restrictive format will permit only a cursory presentation of some noteworthy figures.

   In the 1920s and 1930s, Paris was indeed an important cultural center for émigrés. Prosaists, poets, and artists grouped themselves around leaders in literature and art. Zinaida Gippius and Dmitrii Merezhkovskii held their famous ''Sunday meetings,'' and in February 1927 established the most sophisticated literary group among exiles, ''The Green Lamp.'' Literary groups around Ivan Bunin, Vladislav Khodasevich, and Georgii Adamovich, master of the ''Parisian Note,''[12] exercised significant influence on the younger generation of writers and formed a link between the literature of the beginning of the twentieth century and the writings in Russia Abroad.[13] The older masters transmitted to the younger émigré novices the creative impulse toward modernism while demanding classic clarity, precision, and simplicity in the expression of their new world perception. All masters could boast of a considerable number of faithful followers.

Among women writers, Lidiia Chervinskaia (1907[?]–1988) can be considered the most outstanding disciple of Adamovich's "Parisian Note." In this capacity, she is comparable to many women writers of the preceding periods who eagerly took advice from their male mentors on their literary paths. The precepts of the Parisian school are well represented in her oeuvre. Adamovich requested restraint and honesty, "two lines about the most essential things." Thus, her poetry and prose writings are discreet yet fragmented and formally unpretentious. Her themes focus on faith, love, alienation, and death set against urban imagery. Chervinskaia's work as a whole, although only modestly distinguished, marks an important phase in the evolution of émigré letters.[14]

But there were hosts of women writers who shunned "influences" and followed their individual calling. In spite of their quite personal verses and distinctive styles, certain themes indeed unite them across the continents and even the flow of time. Understandably, Russia and the new foreign environment loom high in their work in addition to the perennial themes of love and death. Within those themes—often painful and nostalgic—the motifs of alienation and loneliness find their natural expression. But most women transcend the ephemeral sense of despondency by turning to religious-philosophical meditation or stoic existentialism tinged with Judeo-Christian metaphysics. Those themes, tabooed in the much regretted homeland, become almost a vocation for all émigré writers. They feel responsible for Russia's downfall and have a need to expiate their neglect of the ruined homeland. Their mission of bringing Russian culture to the West is regarded as a moral obligation on the thorny path of exile. Poets and prosaists alike see themselves as "eternal wanderers" in cosmic dimensions in which the pettiness and bitterness of political divisions fade before the divine magnitude of incomprehensible human destinies.

The émigré concentration on the spiritual and philosophical aspects of existence continues the religious revival of the Silver Age at the turn of the century and is renewed under the pressure of the tragic political events of 1917. This inclination toward spiritual matters explains the large number of religious women writers in emigration. Their work in all ecclesiastical genres is a significant contribution to contemporary Orthodox theological literature. Many of their liturgical verses have been adopted by the Russian Orthodox Church and are currently used in the liturgical yearly cycle. There are about thirty known names of women who are active as writers of theological treatises, lives of recently canonized saints, and liturgical poetry. Some of those writers are known beyond the church and have won due respect throughout intellectual and ecclesiastical circles of professional theologians and historians of religion.[15]

Sensitive literary critics have often observed that émigré literature has been nurtured by the energy of spirituality and of freedom in the diaspora. The dispersion from the Far East through Europe and to the Americas has allowed writers and poets to absorb different cultures with an artistic intensity never before experienced in native literature. "The whole world is our homeland and also an alien land. Our home is everywhere . . . " exclaims Ekaterina Tauber as a spokeswoman for her fellow émigrés.[16] This global absorption of world culture lends émigré literature its peculiar *frissons nouveaux* and turns its basic tragedy into triumphant spiritual success.[17] These *frissons nouveaux* are present in the poetry of Raisa Bloch (1899–1943), who moved from Berlin to Paris and perished in a Nazi camp in 1943, Irina Bulich (1898–1954) from Helsinki, Emiliia Chegrintseva (1904–1989) from Prague, and Alla Golovina (1909–1987), Galina Kuznetsova (1900–1976), Anna Prismanova (1897–1960), Zinaida Shakhovskaia, mostly residing in Paris.[18] These poets share with many other female peers a distinct independent voice resounding in sometimes striking verses.

Ekaterina Tauber (1903–1987) can serve as a prime example of a female independent voice. Her poetry focuses on all formerly adduced themes from her specific perspective as a woman. Her inner experience in facing up to the demands of fate and in transcending life's cruelty produces small masterpieces couched in carefully selected language. Tauber's sense of duty toward her poetic gift is directed to an existential acceptance of destiny and grateful celebration of God's universe. In harmonious stanzas, adorned by various meters, rhythms, and ingenious new rhymes ranging from classic to assonance and blank verse, Tauber captures nature's harmony and presents her intimate, unique experience.[19]

From the other end of the planet the Far East poet, Larisa Andersen (b. 1915?), echoes Tauber's enchantment with nature but perceives it solipsistically. While nature remains the most important source of inspiration for Andersen, it also reminds her constantly of human vulnerability and insecurity, of the impossibility of human perfection. When the apple trees are blooming, Andersen expects miraculous changes for herself through the renewal in nature, but she, eventually, has to accept disappointment:

> They say if you wait and believe
> You'll reach your goal . . .
> Thus I waited . . . [But]
> All is still the same . . .

> Only May, sparkling up
> the apple trees' summits,
> Whirls around white petals. (148)

This disappointment turns into pain when the lyrical persona realizes her instability in the face of nature's constancy: "And nobody knows, how painful it is for me/ That the apple trees are blooming! (149).[20] Andersen also deals with the theme of the artist's impotence at the spectacle of a changing world, of the death of former ideals, of the passing of art's purity: "Gioconda, Gioconda / beauty is dying in the world . . . A world where greed is ruling / A world where beauty is dying . . . Gioconda, is it you? / Is it you? / No, [you're] not the same . . .[21] Andersen has kept her creative authenticity while being a constant member of the Harbin and Shanghai literary communities. She now lives in France and is still contributing to émigré publications. Her voice continues to ring out experimental verses with novel stanzaic structures and original metaphors, but her poetic language is simple and traditional. Andersen is considered one of the finest Far East poets in émigré criticism.

Émigré women prosaists are numerous and versatile throughout the entire period. Many women have written successfully in several genres. Almost all of the earlier named poets have also practiced prose genres from short stories and novels to essays and literary criticism, which are published in magazines and almanacs or as separate editions.[22] Ekaterina Bakunina-Novoselova (1889–1976) was a prolific Parisian prose writer as well as poet. Her writings, in the tradition of the Russian popular erotic novel, reflect the influence of D. H. Lawrence, Freud, and Nietzsche. Her two novels[23] are written in the first person, mostly as an interior monologue, at times digressing into dialogue and descriptive narrative. Both novels are studies of a woman's close self-examination; her sensual and psychological life, her relationships to family, to lovers, to society, are bared to scrutinizing analysis. Bakunina's works represent an interesting attempt at viewing woman's condition with brutal honesty by applying Freudian methods. The books demonstrate psychological skills in unveiling facts usually hidden behind seven seals and only reluctantly exposed. Bakunina anticipates later feminist writings about woman's nature and her self-assessment, notably Simone de Beauvoir's *The Second Sex*. Her novels were "shockers" at the time of writing and received some harsh reviews.[24] Yet, they are representative of the various experimentations by women writers and have enjoyed considerable success among Western readers, having been translated into French, German and Czech.

The Far East has produced many noteworthy prosaists, among them Nina Fedorova (1895–1985), one of the finest historical novelists of the entire emigration.[25] Fedorova's epic novels explore the vicissitudes of "the terrible years of Russia" and the trials of post-revolutionary exile through the eyes and fates of women. Her novel *The Family* was originally written and published in English in 1940 and was subsequently translated into twelve languages. It appeared in Russian only in 1952. *The Family* received the *Atlantic Monthly* "best book" prize and had twenty reprints. The next book, *The Children* (1942), was also first published in English and then translated into Russian by the author and published in 1958. This, too, was translated into several foreign languages. These two books have a universal appeal to readers of any culture. They depict émigré life in China and other foreign countries that are at political and cultural crossroads. The main characters are remarkable women, a grandmother and mother who run the household and sustain "the family," actually a community of chance boarders with whom they share their shaky home and meager fare. They are kind and noble hearted and never forsake their moral commitment to perfect honesty and to charity; they always remain true to basic Christian principles: "to love one's fellow men and one's enemies as oneself."

Fedorova's last novel, *Life*, in three volumes (1946, 1966), juxtaposes women revolutionaries and women aristocrats as they interact before, during, and after the Revolution. Through skillful dialogue Fedorova succeeds in enticing the reader into sympathy with future terrorists and victimizers in order to reveal later their true faces, creating a shattering effect of disappointment and horror. This effect successfully mirrors the tragedy of Russian history. The Soviet holocaust wipes out the entire aristocratic family but neither does it spare their Bolshevik exterminators. Fedorova's novels and short stories are full of irony but steadily abstain from satire, which allows Fedorova to convey fully the complexity of the historical reality. By refraining from ideological censure, Fedorova creates works of Tolstoyan quality highlighting female "domestic" and "political" heroism.

Fedorova emigrated to the United States with her family in 1938, where she wrote and published her prose and taught Russian language and literature. Aleksei Remizov, Aleksandr Benois, and, reportedly, Igor Stravinsky and Vladimir Nabokov admired her novels. She is currently being discovered by readers and publishers in Russia, where all her books are scheduled for publication in the near future.

The "second wave" Russian exodus replenished the ranks of professional women writers, most of whom had moved to the United States after World War II seeking security and freedom for their creative talents. Some were originally members of the "first wave" who retreated before the advancing Red Army. They fled from Serbia, Czechoslovakia, and the Baltic states, and some came directly from Russia. Their writings often reflect the enormity of their experience during the years of terror and on their flight through war-torn Europe. In exquisite idiosyncratic verses, they sing of their losses, their spiritual bond with their native land, their love for God's creation, and their adjustment to a new environment. Most of those poets are profoundly religious. Ol'ga Anstei and Lidiia Alekseeva cannot conceive of life outside the Orthodox Church and write metaphysical verses informed with awe and serenity before the Almighty's divine designs. Their refined mastery of traditional and modern forms reflects their intense devotion to their native language and culture and permits them to give graceful expression to their enjoyment of life in freedom, the "eternal wanderer's essential goal."[26]

Among the many first-rate women writers of the postwar period,[27] the brilliant Irina Bushman (1921–   ) deserves special attention.[28] Born in Tsarskoe Selo, Bushman, in many ways, continues the "Petersburg note" in keeping with the Pushkinian "measure in all things." In her remarkable verses, the eternal themes of love, death, separation, and alienation vibrate in heavy brazen sounds alternating with delicate, almost ethereal, melodious wording. At the same time, her skillfully used modernistic devices, the pauses, broken lines, new metrical and rhythmical variations, as well as innovative rhyme schemes and blank verse promote her into the first ranks of modern poetry. For the past fifteen years, Bushman has been working on a monumental *Poema* on Giordano Bruno (1548?– 1600) to consist of seven parts and nine interludes. Giordano's unusual fate has fascinated Bushman's imagination and creative talent since childhood. Giordano's liberal humanism, his restive roamings, his tragic trial and death, evoke in her a keen sense of affinity with twentieth-century Russian destinies. Lidiia Alekseeva's poetry about Russian refugees, the "eternal [Russian] wanderer," was the immediate inspiration for this monumental work. Bushman has researched Giordano's era and sets twentieth-century Russian wanderings against the background of Giordano Bruno's episodes. Bushman started publishing her poetry and short stories in various literary émigré journals in 1946. Her cycle of novellas, *The Red and the Gray*, [29] reflects the shady and the bright sides of Soviet military personnel's lifestyle in occupied Germany immediately after the end of World War II. Bushman uses wit and sarcasm in her eyewitness accounts of rapes, robberies, and vandalism committed by the Soviet invading forces, but she also reports occasional charitable deeds and humorous situations arising from misunderstandings bordering on the absurd. Her prose is based on light-flowing dialogues in common jargon enlivened with vulgarisms. Her prose compares to Zoshchenko's methods and his use of *skaz*.[30] Bushman's ballads on contemporary and historical motifs, her perceptive literary criticism, her remarkable poetry, should assure her a secure place in the pantheon of twentieth-century Russian literature. Bushman has enough unpublished poetry to fill three books; regrettably, lack of funds, personal pride, and self-respect are responsible for her unpublished writings. This misfortune is shared by many fellow writers of the first two waves. The Metropolis' revived interest in émigrés' works will hopefully change their situation.

Women writers of the third wave have also been very productive in publishing enterprises concentrated in Frankfurt, Munich, Paris, Israel, and the United States.[31] They can boast of decent prosaists and very good poets.[32] Among the most interesting are Ina Bliznetsova (b. 1958) and Vera Zubareva (b. 1958). Ina Bliznetsova is yet little known, but her two published volumes promise an outstanding poetic career.[33] A mathematician by profession, she writes poetry "for herself" while drawing on diverse currents of native and Western poetic trends. Bliznetsova creates entirely novel verses by using an astoundingly wide range of unusual devices and by retaining stern restraint at the peak of lyrical intensity. Several of Bliznetsova's poems explore the myth of woman in Russia. In a 1979 poem she sends an epistle to Akhmatova in the other world. In a mixture of familiarity and reverence, Bliznetsova establishes a feminine poetic sisterhood linking Akhmatova to the poem's lyrical heroine and, through her, to all women poets.[34] Bliznetsova traces the history of poetic inspiration from Lilith through Cleopatra in her lengthy narrative poem, "The Apocrypha of the Sixth Day" ("Apokrif shestogo dnia," 1981). She explores the role of feminine consciousness in the development of a universal poetic tradition. Bliznetsova's lyrical persona embodies a contemporary link in this continuous chain of feminine poetic consciousness.[35] Bliznetsova's very modern, complex, and intellectually charged work is representative of a new generation of young women poets whose poetry embraces ever larger themes and methods. She is inspired by sources that enrich her verses with philosophical depth and universal scope. Among her favorites are St. John's Revelation, Shakespeare, Auden, Pushkin, Tiutchev, the Apocrypha, the Koran, and the Old and the New Testaments. Bliznetsova uses this rich poetic heritage in most ingenious ways.

Vera Zubareva also draws on religious inspiration for her poetry.[36] While adhering to classical versification she toys with innovative methods, especially stanzaic forms and verse lines. Her poems are directed at themes concerning all human endeavors and relationships, but in a special "aura" of her own creation. The essence of this "aura" is Beauty, which ennobles and saves human souls. In "Aura" the interconnectedness of all existence is revealed as a grandiose design of the Almighty Creator in which the human is assigned the responsibility for its cosmic preservation.

Zubareva's poetry resounds in a strong, proud, confident woman's voice asserting her female role of life-giver and conciliator. Interestingly, there are almost no reminiscences of Russia in her verses. She left the homeland only in 1990 seeking total freedom for self-expression, which she felt was impossible in Russia even under *glasnost*.

Emigration has not stifled women's literary talents. Women have never ceased in their energetic, creative activity throughout all the years in the diaspora. Their writings have been a significant contribution to the entire literary process in emigration. They have successfully participated in the émigré mission to preserve and perpetuate authentic, undistorted Russian culture until both literatures—that of the Metropolis and that of the diaspora—can be integrated. Their role and their work is recognized as equal in importance and quality to men's, as the number of women contributors to the many almanacs, anthologies, and journals testifies. Conscious of their obligation to transmit their work to Russia's next generations, émigré women writers and artists in San Francisco have published an almanac, *The Russian Woman in Emigration* (1922–1970), which features about sixty-five articles, poems, and short stories by women and about women. The hope is that their work will, indeed, follow the already begun integration of the two Russian literatures.[37]

NOTES

1. World War I, the 1917 disaster, the Civil War, Leninist-Stalinist holocausts, World War II, the postwar terrorism, and, finally, the instability of government lasting into the present.

2. Pierre Kovalevsky, *Russia Beyond the Borders* (Paris: Librarie des cinq continents, 1971). Kovalevsky, among other commentators, notes: "In world history there is nothing

comparable in volume, numbers and cultural significance to the phenomenon of the Russian Diaspora'' (11); ''The entire population of Russians living outside of their country came to roughly nine to ten millions according to various statistical accounts'' (12).

3. The common division into ''three waves'' is adopted here; the first, after the Bolshevik seizure of power in 1917 and the subsequent terror of Lenin, Stalin, and company, 1917–1940; the second, during and after World War II, when a very large number of Soviet citizens remained in the West (former military personnel, the ''Ostarbeiter'' and people who of their own accord seized the opportunity to abandon their tyrannical homeland and to seek freedom on ''Other Shores''), 1941–1970; the third, still continuing into our post-Soviet era, of émigrés who have been either expelled for ''non-conformity'' to Soviet ideology or have left their country for the same philosophical reasons as their peers of the former ''waves,'' 1970– .

4. Vadim Kreyd, ed., *The Ark. Poetry of the First Emigration (Kovcheg, Poeziia Pervoi Emigratsii)* (Moscow, 1991). In Kreyd's enlightening introduction, 7.

5. There are several studies that assess the Russian exodus and its consequences. Lazar Fleishman et al., eds., *Russian Berlin 1921–1923*, (Paris: YMCA Press, 1983); Pierre Kovalevsky, *Russia Beyond the Borders* (Paris: Librarie des cinq continents, 1971); Marc Raeff, *Russia Abroad—A Cultural History of the Russian Emigration 1919–1939* (New York: Oxford University Press, 1990). These are the most reliable works on this topic. Russian scholars from the Metropolis are feverishly collecting materials to produce their versions of these tragic pages in Russian history.

6. Wolfgang Kasack, ed., Maria Carlson and Jane T. Hedges, trans., *Dictionary of Russian Literature Since 1917* (New York: Columbia University Press, 1988); Vladimir Markov, ed., *Modern Russian Poetry* (Indianapolis: Bobbs-Merrill Press, 1967); Temira Pachmuss, ed. and trans., *A Russian Cultural Revival: A critical anthology of émigré literature before 1939*, (Knoxville: University of Tennessee Press, 1981); Victor Terras, ed., *Handbook of Russian Literature* (abbr. HRL) (New Haven: Yale University Press, 1985); Harry Weber, ed., *Modern Encyclopedia of Russian and Soviet Literature* (abbr. MERSL) (Gulf Breeze, FL: Academic International Press, 1977).

7. M. Ledkovsky, C. Rosenthal, M. Zirin, eds., *Dictionary of Russian Women Writers* (Westport, CT: Greenwood Publishing Group, Inc., 1994).

8. For example, Laszlo Dienes, Boris Filippov, Lazar Fleishman, Simon Karlinsky, Lev Loseff, Olga Matich, Temira Pachmuss, Nicholas Poltoratsky, Olga Raevskaia-Hughes, Leonid Rzhevsky, and Gleb Struve.

9. For example, Ekaterina Bakunina (1889–1976), Nina Berberova (1901–), Ella Bobrova (1911–), Natal'ia Gorbanevskaia (1936–), Tat'iana Goricheva (1947–), Irina Iassen (1893 [?]–1957), Iustina Kruzenshtern-Peterets (1903–1983), Vera Pirozhkova (1921–), Sofiia Pregel' (1894?–1972), Natal'ia Reznikova (1908–), Mariia Rozanova (1930–), Irina Saburova (1907–1979), Zinaida Shakhovskaia (1906–), Valentina Sinkevich (1926–).

10. Dr. Jan-Paul Hinrich, Petra Couvee, Rene Guerra, Efim Etkind.

11. Irina Odoevtseva, (1901–1990), Nina Berberova, Ella Bobrova, Mat' Mariia Skobtsova, (1891–1943). Anthologies of poetry edited by Vladimir Vitkovskii and Vadim Kreyd. Numerous articles, essays, reviews on émigré literature.

12. ''Parisian Note,'' a term that became current in the 1930s to characterize a trend in émigré literature, especially among younger poets and writers. The expression is said to have originated with the poet and writer Boris Poplavskii and was popularized in the literary criticism of Georgii Adamovich, see *HRL*, 330.

13. For more detailed discussion, see *HRL*, 119–24; *MERSL*, 134–40; Vladimir Markov, xiv–xvi; Kreyd, 3–21.

14. Lidiia Chervinskaia, *Approachings* (*Priblizheniia*) (Paris: Chisla, 1956); *Dawns* (*Rassvety*) (Paris: Chisla, 1937); *Twelve Months* (*Dvenadtsat' mesiatsev*) (Paris: Rifma, 1956); "Expectations" ("Ozhidanie"), *Krug* 3(1938):3–42.

15. Abbess Ariadna, Nun Thaisiia, Nadezhda Gorodetskaia (1901–1985), Valeriia Hoecke (1904–1986), Sofiia Kontsevich (1893–1989), Sofiia Koulomizina (1903–   ), Mother Mariia Skobtsova (1891–1945), Nataliia Urusova (d. 1964). See also *Saint Herman Calendar 1992; Featuring Orthodox Women Writers*, St. Herman of Alaska Brotherhood (Patina, CA, 1992).

16. Ekaterina Tauber, *Loyalty* (*Vernost'*), (Paris: Al'batros, 1984), 10.

17. George Fedorov, "About Parisian Poetry," in *The Ark* (New York: Soiuz russkikh pisatelei, 1942), 191; Iurii Ivask, ed., *In the West* (New York: Izd-vo im. Chekhova, 1953), 6–7; Kreyd, 5–6.

18. See Petra Couvee, ed., "Introduction," in *Anna Prismanova* collected works (The Hague: Leuxenhoff, 1990), xii–xxvix; "O poezii Ally Golovinoi," in Alla Golovina, *Gorodskoi Angel* ed. Efim Etkin (Brussels: N. P., 1989), v–x; Marina Ledkovsky, "Paradise Lost to Paradise Regained, Galina Kuznetsova's *Olive Orchard*," *Canadian American Slavic Studies* 27, No. 1–4 (1993): 149–59.

19. Ekaterina Tauber started her writing career in Belgrade and in 1936 moved to France. She became a steady contributor to all major émigré literary journals and almanacs and published five volumes of her own poetry between 1935 and 1984.

20. Larissa Andersen, "The Apple Trees are Blooming," in *Ostrov Larissy*, ed. Emmanuil Sztein (Orange, CT: Antiquary, 1988), 148–49.

21. Sztein, 174.

22. Among those with established reputations are Nina Berberova, Tat'iana Fessenko (1915–   ), Tatiana Smirnova-Maksheeva (1890–1982), Irina Odoevtseva, Georgii Peskov (1885–1977), Irina Saburova, Zinaida Shakhovskaia, Liudmila Shtern (1935–   ), Iuliia Voznesenskaia (1940–), Ruth Zernova (1919–   ).

23. Ekaterina Bakunina-Novoselova, *The Body* (Berlin: Parabola, 1933); *Love for Six Men* (Paris: Impr. EIP, 1935); also *Stikhi* (Paris: Rodnik, 1931).

24. Mikhail Tsetlin, "Ekaterina Bakunina," *Telo*, *Sovremennye Zapiski* 53 (Paris, 1933): 454–56; Zinaida Gippius, "E. Bakunina, Liubov' k shesterym," *Sovremennye zapiski* 58 (Paris, 1935): 478–79.

25. Nina Fedorova, *The Family* (Boston: Little Brown & Co., 1940), translated into twelve languages. *The Children* (Boston: Little Brown & Co., 1942), translated into several languages. *Life* (*Zhizn'*) (Washington, DC: V. Kamkin, 1964–1966).

26. Lidiia Alekseeva (1909–1989) took refuge in Belgrade, Yugoslavia, in 1920 where she graduated from the Faculty of Philosophy at Belgrade University specializing in Slavistics. She eventually resettled to the United States in 1949. Alekseeva's idiosyncratic verses, highly appreciated by her relative Anna Akhmatova, are a lasting contribution to the treasury of Russian poetry. *Sun of the Forest* (*Lesnoe solntse*) (Frankfurt: Possev, 1954); *On the Road* (*V puti*, 1959); reprint (New York, 1964); *A Transparent Trace* (*Prozrachnyi sled*) (New York: Author's Publishing, 1964); *Time of Parting* (*Vremia razluk*) (New York: Author's Publishing, 1971); *Verses* (*Stikhi*) (New York: Author's Publishing, 1980); *Tears of the Prodigal Son* (*Slezy bludnogo syna*), trans. Ivan Gundulic (Washington, DC: Mezhdunarodnoe literaturnoe sodruzhestvo, 1965).

Olga Anstei (1912–1985) was forced out of her native Kiev by World War II events in 1943 and arrived in the United States in 1950. A graduate of the Kiev Foreign Languages Institute (1931), she used her extraordinary literary talents as poet, prosaist, and literary critic. Her work, published in all émigré "thick" journals, almanacs, and anthologies, has been a significant adornment of émigré letters; *Door in the Wall (Dver' v stene)* (Munich: N. P. 1949): *In the Way (Na iuru)* (Pittsburgh: N. P., 1976); *The Devil and Daniel Webster and Other Stories (D'iavol i Daniel Vebster i drugie rasskazy)* (New York: Chaika, 1959).

27. Nonna Belavina (1915–   ), Ella Bobrova, Evgenia Dimer (1925–   ), Iraida Legkaia (1932– ·), Anglaia Shishkova (1923–   ), Valentina Sinkevich, and others.

28. Irina Bushman, a lyric poet, prosaist, literary critic, and translator, belongs to the most gifted Russian writers of the modern era. Events of World War II brought her to the West where she has been publishing her works since 1946. Her poetry appeared in the literary journals *Liberty (Svoboda)* (Munich, 1950s); *Literary Contemporary (Literaturnyi sovremennik)* (Munich, 1950s to 1960s); *New Review (Novyi zhurnal)* (New York, 1950s to 1970s); and almanacs *Bridges (Mosty)* No. 7 (Munich, 1961), *The Concord (Sodruzhestvo)* (Washington, DC: Kamkin, 1966); *In the West (Na zapade)* (New York: Chekhov House Publishers, 1953).

29. Irina Bushman, *The Red and the Gray (Krasnoe i seroe)* (Munich: Svoboda, 1950–1960).

30. The term *Skaz* designates the literary technique of narrative usually told in the first person by a fictitious narrator rather than by the author himself. The narrative is colored by dialecticisms, substandard speech, and slang expressions to produce the illusion of actual speech.

31. Third-wave names, Natal'ia Gorbanevskaia, Tat'iana Goricheva, Mariia Rozanova, and Nina Voronel' (1932–   ), are among many others.

32. In addition to the names above and mentioned earlier the following names are noteworthy: Inna Bogachinskaia (1946–   ), Nora Fainberg (1929–   ), Elena Ignatova (1947–   ), Irina Ratushchinskaia (1954–   ), Dora Shturman (1923–   ), Marina Temkina (1948–   ), Nadezhda Vil'ko (1953–   ), Liia Vladimirova (1938–   ).

33. Ina Bliznetsova, born and raised in Orenburg, Russia, emigrated to the United States in 1979. *Valley of Snares (Dolina tenet)* (Tenafly, NJ: Hermitage, 1988); *A View to a Sky (Vid na nebo)* (Tenafly, NJ: Hermitage, 1991). Her poems were also published in several journals (*Kontinent, The Literary Courier*) and anthologies (*The Blue Lagoon* [Newtonville, MA: Oriental Research Partners, 1986), 5], *Russian Poets in the West* [Paris-New York: Tret'ia volna, 1986]).

34. "Kakuiu vy znali," *Dolina tenet*, 40.

35. Ibid., 63–82.

36. Vera Zubareva, *Aura* (Philadelphia: Black Sea, 1990).

37. *The Russian Woman in Emigration. The Literary Artistic Circle in California, 1922–1970. (Russkaia zhenshchina v emigratsii. Literaturno-khudozhestvennyi kruzhok v Kalifornii, 1922–1970)* (Washington, DC, 1970).

Index

About the Contributors

TOBY W. CLYMAN, Associate Professor of Slavic Languages and Literatures at the State University of New York at Albany, has published studies on Chekhov, Gogol', Babel', and on Russian autobiography. She is the editor of *A Chekhov Companion* and co-translator of Peter M. Bitsilli, *Chekhov's Art: A Stylistic Analysis*.

JANE COSTLOW, Associate Professor of Russian at Bates College, is the author of *Worlds Within Worlds: The Novels of Ivan Turgenev* and co-editor of *Sexuality and the Body in Russian Culture*.

HELENA GOSCILO is the Chairperson of the Department of Slavic Languages and Literatures, and Cultures at the University of Pittsburgh. She is the editor of *Balancing Acts, Glasnost: An Anthology of Literature under Gorbachev, Wild Beach, Skirted Issues: The Discreteness and Indiscretions of Russian Women's Prose*, and *The Fruits of Her Plume: Essays on Contemporary Russian Women's Culture*. She is the translator of Lermontov's *Vadim* and Nagibin's *The Peak of Success and Other Stories* and is currently completing a monograph on Tat'iana Tolstaia.

DIANA GREENE, an independent scholar, is the author of *Insidious Intent: An Interpretation of Fedor Sologub's The Petty Demon* and articles on feminist criticism of Russian literature, the Strugatsky brothers, Anastasiia Chebotarevskaia, and Karolina Pavlova. She is currently working on a book about Karolina Pavlova and other Russian women poets of Pavlova's generation.

BETH HOLMGREN is Assistant Professor of Slavic Literatures at the University of California, San Diego. She is the author of *Women's Works in Stalin's Time:*

272 About the Contributors

On Lidiia Chukovskaia and Nadezhda Mandelstam and articles on Victor Gombrowicz, Andrei Sinyavsky/Abram Tertz, and Nadezhda Mandelstam.

NATALIE KONONENKO is Associate Professor teaching folklore in the Slavic Department at the University of Virginia. She has written studies on epic poetry, minstrels, ritual, embroidery, and folklore patterns in literature. She is currently completing a book on traditional Ukrainian minstrels.

MARINA LEDKOVSKY, Professor of Russian at Barnard College/Columbia University, has published numerous articles on major topics in Russian literature and culture. She is the author of *The Other Turgenev: From Romanticism to Symbolism*, editor of *Russia Through Women's Eyes: An Anthology of Works by Women Writers*, and co-editor of the two-volume *Dictionary of Russian Women Writers*. Her current research focuses on émigré literature, particularly works of Ivan Shmelev, Nadezhda Teffi, and Boris Zaitsev.

CHARLOTTE ROSENTHAL, Assistant Professor of Russian at the University of Southern Maine, has published studies on Remizov, Sologub, Gippius, Lokhvitskaia, and the critic Zinaida Vengerova. She is the co-editor of the *Dictionary of Russian Women Writers*.

MELISSA T. SMITH is Associate Professor of Russian at Youngstown State University. She is the author of many articles on contemporary Russian drama and theater, and is editor of *Ivan Elagin: In Memoriam*.

JANE A. TAUBMAN, Professor of Russian at Amherst College, is the author of *A Life Through Poetry: Marina Tsvetaeva's Lyric Diary*, and co-author of *Moscow Spring*. She is currently writing a study on the works of Ludmila Petrushevskaia and the cinema of Kira Muratova.

CAROL UELAND teaches Russian language and literature at Drew University in New Jersey. She has published articles on Blok, Ivanov, and contemporary Russian poetry and has co-translated with the poet Paul Graves, *Apollo in the Snow: Selected Poems of Aleksandr Kushner*.

JUDITH VOWLES, an independent scholar and translator, is co-editor of *Sexuality and the Body in Russian Culture* and translator of Sophie Dubnov-Erlich, *The Life and Works of S. M. Dubnov*.

MARGARET ZIOLKOWSKI is Associate Professor of Russian at Miami University in Ohio. She is the author of *Hagiography and Modern Russian Literature* and has published articles on contemporary Russian literature.

MARY F. ZIRIN is an independent researcher and translator. She is founder and editor of the AWSS newsletter *Women: East-West*. She is cotranslator of Joseph Shklovsky's *Five Billion Vodka Bottles to the Moon: Tales of a Soviet Scientist*, translator of Nadezhda Durova's *A Cavalry Maiden*, and the co-editor of the *Dictionary of Russian Women Writers*.